The Limited Partnership
Building a Russian–US
Security Community

The Limited Partnership
Building a Russian–US Security Community

Edited by
James E. Goodby and Benoit Morel

sipri

OXFORD UNIVERSITY PRESS

1993

Oxford University Press, Walton Street, Oxford OX2 6DP
Oxford New York Toronto
Delhi Bombay Calcutta Madras Karachi
Kuala Lumpur Singapore Hong Kong Tokyo
Nairobi Dar es Salaam Cape Town
Melbourne Auckland Madrid
and associated companies in
Berlin Ibadan

Oxford is a trade mark of Oxford University Press

Published in the United States
by Oxford University Press Inc., New York

British Library Cataloguing in Publication Data
Data available

Library of Congress Cataloging in Publication Data
The limited partnership: building a Russian–US security community /
edited by James E. Goodby and Benoit Morel.
p. cm.
"SIPRI, Stockholm International Peace Research Institute."
Includes bibliographical references and index.
1. United States—Foreign relations—Russia (Federation)
2. Russia (Federation)—Foreign relations—United States.
I. Goodby, James E. II. Morel, Benoit. III. Stockholm
International Peace Research Institute.
E183.8.R9L55 1992 327.73047—dc20 92–27075
ISBN 0–19–829161–2

Typeset and originated by Stockholm International Peace Research Institute
Printed and bound in Great Britain
on acid-free paper by
Biddles Ltd, Guildford and King's Lynn

Contents

Part IV. Building a new security relationship

16. Some limits on co-operation and transparency: operational security and the use of force   289
William W. Newmann

Preface

This book is part of a larger project—Building a Co-operative Security Regime in and for Europe—which is being carried out jointly by researchers at Carnegie Mellon University and the Stockholm International Peace Research Institute. The project evolved out of joint discussions in both Stockholm and Pittsburgh and was begun at a time when the world was relatively stable— ordered, but at the same time divided. This book was written during the period when along with the dissolution of the Warsaw Treaty Organization and the breakup of the Soviet Union, the bipolar security system was collapsing. It is published at a time when the old order has been buried but the new one has not yet assumed its final shape.

In the past, security was usually identified with stability, and even a certain immobility. Relations between the Soviet Union and the United States were marked by fierce and unrelenting competition tempered only slightly by attempts to limit and reduce arms. Today, fluidity and uncertainty are the main characteristics of international politics. Arms control still has a place in security relations between Russia and the United States, for the dismantling of the cold war levels of weapon inventories will take years to accomplish. However, that is business left over from the cold war.

Today's task is to move from a highly polarized adversarial relationship to one that already, and perhaps prematurely, has been labelled by leaders of the two nations as 'partnership'. That partnership has not yet been achieved. It will require changes in the behaviour of many segments of the two societies, including the financial, commercial, political, and not least, the military.

This transition in behaviour patterns is rather fitfully beginning and needs to proceed more purposefully and urgently. *The partnership is still too limited.* The need for urgency arises from the fact that Russia is passing through a phase that is described in this book as metastable: small inputs into the system can produce large changes. Most of these inputs are bound to be internal in origin. However, policy makers in the West, especially in the administration that has come to power in the United States in 1993, clearly have an opportunity to affect developments in Russia in positive ways and, if they are not careful, in negative ways, too. While the metastable condition in Russia continues to exist, external impulses will have more of an impact than will be the case when Russia stabilizes and more than would be the case were Russia temporarily and tragically to descend into anarchy. A policy of waiting until things settle down would be to miss an opportunity that may not come again. It would be a policy that some have aptly described as 'sleepwalking through history'.

This book describes a series of relatively modest steps that Russia and the United States could take together. Generically, these steps can be thought of as co-operative security, as opposed to arms control and collective security. The latter is important in its own right and is part of the new Russian–US agenda in view of the conflicts that are openly raging in many places across the land mass of Eurasia. It is the subject of study in our larger project and will be explored in future publications.

Co-operative security measures are necessary for two nations that want to move from an adversarial condition to partnership. They are part of the process of building a Russian–US security community. Pronouncements about partnership must quickly be followed by specific policies and actions if disillusionment is not to congeal in Russia and complacency become the order of the day in the United States.

This book recommends such policies and actions but it also seeks to place the current Russian–US relationship in its historical and political context to point out the hurdles that must be overcome and to suggest the consequences of not overcoming them. Therefore, the factors which will inevitably determine the nature of security relations between Russia and the United States are addressed in several chapters. The book focuses on three areas in particular: (*a*) an analysis of the transitional period from the cold war to co-operative security; (*b*) the interaction of military power and international politics; and (*c*) the building of a new security relationship. Within the project a second volume, *A Co-operative Security Order in and for Europe*, is currently being prepared at SIPRI for publication in the near future. It will, of course, examine some of the security issues addressed in this book from a European vantage point.

We want to emphasize that our focus on the Russian–US relationship should not be taken to mean that similar co-operation between Ukraine, for example, and the United States would not be valuable. We think it would be. Some chapters in this book could and we hope will form an agenda for a dialogue between the USA and several of the newly independent states. In fact, co-operative security measures also could find a place in Russian–Ukrainian relations.

It would be naïve to expect that a new security regime embracing much of the Northern Hemisphere would emerge just after the end of the cold war. The shaping of such a regime will be a long and arduous process, not free of wrong decisions taken to meet the needs of the past rather than those of the future. The aim of the joint project, of which this volume is the first fruit, is to inspire new ideas, encourage debate and promote quality decision making.

Adam Daniel Rotfeld
Director
SIPRI

James E. Goodby
Benoit Morel
The Program on International
  Peace and Security
Carnegie Mellon University

January 1993

Acknowledgements

A generous grant from the Ford Foundation to Carnegie Mellon University (CMU) and the Stockholm International Peace Research Institute (SIPRI) made this book possible. The principal investigators of the CMU part of the study were Professors James E. Goodby and Benoit Morel who wish to express their special thanks to Dr Enid Schoettle Okun and Dr Shepard Forman, the former and current directors, respectively, of the Ford Foundation's International Affairs Program. The work on this book was truly collegial. Co-operation is its theme, and this was certainly manifested by all the able men and women who reflected on the nature of a future security regime and dared to write down what they thought, despite the pace of events. The principal investigators want to thank Judyth Twigg and William Newmann not only for the heavy burden of authoring, individually or together, four of the chapters in this book but also for their indispensable help in reviewing and editing the manuscript. Special thanks also are due to Dr Fred Charles Iklé, distinguished scholar and public servant, for his contribution to this book, an adaptation of an article that originally appeared in *The National Interest*. The principal investigators were heartened to find that a man who had served the US Government in very senior positions, including that of Under Secretary of Defense, shared many of their own views about US–Russian security relations. Needless to say, neither Dr Iklé nor any of the authors necessarily endorse anyone's opinions except their own!

SIPRI, under its former Director Dr Walther Stützle and its current Director, Dr Adam Daniel Rotfeld, has provided invaluable help to the CMU team in many ways. Collectively, the SIPRI and CMU team leaders 'brainstormed' a range of ideas and possible emphases for the study. Individually, exchanges of opinion on all manner of problems have contributed wisdom and good humor to the project. The principal investigators particularly thank SIPRI's publication manager, Connie Wall, for timely advice throughout the project, and Jetta Gilligan Borg, for language editing and setting the book in final camera-ready format. Carnegie Mellon was indeed fortunate that its partnership with SIPRI was unlimited in the generously extended help given by the Stockholm team.

The principal investigators wish to thank the Director of the Program on International Peace and Security at Carnegie Mellon University, Dr Granger Morgan, for his confidence that out of this activity might come something useful. The pudding will have to be tasted by many readers before it can be said that he was right, but his faith was comforting and his advice at critical junctures shrewd and penetrating, as always.

Finally, the person on whose shoulders fell the burdens of deadlines, of handling everything from workshops to distributing drafts, and of bringing some semblance of order into the process was Patty Currie. Thanks to her talents and capacity for hard work the project went forward efficiently, swiftly, and pleasurably. May all principal investigators be so blessed!

James E. Goodby and Benoit Morel
Pittsburgh, Pa.
January 1993

Acronyms

ABM	Anti-ballistic missile
ASAT	Anti-satellite
ATBM	Anti-tactical ballistic missile
ATTU	Atlantic-to-the-Urals
AWACS	Airborne warning and control system
C^3	Command, control and communications
C^3I	Command, control, communications and intelligence
CBM	Confidence-building measure
CFE	Conventional Armed Forces in Europe
CIS	Commonwealth of Independent States
CPC	Conflict Prevention Centre
CSBM	Confidence- and security-building measure
CSCE	Conference on Security and Co-operation in Europe
CSO	Committee of Senior Officials
DOD	Department of Defense
EC	European Community
FY	Fiscal year
GPALS	Global Protection Against Limited Strikes
ICBM	Intercontinental ballistic missile
IMF	International Monetary Fund
INF	Intermediate-range nuclear forces
JTIDS	Joint tactical information distribution system
JSTARS	Joint surveillance and target attack radar system
LANTIRN	Low-altitude navigation and targeting with infra-red at night
MFN	Most favored nation
MIRV	Multiple independently targetable re-entry vehicle
MTCR	Missile Technology Control Regime
NATO	North Atlantic Treaty Organization
NPT	Non-Proliferation Treaty
NRRC	Nuclear Risk Reduction Centre
SACEUR	Supreme Allied Commander, Europe
SALT	Strategic Arms Limitation Talks
SLBM	Submarine-launched ballistic missile
START	Strategic Arms Reduction Talks
UNSNF	United Nations Standing Naval Force
WEU	Western European Union
WTO	Warsaw Treaty Organization

Glossary*

Anti-Ballistic Missile
(ABM) Treaty

Treaty signed by the USSR and the USA in 1972 in the SALT I process which prohibits the development, testing and deployment of sea-, air-, space- or mobile land-based ABM systems.

Charter of Paris for a New
Europe

See: Paris Documents.

Commonwealth of
Independent States (CIS)

Established by three of the former Soviet republics in the Agreement on the Commonwealth of Independent States signed in Minsk, Belarus, on 8 December 1991 and joined by eight additional republics in Alma-Ata on 21 December 1991. The CIS Agreement was signed by Armenia, Azerbaijan, Belarus, Kazakhstan, Kyrgyzstan, Moldova, the Russian Federation, Tajikistan, Turkmenistan, Ukraine and Uzbekistan.

Conference on Confidence-
and Security-Building
Measures and Disarmament
in Europe

The Stockholm Conference, part of the CSCE process, was held in 1984–86. The Stockholm Document, in which the confidence-building measures adopted in Helsinki in 1975 are improved and expanded, was signed in 1986.

Conference on Security and
Co-operation in Europe
(CSCE)

A conference which began in 1973 with the participation of all the European states except Albania plus the USA and Canada, and in 1975 adopted a Final Act (also called the Helsinki Declaration), containing, among others, a Document on confidence-building measures and certain aspects of security and disarmament. Follow-up meetings were held in Belgrade (1977–78), Madrid (1980–83), Vienna (1986–89) and Helsinki (1992). A summit meeting of all the CSCE heads of state and government was held in July 1992. As of 1 January 1993, there are 52 CSCE member states including all the former Soviet republics (thereby extending membership outside Europe). The major new CSCE organs created in 1990 are the Council of Foreign Ministers, the Committee of Senior Officials, the Secretariat (seat in Prague), the Conflict Prevention Centre (Vienna), the Office for Democratic Institutions and Human Rights (Warsaw), and the Parliamentary Assembly.

* This glossary is excerpted and adapted from SIPRI, *SIPRI Yearbook 1992: World Armaments and Disarmament* (Oxford University Press: Oxford, 1992), pp. xiv–xxv; and SIPRI, 'Post-cold war security in and for Europe', *SIPRI Fact Sheet*, December 1992.

xvi THE LIMITED PARTNERSHIP

Conventional Armed Forces in Europe (CFE) Treaty	The CFE Treaty was signed by 22 original signatories (members of the WTO and NATO) in Paris in 1990. It sets ceilings on treaty-limited equipment in the ATTU zone. All former Soviet republics agreed later on the principles of the Treaty. The CFE 1A Agreement, setting limits on military manpower, was signed in July 1992. CFE negotiations are now conducted by the CSCE Forum for Security Co-operation in which all member states participate.
North Atlantic Cooperation Council (NACC)	Proposed at the NATO North Atlantic Council meeting in Rome on 8 November 1991, NACC was created as an institution for consultation and co-operation on political and security issues between NATO and the countries of Central and Eastern Europe. As of December 1992, the 37 members included the NATO and former WTO states and all the newly independent former Soviet republics.
Open Skies Treaty	In 1989 President George Bush revived the idea of an Open Skies regime of aerial inspection, first put forth in 1955, and proposed an agreement permitting flights by unarmed military or civilian surveillance aircraft from each alliance over the territory of the USA, the USSR and their NATO and WTO allies. Talks were conducted parallel to the CFE and CFE 1A negotiations in Vienna in 1990–91. In 1990 the USA and the USSR agreed on a basic plan for a treaty at the Ottawa Open Skies Conference. The Treaty on Open Skies was signed by 25 NATO and former WTO states in Vienna on 24 March 1992 and provided also for sharing of data.
Paris Documents	A set of five documents adopted at the November 1990 Paris CSCE summit meeting. They include the CFE Treaty, the Joint Declaration of Twenty-Two States, the Charter of Paris for a New Europe, the Supplementary Document to give new effect to certain provisions contained in the Charter, and the Vienna Document 1990. Several new CSCE institutions were set up in the Paris Documents.
Stockholm Conference	*See*: Conference on Confidence- and Security-Building Measures and Disarmament in Europe.
Strategic Arms Limitation Talks (SALT)	Negotiations between the USSR and the USA which opened in 1969 and sought to limit the strategic nuclear forces, both offensive and defensive, of both sides. The SALT I Interim Agreement and the ABM Treaty were signed in 1972. The negotiations were terminated in 1979, when the SALT II Treaty was signed (it was never ratified).

Strategic Arms Reduction Talks (START) Treaty, START I	US–Soviet treaty, signed in Moscow on 31 July 1991, which reduces US and Soviet offensive strategic nuclear weapons to equal aggregate levels over a seven-year period. It sets numerical limits on deployed strategic nuclear delivery vehicles (SNDVs)—ICBMs, SLBMs and heavy bombers—and the nuclear warheads they carry. The Lisbon Protocol to the START Treaty was signed in Lisbon on 23 May 1992 by the USA, Russia, Belarus, Kazakhstan and Ukraine. Belarus, Kazakhstan and Ukraine pledge to accede to the START Treaty and to join the NPT as non-nuclear states 'in the shortest possible time'. In separate letters, they agree to eliminate all strategic weapons on their territories within the seven-year START reduction period.
START II	Treaty between the Russian Federation and the USA, signed in Moscow on 3 January 1993 by President George Bush and President Boris Yeltsin. The Treaty is to operate concurrently with the START I Treaty, and its entry into force was understood to be dependent on the ratification by Belarus, Kazakhstan and Ukraine of the Lisbon START Protocol (see preceding entry). START II provides for the elimination of US and Russian MIRVed land-based long-range ballistic missiles (ICBMs). It limits the remaining warheads and bomber weapons to between 3000 and 3500. Warheads on submarine-launched ballistic missiles are to be reduced to between 1700 and 1750. These reductions are to be accomplished by the year 2003 or by the end of the year 2000 if the USA can contribute to the financing of the destruction or elimination of strategic offensive arms in Russia. The reductions required by the agreement will be carried out by eliminating missile launchers and heavy bombers using START procedures and, in some cases, by downloading the number of warheads carried by ballistic missiles. These reductions amount to more than two-thirds of the nuclear warheads held by each side as of September 1990.
Vienna Documents on CSBMs	The Vienna Document 1990 on CSBMs, included in the set of Paris Documents and negotiated by all CSCE member states, repeats many of the provisions in the 1986 Stockholm Document and expands several others. It established a communications network and the CSCE Conflict Prevention Centre. The Vienna Document 1992 on new CSBMs was adopted in March 1992. It builds on the Vienna Document 1990 and supplements its provisions with new mechanisms and constraining provisions. The CSBM negotiations are now conducted by the CSCE Forum for Security Co-operation.

Part I
Introduction

1. Introduction

James E. Goodby

I. Regime transition: from cold war to co-operative security

It is a risky business to write about post-cold war, post-Soviet security arrangements in any part of the world and especially foolhardy to write about relations between Washington and Moscow. It is necessary, however, to pause occasionally during the rush of the headlines to ask what might be possible in the days ahead. Otherwise, events will remain in the saddle. The future of international politics is not completely a blank page. It is the product of history, of contemporary events and of human nature. Unpredictable though it is, the future course of Russian–US relations will contain familiar elements—features from contemporary life or from the past. In chapter 2, Dr Fred Charles Iklé refers to the lessons of history as he builds his case for a Russian–US defence community. Part II of this book searches for lessons in the great revolutionary developments that have occurred in what is now, probably transiently, known as the Commonwealth of Independent States. This will be the first step in an effort to define a frame of reference for US relations with the new republics, especially with Russia, in the era beyond deterrence and beyond the self-preservation instinct that motivated the limited co-operation between Moscow and Washington during the cold war.

There was a link between the United States and the Soviet Union during the cold war that required a watchful and wary attention to diplomatic and strategic interactions even though there was hardly any mobility in the basic relationship between the two superpowers. Now the relationship is characterized by a high degree of mobility, which requires close attention to the trajectories on which the two nations are moving. In chapter 3, William W. Newmann analyses the Bush Administration's relations with Mikhail Gorbachev's Government during the Gulf crisis of 1990–91 and during the period of rapid disintegration of Soviet power in late 1991. He suggests that many of the same factors that prompted US–Soviet co-operation in the Gorbachev era will promote US–Russian co-operation in the future; a special relationship between Washington and Moscow already may be emerging.

Daria Fane, in chapter 4, places the collapse of the Soviet Union in the context of the fall of other empires and reminds us that winding down an empire can be a long and agonizing process. Nationalism will remain a threat to order and stability in Russia—the empire within the empire—and the other new republics. The problems of the new states are daunting, but faltering steps towards self-rule suggest that diverse and vibrant societies can emerge from the wreckage. Enormous security implications for the West hinge on how events unfold.

Turning to Russia's external relations, Sergey Rogov writes that the three circles of Russian foreign policy interests will be relations with other republics of the Commonwealth, with the nations around the periphery of the former Soviet Union and with the West, especially the USA and Western Europe. He urges, in chapter 5, that a defence community be established within the Commonwealth of Independent States while US–Russian co-operative military relationships are developing. The difficulties President Boris Yeltsin faced in creating a Russian foreign policy and institutions to run it are the themes developed by Mikhail E. Bezrukov in chapter 6. He welcomes a US policy of vigorous engagement with the new republics, even to the extent of mediating their differences with each other.

In chapter 7, David Kaiser writes about Russian–US relations from the historical perspective of the cold war and great power politics of earlier centuries. Destructive effects have resulted from the image each nation has held of the other during the cold war. Long-term differences between the two countries do not appear to warrant any lasting enmity. As great powers, but no longer as powers holding sway over large parts of the globe, he thinks the US–Russian security agenda has considerable constructive potential but will place severe demands on diplomacy. The general conclusions deriving from the chapters in part II of this book are clear and consistent:

1. Moscow and Washington will continue to interact extensively.
2. Sensitive issues of security will form a significant part of their agenda.
3. There are opportunities for close co-operation between the USA, Russia and the other new republics in the post-Soviet era.

Whether co-operation should take the form of a US–Russian defence community, as Dr Iklé suggests, or some more limited form of partnership, is a question that the rest of this book seeks to illuminate. Regrettably, there is a significant chance that serious security co-operation may not materialize in the future between the two nations. Already there are abundant signs that deep-rooted suspicions will be hard to eradicate. The publics and policy makers in the two nations have a rare opportunity to support and to construct a close Moscow–Washington security relationship. If this moment in history is not seized by those who have the power to do so, the history of missed chances and the wars that have ensued from them may be repeated.

II. Military power and international security

The chapters in part III, military power and international security, develop the theme that the military forces of the USA and some of the post-Soviet republics will interact in a way that will affect international stability and security even though these forces are no longer directed against each other. As actors in an international system common to them both, all the power attributes of the USA and Russia will influence relations between the two nations. The influence may be brought to bear indirectly and may not manifest itself in a competitive sense at all. It may amount to nothing more than how Moscow and Washington are able to go about their business in the world. However, the instabilities inherent in the transition from a bipolar to a multipolar system may heighten the significance of defence-related decisions by Moscow or Washington and send unwanted and unintended tremors through the political structures of the two countries.

Russia will remain a military power of considerable weight during the turbulent years ahead. Other post-Soviet republics, especially Ukraine, also will possess significant military assets. Defence budget cuts in the USA, made possible by the disappearance of a Soviet military threat and necessary by a troubled economic structure, will result in a smaller but still formidable military establishment. The interaction between these military forces will be of an entirely different quality than during the cold war, but it is not likely that interaction, even directly in some respects, will cease to exist. The collision of US and Russian submarines off Murmansk and comments on the incident by both sides provide evidence of that. This is true also for high technology with military applications, as can be seen from the Pentagon's initial reluctance to encourage US purchases of Russian technology and the Russian Government's reflections on the merits of arms sales.

In chapters 8 and 9, Major General Edward B. Atkeson, USA (Ret.) projects the possible shape of the theatre forces of the United States and the republics that emerged from the wreckage of the Soviet state, looking ahead to the year 2000. This is an extraordinarily difficult undertaking in these uncertain times, but the effort is necessary to a comprehension of the kinds of policy options that lie ahead. More important doubtless than the specific numbers of this or that item of military hardware will be the thinking that lies behind development and acquisition and force structure decisions. These projections afford a glimpse of the kinds of considerations that will be in the minds of decision makers in the leadership of the various governments.

High technology will remain a salient part of the US–Russian security relationship and perhaps loom relatively larger than during the cold war. Dr Benoit Morel writes in chapter 10 about the revolution in US defence technology, part of which was revealed in the Persian Gulf War and much of which is still unfolding. The vitality of the technological base of Russia and the other post-Soviet republics is very much in doubt as of 1992, but these assets are national treasures, certainly in Russia, and Moscow will strive mightily to save them for better times ahead. Dr Morel points to the numerous ways in which interaction between the USA and Russia in this area can create tension. He believes that a more open, unrestricted form of co-operation between the technological establishments of the two nations will be necessary to prevent misunderstanding and colliding interests.

For years, scholars and analysts of US–Soviet relations have been using mathematical models as tools to a better understanding of complexities that words alone cannot describe. Irving Lachow argues in chapter 11 that catastrophe theory offers a better tool for modelling purposes than linear methods currently in use. Models that are linear in concept assume a kind of continuity in the interaction of the USA and Russia that no longer exists. Instead, the relationship is marked by discontinuities and is therefore a non-linear system. The general reader should take comfort from realizing that the word 'catastrophe' is not intended to be a prediction of disaster but is used simply to describe a break or jump, in this case in the nature of the US–Russian relationship.

The model advocated by Irving Lachow employs the concept of 'metastability' to describe the situation in Russia and in the system that presently constitutes the Commonwealth of Independent States. This is a condition in which a resolution of the dynamics within the system tends to persist but where the outcome can be altered or overcome even by modest inputs. Instability, of course, is a condition in which there is no tendency for the outcome to persist, and stability is the situation where large inputs are required to revise the resolution of the factors at play. For policy makers as well as analysts these distinctions are highly significant in determining how a particular problem in US–Russian relations should be approached. Understanding these distinctions can mean the difference, for example, between engagement or non-engagement with Russia's shaky government.

III. Building a new security relationship

Turning points in history have not been stories with happy endings. They have been seen as opportunities to overcome mistakes of the past and to lay down the foundations for a new international order. Historically, however, these have been the times when the seeds of future conflict have been planted. Probably this turning point will be no exception, and yet Kant's idea of a Pacific Federation, a zone of peace among democratic states, may be closer to broad realization in the Russian–US world than ever before in history. Many strands of policy must come together in just the right way for this to happen, and one of these strands must be security policy, as Dr Iklé stresses in chapter 2. Part IV of the book presents specific approaches that might forestall renewed competition and build, instead, at least a limited partnership between the USA and Russia.

The ideas of co-operation and competition contended quite unequally during the cold war. Although there were champions of co-operation, in both countries, the rivalry between the two superpowers dominated their relationship. In chapter 12, Steven Kull describes the war of ideas between those advocating co-operation and those who saw competition as the only correct policy. Despite 'new thinking', the legacy of competition still shadows public and official attitudes and may imprison thinking in an outdated straitjacket. *The Pilgrim's Progress* had it right:

And let them that come after have a care
Lest they for trespassing his pris'ners are,
Whose castle's Doubting and whose name's Despair.

Russian and other post-Soviet military forces are in deep crisis; therefore a co-operative security regime should begin by dealing with some near-term problems, for example, those arising from Soviet withdrawal from East and Central Europe. Judyth L. Twigg and William W. Newmann go on from there in chapter 13 to discuss the special role that the United States can play in integrating Russian and other post-Soviet military forces into a Russian–US security community. This, they write, should include military-to-military co-operation and, eventually, joint military operations. Their chapter breaks new ground in conceptualizing about the post-cold war functions of what have been called 'confidence- and security-building measures' (CSBMs). Mechanisms such as transparency still are important in US–Russian relations, not to complicate the task of planning a surprise attack but to facilitate the task of co-operation in operational matters between the military forces of the USA and the post-Soviet republics.

Soviet and US naval forces were left out of most cold war arms control negotiations and agreements. Steven E. Miller argues in chapter 14 that there is little reason now to oppose a co-operative regime at sea, including transparency measures, and that these could help overcome residual mistrust. Arms control, fortunately, no longer defines the outer limits of Russian–US co-operation. Joint Russian–US naval actions should become a part of a security partnership, Miller suggests, noting that the two navies already are beginning to exercise together.

Long-term stability in Russian–US security relations can no longer depend, at least exclusively, on traditional thinking about military balance and arms control, and it cannot be limited simply to political relations. In the post-cold war world, additional methods of ensuring stability are feasible and should be utilized. Judyth L. Twigg writes about these methods in chapter 15. They focus on defence planning in the areas of weapon procurement, budgets, doctrine, strategy and organization. She stresses the difficulties that must be overcome in introducing transparency and habits of co-operation into US–Russian patterns of behaviour in these sensitive matters, but she also offers practical ideas through which progress could be made.

No reader of this book should conclude that even a limited partnership between the United States and the new republics of post-Soviet Eurasia will be easy to achieve. Every chapter highlights that fact while also pointing to policies and methods that seem promising and offer hope. In the final chapter of this book, William W. Newmann discusses one military subject that seems most unpromising, if not hopeless, as an area for transparency and co-operation. When any nation makes a decision to use force, the tightest possible secrecy is imposed to maximize prospects for success. Obviously, the degree of secrecy that is possible differs from case to case and deception frequently substitutes for secrecy. Even in the closest and most long-standing of alliances, however, the possibilities for co-operation and sharing of information fall to practically zero when one of the allies undertakes a unilateral military action against a third country. The same thing can happen within a multinational group where each member is working for the same objective.

Chapter 16 uses case studies to examine the problems posed for co-operative security regimes in such circumstances. Grenada, Panama and the Persian Gulf War are analysed by the author with a view to showing how the requirements of operational security affected US communications with other countries. An effectively functioning partnership is essential to absorb or to deflect the many shocks that are bound to be delivered to the Russian–US relationship by circumstances that neither government will ever fully control.

2. The case for a Russian–US security community

*Fred Charles Iklé**

I. Introduction

The strategic relationship now emerging between the United States and Russia opens a new chapter in world history. During most of this century, these two great nations could change their relationship only incrementally, if at all. But since August 1991, their relations have entered a period of unique malleability, one that offers an epochal opportunity for creative statesmanship.[1]

By far the most promising course of action at this time would be to construct a US–Russian defence community, designed as a growing programme of co-operation that would build progressively closer links between the military establishments of the two sides. Such a relationship with the main heir to Soviet military power would greatly enhance the USA's security in the coming era, when weapons of mass destruction will spread throughout the world.

Since the failed coup in August 1991, much handwringing has been going on in the West about the fragility of the new, democratic government in Moscow. Slowly, some US and European efforts have been organized to provide food and medicine as a form of token humanitarian assistance. And the United States has joined Germany and other European nations in efforts to ease the difficult transition to a market economy in the former Soviet republics. To soothe anxieties about the tens of thousands of nuclear weapons that were scattered among several former Soviet republics, the United States has also offered assistance for nuclear arms transports and storage.

Traversing these near-term hazards is, to be sure, necessary for reaching a better future. But it is not sufficient. The basic transformation of the US–Russian relationship that is so essential for our security cannot be completed within a year or two. Seventy years of Bolshevism and 40 years of cold war have left a hazardous legacy in both East and West—a spiritual, intellectual and material pollution that will require a purposeful effort over many years to be rendered harmless. The old poisons could become virulent again, like an infectious disease that has lain dormant for a long time.

[1] I am referring here to 'Russia' in part because that is the pre-1917 name for the nation that stretched from the Pacific Ocean to the Baltic Sea; in part because the Russian Republic, perhaps in combination with a few other former Soviet republics, will clearly be the most important successor state of the USSR.

* Fred Charles Iklé was US Under Secretary of Defense for Policy in the Reagan Administration and is currently a Distinguished Scholar at the Center for Strategic and International Studies, Washington, DC. This chapter is adapted from an article in *The National Interest*, no. 26 (winter 1991/92).

II. Danger signs

Like no other dimension of the emerging US–Russian relationship, the military interaction remains heavily burdened by the cold war legacy. On both sides old habits of the mind, reinforced by old bureaucratic practices, subtly influence new strategic concepts and new war plans. Throughout the northern hemisphere thousands of military artefacts remain—armaments, electronic instalments, air bases, naval ports, laboratories—that invest the cold war apparitions with tangible reality made of hard metal and reinforced cement. Amidst the detritus of the Soviet Union, the Russian Republic has inherited vast arsenals, huge military forces and an enormous (although presently crippled) military–industrial complex.

Given this context, we should seek to anticipate how things might go wrong in the evolving military relationship between the USA and Russia. At first brush, it may appear reassuring to see how military officers from both sides get along with each other. The military harbours less animosity towards its former cold war adversary than other population groups do. US military leaders are eager to develop cordial and co-operative relations with their Soviet counterparts; to speak to them 'as a friend—no longer as an enemy', as General Colin Powell put it. And the Soviet military has shown that they reciprocate this sentiment.

Underneath this new comity, however, a dangerous dynamic threatens to push the USA and Russia into a new military confrontation. One way in which this dynamic works is through the growing military strength of other nations that are seen as potential adversaries by Washington or Moscow, and hence as compelling the United States, or Russia, to acquire compensating military strength. For example, many in the USA are cautioning against further reductions in the US defence budget, for fear that US forces might not be strong enough later this decade to defeat 'another Iraq'. Similarly, Russia's new military leaders anticipate that their nation will have to be armed against ever more sophisticated weaponry among (unnamed) nations to the south, and perhaps even against independent armies that are being established by some of the former Soviet republics. Strategic planners both in the USA and Russia will surely want to see their own nation's military technology stay well ahead of these potentially threatening new powers.

Alas, with such efforts to arm against emerging 'Third World' military threats, the USA and Russia will stumble into new kinds of arms competition between each other, covering a wide range of weapon developments. And the international arms trade will add fuel to this fire. Because of sharply declining defence budgets at home, arms manufacturers in the United States, Western Europe and the former Soviet republics are all anxious now to find new markets. The few importers in this buyers' market who are still solvent can demand some of the best and latest technologies. It will not take long for nations acquiring such advanced armaments to be seen—either by Washington or Moscow—as new military threats.

The dynamic that could lever the USA and Russia towards a new military confrontation also will include tensions created by secret and possibly illicit weapon developments. In spite of *glasnost*, the political transformation in Moscow and the verification arrangements of recent arms accords, the battle between openness and secrecy is far from over—not only in the Soviet military establishment that is being inherited by Russia and other republics, but in the US military as well.

When the detailed verification provisions of the Treaty Between the United States of America and the Union of Soviet Socialist Republics on the Reduction and Limitation of Strategic Offensive Arms (the START Treaty) were finally being settled, it was the US negotiators more often than the Soviet ones who insisted on limiting access for the other side's inspectors. Indeed, protecting the secrecy of certain military technologies had a higher priority for the USA than enlarging the agreed scope for verification. For example, the United States sought to protect technological secrets of its radar-evading 'stealth' aircraft.

For the Russian military, shielding its latest technology from US 'espionage' may be less important than keeping other kinds of secrets. Quite likely the Russian military establishment still keeps some ugly skeletons in its closet. When former Soviet Foreign Minister Eduard Shevardnadze admitted that the Krasnoyarsk radar station in Siberia violated the Anti-Ballistic Missile (ABM) Treaty, Soviet military officers still sought to deny culpability. And the story has yet to come out, it seems, on violations of the treaty banning biological weapons.

The old penchant of the Soviet military for pushing to the very edge of what arms agreements allow—and sometimes well beyond—may not have been entirely eradicated by the democratic revolution. Besides, the complexities and ambiguities of recent arms agreements will provide ample opportunity for hard-to-prove cheating. In this environment, the cloak of secrecy will do double duty for the self-styled 'patriots' in Moscow. It will shield them from US arms control monitors as well as from budget-conscious economists in their own government. Indeed, in the coming years, some officers and managers of Russia's arms industries may seek to perpetuate old practices of secrecy, not as protection from potential foreign enemies, but to keep their parliament and public in the dark about the burden that their military continues to impose on the nation's economy.

Tensions caused by military secrecy could mar US–Russian relations in many ways. On both sides, it is safe to predict, bureaucracies will show great zest and ingenuity in creating confrontational issues about 'espionage' and 'cheating'. Secrecy is a customary companion of military research projects. And it is to be expected that both the US and Russian military establishments will continue to conduct certain research projects whose purpose, at least in part, will be to stay ahead of the former cold war adversary.

III. Nuclear gridlock

Among Americans associated with nuclear weapon research, there is nearly unanimous conviction that the United States must continue to test nuclear weapons, regardless of what happens to nuclear testing in the former Soviet Union. Since the 1950s Moscow has favoured a ban on all nuclear testing, while Washington's position has shifted back and forth between reluctantly considering such a ban and opposing it outright. In prior decades the US reluctance was due, in part, to the fear that the Soviet Union could easily cheat in ways that would not yield sufficiently unambiguous evidence. Today the former Soviet nuclear weapon establishment is under political pressure not to resume testing for environmental reasons. Should current differences on nuclear testing between Washington and Moscow persist for several years, those in Moscow who want arms spending again to increase will argue that one-sided nuclear testing by the USA is beginning to undermine Russia's nuclear deterrent.

The hoary dispute about nuclear testing is merely a skirmish in a larger battle—the emancipation of nuclear strategy from cold war thinking. The warp and woof of nearly all strategic thought—not only in the United States and the former Soviet Union, but also in France and Great Britain—remains the East–West enmity of the last 40 years. And this strategic thought remains locked into place in each of these countries by their equally dated nuclear arsenals.

To be sure, we have heard some good news after August 1991. President George Bush decided in September to withdraw most of the USA's so-called 'theatre' nuclear weapons, and President Mikhail Gorbachev agreed to reciprocate. In one fell swoop, a large artefact in the cold war museum of nuclear horrors was thus scheduled to be dismantled.

What was the purpose of this artefact? The story reaches back to the early 1950s, when the United States began to deploy theatre nuclear weapons for two reasons: as a means of nuclear retaliation less massive that the strategic bomber force, and to give the US Army—which was jealous of the Navy's and the Air Force's nuclear missions—its own nuclear arms. To keep a long story short, since the late 1950s the various rationales for these weapons have disappeared one by one. In particular, the principal target for US theatre nuclear weapons— the Red Army—has gone home.

As these changes occurred, those who believed strongly in the merits of theatre nuclear weapons reached for a metaphysical rationale: that nuclear weapons based forward on the territory that might be attacked would provide a more credible deterrent than weapons based in the rear. Here is a reminder that military doctrine based on disconfirmed beliefs can survive for decades.

Even though theatre nuclear weapons will cease to burden this relationship, the cold war gridlock is more difficult to overcome for 'strategic' nuclear weapons—the thousands of nuclear arms on missiles and bombers of intercontinental reach. During the last four decades each superpower built an enormously elaborate apparatus capable of totally destroying the other and designed so that this cataclysm could be irrevocably unleashed within minutes—on purpose, or (perhaps) by accident. The risk that this supposedly stable system might end in the superpowers' mutual suicide has not yet been eliminated. While the combination locks on nuclear weapons that many people now confidently promote might ameliorate this risk, they cannot eliminate it. A safeguard system relying on codes that would instantly have to be passed to thousands of command posts needs to be renewed and tested from time to time. (The Chernobyl reactor *did* have safeguards; it exploded because of a mismanaged test of its safeguard system!)

Fortunately, both Washington and Moscow are seeking to overcome these dangers. Already in September 1991, President Bush decided to take all US strategic bombers and part of the land-based US missile force off alert. And early in 1992 he proposed deep cuts on both sides in missiles with multiple warheads. President Boris Yeltsin seemed eager to respond to these proposals and to find ways to overcome the US–Russian nuclear confrontation entirely.

Unless these efforts succeed and the cold war legacy of the confrontational nuclear deterrence postures can be eliminated, new tensions and conflicts would arise between Moscow and Washington. Whenever one side might modernize elements of its strategic forces, the other side would find reason to worry. Military staffs on each side would continue to perform calculations to estimate whether the Other Side (who used to be The Enemy) could somehow launch a first strike without having to fear massive and certain retaliation. On each side, estimates would also be prepared on the number of minutes within which the retaliatory strike would have to be launched before the codes to unlock nuclear weapons could no longer be transmitted to the missile and bomber crews. Such cold war imagery would thus persist, like a genetic defect, long after the conflict itself has ended.

IV. Woe and wickedness

Threats from third nations, competition in military research and contradictions in nuclear strategy all have potential to ratchet the United States and Russia towards a new enmity. To make matters worse, as these pressures and tensions do their work, they will be exacerbated on occasion by accidents, mistakes or mischief—the woeful triplets that always intrude into human affairs.

A future dispute between Washington and Moscow about some secret military research project, for example, might suddenly become inflamed because of an accident that, to the USA, looked like a hostile act planned in Moscow at the highest level—the Soviet shooting-down of a Korean airliner in 1983 comes to mind. Disagreements about a new arms programme (ostensibly directed against third country threats) might be aggravated by incidents involving 'spies' and denial of legitimate access for arms control inspectors. Such incidents, perhaps started by junior officers, could well be magnified by mistakes higher up in the decision chain.

To make matters worse, scattered amidst all these combustible tensions between Moscow and Washington will be plenty of mischief-makers. Like smouldering embers, Bolshevik hatred of the West will linger on in the minds of many senior officials in Russia. In all the former Soviet republics, the older generation had to spend its formative years in a din of anti-Western locutions, distortions and lies. One recalls that several years after *glasnost* had swept such old-think aside, then KGB Chief Vladimir Kryuchkov and Prime Minister Valentin Pavlov still gave speeches bristling with hostility towards the West. Although these two men are facing trial as leaders of the August coup, years from now like-minded Bolsheviks might again—or still—occupy positions of influence in the lands that Stalin ruled.

In 1920, Lenin asserted that 'the real basis of contemporary international politics is the coalition of all powerful capitalist countries of the world against Soviet Russia'; and Stalin in 1925 foreshadowed the cold war era by declaring that 'the world is now divided into two camps'. Two camps—'us' and 'them'— who will destroy whom? Paint these old fighting words with new lush colours of Russian nationalism, omit that tedious Marxist theorizing, and one has the core of new ideology for Russia's unreconstructed Bolsheviks to rally throngs of discontented youths—that essential ingredient for a political mass movement.

If, sometime during this decade, such a political movement were to become influential in Russia or to gain controlling power, much of the enormous Soviet military establishment would still exist. It will take many years and strong political leadership (both in short supply) to transform a major part of the gigantic Soviet arms industries into genuine civilian enterprises, to deactivate substantial military forces and to dismantle excess armaments, bases and military infrastructure. The US–Russian military relationship would therefore have a decisive influence—for better or for worse—if a reactionary political movement in Russia sought to stir up tensions with the United States. Unless most of the cold war legacy had been cleared away in the meantime, a new Bolshevik-nationalist–fascist movement could readily gain ardent support throughout the Russian military establishment. A long list of growing US 'threats' could easily be compiled: continued US nuclear tests, undiminished US naval superiority, expanded deployment of the 'stealth' and precision technologies that won the Persian Gulf War, and the survival of the North Atlantic Treaty Organization (NATO) and of most US bases that are 'encircling' Russia even though the Warsaw Pact has been abolished.

V. A gathering storm

One recalls that after World War I, Germany became a democratic nation free of its imperial burdens. During its first four years, to be sure, the new Weimar Republic had a troubled time. It suffered a string of disasters—a Communist *putsch*, a Nazi *putsch*, hyperinflation, food riots—the kind of tribulations that people in Moscow are now worried about. During the following five years, however, Germany enjoyed stable democratic government, vigorous economic growth, minimal unemployment, friendly relations with all its neighbours and a burst of extraordinary cultural creativity. Europe and the world seemed at peace. Suddenly, the Great Depression and its wave of massive unemployment tilted the political forces in Germany (and in Japan as well) in favour of an ideology of violence and expansion.

Yet Adolf Hitler could not have consolidated his power, much less launched his sweeping territorial conquests a mere seven years later, had the German military establish:nent not been so willing and so well prepared to revert to a policy of imperial expansion. Throughout the seemingly peaceful Weimar years, the German military, stuck in their 1914 mentality, saw the world as divided into two camps—and readied themselves accordingly.

History, of course, will not repeat itself—not exactly. And every lesson from history can be contradicted with another one. Should we heed today the lessons from the 1920s, or the lessons from the 1930s? Were France and Great Britain too slow in the 1920s in weaving closer ties with Weimar Germany, especially with its military? Or were they too slow in rearming themselves in the 1930s? If again 'the Russians are coming,' how should the United States respond?

The Pentagon's answer today is 'reconstitution,' by which is meant the rebuilding and refurbishing of the USA's armed forces. Defense Secretary Dick Cheney has rightly emphasized that such a rearmament effort would entail building 'wholly new forces' whose equipment and weaponry would have to be developed long in advance. Much of the equipment that played a crucial role in the US victory over Iraq, Cheney pointed out, 'was developed 20 or 30 years ago'. Unless the Pentagon keeps funding a wide range of research and development projects, the United States will be ill prepared to rebuild its military strength if it had to meet a global crisis in the future.

In this age of turmoil throughout vast reaches of Eurasia, to maintain a capacity for reconstituting military strength is prudent. But to rely on this capacity as the main guardian of the USA's security and world peace would be reckless. If the storm should gather again, a rearmament programme would not offer a safe haven to which the United States could comfortably retreat.

A policy of rearming would have to gain the co-operation of allies, be guided by agreed strategic concepts and be supported by the American people. Questions regarding nuclear arms and nuclear strategy would arise at the outset. Conflicting ideas about a policy of nuclear deterrence—which originally emerged gradually during the cold war and hence rarely stirred up public anxiety—would be hurled into the political arena. Some would want to rely mainly on new defensive technologies, others would want to reconstruct a stable balance between offensive forces; some would want to rearm full speed and without any restraints, others would want to negotiate new arms agreements.

Such discord would revive the profound—and justified—fear of nuclear destruction that has lain dormant since the worst years of the cold war. Washington's political climate would very likely resemble the Viet Nam years during the Johnson and Nixon administrations, rather than the Truman and Eisenhower years when the policies of containment and peace–through–strength could be so successfully launched and promoted with substantial consensual support. The nation's resoluteness and confidence would be sapped by recriminations. Americans and their remaining allies would ask how the victory of democracy that ended the cold war could have been so foolishly squandered. They would blame their leaders for having failed to build an enduring peace with Russia after the attempted coup, during those few years of great opportunity.

Enough of this nightmare! Our opportunity is not yet lost.

VI. The problem is the solution

In 1991, the Union of Soviet Socialist Republics expired, and the autopsy revealed that it died of three chronic illnesses. Most visible after the failed coup in 1991 was its death by terminal imperialism. The world's last empire could no longer hold its independent-minded nationalities together. The second chronic illness was communism. As the world's first 'socialist' state, the USSR was afflicted for over 70 years—longer than any other country—with the economic inefficiency, political stultification and human cruelty of the communist system of government. The third cause of the USSR's demise was militarism. No other industrialized state in the world has for so long spent so much of its national wealth on armaments and military forces. Soviet militarism, in harness with communism, destroyed the Soviet economy and thus hastened the self-destruction of the Soviet Empire.

Of the Soviet Union's three mortal illnesses, militarism poses the greatest danger of being passed on to the successor states; not because Russians (and Ukrainians, etc.) are a particularly militaristic people, but because militarism has become so entrenched in society. Both figuratively and literally it is cemented into the landscape.

The US–Russian military relationship, therefore, presents the greatest challenge for statesmanship. By contrast, economic relations will have much less sway, either to hurt or to help. To help, US economic assistance can play only a small role, since conditions on both sides preclude 'another Marshall Plan'. To hurt, economic relations are too crushingly one-sided. We need not fear the day when 'Russia-bashers' in Congress accuse Russia of flooding the US market with automobiles or computers.

Similarly, diplomatic relations by themselves are unlikely to cause a new enmity. Mistakes in diplomacy could bring a new cold war only if accompanied, or followed, by moves in the military sphere—such as Russian security guarantees or arms shipments to an aggressor nation, Russian covert military assistance to terrorists or troublemakers, hints from Moscow of nuclear blackmail or an outright attack by Russian forces on another nation.

While the military interaction between the USA and Russia in the coming years is pregnant with danger, paradoxically it also offers the most promising opportunity for building a solid structure of peaceful co-operation. The new, friendly links between Washington and Moscow are still fragile, without roots in the two governments and overly dependent on changing personnel in positions of leadership. For improved relations to become enduring, they must be anchored in institutions that are endowed with steadiness, influence and continuity. On the Russian side, only the military institutions can currently meet this bureaucratic requirement. The Foreign Ministry in Moscow lacks power and permanence, and the trade and financial institutions for the post-communist market economy have yet to emerge from the vortex of change.

Proposals for joint activities and common structures between the US and the Russian military establishments do not have to sail against the wind these days. Presidents Bush and Yeltsin agreed that their two nations 'do not regard each other as potential adversaries'. Indeed, both used the word 'ally' to refer to the prospects of the new relationship. Moreover, starting February 1992, concrete steps have been agreed to for co-operating on the dismantling of nuclear weapons, on the conversion of arms industries, and on missile defence and warning systems.

In the present atmosphere of good will between the two militaries, there is no lack of ideas for joint projects. Lacking still is a sense of direction—or, more to the point, a sense of destination. Without an agreed destination, all these joint projects would merely provide occasions for good fellowship between US and Russian military people. Without institutional links animated by a common purpose, these fraternal relations offer scant protection against a new enmity. One is reminded of those yellow photographs from around 1910, depicting German, French, Russian and Austrian generals enjoying lavish picnics together while watching through binoculars their splendidly dressed troops executing a joint manœuvre—better to kill each other in World War I.

VII. Towards a defence community

A clear and ambitious destination should guide the United States and the new Russia in shaping their military relationship. The common goal should be to eradicate the adversarial confrontation throughout the two military establishments. This endeavour will take many years, moving forward step by step through changes in the deployment of forces, their armaments, their exercises and training, and in each side's preparation for war. Great strides have already been made; most significantly, the dismantling of the military confrontation in the centre of Europe and, recently, the reduction on both sides of nuclear forces that are kept on alert.

To describe the destination of the evolving military relationship as a 'defence community' serves to evoke a useful analogy with the 'economic communities' that began to link former enemies in Europe 40 years ago, starting with the Coal and Steel Community launched in May 1950 to promote lasting reconciliation between France and Germany. The analogy, of course, must not be pushed too far; and like all enterprises that seek to shape international affairs, the attempt to create a US–Russian defence community might fail.

Failure, though, is more likely for a policy that would cling to the tried and old. Denied a constructive long-term goal, such a policy would lack the calendar to force a process of step-by-step improvement. The USA and Russia, in their security relationship, would sail ahead without a compass, bobbing and weaving between partnership and confrontation, anxiously focused on some quivering balance of armaments, forever undecided whether to live with each other as friend or foe.

The nuclear arsenals on both sides will provide the lever and the fulcrum to create a defence community. On nuclear arms, Washington and Moscow are accustomed to the idea of co-operation, and the USA's allies favour, or at least do not oppose, such co-operation. Prudent policy makers will continue to be burdened with the threat to national survival that lurks behind the continuing 'balance of terror'. And from time to time, incidents will occur to stir up public anxiety about nuclear war.

The idea that someday, somehow, this latent threat of massive nuclear destruction should be 'abolished' is neither new nor the brainchild only of pacifists and left-wingers. When the nuclear age was only nine years old and proliferation had not yet started, even a realist like John Foster Dulles could speak of 'nuclear abolition' as at least a distant possibility.[2] Today, in a literal sense, abolition appears to have become impossible. But the political transformation in Moscow has now opened the door to other solutions—although it may not stay open for long. While the United States and Russia cannot abolish nuclear weapons, they can overcome the nuclear confrontation; and in doing so, they will go a long way towards establishing a defence community.

Too much has been made of reducing the number of nuclear weapons, and not enough of the need to reduce the adversarial postures of the strategic forces on both sides. Without a fundamental change in these postures, even the most drastic reductions in the number of weapons would still leave the USA and Russia in a potentially mortal confrontation. Senior defence officials have reminded us that Soviet missiles could destroy the USA in 30 minutes. This would be true if the 4900 nuclear missile warheads permitted by START were reduced tenfold.

To overcome this confrontation, both sides must abolish the hair-trigger launch procedures of their strategic forces and abandon their constant readiness to unleash nuclear cataclysm. Early in 1992, Presidents Bush and Yeltsin began to take encouraging steps in this direction. The reduction in alert states of

---

[2] In 1954, Dulles conveyed to President Eisenhower the thought that even if the United States could break up the Soviet control over Eastern Europe and China, 'this in itself would not actually touch the heart of the problem: Soviet atomic plenty'. Secretary of State Dulles knew that the only real solution might be 'nuclear abolition'. Gaddis, J. L., 'The unexpected John Foster Dulles', ed. R. H. Immerman, *John Foster Dulles and the Diplomacy of the Cold War* (Princeton University Press: Princeton, N.J., 1990), p. 55.

nuclear forces, however, must be expanded and complemented with a reliable monitoring system. President Yeltsin had a point when he remarked on the 'absurdity' that the new political reality is now separated from the 'military–technological situation' which keeps the strategic forces targeted on each other's countries.

Nuclear planners schooled in cold war theories might reject as heresy a nuclear strategy that would be without its thousands of missiles, primed to retaliate instantly against an enemy first strike. The US–Russian defence community, by bringing about a wide range of military reforms, will make the abolition of the nuclear confrontation both safe and psychologically acceptable. At the end of this road, the remaining restructured nuclear forces of the United States and Russia will coexist side by side—much like the French and British nuclear forces—without the adversarial concern about the 'stability' of mutual deterrence. Are any French generals worried whether their nuclear forces are up to the task of deterring perfidious Albion from launching a first strike against France?

In harmony with this strategic transformation, an old, contentious issue between Washington and Moscow will quietly fade away—NATO's doctrine of using nuclear weapons first to stem a conventional attack by the Warsaw Pact. As the US nuclear advantage kept shrinking, this doctrine kept losing credibility; as the Warsaw Pact collapsed, it lost its purpose; and now, as theatre nuclear weapons have been withdrawn, it has lost its chosen instrument.

Instead of the vanished cold war issue of 'first use,' the United States, its allies and Russia together will have to cope with a different and growing problem of first use stemming from the proliferation of weapons of mass destruction. If a 'future Iraq' used poison gas or biological weapons against an international peace-keeping coalition, should the United States and Russia respond with a nuclear strike? The answer might not be easy. On the one hand, any use of weapons of mass destruction by some tyrant ought to be deterred; on the other hand, the tradition of not using nuclear weapons since 1945 is of immense value for democratic nations.[3]

The scope of a defence community linking the USA and Russia should not be confined to bilateral nuclear issues and to issues raised by the global proliferation of weapons of mass destruction. The community must also serve to develop a constructive relationship between the conventional forces of both sides. To this end, continued progress in reducing military secrecy is essential, and progress here can have mutually reinforcing benefits. If the two nations no longer see each other as potential enemies, the need for military secrecy could nearly vanish; and if military secrecy between them is nearly eliminated, they will have removed a key source of military tension that could cause a new enmity.

---

[3] This problem has already raised its ugly head during the Persian Gulf War. See Bundy, McG., 'Nuclear weapons and the Gulf', *Foreign Affairs*, vol. 70, no. 4 (fall 1991), pp. 83–94.

A particularly inspiring purpose of the defence community, both for the USA and for the new democratic forces in Russia, is the promotion of democratic practices and traditions for civilian control of the military. These days such an effort will find open doors in Russia. Most of the military officers now in charge there want their nation to become a modern state with stable civilian control of the armed forces, and the political authorities in Moscow today, of course, share this objective. For the sake of the Russian people, for the sake of world peace, Russia must not become a 'giant Burma'—a huge country with a backward civilian economy and a brutal, highly armed military dictatorship.

To construct meaningful institutional links in the military sphere, Washington and Moscow will have to design projects that can benefit from intensive co-operation and, at the same time, are important for the security of both sides. Some of these projects may be temporary (such as the safe disposal of nuclear weapons) and will be followed by new common tasks. Other joint missions will grow in importance and be long-lasting (such as coping with continued proliferation of new technologies for mass destruction).

The common military projects that, collectively, will constitute the defence community must not be confused with contrived clusters of bureaucrats, forever in search of a real purpose but always busy with organization charts and acronyms. A sense of urgency in tackling the most dangerous problems will have to be complemented by a sense of organic evolutionary growth. When the European Coal and Steel Community was created, the founders did not seek to establish a monetary union—it will be 40 years later when (and if) such a union materializes.

At this time, four broad missions of the defence community can be identified: first, eliminating the adversarial confrontation of nuclear forces—above all, the hair trigger posture of these forces; second, gradually abolishing secrecy between the two military establishments; third, balancing measures against proliferation with the need to respect the legitimate sovereignty and independence of all nations; and fourth, cultivating responsible civilian control of the Russian military and—in both militaries—a sense of dedication to make the community serve the interests of both nations.

VIII. No hegemony

The more the defence community can promote democratic, civilian control of Russia's military, the less the USA's allies and friends in Europe and in Asia will have to fear an expansionist Muscovite Empire that would again coerce and invade its neighbours. The concept here for a new Russian–US military relationship stands in total contrast to Franklin D. Roosevelt's ill-fated concept for a security relationship with the Soviet Union after World War II. FDR's concept linked up (by necessity) with a Soviet Union that was advancing to conquer other nations, not with a Russia that had recently withdrawn and set other nations free. It was a relationship that floated on air, without any institutional links. It entailed an extreme tightening, not a reduction, in Soviet secrecy, and thus covered up unending Soviet lying. And worst of all, FDR based his attempted new relationship with the Soviet Union on his trust in Stalin's good will.

After World War I, leading concepts for securing world peace were equally mistaken. The major powers in the 1920s sought, by negotiating several naval treaties, to stabilize the balance in the global strategic armaments of that time— the very purpose of the Strategic Arms Limitation Talks (SALT) and START agreements of recent years. After much hostile haggling among technical experts, treaties were concluded that incorporated elaborate definitions and restrictions designed to fix parity (and other ratios) in naval armaments. The goal was to keep the military confrontation peaceful, not to keep the peace by overcoming the military confrontation. Hence, the naval staffs continued to see each other as adversaries—even between the United States and Great Britain! And seeing each other as adversaries, they modernized their navies and planned for war.

As if to put some icing on this crumbling cake, the major powers of the 1920s tried another concept—renouncing war as an instrument of national policy. Eleven years and five days before Hitler started World War II, the US Secretary of State Frank Kellogg and his French counterpart, Aristide Briand, signed with plenipotentiaries from Germany and a dozen other major powers the Kellogg–Briand Pact, which has since become an object of ridicule among historians. By contrast, Jean Monnet's idea for a European economic community provides a historic example of a successful concept. Monnet's main goal was to start building a viable, meaningful institution to link France and Germany—nations that had fought three wars in the span of 70 years—and to let other European nations join. 'The life of institutions', wrote Monnet in 1955, 'is longer than that of people, and institutions can thus, if they are well-constructed, accumulate and transmit the wisdom of successive generations'.

After World War II, meaningful links between France and Germany could best be established in the economic sphere; after the cold war, links between the United States and Russia can best be established in the military sphere. Economically, Russia is a supplicant. By contrast, in a military concordat with the United States, Russia can play a global role constructively. However, the national interests that the two nations could now pursue in common through a defence community remain strictly limited. When Russia's economic relations with the outside world gain in importance, its principal partners are likely to be Germany and Japan, not the United States. It is inconceivable that the United States and Russia would ever be seized by a convergent imperialist frenzy, to form a Washington–Moscow axis for global hegemony.

The purpose of the US–Russian defence community will not only remain limited, it will remain fully supportive of the enduring national interests of the USA's allies. Russia and the USA will want to eliminate the risk of global nuclear war—the paramount interest of every nation in the northern hemisphere. And their new military relationship will also serve to prevent military developments between them that would either threaten the USA's allies or Russia's national interests and territory. These purposes cannot be achieved by some vast multilateral conglomerate, such as the Conference on Security and Co-operation in Europe (CSCE) or the United Nations.

The USA's Atlantic and Pacific alliances have emerged from the cold war as viable and valued security structures for the new era, linking old allies as well as enemies that fought each other in World War II. The USA's and Russia's armed forces have never fought a war against each other; they fought together as allies in two world wars. Their day has come to work together for the sake of both their nations and the world at large.

Part II

Regime transition: from cold war to co-operative security

3. History accelerates: the diplomacy of co-operation and fragmentation

William W. Newmann

I. Introduction[1]

This volume explores the changes in the world since the collapse of communism in Europe; this chapter examines the growth of co-operation between the USA and the USSR and the changes in that co-operative relationship following the attempted coup of August 1991. At this early stage of post-cold war US–Russian or US–Commonwealth relations, analyses of recent history can only illustrate the current patterns in these relations. To suggest that more is possible would be wishful thinking.

This chapter traces the political bargaining that has marked post-cold war US relations with the USSR and its successor nations. Its primary purpose is to reveal how the US–Soviet partnership that was formed during the Persian Gulf War influenced the US response to the continued disintegration of the USSR and Gorbachev's authority. First, this chapter discusses several themes or patterns present in the post-cold war relationship between the Bush Administration and Gorbachev's USSR that made the Gulf War partnership possible and, in many ways, established the ground rules for future co-operation. Second, the unprecedented Gulf War co-operation, which sealed the bargain that defined the new US–Soviet and US–Commonwealth relationships, is illustrated. Following this, the chapter examines the political bargaining concerning UN Security Council Resolution 678 (authorizing the use of force against Iraq) and the events leading up to the initiation of air and ground operations; that section highlights a period during which the USA and the USSR, although allied, seemed to be working at cross-purposes. The analysis continues by exploring the beginnings of a US–Soviet post-war economic relationship. Next, the US response to the attempted August 1991 Soviet coup and the disintegration of the USSR are outlined. The chapter concludes with a discussion of the future of US relations with the newly independent nations that were once the USSR.

---

[1] Secondary journalistic sources were used in the collection of some data on recent events. Individual articles are cited only as necessary. These sources are: *New York Times, Washington Post* and *Los Angeles Times.*

II. Basic themes in post-cold war US–Soviet relations

With many important issues still unresolved, analysis of such recent history merely consists of an illustration of several themes in the relations between the USA and its powerful nemesis turned uncertain partner, turned shattered empire.

The first theme illustrates what seems to be a paradox in US foreign policy. In the post-cold war world it is generally agreed that the USA is the only complete superpower. While Japan may be the economic giant of our times, it possesses neither the capability nor the will to transform that financial power into global military power. Germany, as well, seems more concerned with redesigning Europe through the evolving European Community (EC) than with exercising its military might. Both nations were reluctant partners in the coalition against Iraq during the 1990–91 Persian Gulf War.

In contrast, as the Soviet empire began to crumble, the USA felt more free to exert its military power. The vacuum created by the decline of the USSR was eagerly filled by the USA as it deployed over 500 000 troops to the Middle East—a move that would surely have conjured up visions of Armageddon only a few years earlier. If the post-cold war world was one of unipolarity in which a single superpower could reshape a 'new world order' in its own image, why did the USA make such an effort to form a partnership with the USSR at the dawn of a new 'American century'?

As a look at the diplomacy of the Gulf War will reveal, there are three reasons that the USA may have chosen to form a partnership with the USSR in the Gulf instead of flaunting the decline of Soviet power and the corresponding elevation of US superpower status. The first and most basic reason for forming a partnership with the USSR was the continued existence of Soviet nuclear weapons. Though Soviet President Mikhail Gorbachev had signed the Intermediate-range Nuclear Forces (INF) Treaty, allowed Eastern Europe to throw off the communist yoke and announced unilateral cuts in Soviet conventional forces and changes in Soviet military doctrine, the strategic nuclear relationship had changed little. Wrangling over the START Treaty continued until the summer of 1991. Soviet nuclear warheads were still targeted at US military facilities and cities; this simple fact reminded US decision makers to seek some type of Soviet consent on any moves in the Middle East.

A second reason for the USA to court the USSR for support in the Gulf War stemmed from the long-standing Soviet relationship with Iraq. From the outset of the conflict it was clear that, although the USSR supported US efforts to reverse the Iraqi invasion of Kuwait, there was decidedly less Soviet support for the means the USA had chosen to attain those ends. Soviet efforts to negotiate a political settlement that would remove Iraqi forces from Kuwait, culminating with a Soviet–Iraqi peace plan on the eve of the ground war, were a constant worry to the USA. The Bush Administration set its policy of unconditional withdrawal in stone and operated under constant fear that the USSR would allow Iraq to retreat from Kuwait under favourable conditions. Although the USSR could not stop the USA from acting against Iraq, it could make those actions more difficult.

The third reason the USA sought to establish a partnership with the USSR was to bring an air of legitimacy to the US decision to oppose Iraq. As is illustrated below, the recent resurgence of the notion of using the United Nations as a forum for multilateral security in a new world order stems from Soviet rhetoric during the Gorbachev era. Originally designed for collective security, the UN had been hostage to the cold war stand-off within the Security Council. The inability of the USA and the USSR, permanent members of the Security Council each armed with a veto, to reach consensus prevented the Security Council from acting on the very issues the UN was intended to address—security threats to the community of nations.

Since 1986, Gorbachev had turned Soviet policy at the UN around, allowing for an expansion of the type of peace-keeping and election supervision operations that the Security Council, unable to perform its mandated mission, had made its primary tasks. The UN had become active in regional conflicts in Africa, East Asia and Latin America, but still cold war suspicions prevented it from redefining and redesigning itself to complete its original assignment—collective security. Gorbachev's hope to bring the USSR into the West, into a 'common European home', was accompanied by Soviet support for resurrecting the UN's unfulfilled role as a multilateral security forum. Like many of the abrupt Soviet turnarounds during the years of *perestroika*, the Soviet Union became the international advocate for a UN with intrusive and expansive powers.

Gorbachev and Soviet Foreign Minister Eduard Shevardnadze's harsh condemnation of Iraq and alliance with the USA would have seemed like abandonment of an ally if not understood within the context of Gorbachev's push for the rule of law in international affairs and a greater role for the United Nations. The Bush Administration's emphasis on the UN and the multilateral nature of the effort against Iraq saved the USA not only from protests within the world community that the USA was acting in its traditional role of imperialist power but also from similar criticism of the Bush Administration that might have come from the US Congress.

A related aspect of that legitimacy is the US desire to gain Soviet acceptance of its new role in world affairs. The USA had led the West in its conflict with the USSR during the cold war; the USA leading the USSR into battle in the early days of the post-cold war world implied that the USSR not only accepted but supported the new US role as the dominant power in that new world order. This undisputed role as world hegemon earned the USA tremendous political capital as bargaining for the shape of the post-cold war world began. Legitimizing the new world order by bringing the powers of the old world order into the fold is an old tradition. The Gulf War was a prime example.

Moving past the Gulf War to US–Soviet relations in 1991 reveals the Soviet motivations for forming a partnership with the USA. These reasons are more obvious and less complex than those of the USA. Whatever Moscow's initial reasons for ending the cold war and moving towards better relations with the West (the debate on this point will continue for decades), by 1990 the motivations for forming a partnership with an old adversary were relatively clear-cut. In order to proceed with the transformation of the Soviet Union, the Soviet leadership needed not only economic assistance from the West, but an end to the economic and political isolation of the USSR. To be blunt, the USSR required massive infusions of Western aid to resurrect an economy ruined by decades of communist control and to move towards a market-oriented system.

A second reason for the USSR to form a partnership with the USA stemmed from the new international balance of power after the cold war. With Soviet power in rapid decline, Moscow feared that it would be eclipsed on the world stage by the USA. The age of bipolarity and superpower rivalry might give way to an age of unipolarity and US domination in which the USSR might suffer the fate of other collapsed empires—becoming a second-tier power with a foreign policy that consisted primarily of balancing alliance with and independence from Washington. Forming a special relationship with Washington might enable Moscow to maintain its pre-eminence in the world even as the USSR retreated from its traditional global entanglements. To remain a leader in world affairs, Moscow employed a strategy that hoped to remake international politics in terms of international legal norms, peaceful settlement of disputes and an expanded role for the UN. By portraying itself as the champion of a peaceful world order, Moscow hoped to replace its military power with a more intangible moral, legal and intellectual power, while at the same time restricting US unilateralism by elevating the UN to the centre of the new world order. As illustrated below, these policies of Gorbachev and Shevardnadze also gave the USA an ideal method of cementing a partnership with the USSR while pursuing its own foreign policy goals.

The rewards the USSR was promised by the West in exchange for its co-operation in the Gulf are illustrated below. Essentially, they were twofold: (a) Gorbachev was invited to the July 1991 Group of 7 (G-7) summit to plead his case for a substantial programme of Western aide into the anaemic Soviet economy; and (b) the USA went out of its way to give Gorbachev the benefit of the doubt in the struggle between the Union Government and the forces attempting to split the Union apart. This was particularly evident in the case of the Baltic states and Ukraine. The US relationship with Gorbachev caused the USA to appear to support territorial integrity at the expense of the concept of self-determination and independence for the Soviet republics.

The August 1991 attempted coup changed the nature of power in the USSR as Moscow's disarray became the impetus for a new republic-centred order. The USA still leaned towards Gorbachev's Union even as the Union and the man himself became more and more irrelevant. It was not until late November that the Bush Administration abandoned Gorbachev, announcing that it would recognize an independent Ukraine. By mid-December, the Commonwealth of Independent States (CIS) was born, and the new nations of the former USSR began the diplomatic task of seeking better relations with and economic aid from the West as a path to greater independence from Russia. The early trend in US policy is rather straightforward: the Bush Administration seems intent on building a relationship with Boris Yeltsin's Russia that will build upon the partnership formed with Gorbachev's USSR. For all the changes in the USSR, now the Commonwealth, continuity rather than change seems to be the early trend in relations between Moscow and Washington.

III. The new world order

Since the 27th Communist Party Congress in 1986, Gorbachev had been redefining the USSR's role in world affairs and its view of the shape of international politics to come. Gorbachev outlined these ideas in more detail in 1987, calling for a 'comprehensive system of international security' that included a UN-centred system (Secretary-General and Security Council) in maintaining peace around the globe.[2] Foreshadowing the role the UN would play in the Gulf conflict, Gorbachev specifically called for the permanent members of the Security Council to become the 'guarantors of regional security'.[3] Throughout the mid- to late 1980s the USSR championed the UN as the proper forum for solving the political problems of the world, preventing war and stemming the spread of political violence. It saw the Security Council's role as one not simply of crisis management or peace-keeping after a conflict had begun, but of crisis prevention—preventing a political conflict from becoming war.[4] Included in an expanded role for UN peace-keeping forces (possibly contributed by UN Security Council members) would be a new role in crisis prevention in which a nation could ask for UN troops to be deployed to protect that nation from the aggressive designs of another.[5]

These ideas could be viewed as idealistic 'new thinking' or as the next generation of Soviet propaganda. It is more useful, however, to see them as part of a Soviet strategy to maintain international influence.[6] As the Soviets' ability to act on the global scene unilaterally continued to decline, the USSR could still

[2] Gorbachev M. S., 'The reality and guarantees of a secure world', *Pravda*, 17 Sep. 1987, in Foreign Broadcast Information Service, *Daily Report–Soviet Union (FBIS-SOV)*, FBIS-SOV-87-180, 17 Sep. 1987, pp. 23–28. Further Soviet outlines of 'new thinking' on international affairs can be found in Eduard Shevardnadze's speech to the UN General Assembly, 'Striving for comprehensive security', *Pravda*, 28 Sep. 1988, in FBIS-SOV-88-188, 28 Sep. 1988, pp. 2–9; and Gorbachev's speech to the UN General Assembly, *Pravda*, 8 Dec. 1988, in FBIS-SOV-88-236, 8 Dec. 1988, pp. 11–19.

[3] See Gorbachev, 17 Sep. 1987 (note 2), p. 25.

[4] Belonogov, A., 'Soviet peace-keeping proposals', *Survival*, May/June 1990, p. 208.

[5] Nolan, A. R. and Weiss, T. G., 'Superpowers and peacekeepers', *Survival*, May/June 1990, p. 215. If such a UN mechanism had existed at the time of the Gulf War, Kuwait could have asked for and received a contingent of UN peace-keeping forces for deployment on its northern border in July of 1990. This deployment would have acted as a much stronger signal of the world's opinion than warnings to Baghdad before an invasion or deployments in Saudi Arabia after the fact. In a speech before the UN General Assembly in Sep. 1988, Shevardnadze also suggested that the UN create its own reserve force for rapid deployment wherever needed. These forces would be commanded by an active Military Staff Command. See Johansen, R. C., 'UN peacekeeping: the changing utility of military force', *Third World Quarterly* (Apr. 1990), p. 63; and Belonogov (note 4), p. 210.

[6] This argument is outlined in Weiss, T. G. and Kessler, M. A., 'Moscow's UN Policy', *Foreign Policy*, no. 79 (summer 1990), pp. 94–112.

retain a major role in world affairs through its Security Council seat if the UN became an important actor in international politics. Not only was this a way to increase Moscow's declining influence, but it could also serve to restrain unilateral US actions by linking events to the UN and international law. In essence, Moscow hoped to create a new multilateralism since it no longer had the power to influence events unilaterally.[7]

As Iraqi forces rolled southward, the creation of a US–Soviet partnership achieved precisely these goals for Moscow. If the USA wanted Soviet support for any actions taken in the Gulf, it would have to use the UN to co-ordinate an international response. Moving the centre of decision from Washington to New York also allowed the UN Security Council to act as a ball and chain that might restrain the US response to Iraqi actions. Such was the case early in the Gulf stand-off, as ships bound for Iraq appeared to be on their way to challenging the UN naval blockade. The USA wanted to act decisively and militarily, but had to delay any military moves until all permanent members of the Security Council could agree on the use of force in support of the blockade.[8]

The veto of the permanent members of the Security Council acted as a brake on US designs throughout the conflict. To maintain the appearance of international solidarity, the USA was forced to move only as fast as the other permanent members would allow. Since Britain and France were allied with the US position (although some minor disagreements did spring up), it was up to the USA to bargain out the positions of the international coalition with China and the USSR. The USA aimed its diplomacy primarily at the USSR. The Bush Administration believed that it would be easier to deal with Moscow than Beijing, and that China would not want to isolate itself by vetoing resolutions if the USA could first gain approval from the other permanent members.[9] This analysis seems to have been correct: China voted with the other UN Security Council members on all votes leading up to Resolution 678 authorizing the use of force against Iraq; it abstained from voting on that resolution.[10]

The stature of a superpower in decline was therefore elevated, and Moscow sought to use the Gulf War as a way to secure favours from the West. For this reason, US–Soviet relations during the Gulf War became the politics of horse-trading and logrolling more reminiscent of alliance than superpower politics. The use of the UN as the representative of the international stand against Saddam Hussein cemented an unlikely partnership. The USA's need to legitimize

[7] The Soviets used a similar strategy of multilateralism in their policies towards European international relations. See Flynn, G. and Scheffer, D., 'Limited collective security', *Foreign Policy*, no. 80 (fall 1990), pp. 77–101.

[8] For details on the initial agreement to use the UN Security Council and the international bargaining over the use of force to maintain the blockade of Iraq see Newmann, W. W., 'Intervention and the new world order: the US use of force in Latin America and the Persian Gulf', ed. J. E. Goodby, *From Hegemony to Co-operation* (Oxford University Press: Oxford, forthcoming).

[9] The author would like to thank Jim Goodby for these insights into Security Council politics.

[10] The voting behaviour of nations on the Security Council on all resolutions leading up to Resolution 678 on the use of force is reprinted in *The Persian Gulf Crisis: Relevant Documents, Correspondence, Reports*, Report prepared by the Subcommittee on Arms Control and International Security and Science of the Committee on Foreign Affairs, US House of Representatives, 102nd Congress (US Government Printing Office: Washington, DC, 1991), p. 153.

its moves in the Gulf, and the Soviet Union's need to maintain its international position and hopefully to garner some benefits from its new relationship with the West, ensured the solidarity of the coalition.

The Bush Administration also worried about potential Soviet actions that could undermine US goals in the Gulf. While the Gulf War could be seen as a test of Gorbachev's commitment to new thinking, it also served to test the depth to which that new thinking had become a part of the Soviet Government and military bureaucracies.[11] Even as the coalition was formed, many in the USSR publicly railed against US policy.[12] These public criticisms, the inherent uncertainty over whether an old adversary could so swiftly become an ally and the fact that 8000 Soviets, including 1000 military advisers, remained in Iraq gave the Bush Administration a recurring nightmare of the USSR switching its position and striking a deal with Iraq for the withdrawal of Iraqi troops behind the back of the USA.[13] As the record shows, this fear was warranted. There existed a real and growing disagreement within the USSR over its interests in the Gulf and its role in the world in general. The debate within the USSR over the Gulf War has been seen as a rift between the 'Westernizers' and the 'Arabists.'[14] Essentially, this was a political conflict between the Westernizers who took a tougher stand against Iraq and aligned themselves closer to the US and British position, and the Arabists who sought a political settlement of the conflict even if this called for making concessions to Baghdad.

Another way of characterizing the debate would be to describe it as an ideological struggle between old thinkers and new thinkers, or conservatives and reformers.[15] This characterization places the debate over the Soviet role in the Gulf within the context of larger political conflict within the USSR that came to a climax with the coup of August 1991. The new thinkers or reformers supported the use of the UN in the conflict and truly believed that, in a more peaceful world, such aggressions as the Iraqi invasion of Kuwait could not be tolerated. The old thinkers or conservatives saw the USSR's condemnation of Iraq as the abandonment of an ally and a complete reversal of Moscow's traditional Middle East policy of supporting radical Arab regimes. This debate would manifest itself in a two-track Soviet policy of supporting the UN's demands for unconditional Iraqi withdrawal from Kuwait and the threat of military action,

---

[11] In particular, the Gulf War allowed the world to witness the politics of the Soviet bureaucracies for the first time. On this point see Fuller, G. E., 'Moscow and the Gulf War', *Foreign Affairs*, vol. 70, no. 3 (summer 1991), pp. 55–57.

[12] Even as the USA and USSR were forming their unprecedented partnership many statements by Soviet officials were reminiscent of the cold war. See Fuller (note 11), pp. 63–64; and Freedman, R. O., 'Moscow and the Gulf War', *Problems of Communism*, July/Aug. 1991, p. 7.

[13] Keller, B., 'US and the Soviets as allies? It's the first time since 1945', *New York Times*, 8 Aug. 1990, p. 1.

[14] For this analysis see Crow, S., 'Primakov and the Soviet peace initiative', *Report on the USSR*, vol. 3, no. 9 (1 Mar. 1991), pp. 14–17.

[15] On this debate see Weitz, R., 'The USSR and the confrontation in the Gulf', *Report on the USSR*, vol. 2, no. 23 (17 Aug. 1990), pp. 1–7; and Crow, S., 'The Gulf Conflict and the debate over Soviet national interests', *Report on the USSR*, vol. 3, no. 6 (8 Feb. 1991), pp. 15–17.

while maintaining a continuous effort to reach a political settlement with Baghdad.[16]

Although the USA and the USSR began to act in concert from the outset of the conflict, the real partnership was not fully formed until the Helsinki summit of 9 September 1991. What the USA desired most from this summit was a public demonstration of the solidarity between the USA and the USSR. The USA also hoped to convince the USSR to contribute military forces and to withdraw their advisers from Iraq.

In exchange for supporting the USA, the USSR wanted a number of things. Several days before the summit, while in Vladivostok, Shevardnadze gave a speech calling for an international Middle East peace conference that would address the Iraqi-Kuwait and Arab–Israeli disputes.[17] This request essentially asked the USA to reverse its decades-old policy that sought to limit the influence of the USSR in the Middle East. Predictably, US officials spoke out against a Middle East conference, contending that such a conference would link the Iraqi invasion of Kuwait with the Arab–Israeli conflict.[18] Gorbachev also hoped to convince the USA to seek a political solution to the conflict and to gain reassurance from the USA that any deployments to the Middle East would be temporary.[19]

A long-term objective of the USSR, going into the summit, was to secure access to Western aid. Reportedly, Gorbachev hoped that the USSR's co-operation in the Gulf would be rewarded just as the USSR was rewarded by Germany for its support of German reunification (Bonn had promised Moscow a massive aid package amounting to nearly $31 billion).[20] US officials were working on just such an aid package in preparation for the summit. The aid would come as part of an international package in exchange for the removal of Soviet advisers from Iraq and a Soviet contribution of troops and equipment. Essentially, the USA linked the amount of international aid to the amount of Soviet co-operation.

Both sides received what they desired from the summit. Bush sent Gorbachev several reassuring signs on economic aid following the summit. The USA brokered deals for Saudi Arabia and Bahrain to establish relations with the USSR in late September;[21] this opened the door for the USSR to receive aid from the wealthy oil states of the Arabian peninsula. The Bush Administration also agreed to approve 'special invitee' status for the USSR at the International

---

[16] For a discussion of this policy see Crow, S., 'Soviet Union pursues dual policy on Iraq', *Report on the USSR*, vol. 2, no. 40 (5 Oct. 1990), pp. 6–9.

[17] TASS, 4 Sep. 1990, in FBIS-SOV-90-172, 5 Sep. 1990, pp. 3–10.

[18] This linkage was the essence of Saddam Hussein's peace proposal of 12 Aug. which was unacceptable to both the USA and USSR. To the USSR, its proposal for a Middle East conference amounted to an indirect linkage between the two issues which, for the USSR, distanced it from a direct linkage that rewarded aggression. For more details of the Soviet position see the articles by Gorbachev's Special Envoy in the Gulf conflict, Yevgeniy Primakov, 'The war which might not have been', *Pravda*, 7 Feb.–2 Mar. 1991, in FBIS-SOV-91-048, 12 Mar. 1991, p. 7.

[19] See Primakov (note 18), p. 8.

[20] Whitney, C., '7 arrive with Soviets on their mind', *New York Times*, 15 July 1991, p. A4.

[21] Freedman (note 12), p. 9.

Monetary Fund (IMF) and the World Bank soon after the summit. Although this only allowed them to observe these two institutions without membership, it established a relationship that could lead to the acceptance of the USSR in Western financial circles. The trade-off of Soviet support for international aid was all but explicitly announced by Bush in remarks made at the summit press conference. While gaining access to potential credit seemed like a major victory for Gorbachev, the Bush Administration also reversed its long-standing policy on the Middle East and agreed not only to a Soviet role in the Middle East peace process, but also to an international conference of the type Moscow had supported. By advocating an increased Soviet role in the Middle East, the summit paved the way for the opening of relations between the USSR and Israel.[22]

The benefits the USA received from the summit were less tangible. The simple reality of a joint Bush–Gorbachev press conference gave the world a prime-time illustration of the solidarity between the USA and the USSR and the legitimacy of the US actions in the Gulf. Although the struggle against Iraq was undertaken through the UN and an international coalition, the fact that the USA led this coalition was obvious. US troops made up the majority of the forces deployed to Saudi Arabia and conducting military operations against Iraq. US Secretary of State James Baker travelled the globe in maintenance of the coalition, and President Bush used diplomatic channels and historic visits to various nations to ensure its solidarity. Moscow's secondary role was evident even as Bush and Gorbachev stood side by side in Helsinki. The fact that the USSR tolerated a massive deployment of US troops so close to its borders and in opposition to a traditional Soviet ally illustrated the weakness of Moscow's position. One Administration official explained that National Security Advisor Brent Scowcroft viewed co-operation with the USSR as a way to illustrate 'the United States and the Soviet Union working together, with the Soviet Union clearly the junior partner'.[23] In spite of the concessions made to Moscow, the impression was clearly one of US dominance.

The disagreements that arose between Bush and Gorbachev during the summit illustrated this fact even more. It was clear that the USSR did not yet support the use of force if UN sanctions failed, while the USA went out of its way to impress upon Iraq that force would be employed if Iraq did not withdraw from Kuwait. The fact that US forces continued to be rushed to the Middle East in an unprecedented deployment was a constant reminder that the USA and its military potential were the key element in the struggle.

---

[22] Transcript of Bush–Gorbachev news conference, *Washington Post*, 10 Sep. 1990, p. A20. Gorbachev was dismayed at all the allusions to such a trade-off and the notion that Soviet support could be bought. During the press conference he argued that the summit meeting was not a case in which the US could 'align a certain sum with a certain behavior'. In spite of the protests, this seems exactly the case. In fact, it is another example of the non-linkage linkages during the Gulf War. The linkage between sudden US support for an international Middle East peace conference and the Iraqi invasion of Kuwait was denied by all members of the coalition despite the fact that the invasion did lead to the peace conference.

[23] Warner, M. G., 'The Moscow connection', *Newsweek*, 17 Sep. 1990, p. 25.

The USA was not, however, entirely against a political settlement. If the USSR could convince Baghdad to withdraw unconditionally, the USA would accept those terms. The USA and the USSR reportedly formed an implicit agreement: the coalition would maintain a dialogue with Iraq through the travels of Gorbachev's Special Envoy Yevgeniy Primakov in exchange for a Soviet promise not to obstruct US efforts to pressure Iraq at the UN.[24] This agreement allowed Gorbachev to play both sides of the political debate in the USSR; he could support the world's unified stance against aggression while maintaining a relationship with Baghdad.

IV. Resolution 678 and Soviet peace proposals

As events unfolded throughout the autumn, the Bush Administration became less and less inclined to support any negotiated settlement, while the Primakov–Gorbachev diplomatic channel to Baghdad grew more and more active in support of a negotiated withdrawal even if it allowed some concessions to Baghdad. The Bush Administration made its decision to go to war in mid-October; it did not, however, formally announce that it would cancel scheduled troop rotations and instead deploy additional forces to the Gulf until early November (after the congressional elections).[25] Once it concluded that Iraq did not intend to withdraw its troops, the Bush Administration began to lay the groundwork for gaining UN acceptance of what seemed to be the only option left—militarily forcing Iraq's troops out of Kuwait. Since the USA had decided to use the UN as the instrument for forging international solidarity, the Bush Administration needed to gain Soviet agreement on a Security Council resolution approving the use of force to expel Iraq from Kuwait.

This was not an easy task. Although Shevardnadze had given a speech at the UN General Assembly condemning the Iraqi invasion and implying that the USSR would support the use of force, Gorbachev only a month later insisted that the coalition 'cannot accept a military solution'.[26] The Soviets, seemingly of two minds, wanted two UN resolutions.[27] The first would set a deadline for Iraqi withdrawal from Kuwait. If Iraq had not withdrawn its forces by that deadline, then the UN would vote again to authorize the use of force to remove Iraqi troops. The USA preferred setting a deadline for withdrawal, the

---

[24] Cooley, J. K., 'Prewar Gulf diplomacy', *Survival*, Mar./Apr. 1991, p. 133. One of Primakov's objectives during his first visit to Baghdad would be to secure safe passage back to the USSR for Soviet citizens and advisers in Iraq. See Primakov (note 18), p. 9.

[25] An analysis of this decision can be found in Newmann (note 8).

[26] Shevardnadze speech at the General Assembly, TASS, 25 Sep. 1990, in FBIS-SOV-90-187, 26 Sep. 1990, pp. 2–7; Gorbachev's news conference in Paris, TASS, 29 Oct. 1990, in FBIS-SOV-90-209, 29 Oct. 1990, pp. 40–42. Gorbachev had also sent Primakov to Baghdad for discussions with Saddam Hussein twice in the autumn. For details, see Primakov (note 18), pp. 9–20.

[27] Reportedly, this two-resolution approach was designed with the influence of Primakov. He has been labelled one of the leading Arabists in the Soviet leadership: see Crow (note 15), p. 15. Primakov also created a small fire-storm by announcing during a trip to the UN that it should delay a resolution approving the use of force and even offer Saddam Hussein a 'face-saving' option for withdrawing from Kuwait: Lewis, P., 'Soviet aide urges delay of UN move on force In Gulf', *New York Times*, 16 Nov. 1990, p. 1.

expiration of which automatically authorized the use of force. In this way a UN deadline would carry an explicit threat of military action and not a softer and more ambiguous message that if forces were not withdrawn by a specific date, the coalition might consider whether to use force. Having decided that force was going to be the ultimate answer, the USA wanted to gain authorization as quickly as possible as a way of removing the UN from the decision loop; once a deadline was set and authorization was given, the USA, commanding the multi-national forces, could set its own timetable for military action. The USA hoped to gain Soviet acceptance of a single UN authorization at the November CSCE summit in Paris.

At the CSCE summit, Bush and Baker convinced Gorbachev and Shevard-nadze to drop the idea of two resolutions, but did not secure Soviet agreement on a draft resolution until the following week. Once the final differences in the draft resolution were settled, UN Security Council Resolution 678, setting a deadline for withdrawal of Iraqi troops from Kuwait of 15 January 1991 and authorizing the use of force to expel those troops after the passing of the deadline, was adopted by the Security Council on 29 November 1990.[28]

Although the Bush Administration attempted to gain Soviet approval of the resolution in a number of ways, underlying the entire bargaining process was the promise of economic aid to Moscow.[29] As the USA and the USSR negotiated the resolution, Saudi Arabia and the USSR completed negotiations for a $1–4 billion loan to the USSR.[30] This followed a number of other aid packages to the USSR which were put together as negotiations between the USA and the USSR took place. Economic aid to the USSR included credits of $1 billion from France, food aid amounting to $1.5 billion from Spain, an overall package of $6.3 billion from Italy and a total of $6 billion from the Gulf states.[31]

President Bush also suspended some aspects of the Jackson–Vanik amendment restricting trade with Moscow. In June of 1990, Bush and Gorbachev had signed a treaty granting the USSR most favored nation (MFN) trade status. Bush had yet to give the treaty to the Senate for approval, which would override the Jackson–Vanik amendment. As a reward for co-operation in the Gulf, Bush gave the Soviets as much as he could on his own, without making a domestic political issue of Soviet aid by including Congress in the decision. In January 1991, the USA began a grain credit programme, renewable every six months,

---

[28] The text of Resolution 678 is printed in *New York Times*, 30 Nov. 1990, p. A6. Initially, the USA wanted a deadline of 1 Jan., but conceded the point to the USSR by setting the Soviet-preferred deadline of 15 Jan.; in another concession to the Soviets, the USA also altered its draft resolution to authorize 'all means necessary', not 'military force'. Lewis, P., 'UN draft offers one "final" chance for Iraqi pullout', *New York Times*, 27 Nov. 1990, p. 1.

[29] In several meetings with Gorbachev, Baker portrayed a unified stance against Iraq as a test of a UN-centred security system. The Bush Administration also agreed to set up meetings between Baker and Iraqi Foreign Minister Tariq Aziz. Meeting with Aziz, a frequent visitor to Moscow, was a clear concession to Gorbachev. The Soviets had continued to maintain a dialogue with Iraq, and opening such a dialogue between Washington and Baghdad gave new life to the possibility of the political settlement Moscow hoped for. This led to the 9 Jan. 1991 meeting in Geneva between Baker and Aziz.

[30] Murphy, C., 'Saudis rewarding Soviets with loan of 1 billion', *Washington Post*, 29 Nov. 1990, p. A37.

[31] See Murphy (note 30), p. A37.

that would provide the USSR with loans to buy US grain. The programme began with a $1 billion loan.[32]

The USSR attempted to avert both the initiation of combat operations as the deadline approached and the escalation to ground operations in February. A Moscow-designed peace proposal was in the works in early January, but never materialized due to what Shevardnadze, following his resignation, called 'organizational problems'.[33] These organizational problems were actually policy disputes reflecting the divisions within the USSR over Soviet interests in the Gulf.[34] Gorbachev did manage to put together a peace plan that was intended to avert a ground war. The organizational problems that had prevented a comprehensive Soviet proposal in early January may have disappeared along with Foreign Minister Shevardnadze, and allowed the USSR to offer a political settlement to Iraq without consulting the USA. Gorbachev had remained silent during the air war until US officials began discussing the timing of ground operations. In criticizing US conduct of the air war as possibly exceeding the UN mandate and announcing a third Primakov trip to Baghdad, Gorbachev began two weeks of diplomacy that seemed to end the US–Soviet partnership on the Gulf. At every turn, Soviet peace initiatives and Iraqi responses were blasted by the Bush Administration as too little, too late.

In response both to a letter from Gorbachev and Primakov's visit to Baghdad, Iraqi radio announced, on 15 February, that Iraq would withdraw in exchange for a repeal of UN sanctions, a withdrawal of US troops from the Middle East and negotiations to resolve elements of the Arab–Israeli conflict.[35] President Bush denounced the proposal as a 'cruel hoax'.[36] Although the Soviet leadership realized that Iraq had attached conditions to a potential withdrawal, Moscow was optimistic. The USA, however, was not on the same page as the USSR; the Bush Administration wanted Saddam Hussein politically humiliated and discredited within the Arab world, not given concessions on the basis of a negotiated settlement. For the USA, the Gulf War was no longer simply about removing Iraqi forces from Kuwait. It was among other things a test of the Bush Administration's resolve, a demonstration of the pre-eminence of the USA in the new world order, and a way to destroy Iraq's conventional and nuclear weaponry capabilities. Never before had the USA had an opportunity to gain favour with the Arab states and Israel at the same time, while also gaining a foothold on the Arabian peninsula and establishing itself as the undisputed

---

[32] Gugliotta, G., 'US continuing grain credits for Soviets', *Washington Post*, 13 Dec. 1991, p. A39.

[33] See Crow (note 14), p. 16.

[34] It is unclear how those disputes played out bureaucratically. However, the old-fashioned (or new-fangled) Kremlin intrigue that led to Shevardnadze's resignation played some part. He leaned decidedly towards the harder line on Iraq, while the more conservative elements of the Soviet leadership continued to pressure him towards a diplomatic settlement. Since Shevardnadze resigned on 20 Dec., but stayed on until Jan. 1991, it is unclear what role he played in formulating or scuttling possible peace initiatives. See Fuller (note 11), pp. 56–59; and Crow, S., 'The resignation of Shevardnadze', *Report on the USSR*, vol. 3, no. 2 (11 Jan. 1991), p. 6.

[35] See Primakov (note 18), pp. 24–25.

[36] Tyler, P., 'Iraqi's speak of a withdrawal but impose a list of conditions', *New York Times*, 16 Feb. 1991, p. 1.

military power in the region. Once it had a massive military force perched on the edge of achieving those goals, the USA was not going to let the opportunity slip away.

A last effort to negotiate a withdrawal brought Foreign Minister Tariq Aziz to Moscow twice and led to Iraqi acceptance of a Soviet peace plan on 21 February.[37] The USA swiftly rejected the plan.[38] A modified peace plan was negotiated the night of 22 February between Baghdad and Moscow but rejected by Washington after a conversation between Bush and Gorbachev; immediately after the conversation, Bush effectively ended the peace negotiations by setting a deadline of noon Washington time on 23 February for the withdrawal of Iraqi forces. The deadline passed and in the early evening of 23 February, the ground war began.

The differences between the USA and the USSR after the war with Iraq began did not destroy the new partnership; they were simply reflections of its nature. Clearly the USA was the more powerful of the two, and the Bush Administration was eager to use that power. The USSR could do nothing to stop the USA from pursuing military operations except negotiate an end to the war before military force was necessary. Since Iraq would not comply with US conditions for withdrawal, the Soviet role as intermediary failed.

V. Building an economic partnership

The USA did not penalize the USSR for its diplomatic activity. The benefits of a short, relatively painless war to President Bush's popularity allowed him to be generous towards the USSR. Of course, the USSR still possessed nuclear weapons aimed at the USA; political chaos caused by economic collapse in a nuclear-armed nation could be a catastrophe. The nuclear issue was an implicit one. More explicit were the requests for economic aid—requests that Moscow saw as its just rewards for participation in the Gulf War.

At the July 1990 G-7 summit in Houston, the USA had rejected the notion of a massive aid grant to the USSR by arguing that the Soviet economy was not ready for a large infusion of capital; the money would simply be wasted. The US position carried the day and the issue of aid to the USSR was deferred. Although the Bush Administration had begun to channel aid from the USA (grain credits) and the Gulf states as a result of the Helsinki summit, Bush had not yet submitted the MFN treaty to the Senate by the spring of 1991. Without Senate approval the USSR would not be granted MFN status, and the Jackson–Vanik amendment would still cap the amount of trade and aid the USA could grant Moscow.

[37] The plan is outlined in *New York Times*, 22 Feb. 1991, p. 1.
[38] The sticking point in the proposal was an unspecified time-frame for the Iraqi withdrawal. Aziz, in consultations with Gorbachev, claimed that it would take a long period for Iraq to withdraw since most of the Iraqi equipment in Kuwait had been brought in over a period of months between Aug. and Jan.. The Bush Administration wanted a swift withdrawal of Iraqi forces, stating that Iraqi forces should be completely out of Kuwait within four days of an agreement to withdraw. See Primakov (note 18), pp. 26–27; and Hoffman, D., 'Bush urged Soviets to stiffen offer', *Washington Post*, 21 Jan. 1991, p. 1.

On 22 May 1991, the USSR began to ask for what it perceived as its just rewards. In anticipation of the July 1991 G-7 summit in London, Gorbachev requested a multi-year $100 billion aid plan and a chance to participate in the upcoming summit.[39] Gorbachev was blunt about how he viewed Western aid. During his speech accepting the Nobel Peace Prize, he stated: 'We are now approaching what might be the crucial point, when the world community, and above all, the states with the greatest potential to influence world developments will have to decide on their stance with regard to the Soviet Union and to act on that basis'.[40]

The aid request was a test for the West. If the West really wanted to bring the USSR into the free world as a politically and economically stable ally, it would have to put its money where its rhetoric was.

A meeting between Gorbachev and the leaders of the G-7 nations was scheduled for the conclusion of the summit on 17 July. Gorbachev presented his aid request to the G-7 leaders at the start of the summit in the form of an extensive document which consisted of a 23-page letter from Gorbachev detailing his economic reforms for the USSR and an accompanying 31-page compilation of proposals for economic assistance.[41] It asked the West to forgive the USSR's $65 billion debt and to create a $10–12 billion rouble-stabilization fund. Before meeting with Gorbachev, the Western leaders made it clear that they did not think his proposals went far enough. They seemed to be nothing more than a conglomeration of a number of old plans and, more importantly, did not include selling off the huge Soviet Government holdings. The USA was the most critical of Gorbachev's plans, arguing that straight financial aid (even loans from the European Bank for Reconstruction and Development) would be wasted on an economy not yet market-oriented. Japan supported the US line, while France, Germany and Italy argued for increased aid.

Gorbachev did come away from the summit with a small amount of economic aid. The G-7 plan included special status in the IMF (promised in the autumn of 1990 after the Helsinki summit), technical assistance from the West and regular visits to Moscow by officials from the G-7 finance ministries for economic consultation and advice. Essentially, the G-7 leaders decided that they would act as the midwives, not the parents, of Soviet economic reform.

Although certainly not what Gorbachev had hoped for, the USSR had slid its foot in the door of a very exclusive club. If the end of the cold war would usher in an era during which the most prominent world struggle would be to increase world prosperity and economic stability (as the real path to political stability), then the G-7 would be the most important multinational actor.[42] As a body designed primarily for defence of the West from the USSR, NATO appears to

[39] Dobbs, M., 'Gorbachev asks for aid, seat at economic summit', *Washington Post*, 23 May 1991, p. A42.

[40] Parks, M., 'Gorbachev ready to hand West a bill for Perestroika', *Los Angeles Times*, 9 June 1991, p. A1.

[41] 'Cinderella Gorbachev', *The Economist*, 20 July 1991, pp. 47–48.

[42] An insightful discussion of this notion can be found in Lewis, F., 'The G-7 1/2 directorate', *Foreign Policy*, no. 85 (winter 1991–92), pp. 25–40.

be obsolete; the CSCE includes non-security issues, but Japan is not a member; the UN Security Council fails to reflect the realities of power in the world by excluding Japan and Germany. The G-7, however, represents the major economic powers of the world. Gaining entry into the inner sanctum of the G-7 could lead the USSR towards real economic assistance and acceptance in the Western world.

It seemed to Moscow that the USSR had earned what it received at the G-7 summit through its participation in the Gulf War; the Bush Administration, however, asked for more from Gorbachev in return for that aid. The USA and the USSR had begun another round of START negotiations several days before the G-7 summit began. During the G-7 meeting, US and Soviet negotiators reached an agreement and set a date to sign the START Treaty at a summit later that month in Moscow. Although Bush explicitly denied that the negotiations on nuclear weapons were linked to the negotiations on economic assistance, the timing of the events made it appear that Gorbachev travelled to the bank to request a loan and was asked to put his nuclear weapons up for collateral.[43]

Once Bush and Gorbachev were committed to a START agreement and a high profile Moscow summit, the USSR attempted to pressure the USA for more economic aid. In a surprise move, the USSR asked for full IMF status only a week before the Moscow summit. The G-7 had granted the USSR special status, and it was thought to be understood by all who were present at the G-7 summit that the USSR was not yet ready for full IMF membership. The surprise announcement placed President Bush in the difficult position of having to travel to Moscow to sign the START agreement and refuse Moscow's continued request for aid. The Soviet tactic may have worked. At the summit, Bush agreed to ask Congress for MFN status for the USSR and called for $20 million in aid for fiscal year 1992.[44] The USA did not, however, agree to lobby for full Soviet IMF status, instead listing several more obstacles, including Moscow's relationship with Cuba, Soviet possession of the Kurile Islands, Soviet activities in the Baltic states and Soviet defence spending.

National Security Advisor Scowcroft commented during the Moscow summit that this would be the last summit at which arms control dominated the agenda; it was the end of an era, 'the first post-Cold War summit'.[45] Scowcroft's analysis turned out to be an understatement. The late-August attempted coup in the USSR led to the end of the USSR and the birth or rebirth of nations that had been engulfed by Moscow over the last several centuries. The July Moscow summit was the last time any US president visited the Soviet Union. By late autumn, the Soviet empire had collapsed.

---

[43] President Bush's denial that the arms and economic aid talks were linked is discussed in Hoffman, D., '1st day of renewed arms talks fails to end impasse', *Washington Post*, 12 July 1991, p. A14.

[44] Apple, R. W., 'Bush vows to put Soviets in group favored in trade', *New York Times*, 31 July 1991, p. 1.

[45] Rosenthal, A., 'Where do interests of US lie: in united or divided USSR?', *New York Times*, 28 July 1991, p. 1; and Smith, R. J., 'Treaty looks backward, forward', *Washington Post*, 1 Aug. 1991, p. A23.

VI. US policy and the disintegration of the USSR

In the aftermath of the failed coup, as republics declared independence and the cracks in the empire began to grow, the USA was faced with a difficult dilemma: should it support the right of peoples to self-determination by supporting the republics in their struggle with the Kremlin, or should it continue to base its policy on relations with Gorbachev's Union for the sake of stability? Before the coup, the Bush Administration's approach had been to support Gorbachev in spite of the inconsistencies of his policies. To many Western analysts, the success of reform was inextricably linked to Gorbachev's ability to stay in power. Reform in the USSR, the end of the cold war and freedom in Eastern Europe were personified by Gorbachev; it was believed that only he would be able to maintain the current direction of Soviet policy. In many cases, he was given the benefit of the doubt as the West hoped that continued support from abroad would translate into staying power in Moscow.[46] As things turned from bad to worse within the USSR, it was hoped that the maintenance of Gorbachev's stature as a world leader would keep the conservatives in line. The West wanted to make it clear that the warming of Western relations with the USSR might not continue if Gorbachev were removed from power. One US official described the US support of Gorbachev as a 'geopolitical massage'.[47]

Even before the Gulf War, the USA was noticeably quiet in its criticism of Gorbachev's pressure tactics and economic blockade against Lithuania following its declaration of independence in March of 1990.[48] Washington's only response was to delay by one month the signing of a treaty granting the USSR MFN status. During the Gulf War, US responses to the actions of Soviet troops in the Baltics were even more muted. In early January, in the days preceding the UN deadline for Iraqi withdrawal and following the start of coalition air operations, Soviet troops sent to enforce the draft seized buildings in armed clashes with Lithuanian and Latvian nationalists in both Vilnius and Riga. A number of deaths resulted. The EC quickly suspended $1 billion of aid to the USSR.[49] However, the USA remained cautious—Soviet support for US Gulf operations were of higher priority. While the USA considered sanctions and held repeated meetings with high level Soviet officials in both Moscow and Washington, its public stance was represented by repeated official statements that the USA was 'seriously concerned' and that the USA would 'continue to

---

[46] An example of such thinking can be found in: 'Help for Russia', *The Economist*, 1 Dec. 1990, pp. 14–15. Even academic sources considered the changes in the Soviet Union to be linked to Gorbachev's leadership: Meyer, S. M., 'The sources and prospects of Gorbachev's new thinking on security', *International Security*, vol. 13, no. 2 (fall 1988), pp. 124–63. Some speculated about how the West could help Gorbachev succeed in his reform programme: Snyder, J., 'International leverage on Soviet domestic change', *World Politics*, vol. 42, no. 1 (Oct. 1989), pp. 1–30.

[47] Friedman, T. L., 'Will the US miss its partner, the Kremlin', *New York Times*, 8 Sep. 1991, p. E2.

[48] For the details of Lithuania's drive for independence and Gorbachev's response see: Girnius, K., 'Lithuania and the Soviet Union: negotiating a settlement', *Report on the USSR*, vol. 2, no. 19 (11 May 1990), pp. 22–24; and Goble, P., 'Gorbachev's Baltic policy backfires', *Report on the USSR*, vol. 2, no. 21 (25 May 1990), pp. 1–3.

[49] Riding, A., 'Baltic assaults lead Europe and to hold off aid', *New York Times*, 23 Jan. 1991, p. 1.

view this matter very seriously'.[50] Even when a US–Soviet summit scheduled for February was cancelled, the USA repeatedly denied that the postponement had any relation to Soviet actions in the Baltics.

Congressional criticism of Moscow was much stronger. During a congressional visit to Riga in mid-February, however, the US legislators stated US policy explicitly: although the USA supported the Baltic drive for independence, it was not ready to disrupt US–Soviet relations during the Gulf War.[51] Essentially, the USSR was being treated as an ally that was misbehaving; friendly diplomacy would solve the problem.

This moderate response to a case in which the USSR was engaged in military action against sovereign nations (the USA had never recognized the Baltic incorporation into the USSR) foreshadowed the US response to the hopes for independence of Soviet republics the USA did consider legal territory of the USSR. President Bush let the world know exactly who the US supported in the struggle between the centre and the republics during his now-famous 1 August speech in Kiev. He stated that the USA: 'will not support those who seek independence in order to replace a far-off tyranny with a local despotism . . . will not aid those who promote a suicidal nationalism based on ethnic hatred'.[52]

The USA stood firmly in alliance with the centre, in part because of the Bush–Gorbachev Gulf War partnership, but also owing to fear of the potential for trouble if the USSR dissolved into multiple nations that possessed nuclear weapons.

During the August coup attempt, the Bush Administration repeated its support for Gorbachev and Russian President Yeltsin's defiance of the coup in the Russian White House. The Administration suspended aid to Moscow, maintained contact with Yeltsin and refused to send newly appointed Ambassador Robert Strauss to meet with the new leadership. Although Gorbachev had returned to Moscow, a tremendous shift in power had taken place. The Communist Party became a relic of history, and republic after republic declared its independence from Moscow. Yeltsin became the new symbol for the aspirations of the Russian people; the coup was partially blamed on Gorbachev's short-sightedness and failure to reform the economy.

The Bush Administration, however, continued to support Gorbachev's attempts to hold the Union together. The first test for the US relationship with Gorbachev was the Baltic insistence on gaining independence immediately after the coup. Germany took the lead, pushing other Western nations to recognize the Baltics even before the coup attempt had fallen apart. At the EC ministerial meeting on 27 August, the Baltics were officially recognized by all 12 EC

[50] Bungs, D., 'Baltic notebook', *Report on the USSR*, vol. 3, no. 2 (11 Jan. 1991), p. 25; and Oberdorfer, D., 'Bush remains cautious on Baltic events', *Washington Post*, 12 Jan. 1991, p. A18.

[51] Bungs, D., 'Baltic notebook', *Report on the USSR*, vol. 3, no. 8 (22 Feb. 1991), p. 27.

[52] This speech is often referred to as the 'Chicken Kiev' speech, an allusion to criticisms that Bush lacked the courage to ally himself with the forces of freedom. After hearing this speech, Ivan Drach, leader of the Rukh movement for Ukrainian independence, commented that President Bush travelled to Kiev 'as a messenger for Gorbachev'. See Devroy, A. and Dobbs, M., 'Bush warns Ukraine on independence', *Washington Post*, 2 Aug. 1991, p. A1.

member states. President Bush did not want to embarrass Gorbachev by further legitimizing the breakup of the USSR and instead urged him to grant independence to the Baltics, stating that the USA would wait until this was done before extending US recognition. Pressure on President Bush to recognize the Baltics, however, grew to the point where he could no longer wait. In a deal with Gorbachev, Bush promised to delay recognition from 30 August to 2 September to give Gorbachev time to introduce Baltic independence legislation into the Soviet parliament.[53] Gorbachev failed to secure passage of the legislation, and the USA went ahead with recognition.

The Bush Administration moved a step further by outlining what amounted to requirements that Soviet republics seeking independence would have to meet before the USA would consider recognizing them as independent states. Secretary Baker's five principles of US policy towards the republics did not apply to the Baltics (the USA had never recognized their incorporation into the USSR). These following principles were discussed with Soviet and republican leaders at a CSCE conference on human rights in mid-September:

1. The future of the USSR must be decided peacefully by the peoples of each republic in accordance with the Helsinki Final Act.
2. Present borders must be respected, and any changes must be 'consistent with CSCE principles'.
3. Change within the USSR and republics must be through democratic elections.
4. Basic human rights, especially 'equal treatment of minorities', must be established within the republics.
5. All republics must adhere to international law, in particular provisions within the Helsinki Final Act and the Charter of Paris.[54]

Essentially, these guidelines for US policy made it clear to republican leaders that if they expected the USA to welcome them into the community of nations in the West, they must first prove themselves able to adhere to Western notions of democratic political behaviour. As discussed below, these principles were reiterated following the establishment of the CIS.

The Bush Administration's views on giving the USSR economic aid remained mostly unchanged after the coup. Congress took the lead in proposing massive aid packages to the USSR. Congressman Richard Gephardt called for a $1–3 billion fund for the USSR, while House Armed Services Committee Chairman Les Aspin supported a similar $1 billion of aid for food, medicine and other humanitarian needs.[55] Both proposals suggested drawing these funds

[53] Rosenthal, A., 'Baltics recognized', *New York Times*, 3 Sep. 1991, p. 1.

[54] See 'Baker's remarks: policy on Soviets', *New York Times*, 5 Sep. 1991, p. A8.

[55] Dewar, H., 'Gephardt backs using defense funds to aid Soviets', *Washington Post*, 28 Aug. 1991, p. A17; and Dewar, H., 'Aspin: tap Pentagon for Soviet aid money', *Washington Post*, 29 Aug. 1991, p. A43. Aspin termed a policy of redirecting Pentagon funds 'defense by different means'. This characterization foreshadowed a continuing debate within the USA: is it better to spend relatively smaller amounts of US tax dollars in hope of stabilizing the situation in the CIS or spend nothing and risk the rise of an authoritarian leader who might impose order forcefully and bring on a new cold war? In the long run, a

from the Pentagon budget, in effect using the 'peace dividend' as a new type of defence spending that would enhance US security by helping the USSR undergo a stable transformation. Secretary of Defense Dick Cheney led the Administration assault on these plans, calling them 'foolish' and 'a serious mistake'; President Bush merely called them 'premature'.[56] To the Administration, the situation in the USSR was too unstable for the USA to make any major adjustments in policy especially if they consisted of financial aid. Accordingly, in spite of German support for a vast increase in aid to the USSR, the US position prevailed. G-7 officials, meeting in London in late August, again rejected financial aid, instead recommending additional shipments of food and medicine.

However, the G-7 did begin to develop a more focused approach towards aid to the USSR as Gorbachev's attempts to form a new Union and develop new economic relationships between the republics repeatedly failed. At the annual meeting of the IMF in Bangkok in mid-October, a Soviet delegation held two days of talks with G-7 finance ministers. It was agreed that the G-7 would begin a series of advisory missions to the USSR to help the Soviets sort out their economic problems. Although the West still was not ready to grant large financial aid packages, US Treasury Secretary Nicholas Brady developed a five-point plan consisting of medical supplies, food aid, business training programmes, pipeline infrastructure repairs and environmental aid.[57]

The G-7 also began to deal directly with the republics. In late October representatives from the G-7 finance ministries met with the prime ministers (or equivalents) of the republics to discuss how to divide up the cumulative debt of the Soviet Union.[58] A second round of what had been called the '12 plus 7 talks' resulted in an agreement regarding outstanding debt and structural adjustments to the republic economies. These were seen both as necessary for real economic reform and as requirements for Western rescheduling of Soviet debt.[59] These reforms would be recommended and assisted by the IMF. Essentially, it was business-as-usual for the IMF in dealing with problem economies—requirements of deficit reduction, exchange rate adjustments and government spending cuts in exchange for debt restructuring and potential credit access.

Within the USA, plans for economic aid to the USSR fell prey to the continued recession. A plan designed by Congressman Aspin and Chairman of the Senate Armed Services Committee Sam Nunn was abandoned as criticism from both Republicans and Democrats grew; critics argued that the money was

new cold war would be far costlier. In this broader sense of national security, the preventive measures of economic aid are better long-term investments of US tax dollars than a renewed defence buildup.

[56] Lancaster, J. and Gellman, B., 'Citing Soviet strife, Cheney resists cuts', *Washington Post*, 30 Aug. 1991, p. 1; Devroy, A., 'Bush: defense restructuring possible', *Washington Post*, 30 Aug. 1991, p. 1.

[57] 'The perils of togetherness', *The Economist*, 12 Oct. 1991, pp. 15–16.

[58] 'G-7 representatives meet republic delegates', TASS, 27 Oct. 1991, in FBIS-SOV-91-208, 28 Oct. 1991, p. 6; and 'Serious differences emerge', Moscow Interfax, 29 Oct. 1991, in FBIS-SOV-91-209, 30 Oct. 1991, p. 8.

[59] A text of the agreement was published in TASS, 21 Nov. 1991, in FBIS-SOV-91-226, 22 Nov. 1991, pp. 4–5.

needed at home, to revive the US economy. Although the Administration no longer opposed a billion dollar diversion of Pentagon funds, it did not openly support the plan for fear of protest from those who railed against Bush's inattention to domestic affairs. Aid to the Soviet Union became a problem issue in US politics, as many leaders in and out of government argued that foreign aid to the USSR was inexcusable during a period in which the US education, health care and economic infrastructures were in such poor condition. For the moment, anything beyond emergency aid was out of the question. Even the aid already promised earlier in 1991 was not finding its way to Moscow; reportedly, US officials feared that publicity surrounding aid to the USSR would create a backlash against the Administration for being more responsive to Soviet than US economic needs.[60]

At this point, the USA seemed more concerned with dismantling some of the remnants of the cold war military posture. In late September, President Bush announced major cuts in US nuclear forces and challenged Gorbachev to match them. Gorbachev responded quickly, meeting Bush's challenge and announcing his own proposals for further cuts.[61]

US policies that seemed to tilt decidedly towards the centre in its struggle with the republics took an abrupt about face near the end of November. Although the Bush Administration had followed the lead of the G-7 and negoti- ated the autumn renewal of grain credits with the 12 republics, the USA still recognized Moscow as the political power centre and Gorbachev as the legit- imate, even preferred, leader of the USSR.[62] Since the August coup, policy makers within the Bush Administration had been arguing over whether the USA should stick with Gorbachev or throw its support towards the republics. Secretary Baker had urged continued backing of Gorbachev's efforts to remake the Union, while Secretary of Defense Dick Cheney saw recognition of the republics as the more realistic approach. By the end of November, Cheney's faction seemed to win out.[63] A change in the Administration's policy was not signalled until a meeting with Ukrainian-Americans at the White House on 26 November. At the meeting, President Bush indicated that the USA would recognize an independent Ukraine shortly after the scheduled referendum on

[60] McManus, D., 'US promises to aid Soviets still that—only a promise', *Los Angeles Times*, 16 Nov. 1991, p. A1.

[61] For the details of these arms control proposals see Devroy, A. and Smith, R. J., 'President orders sweeping reductions in strategic and tactical nuclear arms', *Washington Post*, 28 Sep. 1991, p. 1; and Clarke, D. L., 'Gorbachev replies to Bush's nuclear arms initiative', *Report on the USSR*, vol. 3, no. 43 (25 Oct. 1991), pp. 11–17.

[62] The Nov. grain credit programme renewal is discussed in Gugliotta (note 32), p. A39.

[63] On disagreements within the Administration see Rosenthal, A., 'US, turning from Moscow, would grant recognition to an independent Ukraine', *New York Times*, 28 Nov. 1991, p. 1. Some analysts suggested that the turnaround was caused to a large extent by the results of the Pennsylvania Senatorial election. Reportedly, Pennsylvania voters of Eastern European descent voted against ex-Bush Attorney General Richard Thornburgh to protest the slow response of the President to the republics' declarations of independence. If this did play a part in the Administration's calculus, the President must have hoped that the shift in policy would give a boost to his flagging popularity at the start of an election year. Jehl, D. and McManus, D., 'US to recognize Ukraine in policy shift, officials say', *Los Angeles Times*, 28 Nov. 1991, p. 1; and Rosenthal, A., 'Aides say Bush is shifting focus from Gorbachev to republics', *New York Times*, 30 Nov. 1991, p. 1.

independence to take place on 1 December. The USA made no formal announcement; the previous day the State Department had reiterated the standard US policy line that the Bush Administration would not recognize any changes in the make-up of the USSR until the Moscow Government did. The content of the President's pledge to the Ukrainian-Americans, however, was soon reported in the press, and the Administration then began to talk openly of a shift in policy towards the republics.

This shift, coming before the Ukrainians themselves had voted for independence, illustrated not only a sharp turn in US policy but a willingness to become involved in the conflict between Gorbachev and the republics. The Administration displayed further evidence of its new conception of where power rested in the USSR when, in an attempt to soothe Yeltsin's irritation at US acceptance of Ukrainian independence, the Bush Administration promised not to officially recognize Ukraine until Russia had done so. Like Gorbachev, Yeltsin felt that Ukraine and Russia would have to remain together—a point that was a source of irritation to the independence-minded leaders of Ukraine.

This late-November shift was a major step towards recognizing 12 sovereign nations instead of one Soviet empire. Ukrainians overwhelmingly approved independence on 1 December 1991 and although the USA withheld diplomatic recognition it did quickly dispatch Assistant Secretary of State Thomas Niles to Kiev and scheduled a similar trip for Secretary Baker that also included a stop in Moscow. The Bush Administration spoke to both Gorbachev and Yeltsin before commenting on the Ukrainian independence vote, in an attempt to balance out a shifting policy. It was clear, however, that if Gorbachev's standing in the international community was what maintained his power in Moscow (he had become increasingly unpopular after the coup), the new US policy undermined Gorbachev almost completely. Official recognition of Ukraine waited until the USA had assurances from President Leonid Kravchuk's Government in Kiev on the principles outlined by Secretary Baker in early September and additional US concerns about adherence to agreements signed by the USSR, such as the Conventional Armed Forces in Europe (CFE) Treaty and the Nuclear Non-Proliferation Treaty (NPT).

More importantly, the Bush Administration wanted to prevent an independent Ukraine from becoming an independent nuclear state. In the early autumn, Ukrainian leaders had issued many seemingly contradictory statements about the nuclear weapons long deployed on Ukrainian soil by the Soviet Government.[64] With Soviet nuclear weapons on the territory of Belarus and Kazakhstan, in addition to Russia and Ukraine, the Bush Administration feared that the breakup of the USSR would leave the USA to deal with four independent, possibly feuding, nuclear states. Accordingly, the Bush Administration

---

[64] Statements by Ukrainian leaders alternated between declaring the region a nuclear-free zone and demanding operational control over 'Soviet' weapons deployed on Ukrainian soil. These pronouncements were actually a reflection of the bargaining process between Russia and Ukraine over the assets of the Soviet Union. Though Ukrainians have held a special aversion to nuclear weapons since the Chernobyl accident, they realized that the possession of nuclear weapons might be the key to preventing Moscow from dominating its smaller neighbour.

made it clear that US recognition of Ukraine depended on Ukrainian support for a single, unified command of nuclear weapons on what had been Soviet territory.

The Bush Administration's focus on the nuclear issue was the main thrust of Baker's trip to Moscow and republic capitals in December. At best, the Administration hoped that only the Russian republic (or nation) would retain nuclear capability. Whether these weapons were destroyed or simply moved to Russia was not as important. Of course, the USA and other NATO allies realized that this could not occur overnight. Soviet officials were briefed in Brussels on NATO decision-making procedures for nuclear weapons release. NATO hoped its procedures could become the model for a stable collective decision process among the nuclear republics of Belarus, Kazakhstan, Russia and Ukraine.

Ukrainian leaders were quick to reassure the USA, most likely in hopes of gaining favour with the Bush Administration that could lead to diplomatic recognition, economic aid and US investment. Both Kravchuk and Defence Minister Konstantin Morozov publicly stated, shortly after the referendum, that Ukraine intended to become a nuclear-free zone (even before the US diplomatic barrage on maintaining joint command and possible denuclearization).[65]

Before US policy could truly take shape, the breakup of the USSR accelerated. During a weekend meeting between the leaders of the three Slavic republics (President Yeltsin of Russia, President Kravchuk of Ukraine and Supreme Soviet Chairman Stanislav Shushkevich of Belarus) in the Belarus town of Viskuoi, near Brest, on 8–9 December, the Commonwealth of Independent States was established. Essentially, it was an alternative to Gorbachev's Union in which the 'centre', located in Minsk, Belarus, would play merely a coordinating role instead of retaining major decision-making powers similar to those of the USSR central government. Other republics were invited to join the CIS in the hope that the CIS would completely replace the USSR. The text of the Brest Declaration explicitly stated that the 'USSR is ceasing its existence as a subject of international law and geopolitical reality'.[66]

Although Gorbachev called this move a 'catastrophe' leading to 'anarchy', the Bush Administration illustrated its almost total abandonment of Gorbachev by reiterating the CIS declaration as Secretary Baker agreed that the USSR 'no longer exists'.[67] Gorbachev had spent all his energies since the coup attempting to reconstruct the USSR and even felt that the Ukrainian independence vote did

[65] Hiatt, F., 'Ukraine vote leaves Union shattered', *Washington Post*, 3 Dec. 1991, p. 1; and Thor-Dahlberg, J., 'Ukraine vows to become nuclear-free', *Los Angeles Times*, 4 Dec. 1991, p. A4. Ukraine's desire to remove nuclear weapons from its soil seems to stem from the trauma caused by the Chernobyl nuclear accident. The accident, so close to Kiev, may have more to do with Ukraine's single-minded drive for independence than centuries of Russian domination. Members of the Ukrainian Parliament have even called for placing Gorbachev on trial for failing to make the accident public after radiation had begun to leak into the Ukrainian countryside; see 'Ukrainians ask Gorbachev trial, asserting cover-up at Chernobyl', *New York Times*, 12 Dec. 1991, p. A10.

[66] The text of the agreement between Russia, Belarus and Ukraine, which has been called the Brest Declaration, was reprinted in *Washington Post*, 10 Dec. 1991, p. A32.

[67] Hoffman, D., "'Soviet Union as we've known it" is gone, Baker says', *Washington Post*, 9 Dec. 1991, p. A16.

not preclude a new union. Suddenly, with no warning, a new union was formed without him, and his Bush Administration allies seem to be aligning themselves with that new union. Gorbachev even complained of the Bush Administration's disloyalty in an interview conducted shortly before his resignation.[68] The Bush Administration was not eager to become more deeply embroiled in the struggle between Gorbachev's union and what soon came to be seen as Yeltsin's union. Explicitly, US policy would be static, neither severing relations with Gorbachev's USSR nor initiating relations with the Commonwealth. Unless the Bush Administration completely ignored the Commonwealth, however, it would be choosing sides. Furthermore, US policy towards Ukraine had already done permanent damage to US relations with the USSR.

On 12 December, in a speech at Princeton University, Secretary Baker outlined the essence of the new US policy towards the breakup of the USSR and the independence of the republics. Among the elements of this new policy were: (a) dealing directly with the republic governments, bringing them into the 'Euro-Atlantic Community'; (b) a call for an international co-ordinating conference on aid to nations of the former Soviet Union that would include representatives from donor nations of Western Europe, East Asia and the Persian Gulf; (c) the sending of US experts on non-proliferation and nuclear weapon safety and dismantlement; (d) expansion of IMF and World Bank ties to the republics; and (e) reiteration of the requirements for recognition of 4 September.[69]

Baker's speech described US priorities in the following order: (a) managing the military situation within the republics, in particular nuclear weapons; (b) bringing democracy to the nations of the former Soviet Union; and (c) encouraging and assisting in the creation of market-oriented economies. The speech was given shortly before Baker left on a trip that would take him to Moscow, Kiev, Alma-Ata (Kazakhstan's capital), Bishkek (Kyrgyzstan's capital) and Minsk to meet with the leaders of each republic. The trip to other capitals in addition to Moscow signified US acceptance of the new balance of power within the former USSR, now the budding Commonwealth.

The latest developments made the nuclear issue even more of a priority for the USA. The potential existed for four independent nuclear powers. While travelling from capital to capital, Baker spelled out explicit requirements that the republics possessing nuclear weapons must satisfy, including collective control of nuclear weapons, signing of the NPT, inspections of and advice on dismantlement and disabling procedures for nuclear weapons, export controls on nuclear technology and materials, and the continuity of arms control agreements signed with the USSR.

On 17 December, Gorbachev met with Yeltsin and the two agreed that pending the acceptance of the Commonwealth by the remaining republics, the USSR would come to an end on 31 December 1991. Shortly afterwards, all remaining republics with the exception of Georgia (where a rebellion against

---

[68] Kohan, J. and Talbott, S., *Time*, 23 Dec. 1991, p. 26.
[69] The text of Baker's speech is reprinted in 'Baker sees opportunities and risks as Soviet republics grope for stability', *New York Times*, 13 Dec. 1991, p. A10.

the Government was underway) signed a second, more detailed treaty establishing the Commonwealth of Independent States on 21 December.[70] In one last concession to Gorbachev, President Bush waited until after Gorbachev had resigned on 24 December to recognize Armenia, Belarus, Kazakhstan, Kyrgyzstan, Russia and Ukraine as independent nations. The other republics of the CIS had not yet satisfied the standards set by the USA in September and December.

VII. The USA, the Commonwealth and beyond

At the time of writing, it is too early to tell what shape US relations with the new states of the former Soviet Union will take. Several patterns, however, have already emerged. Whether these will last depends upon the highly uncertain relationships among the nations of the Commonwealth and the success their leaders will have in stabilizing the economic and political life of these nations. Above all, it seems clear that the Bush Administration prefers to maintain the partnership with Moscow that formed during the Gorbachev era, and that Yeltsin's Government is more than willing to be viewed as first among equals in the new Commonwealth. The next few years may witness more continuity between US relations with Russia and US relations with Gorbachev's USSR than might have been expected.

The Soviet, now Commonwealth, nuclear arsenal remains the primary concern of the USA, as it had been throughout the cold war. The threat of a Soviet invasion of Western Europe passed into history even before the Soviet empire disintegrated. As far as the USA knows, however, strategic nuclear weapons in the four nuclear republics are still aimed at targets in the USA, although the likelihood of use against the USA is extremely low.[71]

Many are concerned that nuclear weapons may be used if squabbles such as the dispute between Russia and Ukraine over the Black Sea Fleet escalate out of control. In a televised interview, Secretary Baker warned of a Yugoslavia-type conflict with nuclear weapons in the arsenal.[72] Even this, however, may be exaggerated. Any war between Commonwealth states would start as a conventional war, and like any war in history, basic territorial, ethnic, political or ideological conflicts would be at the root of hostility. It is in solving these basic disagreements and problems from the Soviet years that the path to stability lies. The most problematic issue seems to be old republic, now national, borders that do not reflect ethnic realities. In this sense, the problems of the Commonwealth are similar to those that have plagued Africa since independence.

---

[70] The text of this agreement among the 11 remaining republics is reprinted in *New York Times*, 23 Dec. 1991, p. A6.

[71] Although the Bush Administration clearly focused its policies on helping Russia, Ukraine, Belarus and Kazakhstan maintain control of CIS nuclear capability, almost as an urgent priority, not everyone agreed that this was the most pressing issue the world faced as the USSR came to an end. For a particularly incisive look at how the nuclear threat may be exaggerated see Meyer, S. M., 'Hyping the Soviet nuclear peril', *New York Times*, 12 Dec. 1991, p. A10.

[72] Hoffman (note 67), p. A16.

As discussed above, the USA has set many guidelines for how the Common-wealth nuclear arsenal should evolve from the Soviet arsenal. Most importantly, the USA wishes to deal with only one nuclear weapon state—Russia. US policy did not seek the disarmament of Russia, simply the continued maintenance of the nuclear deterrent relationship that had existed between the USSR and the USA; this deterrent relationship would now exist between Russia and the USA. The Administration has also spelled out a condition for recognition: that Russia join the non-proliferation regime as a nuclear state, while Belarus, Kazakhstan and Ukraine join as non-nuclear nations. Whether nuclear weapons in the hands of the four nations are a source of instability, in which ethnic conflicts could become nuclear war, or a source of stability, in which nuclear capability becomes a deterrent to armed conflict, is unclear.

It may also be academic. Ukraine, suffering from the trauma of the Chernobyl accident, seems eager to rid itself of all nuclear weapons. Although Nursultan Nazarbayev, President of Kazakhstan, has stated that his nation will maintain nuclear weapons as long as Russia does, he reportedly told Baker that Kazakhstan will eventually be nuclear free.[73] Belarus, as well, seems ready to denuclearize, and all four nations signed an annexe to the Commonwealth treaty calling for the removal of all tactical nuclear weapons from Belarus, Kazakhstan and Ukraine either to be destroyed or moved to Russia) by July 1992.[74]

The Bush Administration also planned to use $400 million in aid to the Commonwealth appropriated by Congress early in the autumn of 1991 for the destruction and storage of nuclear weapons on the territory of the former Soviet Union. Earlier, it was unclear whether the Administration had intended to spend this money or not. Money taken out of the Pentagon budget, to be used for dis-mantling and destroying Commonwealth nuclear weapons, seems to be money well spent towards enhancing US security. There have even been suggestions by officials of the Commonwealth, including some from the Ministry of Atomic Power and Industry, that the US funds should be used to build one of several storage depots for nuclear weapons scheduled for destruction, and that keys to these facilities should be shared with the USA.[75] If US policy takes such a hands-on approach, it will necessitate a long-term commitment.

The Bush Administration seemed to be taking the longer term view during the early days of the Commonwealth. It was clear that the Administration hoped to maintain the partnership that it formed with the USSR during the latter years of the Gorbachev era and cemented during the Gulf War with the new Russian nation under the leadership of Boris Yeltsin. Administration officials made it known that the USA planned to treat Russia as the successor state to the USSR, supporting Russia's bid to take the Soviet seat at the UN and naming Robert

[73] Hoffman, D., 'Kazakhstan keeping nuclear arms, republic's president tells Baker', *Washington Post*, 18 Dec. 1991, p. A30.
[74] See the Alma-Ata Declaration reprinted in the *New York Times*, 23 Dec. 1991, p. A6.
[75] Broad, W., 'Soviets say arms scuttling will take ten years', *New York Times*, 18 Dec. 1991, p. A29; and Smith, R. J., 'Soviets suggest giving US keys to nuclear sites', *Washington Post*, 19 Dec. 1991, p. A42.

Strauss, US Ambassador to the USSR as the new Ambassador to Russia. Although the USA may now be the only superpower, the Bush Administration's new world order demands a UN Security Council that is allied and even somewhat compliant. Awarding Russia—a nation in need of US economic assistance—the Soviet seat gives the USA another ally on the Security Council. It also forces the USA either to maintain its partnership with Russia, if the UN will be used as an instrument of multilateral (although often US-led) policy, or face the charge of unilateralism.

At the Heads of State UN Security Council Summit, held on 31 January 1992, Yeltsin was welcomed into the exclusive club of permanent Security Council members. His participation in the summit at which the Security Council charted the post-cold war role of the UN in world affairs was a symbol of Russia's role as the inheritor of the USSR's power. Ironically, only after the ousting of Gorbachev, the first head of state to resurrect hopes for the UN's role in preventive diplomacy and peace-keeping, did the UN begin to develop ways to fulfil its original mandate as a collective security organization.[76]

The USA recognized quickly that Russia and Yeltsin remained the first among equals within the Commonwealth. The Commonwealth treaty gave nuclear control decisions to Yeltsin (with approval from the other nuclear republics), conceded the UN Security Council seat to Russia and turned over command of new Commonwealth joint forces to the last Soviet Minister of Defence Yevgeniy Shaposhnikov.[77] For both the nations of the Commonwealth and the Bush Administration it was simply a recognition of reality. Russia, by its sheer size and extent of resources, will dominate the other republics economically and politically unless it crumbles from within just as the Soviet empire did.

Only Ukraine seems to desire to move away from Moscow and towards the West. Since the attempted coup in August, the leaders of Ukraine and Russia have been at odds over whether the forces deployed on Ukrainian territory should be commanded by Kiev or Moscow. The Black Sea Fleet has become a particularly contentious issue.[78] Kazakhstan seems to be a strong believer in unity. President Nazarbayev supported Gorbachev's union attempts even after Belarus, Russia and Ukraine formed the Commonwealth, but quickly moved to embrace the Commonwealth. With such a large proportion of ethnic Russians in Kazakhstan, nearly 38 per cent compared with only 40 per cent ethnic

[76] At the Security Council summit, the heads of state asked UN Secretary-General Boutros Boutros Ghali to report on the 'capacity of the UN for preventive diplomacy, for peacemaking and for peace-keeping' and the 'role of the UN in identifying potential crises and areas of instability as well as the contribution to be made by regional organizations'. The text of the Security Council's declaration is reprinted in *New York Times*, 1 Feb. 1992, p. 4.

[77] The problem of what forces actually are included in the 'joint forces' is contentious. Nations within the Commonwealth have been wavering back and forth over whether they want Soviet units stationed on their soil to be turned over to joint command or be remodelled into national forces. For further details, see chapter 12 in this volume.

[78] The Commonwealth treaty of 21 Dec. gives Moscow control of all 'strategic' forces. However, 'strategic' is never defined. Kiev argues that the term refers only to nuclear weapons, and therefore the Black Sea Fleet belongs to Ukraine. Moscow defines 'strategic' as all those forces that would be used to engage foreign powers outside of Soviet territory; therefore all naval forces fit this description, no matter where deployed.

Kazakhs, Alma-Ata seems firmly aligned with Moscow.[79] Belarus was given the honour of having its capital, Minsk, named as the Commonwealth capital. Among other things, such as economic realities, this should keep Belarus aligned with Moscow. The other republics are simply too small to go it alone. That, however, does not exclude the possibility that a nation like Moldova might move to unite with the more ethnically similar Romania, or that as time goes on, the Central Asian nations might seek stronger ties to Turkey or Iran at the expense of Moscow's influence.

This second possibility is becoming a preoccupation within the Bush Administration. Many ethnic Muslims in the Central Asian nations dream of unification with territory in Iran and Turkey to create a large and powerful nation—Turkestan. While this seems an unlikely development (and could probably not proceed without violent conflict, given that such a change would necessitate the dismemberment of ethnically diverse Kazakhstan), the USA does fear that Iran might gain tremendous influence through the appeal of Islamic fundamentalism. A loss of influence in this region would be a great blow for Western hopes to expand democratic and free-market principles to all territories of the former USSR. It would also jeopardize Western strategic interests in containing instability, and anti-Western forces in South-West Asia. In February 1992, Secretary Baker was dispatched to the Commonwealth for a tour of the Central Asian capitals. Although the explicit purpose of his mission was to build better ties between these nations and Washington, an implicit purpose was to persuade these nations to see Turkey, not Iran, as the model for nation building.

In many ways, Yeltsin and the Russian leadership achieved in December what the conservatives failed to achieve in August: the overthrow of Gorbachev and his Government. Yeltsin now has control of the Kremlin, the Treasury, the Defence and Foreign Ministries, the intelligence apparatus, the UN Security Council seat and the nuclear weapons. In spite of the Commonwealth's co-ordinating institutions being located in Minsk, US policy will focus on Moscow as it did in the past.

All of the new nations understand that their future relies heavily upon securing Western aid, and that aid depends upon satisfying the many conditions outlined by Washington and multilateral institutions such as the IMF and the World Bank. Though Russia may still be able to dominate the nations of the Commonwealth, it does not have the power to stabilize (or resurrect) their economies. Russia's economy may be in the worst shape of all. Since economic reform is the first order of business, the Commonwealth looks to the West for aid, acceptance and approval.

The USA had set out the many conditions for recognition in speeches by Baker in September and December of 1991. The nuclear nations responded quickly with their declaration of intent to remove tactical nuclear weapons to Russia, to create a single nuclear command, to renounce first use of nuclear weapons, to adhere to all agreements signed by Gorbachev and to welcome a

---

[79] 'The Soviet Union's republics in 1991', *New York Times*, 29 Aug. 1991, p. A7.

US advisory role in the destruction of nuclear capable systems. Even more indicative of how the new nations view the USA were leaders' attempts to court favour with Baker during his travels to the former Soviet Union in December of 1991.[80] President Nazarbayev reportedly told Baker that he keeps a copy of Baker's five principles of 4 September in his office. President Askar Akayev of Kyrgyzstan also commented to Baker on the importance of Baker's 12 December speech.

The Bush Administration had made it clear in its choice of which nations to recognize first that it intended to stick to its requirements before recognition would be granted. The four nuclear nations were recognized, as were resource rich (and eager to please) Kyrgyzstan and Armenia (the latter was recognized for domestic political reasons).[81] Although Administration officials let it be known, on 23 December, that the USA intended to recommend full membership in the IMF and the World Bank for some of these nations, it did not make the formal announcement until 3 January, one day after the Commonwealth lifted price controls. As detailed above, the USA had previously been against Soviet membership in these institutions. The recommendation that Armenia, Belarus, Kazakhstan, Kyrgyzstan, Russia and Ukraine should be allowed to join illustrates what some officials explained was a belief that these nations, as individual sovereign states, would have an easier time satisfying IMF and World Bank conditions for membership than the USSR would have had.[82]

This also illustrates a Bush Administration tactic used in recognizing Ukraine—announcing informally what the USA intended to do, but making it clear that these promised rewards would have to be earned. The Administration would then wait until the necessary conditions were satisfied before formally giving the new nations what they desired. Within the Administration, the debate on the proper response to the Ukrainian referendum included disagreement about how best to gain political influence within the new nations.[83] Secretary of Defense Cheney felt that quick recognition would gain the USA the most influence, while Secretary of State Baker argued that withholding recognition would allow the USA to use recognition as a reward for good behaviour. It seems that the Administration chose a compromise strategy of holding out a carrot, but not giving it officially until it was deemed a proper reward.

In the long term, the Bush Administration hoped that the USA could maintain its leadership role in the new policy of rebuilding the crumbled empire of the USSR, just as it had led the West in the old policy of defence against the Soviet Union. Baker's 12 December speech was an attempt by the USA at

[80] Friedman, T. L., 'Baker doubtful Commonwealth will last long', *New York Times*, 22 Dec. 1991, p. 1.

[81] The Armenian community in the USA is somewhat powerful, possessing great influence within the US Congress. If the Administration had ignored Armenia, it would have faced opposition similar to that which met its Baltic policy before the Sep. 1991 recognition of Lithuania, Latvia and Estonia.

[82] Tumulty, K. and McManus, D., 'Officials say US will recognize all 12 Soviet states', *Los Angeles Times*, 24 Dec. 1991, p. 1.

[83] On this debate, see Hoffman, D., 'Bush to "welcome" Ukraine vote, skirting immediate recognition', *Washington Post*, 1 Dec. 1991, p. 1.

international agenda setting. Even Baker's rhetoric compared an international effort at 'collective engagement' to aid the Commonwealth to the NATO alliance collective defence against Stalin's USSR.[84] Although reportedly a last-minute addition to Baker's speech, the idea of an international conference to co-ordinate aid to the Commonwealth nations was a way in which the USA might spell out how responsibility for reform of the Commonwealth economy will be shared by the nations of North America, Western Europe, East Asia and the Gulf Co-operation Council.[85] This effort at assuming a leadership role stems from the US fear that its presence in Europe is becoming obsolete. The USA became a major actor in European affairs to defend European democracy, first from Nazi Germany, then from the communist Soviet Union and, some might say, from the potential reunification of Germany. The Nazi and Soviet threats are gone, and Germany has reunified under the leadership of a government that seeks economic, not military, mastery.

The USA hopes to maintain a special relationship with Russia (similar to that it had with Gorbachev's USSR) are a bid to maintain relevance in the new Europe. The international aid conference is a similar effort, as well as an attempt to repeat in peacetime the successful leadership role the USA assumed during the Gulf War. The USA did have the guns to lead the world into battle against Iraq, but it does not have the butter to help the CIS out of its ruinous economic state. The Bush Administration does not intend to put together a large aid package to the USSR. The US recession and criticism that President Bush pays too much attention to foreign affairs will preclude the USA from transferring major resources away from its domestic economy in the short term. The Bush Administration seems to desire to assume the lead role in telling others how to spend their money. Over 70 per cent of the aid given to the USSR has come from the European Community.[86] Although the aid conference was welcomed by Germany, French President François Mitterrand criticized the USA, contending that the US-sponsored aid conference was simply a bid for political influence in a changing Europe. Mitterrand argued that the G-7 already had assumed the leadership role in co-ordinating aid to the USSR, and now the Commonwealth. Given that a major source of aid to the Commonwealth may come from the oil states of the Persian Gulf (a channel opened up by the USA as reward for Soviet co-operation in the struggle against Iraq), which are not represented by the G-7, the USA does have the opportunity to play a unique facilitating role. It is also unclear if Germany, the other leading contender for a leadership role, will be able to deal simultaneously with Commonwealth troubles, the incorporation of eastern Germany and the formation and stabilization of the EC.

[84] Hoffman, D., 'US calls conference to coordinate aid', *Washington Post*, 13 Dec. 1991, p. 1.

[85] On the aid conference as a last minute addition, see Bradsher, K., 'Aid panel stalls on former Soviets', *New York Times*, 8 Jan. 1992, p. A4.

[86] McManus, D. and Tumulty, K., 'Doubts grow on conference to aid Soviets', *Los Angeles Times*, 19 Dec. 1991, p. 1.

The conference, held at the US State Department on 22–23 January 1992, seemed to accomplish little. Although many of the 47 nations attending pledged more aid for the Commonwealth, and five co-ordinating groups were created to manage different categories of aid, the conference was marked more by acrimony at the role of the USA. The Bush Administration did open the conference with a pledge to ask Congress for authority to spend $645 million to aid the Commonwealth, bringing total US aid, including the grain credit programme, to nearly $5 billion.[87] However, a Marshall Plan for the Commonwealth does not seem likely.

After all the sweeping changes in the former Soviet Union during 1991, US policy towards Moscow, at least, seems remarkably unchanged. The Bush Administration has focused first on stabilizing its nuclear deterrent relationship with Russia. President Bush, at least at this early stage, still sees a partnership with Russia as a key element of the new world order.

[87] Friedman, T. L., 'Bush to press Congress to approve $645 million for ex-Soviet lands', *New York Times*, 23 Jan. 1992, p. 1.

4. Moscow's nationalities problem: the collapse of empire and the challenges ahead

Daria Fane

I. Introduction: the multinational Soviet Union

One of the most dramatic developments on the contemporary world stage was the emergence of the Soviet 'nationalities question' and its transformation into the force behind the disintegration of the Soviet central government. Nationalities issues, however, have long been poorly understood in the West; throughout the Soviet Union's history it was common to hear people from the area referred to as 'Russians', when in fact almost half of the Union's 286 million population was non-Russian.[1] The nationalities question now eclipses virtually all other domestic and international issues in its threat to the very idea of community, as the republics seek to define the future arrangements that will reign over the former Soviet land mass.

The Soviet Union after World War II was comprised of some 100 ethnic groups with their own distinct languages and cultures; of these, 22 ethnic groups have populations over one million.[2] Some but not all of these groups are the titular nationality in their own territories. Before the disintegration began, the Soviet Constitution had spelled out a federal structure of 15 Union republics, 20 autonomous republics (of which 16 were to be found in the Russian Federation), 8 autonomous oblasts (of which 5 were in the Russian Soviet Federated Socialist Republic, RSFSR), and 10 national districts or okrugs (all in the RSFSR).[3] This constitution was declared invalid in August 1991. First, Baltic independence reduced the number of Union republics, and then a spate of declarations of change of status left a confusion of identities and levels of subordination.

After the Baltics, the remaining 12 republics declared their independence. Most of the autonomous republics within the RSFSR proclaimed themselves to be Union republics, and a variety of oblasts and okrugs have declared themselves to be autonomous republics. Even some regions and cities that formerly had no autonomous status have announced their own structures; some, such as the Gagauz of Moldova, have even proclaimed themselves independent repub-

[1] According to the 1989 census, 145 million of the Soviet Union's 285.7 million population are Russian. These figures include the Baltic states which are now recognized as independent.
[2] The 1989 census lists these 22 ethnic groups and their populations in millions as: Russians 145, Ukrainians 44, Uzbeks 16.7, Belorussians 10, Kazakhs 8.1, Azeris 6.8, Tatars 6.6, Armenians 4.6, Tajiks 4.2, Georgians 3.9, Moldovans 3.8, Lithuanians 3.1, Turkmen 2.7, Kirghiz 2.5, Germans 2.0, Chuvash 1.8, Bashkirs 1.5, Latvians 1.5, Jews 1.4, Mordvinians 1.2, Polish 1.1 and Estonians 1.0.
[3] See chapters 8–11 of the 1977 Constitution.

lics. It is therefore difficult to determine the current status of various units, and even harder to predict the future. On 8 December 1991 the three Slavic republics, Belarus, Russia and Ukraine, met in Minsk and decided to form a Commonwealth of Independent States (CIS).[4] Following a 12 December meeting in Ashkhabad, they were joined by the Central Asian republics. At the time of writing, all of the former republics except Georgia have joined the CIS, but it is too early to know how viable the Commonwealth will prove to be.

This chapter outlines some of the problems and opportunities posed by the multi-ethnic nature of the former Soviet Union as national forces change the Eurasian political landscape. It begins with some general lessons about empires and their applicability to the Soviet case. It then chronicles the creation and disintegration of the Soviet empire, and assesses the challenges faced by the newly-independent republics and the international implications of the new political geography.

II. Lessons about empires

Throughout the span of history, empires have risen and collapsed. Despite the uniqueness of the Soviet situation, certain principles relevant to it can be extrapolated from the experiences of other empires.

1. *Empires do break up, leading to independence for the former colonies.* As anyone who is familiar with Edward Gibbons' classic *The Decline and Fall of the Roman Empire* knows, empires do decline and fall. Some of these transitions lead to stable independence on the part of the former colony as in the case of the United States. When the United Nations was founded in 1945, it had only 55 members. With the addition of the 3 Baltic nations on 17 September 1991, membership in the world body rose to 166 states. In 1945 the only completely independent countries in Africa were Egypt, Ethiopia and Liberia; now, with the addition of Namibia, 56 newly independent nations in Africa are UN members. Breakup is part of the empire-building process. Sooner or later empires fall. New nations appear on the world map. New nations have now emerged on the territory of the former Soviet Union as part of this historical process in the course of empire.

2. *In most cases independence is achieved through armed struggle.* Most newly independent nations emerge via birth pangs that are bloody and violent— the consequence of a successful separatist movement. When the intensity of the revolt of colonial peoples reaches the point where empire is no longer cost-effective, the centre gives up. Ultimately the final cause of breakup is that the central power loses its will to rule and lets go. Algeria is a classic example of independence via armed struggle. France initially resisted Algerian independence but changed its decision as the cost of this policy rose. In cases where the imperial power pulls out abruptly, such as the Portuguese withdrawal from

---

[4] Known in Russian by the acronym SNG (Sodruzhestvo Nezavisimykh Gosudarstov).

Africa in the mid-1970s, the lack of advance planning for post-imperial transition often leads to civil war and chaos.

Armed struggle is not always the case. Independence can emerge by mutual consensus among the relevant actors. However, there must be some incentive for the imperial power to let go. This incentive may be related to loss of the will to maintain an empire or to a settlement that provides other compensation, be it monetary, trade of territory, prestige or good will. Few would have suggested in the pre-*glasnost* era that the Soviet Union would let go of its republics without major bloodshed. Instead, the centre lost its will and the power to enforce it. First, the Baltics slipped out of the Union with a minimum of bloodshed, although the argument could be made that their incorporation into the empire had never been internationally recognized. Then, without even 'last gasp' violence, the centre faded away leaving independent republics. Within the Russian Federation, however, current indications are that President Yeltsin has no intention of letting go of secessionist autonomous republics. Yeltsin's response to events in the Chechen-Ingush autonomous republic suggests a will to preserve the 'empire within the empire'.

3. *Armed struggle may occur not just against a former power, but between both political and ethnic subgroups.* The removal of a colonial power may reveal an underlying contradiction between two ethnic groups. In some cases bloody struggles result as factions of a former colony struggle for hegemony. Two well-known examples from the breakup of the British empire are India–Pakistan and Israel–Palestine. Conflicts remaining after the departure of the imperial power have the potential to emerge as intractable struggles lasting for generations.

A wide range of border conflicts and territorial disputes exists between the former Soviet republics. Unresolved claims are numerous. To a greater or lesser extent these were kept under control by central power, but a new era of upheaval is likely to begin as the centre's power recedes and the republics struggle to determine these borders. Some have already been quite violent, such as the struggle between Armenia and Azerbaijan, while in others simmering irredentist claims persist and hold the potential for future violence. In some cases, such as Georgia, political factions within an ethnic group vie for control in a virtual civil war. Such conflicts and unresolved claims hold the potential for mass discontent, political mobilization and possible violence in the future.

4. *Another great power may step in to fill the power vacuum left by the withdrawal of a colonial power.* When an empire is in decline, other regional powers may see an opportunity to move in. This was the situation at the end of the Ottoman empire, when other powers looking to carve it up took parts from the 'sick man of Europe'. Other examples can be found in the case of French Indo-China; when the French left, the USA stepped in. In Central Asia there is already competition between Iran and Turkey for influence. In the absence of Soviet power, these regional neighbours are eyeing the potential for greater influence. One possible scenario could be an Iranian attempt to take Azerbaijan.

Another might involve a union of Persian speakers. Alternatively, the Turkic republics could form a confederation with Turkey.

5. *Former colonies may set up different types of states.* Variations in political systems and economic conditions will most likely emerge as the different parts of an empire achieve independence. Of the former French colonies in Africa, the 13 countries of the Communité Français Africain (CFA) vary in their political systems and in their economic circumstances. Some have set up Marxist states; others are ruled by conservatives. Economically, a few are relatively prosperous; others are on the verge of national bankruptcy. While the Côte d'Ivoire (Ivory Coast) has grown economically, the mostly Muslim societies of Burkina Faso, Mali and Niger have suffered greatly from the drought in the Sahel and face famine and grinding poverty.

One should not therefore expect the states resulting from the Soviet breakup all to have the same type of political and economic system. Some may opt for Western-style democracies; some may not. The Soviet empire covered a vast territory, and its republics' cultures differ widely. Regional differences will likely emerge as the republics set up independent states, some looking to Islamic states for inspiration, others looking to Europe. Newly independent nations can institute a variety of different types of government: communist dictatorships, non-communist authoritarian regimes, military regimes, democracies or even constitutional monarchies. Unfortunately, newly emerging systems often lack historical traditions adequate to provide for democratic governments; these states are vulnerable to strongman leaders or governments with fascist orientation.

6. *A variety of different post-empire regimes link former empires.* The British set up a commonwealth, while the former colonies of francophone Africa are members of the CFA, a customs union most of whose members share a currency that is tied to the French franc. These may provide models for the post-Soviet Commonwealth. Most post-colonial republics have opted to retain some form of federated economic union. Members of an empire may, however, select different levels of participation in a post-empire regime. In the case of the CFA, some, such as Senegal and the Côte d'Ivoire, maintain unusually close ties with France, while others have looser ties with the former colonial power. Similarly, in the Soviet context, most republics have chosen to participate in the Commonwealth, but some want no part of either the CIS or any other post-Union economic community.

7. *Long-term effects linger.* Even after full independence is achieved, some long-term imperial political and cultural effect on the colony is likely to endure. Language, religion, judicial system and some aspects of the technological base are typically areas which are subject to long-term influence. The English spoken in the United States is, of course, a long-term lingering effect of British colonialism, just as it is in India. The British-built rail and postal systems still function in India. In Latin America the split between the Spanish-speaking countries and Portuguese-speaking Brazil remains, hundreds of years after

Spain and Portugal drew the line of demarcation, and almost two centuries after the end of those colonial empires.

The effect of the Soviet years on the Union republics will be visible for years to come. Even with the establishment of full independence, these areas cannot escape the cultural and linguistic effects of decades of Russification. Seventy-four years of socialism have left scars on society and on national culture. The impact of socialist education on the current generation cannot be wiped out overnight.

III. Creation of the Russian empire

European empire building began in the 15th century as the Dutch, English, French, Portuguese and Spanish set out across the seas in search of new worlds. They set up colonies because of the access to raw materials, precious metals, new markets and the power that stemmed from greater dominion. Muscovy began its expansion at much the same time. Russia became a multinational empire in 1552 when it succeeded in conquering the Khanate of Kazan. The fall of the Khanate of Astrakhan soon after in 1556 further expanded Russia's territory. This brought under Russian control Tatars, Chuvash, Mordvinians, Maris, Udmurts and Bashkirs, peoples which later became in each case the titular nationality of an autonomous republic within the RSFSR.

Eastward expansion between the 1580s and 1689 brought the Siberian area reaching to the Pacific Ocean under Russian control, establishing the Amur River as the border with China, and bringing a variety of Turkic, Mongol and Finnish tribes also under Russian control. The 18th century saw westward expansion into the Baltics, while in the 19th century Russia moved southward into the Caucasus and Central Asia. Like the classic empires, Russian expansion was fuelled by a mixture of political and economic motives. Fur trade was no doubt one of the reasons for moving into Siberia, while the prospect of political and strategic gain appears to have driven the conquest of Kazan.[5] By the time of the first census in 1897, non-Russians were already a majority in the empire.[6]

Unlike the European colonial empires, such as the British empire where London ruled a far-flung territory upon which the sun never set, the Russian empire formed a contiguous land mass. This is a structural difference from the other non-contiguous European empires that lasted until the 20th century. This distinction could be viewed as part of a typology, perhaps the beginnings of an empire theory, suggesting two types of empire: contiguous and non-contiguous.

---

[5] Discussed by Kollman, N. S., 'Historical perspectives on Russian nationality policy', eds I. Bremmer and N. Naimark, *Soviet Nationalities Problems* (Stanford University Press: Stanford, Calif., 1990).
[6] According to the census figures given in Pipes, R., *The Formation of the Soviet Union: Communism and Nationalism 1917–1923* (Harvard University Press: Cambridge, 1964), rev. edn, p. 2, in 1897 Russians constituted only 44.3 per cent of the population. Since these figures reflect linguistic preference, not nationality, and some non-Russians had adopted Russian as their mother tongue, the actual number of Russians is somewhat lower.

Other contiguous empires have been the Roman empire, the Ottoman empire, and the Austro-Hungarian empire.

In contiguous empires such as the Russian/Soviet empire it can be difficult to determine where the centre ends and the colonies begin. Take, for example, the Kazan Tatars who were conquered in 1552; for over 400 years colonizers and colonized have lived side by side, intertwined, with much intermarriage. It was often assumed that it would be too difficult to separate the two—there is too much mixed blood, too long a mutual history—and yet Tatar nationalism is now rising. Tatar activists such as the Ittifaq Party are pushing for full independence, while the nationalist government seeks to secede from Russia but remain as an independent signatory to the Commonwealth treaty. While it is unlikely that Tatarstan, which is surrounded by other parts of Russia, could actually gain its independence, the lesson is that the collective Tatar nation maintained a separate ethnic identity for over four centuries. Tatar independence activists name San Marino, which is surrounded by Italy, and Swaziland, which is surrounded by South Africa, as historical precedents for this type of arrangement.

IV. The Soviet Union as empire

The Soviet Union as it had existed until 1991 was formed by Lenin and Stalin on the ruins of the collapsed Russian empire. Political scientists and historians accept the pre-1917 tsarist regime as an empire, and yet these same scholars usually choose to view the Soviet Union as a new entity that began in 1917. *Perestroika* brought about a collapse of the ideological underpinnings that propped up the Soviet Union, revealing the old Russian empire underneath the Soviet surface.

The earlier Russian empire which broke apart in 1917 had encompassed most of the land that came to be known as the Soviet Union, although the empire continued to expand to include additional territories added in the 1940s.[7] As a successor state to the tsarist empire, the Soviet Union was a new regime, a new political system with a new name but located on basically the same territory. When a new regime takes power after a revolution, this does not necessarily signify the existence of a new state so much as a new order within the same state. The post-revolution state is usually a successor state to the previous regime, inheriting its structures as well as becoming responsible for its international commitments and obligations. Though the 1917 revolutionary Soviet Government renounced tsarist debts, claiming it was not a successor state, its

---

[7] The specific areas that were added in addition to the Baltic states and Moldova are Bukovina, which had been part of Romania; Transcarpathia from Czechoslovakia (including the Mukachev area that had been part of Hungary before 1918); Western Ukraine and Western Belarus from Poland; Königsberg from Germany (Kaliningrad oblast); Southern Sakhalin and the Kurile Islands from Japan; several parts of Karelia from Finland and the previously independent state of Tannu-Tuva. Of these areas only Bukovina, Königsberg, Transcarpathia and Sakhalin were not part of the old Russian empire.

territory was largely coterminous with the former Russian empire and thus had a historical continuity with the empire that preceded it.

When the Bolshevik regime came to power in 1917 and the civil war started, the disintegration of the Russian empire began. Some of its constituent parts declared independence. Of the states hatched out of the Russian empire that gained independence in the 1917–20 period, only a few succeeded in staying outside the reconstituted empire, namely Estonia, Finland, Latvia, Lithuania, Moldavia (Moldova) and Poland. Independence was short-lived for the other states that had proclaimed their independence as the tsarist empire broke up— Armenia, Azerbaijan, Georgia, the Mountain Republic in the Caucasus, Ukraine and the Far Eastern Republic (FER). These were quickly reincorporated as Moscow reconquered most of the empire. A few areas were not retaken until the World War II period when, as a result of the Molotov–Ribbentrop Pact, Moldavia and the three Baltics were reincorporated into the Union, and several districts from Finland were added to Soviet Karelia.

Built on the ruins of the tsarist empire, the Soviet Union emerged, claiming a new identity but really functioning as a continuation of the empire under a new regime. Using the ideological justifications of communism, the Bolsheviks were able to establish control over the territory. A legal fiction was created of voluntary participation of 'independent' republics in this Union. The republics supposedly had the right to secede, but in practice this was not true.

The 'nationalities problem' has had different meanings in different eras of Russian and Soviet history. Although Lenin first approached the nationalities issue from an orthodox Marxist point of view, he understood that ethnic issues played a key role in popular discontent under the tsar, and thus he supported territorial autonomy for national groups. After the revolution there was a period referred to as the 'flowering of nationalities'; while maintaining political control over the republics, Lenin encouraged them to preserve their national languages. He established a Commissariat of Nationalities, headed by a Georgian—Joseph Stalin. By the time Stalin came to power, things had changed, and by the 1930s any 'flowering' of national culture had been cruelly sacrificed to the goals of rapid industrialization and state centralization. Under Stalin many nationalists pressing for greater republic sovereignty were either killed or sent to Siberia.

Sovietologists have traditionally overlooked the view that the Soviet Union was indeed an empire, viewing it instead as a federation. Because of this tendency Soviet nationalities problems have generally been misunderstood. The periodic, escalating outbreaks of violence have been viewed in a context of inter-ethnic tension, rather than as an issue of decolonization. Now it is clear that a systemic approach was needed for examining Soviet nationalities problems. Rather than regarding each problem separately, these issues should be linked to the broader question of the formation, structure and disintegration of the Union. The outbreaks of violence were not merely ethnic differences, but part of the process of nations asserting their identity.

The Russian Federation: empire within empire

Another aspect of the former Soviet structure also leaves a unique legacy. Like the peeled layers of an onion, there was another empire within the empire—the Russian Federation, the RSFSR. There is a tendency to view Russia as the 'home territory' and the 14 non-Russian republics as colonies. This is a myth, as Russia too is built of conquered nations. As the trend towards disintegration of the USSR grew, this instability began to be felt within the RSFSR as well.

Like the former Soviet Union, the Russian Federation is also a multinational empire. In addition to Russians, it is home to such diverse peoples as the Buryats, Tatars, Yakuts and Chechen. Boris Yeltsin, as President of the Russian Federation, now confronts some of the same nationalities challenges that Gorbachev faced. Like the Union republics, these autonomous republics have begun to seek greater economic and political sovereignty. Rising nationalism in the autonomous units within the Russian Federation is a key part of their political agenda.

The autonomous republics now challenge the continuity of Moscow's dominance in much the same way that the republics of the former Soviet Union challenged the Kremlin. Some seek to secede from the Russian Federation but remain in the Commonwealth, while in certain autonomous republics there are even independence movements. The secessionist challenge that could be posed by certain autonomous republics is quite legitimate, particularly in the more recent 20th century acquisitions such as Karelia, parts of which were taken from Finland, or Tuva, which was independent until 1944.

In the Soviet Union the RSFSR played a dual role. Like nested matroshka dolls, it was an empire nested within the Union. Yet at the same time Russia is the challenger that became the legal successor to the Union, adopting the Soviet Ministry of Foreign Affairs and the Soviet embassies abroad as its own. As the pretender to Gorbachev's 'throne', the Russian Government took control of most Soviet ministries and agreed to become responsible for assuming Soviet debt. The situation is unique. Yeltsin stepped into the disintegrating centre and to some degree assumed the role of its successor, while at the same time Russia too is threatened by the centrifugal challenges of its own nationalities. Indeed, the Soviet Union was unique as an empire, and the circumstances surrounding its collapse are unique.

V. The collapse of the Soviet empire

The basic dilemma which was faced by the Soviet Union was that it could not sustain the continuity of its empire in the presence of democratic change. Previously, socialist ideology had been a unifying factor. The breakdown of the communist ideal was an erosion of the central value structure of the Soviet system, leaving the centre without an ideological justification. *Perestroika* allowed the emergence of freer expression, which unleashed uncontainable centrifugal forces. The greater openness under *glasnost* has permitted long-simmering aspirations of the non-Russian nationalities to come to the surface. Early in the Gorbachev period, several waves of ethnic unrest swept the Union, and the term 'nationalities problem' evoked images of inter-ethnic violence. One of the first such outbursts was in Alma-Ata in December 1986. One after another, outbreaks in such places as Tbilisi and the Fergana Valley in 1989, and Baku, Dushanbe and Osh in 1990, revealed dramatically that the nationalities problem had not been solved.

By 1988–89, Popular Front movements had been formed in most republics. These fronts began to articulate an agenda of national self-determination, casting the nationalities problem in broader terms and pushing for greater sovereignty. Estonia's initial demands were for economic autonomy, not independence. A new stage was ushered in on 11 March 1990, when Lithuania declared its independence. This began the struggle between centre and periphery—a test of wills to determine whether or not the republics would succeed at secession.

In 1991 the historical structures of the Soviet empire disintegrated. Once again Estonia, Latvia and Lithuania regained their independence; then the other republics gained their independence as well. The August 1991 coup attempt was the decisive turning point in the history of the Soviet Union. The empire's nationalities problems were the trigger for this coup attempt. Its timing, on the eve of the signing of the Union treaty scheduled for 20 August, was an attempt to keep the new Union treaty from moving forward. Ironically, the coup hastened the very changes it sought to prevent. The coup was like the first shot in a revolution, triggering a series of major changes that accelerated the overthrow of the communist system.

Rapid change followed the failure of the coup. A major collapse was set in motion as the administrative structure of the Union and its central institutions began to fall apart.

The initial euphoria following the coup was soon replaced by anxious uncertainty about the future. The coup triggered upheavals in many of the republics and intensified their underlying problems. In Tajikistan the republic leadership was quickly toppled; the republic president was forced to resign after demonstrating crowds spent weeks in the streets. Ironically, the president who replaced him was the old-line Brezhnevian Communist Party leader. In Uzbekistan, determined to prevent a similar fate, the republic president, Islam Karimov, began to espouse what he called 'the China model'—economic reform, but refusal to permit demonstrations. Attempts in Tashkent to hold demonstrations, first on 26 August 1991 and again on 8 September, were squelched by local authorities. In other republics, the accelerating push for independence caused strains and uncertainty clouded by a gloomy economic picture.

The Ukrainian independence referendum of 1 December 1991 triggered a domino effect. The 8 December Minsk meeting which formed the Commonwealth of Independent States officially pronounced the central structures of the

Union defunct. Although initially the republics proclaimed themselves independent within the borders established during the Soviet era, they will not necessarily remain within those borders. There is likely to be a period of upheaval and fighting as at least some of the states struggle to determine new boundaries.

VI. The challenge of national independence

This enormous land mass now faces several major challenges in its struggle for survival. It must reorganize its economic system if it is to feed its people. It must continue on the path of political reform if it is to create a pluralist democracy. Yet in addition to these two almost insurmountable challenges is the far greater problem of dismantling the empire and establishing a new federal structure.

Many new post-colonial nations remain in a period of prolonged economic dependency while they struggle to establish an independent system. These nations exist in a contradictory limbo, nominally independent but unable to sustain themselves without significant support from the outside. This economic dependency can generate cognitive dissonance caused by the contradiction between the ideal of independence and the reality of dependence. The frustration and discontent can lead to uprisings and instability.

Newly independent nations often lack the stability provided by an established political culture. This is likely to be true for the former Soviet republics, emerging from 70 years of communism within the Soviet Union. Neither elites nor masses are familiar with Western concepts; the limited understanding of notions such as democracy and free markets suggest the difficulties that newly independent states will face in attempting to set up such systems. Lacking adequate industrial bases, they are likely to be mired in poverty and the social instability engendered by it.

These states face a host of economic and social problems. The old central authorities often cited these problems as a way of asserting that the republics would not seek or could not maintain independence. Economic problems lie ahead and are part of the difficulties these states face, but they were insufficient to persuade nationalists to hold back on independence. Economic interdependence, however, did provide much of the force behind the emerging Commonwealth, and will likely continue to play a defining role in its cohesion.

Economically the post-Soviet leaders must now direct the region out of one of the bleakest periods of its history. Shortages of food and medicine are critical and show signs of worsening. Political chaos is likely to accompany further economic decline if the leaders are unable to resolve these problems. Part of the dilemma of the erosion of central authority is that as power devolved from the centre to the republics, increasingly the burden for resolving these problems fell on the republic level authorities and not on the centre. Yet the structures of the newly independent states also lack the means to control successfully the food riots, labour strikes and ethnic disturbances that are likely to occur. The potential for unrest remains high throughout the territory once ruled from Moscow. Fearing this, the world community has moved to airlift international humanitarian assistance of food and medical relief. Economic assistance is being offered and accepted.

Control over resources: the war of laws

Between the central governments and the regional units of the newly independent states lies the particularly thorny unresolved question of control over natural resources. The central administrations are now trying to gain access to a larger share of revenues from the sales of these resources, while the regions that contain the resources are asserting their rights to full control over their extraction and sale. This conflict over resources was part of an overall struggle for primacy dubbed the 'war of laws' by the Soviet press, and is particularly vivid in the Russian Federation where subrepublic level autonomous units are particularly numerous.

The war of laws has enormous economic implications for the future. A vivid example that foreshadowed serious tensions between central administrations and regional units was the diamond controversy between the Soviet Government, the RSFSR, the Yakut autonomous republic (ASSR), and the Mirnyy city soviet. Diamonds had long been controlled by the all-Union ministries. On 25 July 1990, the USSR announced a multibillion dollar hard-currency deal granting the South African firm DeBeers the exclusive right to sell Soviet diamonds on the world market, for which DeBeers agreed to pay the Soviet Union $1 billion in advance. The majority of these diamonds come from mines in the Yakut ASSR of the RSFSR.

In a direct attack on the DeBeers deal, the Presidium of the Russian Supreme Soviet issued a decree on 9 August 1990 declaring all-Union diamond and gold deals affecting its resources invalid, unless approved by the RSFSR. Gorbachev responded on 23 August by annulling the RSFSR decree, and the RSFSR Supreme Soviet Presidium two days later declared Gorbachev's decree invalid. Finally the Yakuts asserted their sovereignty, passing a declaration on 27 September 1990 claiming all natural resources on Yakutia's territory as its 'exclusive property'. Then the debate went one step further: the diamond centre around the town of Mirnyy decided to hold a referendum on secession from Yakutia and the setting up of its own independent, autonomous administrative unit.

The example of the Yakut diamonds is indicative of the complex, multi-tiered war of laws debate. It demonstrates the type of difficulties that lie ahead in changing over from the old centralized system, when the Union controlled all.

Problems of economic reorganization

One of the most difficult problems facing the newly independent states is the question of their economic viability. These states face enormous problems in converting the old Union enterprises into profitable ventures. The lack of a management sector familiar with market principles and the low level of skills of the work force are part of the legacy of years of communism. Both managers and workers must be retrained to function in a new economic environment. The difficulty of establishing convertible currencies and stable monetary systems also makes it likely that the newly independent states will enter into a period of unchecked inflation.

Most of these states are trying to take the steps necessary to make the transition to market economies. This requires the establishment of new legal structures and societal values, and most states have begun drafting new economic laws. Such laws must make provision for foreign capital, tax legislation, regulation of the business environment and privatization. Some republics are also setting up their own customs posts to protect their scarce goods.

A major obstacle is the currency issue. The leaderships of the newly independent states realize that use of the non-convertible rouble hampers their attempts to set up foreign trade. Price reform has initiated a process of trying to set values closer to the world market. The value of the rouble against world currencies has dropped radically from its former artificial level. Some states have announced their intentions to set up their own currencies; having its own currency is one attribute of an independent state. Kyrgyzstan, for example, announced that it seeks an independent monetary system, and began preparations for issuing its own money. Other republics such as Armenia have expressed an interest in preserving the rouble as a unified currency. Kazakhstan has wavered, first announcing its continued adherence to the rouble, and then on 1 November 1991 announcing plans to develop its own currency.

Initial announcements show little indication that the newly independent states have planned backing for their currencies; the creation of a new currency seems to be viewed more as a printing job than as the establishment of a fiscally sound unit of value. Some states have more backing than others. Uzbekistan with its gold resources, for example, might succeed in establishing a convertible currency.

Divorce: dividing up the property

A related issue is the problem of dividing both the assets and liabilities of the former Union. The newly independent states have commenced wrangling over both resources, such as the gold reserves, and liabilities, such as the national debt. Like the issues surrounding a divorce, the common 'marital' property must be reassigned to the members of the previous Union.

As in any divorce, there are unresolved grievances. The split involves a division of property and resolution of claims and counter-claims about who owes how much to whom for what. These questions came up in the Baltics during the period in 1990 when negotiations with the centre took place. The Soviets discussed charging the Lithuanians for investments in infrastructure. The Lithuanians countered that they would present a bill of their own, including compensation for those citizens who were deported. These issues, of course, cannot really be solved. What is the value of a human life? How does one place a monetary price on human suffering, on the value of a person sent to Siberia? The task is daunting.

Problems of ethnic minorities

One of the logical outgrowths of the principle of self-determination is the problem of ethnic minorities. If the international system accepts the principle that an ethnic group has the right to its own nation-state, what about an ethnic minority living among that group? Do they too have the same right? This type of multi-tiered ethnic fragmentation is emerging in some of the newly independent states. Most of these states are also multi-ethnic; independence is therefore not only for the 'titular' nationality, but for all the other peoples within the state's borders. In many states the other nationalities opposed republic independence for fear that their rights would not be respected by the new nation. When nationalism is the basis for new independence, the possibility of hostile ethnic chauvinism is strong.

The recent resurfacing of ethnic identity and national feeling among Russians and non-Russians alike has turned up the heat in these inter-ethnic cauldrons. Rising nationalism fuels movements for greater sovereignty for the titular nationality, which usually generates ethnic tension between the titular nationality and the Russians. In other cases there are problems with another non-Russian minority threatened by the nationalism of the titular nationality.

Events in various of the newly independent states demonstrate the pattern of conflict between the titular nationality and the Russians. In states such as Moldova and Tajikistan, the passage of language laws requiring business to be transacted in the language of the titular nationality has triggered a flow of Russian emigration out of these states.

Tensions between titular nationalities and local Russians have even occurred in the autonomous republics within the Russian Federation. In Tuva a round of clashes broke out in May 1990, where Russians were the targets of attacks in which motor cars were stoned and entire blocks of flats burned. More than 3000 Russians fled the republic in the first six months of 1990.

Another example is the Moldovans, who as a 'nation' want an independent state. Within that nation, however, are other ethnic groups, such as the Gagauz. A new pattern of nationalities problems has emerged, 'the Gagauz model', where a minority group declares its own independence or looks outside the state for protection against the aspirations of the titular nationality. Along the line of the Gagauz model, for example, are such other problems as the Pamiris in Tajikistan who proclaimed their region, the Gorno-Badakhshan autonomous oblast, to be an autonomous republic. Many Pamiri intellectuals now support total independence. Similarly, the Chechen and the Ingush in the former Chechen-Ingush ASSR are each forming their own independent state institutions. The problem lies in the principle of 'self-determination of peoples' as recognized in the Charter of the United Nations. No limit or counter-principle has been established. In practice the limit lies in *realpolitik*; the limit on self-determination is the capacity of the larger group to use force to deny independence to the group seeking it.

Border problems and territorial conflict

Some of the newly independent states are embroiled in border disputes with their neighbours. A new era of upheaval has begun as Moscow's domination recedes and the newly independent states struggle to determine these borders. These unresolved claims hold the potential for mass discontent, political mobilization and possible violence in the future. Such complex claims as the conflict between Armenia and Azerbaijan over Nagorno-Karabakh will be resolved, if at all, only after much blood has been spilled and more seeds of hatred sown.

A multitude of other conflicts lurk. Tajik minorities in Uzbekistan live mostly in the cities of Samarkand and Bukhara, and many Tajiks feel this territory is Tajik, not Uzbek. The question of the Crimea has complicated relations between Russia and Ukraine. Although the two governments are seeking to avoid conflict, the Russian Parliament reopened the question of the legality of this 'gift to the Ukrainian people'. The northern oblasts of Kazakhstan could become a bone of contention with Russia, as they are inhabited mainly by Russians, and the borders were initially arbitrarily drawn. Moldova and Ukraine have a potential border conflict over 'South Bessarabia'. Kazakhstan and Uzbekistan could yet come to blows over Karakalpakistan.

Reclaiming pre-Soviet culture

One of the tasks facing the newly independent states is the reforging of an ethnic identity that had been destroyed by the Soviet years. Reclaiming a cultural identity involves language reform, rewriting history and in some cases a resurgence of fundamentalist religion.

Language reform was in most republics the beginning of national resurgence. The use of Russian had been part of a policy to create a new 'Soviet' man. A return to the traditional national language permits a reclaiming of ethnic identity separate from the Russians.

Many of the states face the task of rewriting their own histories. One, two or even three generations have lived under communist rule, been educated under that system and been fed concepts produced by the Party. The generations raised in communist schools need to relearn the stories of their own cultures. Certain themes need to be rewritten. In Central Asia, for example, the communist presentation of the region's incorporation into the Soviet Union, of the Basmachi or of topics such as deportations, all represent seminal moments in the nation's history that need to be rewritten. In some newly independent states local nationalists have begun writing about their nation's pre-Soviet history to help their readers build a better understanding of where they have come from.[8]

The resurgence of religion affects Muslims, Christians, Buddhists and Jews. Adherents of each of the major religions are experiencing a blossoming religious commitment as a vehicle for an alternate non-Soviet identity.

VII. The future of the Commonwealth: centripetal and centrifugal forces

Although Gorbachev failed in his effort to pull together a new Union treaty, centripetal forces pulled most of the newly independent states together into a 'centreless' Commonwealth. Several key forces provided the drive to bring about this new order. At the heart of the Commonwealth is economic interdependence; trade is thus a unifying factor. Another key issue is the world-wide interest in maintaining the stability of weapons of mass destruction, to ensure that they remain under the authority of a single unified command that continues to respect existing obligations contracted by the Union. Fragmentation of control over the nuclear arsenal would open a dangerous Pandora's box of threatening instability.

Looking ahead, however, the territories of the former Soviet Union still face an uncertain future, and the current fragmentation may lead to several different possible outcomes. At one extreme is complete viable independence for all the constituent parts of the Union that have set out on their own. At the other extreme is a resurgence of conservative forces, perhaps led by the army, and a return to another form of centralized union.

Complete fragmentation

One scenario is complete fragmentation of the empire into component parts based on nationality. Independence movements initially were based on a separation of the former Soviet republics from the centre, but an eventual breakup would most likely not follow the borders of the old Soviet republics. There would probably be a process of recombining and realigning, some of which may involve civil wars and border struggles.

---

[8] For example, in Uzbekistan the writer Pirimqul Qodirov began even before *glasnost* to write a history of Babur—with the goal of providing the Uzbek people with more information about their own prehistory. Similarly, Sotim Ulughzodah in Tajikistan was written about the Sogdians to provide a deeper historical context.

Some regional alliances are already forming, suggesting the possible border-lines of potential future countries. The peoples of the North Caucasus announced a unified structure at the Congress of Mountain Peoples, while the peoples of Central Asia may merge into a single united Turkestan. Approximately 60 million peoples of various Turkic nationalities might form a federation, possibly linked with Turkey.

These changes would likely involve enormous movement of peoples. There are currently about 50–60 million people living outside their home nation-states. In early 1991, about 5000 Russians per month were departing from the RSFSR; by early 1992 it was up to 150 000–200 000 per month.

The newly emerged countries would likely set up new forms of government, and not all would be attracted to liberal democracies. Some of the newly inde-pendent states are likely to set up regimes headed by a nationalist fascist strong-man. Some may end up preserving forms of communism. In addition, there are different types of arrangements between these states, some political, some eco-nomic. The reality of the Soviet economy was a high degree of interdependence among the republics; even with the achievement of national independence, the newly independent states are likely to continue to have trade relations.

What about the situation in Russia? Even without the former Union repub-lics, Russia alone as a successor state is still a great power with a population of 150 million people, the largest in Europe. As the guardian of the nuclear arsenal, Russia's status as a nuclear superpower in its own right is assured.

As the former Union republics go their own way, the remaining Russian population might begin to be attracted to a highly nationalist pro-Russian ideology, possibly led by a charismatic fascist nationalist. Right-wing groups such as Pamyat, notorious for its Russian chauvinism and open anti-Semitic, anti-Western views, would be expected to gain wide appeal among Russians. Many Russians would likely support campaigns to protect the rights of Russians in the newly independent states, or even to reconquer those areas in order to protect the Russians living there. This could easily lead to fighting between the Russian state and the newly independent states of the former Union. As in 1917, this could lead to a fight to regain control of those states.

Re-emergence of the right wing

While a return to the pre-*glasnost* party structure now seems highly unlikely given the discrediting of the party, right-wing resurgence remains a possibility. As economic difficulties set in and chaos accelerates, right-wing ideologies could have growing appeal for many. Generations raised under the Communist Party system will find the new events alarming.

There are many in the territory of the former Soviet Union who long for strong leaders to re-establish law and order and break the spiral of disintegra-tion. A sign of the appeal for many Russians of a 'law and order' candidate is that of the Russian presidential elections of June 1991, where the virulent nationalist Vladimir Zhirinovskiy won 6 million votes. His platform would likely generate far greater support today; the potential appeal of Russian nationalism is great.

Regrouping into federation

Another possibility is a temporary split, and then a voluntary regrouping into a federation or commonwealth. The future of the CIS is uncertain. As in 1917 following the breakup of the empire, the parts could join together once again. Last time the parts were pulled together by force; this time they may be led by economic interest and force of habit.

A less centralized federation or confederation might join some of the newly independent states into a 'unified economic space'. One might imagine an association like the European Community, in its post-1992 variant, with greater political unity. It is likely that what will emerge will be a patchwork of relationships held together by an umbrella agreement. These interconnections may vary—some looser, some closer; some friendly, some hostile.

Chaos

The image of 'a Yugoslavia with nuclear weapons' has been used to underscore the potential for catastrophe as the old centralized controls over advanced weapons dissolve. International concerns focused on the question of a singular nuclear command, since among the republics of the former Union, temporarily at least, there were four nuclear powers—Belarus, Kazakhstan, Russia and Ukraine. A variety of unpleasant scenarios can be imagined for both nuclear and conventional chaos.

VIII. The international implications of the Soviet breakup

The disintegration of the Soviet Union is a major shift in the nature of the international system, signalling the official end of the bipolar structure of the post-World War II era upon which international relations have rested for the past 45 years. As East and West Europe achieve increasing integration and break down the wall between them, this shifting superpower relationship leaves the United States playing the role of the unipolar superpower. The breakup of a large superpower empire and the demise of bipolarity are intrinsically destabilizing. If change is not well-managed in a co-operative spirit, the numerous international implications of the Soviet breakup could easily trigger a domino effect. Nearly every country that shares a border with the newly independent Eurasian states could be affected.

Implications for Europe

Denmark, Finland, Iceland and Sweden became involved in the recent Baltic struggle for independence, giving these Nordic countries a more active role in the international arena than they were accustomed to playing. While the Government of Finland, whose prior accommodation with the Soviet Union gave rise to the term 'Finlandization', denies interest in pressing its territorial claim on Karelia, if territorial disintegration begins in the Russian federation as well, Karelia might eventually revert to Finland. The Finns have already begun pouring monetary aid into the area. However, the nightmare of absorbing the large Russian population now residing in the Karelian peninsula causes considerable hesitancy in Helsinki.

The possibility of changes in the western border of the former Soviet Union is another potential source of instability that could affect the entire region of Central and Eastern Europe. Several countries in Eastern Europe have territorial claims dating from the interwar period that could easily resurface: Czechoslovakia and Hungary have historic claims in the Transcarpathia; Germany in Königsberg (Kaliningrad oblast); Poland not only in Western Ukraine and Western Belarus, but historically in Lithuania and its capital Vilnius (Wilno). All of these could produce eventual territorial conflict. For Romania the territorial interest is even more direct, as Moldova might well reunite at some point with Romania.

Implications for the Islamic states

To the south, the independence of Azerbaijan and the Muslim republics of Central Asia directly affect the interests of the various Islamic countries in the region. The six new Muslim nations have more in common culturally with their co-religionists in the region than with Moscow. The rapid changes in Central Asia have set in motion a competition for influence, as Iran, Pakistan, Turkey and the Arab states, especially Saudi Arabia, seek to position themselves for the upcoming opportunities.

Independence in the Transcaucasus and Central Asian republics could easily exert a direct impact on Iran and Turkey; the latter nations might be brought into conflict as they struggle for influence in the area. Tehran's concern is heightened by its common border with former Soviet territory. Independence in Azerbaijan could spill over, stimulating the Azeris in Northern Iran to try to break away. Despite its concern about Azeri irredentism, Iran is encouraging the movements for greater religious expression in Central Asia, seeking to influence the newly independent states to move in an Islamic direction.

The relations of these new states with Iran are important for the region. These states are not well situated for trade with the outside world. Iran is the only route providing a transportation outlet to the sea for Turkmenia and Azerbaijan; the development of trade relations is therefore critical.

The effect on Turkey is dramatic. Four of the five new Central Asian nations, as well as Azerbaijan and several of the autonomous republics, are Turkic speaking. The independence of nearly 50 million Turkic-speaking people is definitely a significant event for Turkey, their ethnically similar neighbour. Turkey is eager to pre-empt the influence of Iran and Saudi Arabia, and is fostering increased ties. Meanwhile, Armenia still lays claim to the Mount Ararat region in Turkey, and harbours resentment against Turkey over historic injustices.

For now, Turkey is viewed as a stronger influence in Central Asia than Iran. The ethnic connection is a major factor, and some people in Central Asia support a single, united Turkestan. While Turkestan may be only a dream, contacts are expanding. With the exception of Tajikistan, the Central Asian states have all formulated trade agreements with Turkey.

If the Turkic states of Central Asia look towards Turkey for a possible Turkestan, this would leave Tajikistan looking towards Iran and Afghanistan, the latter with a large Tajik population, for a union of Persian speakers. This might threaten the territorial integrity of today's Afghanistan. If the Tajiks of Afghanistan and Tajikistan were to unite, this could cause territorial realignments inside Afghanistan that would in turn spill over into Pakistan. The Pushtoons of Pakistan and those of Afghanistan might look for unification into a Pushtoon state, possibly affecting the Baluch of Afghanistan, Iran and Pakistan.

Implications for Asia

China, with its own Muslim population, will likely be affected by increasing Central Asian independence from Moscow. The Kazakhs, Uzbeks and Uigurs of China might begin to look to their brethren in Central Asia for inspiration, and perhaps Beijing's hold on the area would be threatened. Mongolia, where an irredentist movement has already begun talking about unity with the Buryat Mongols of the former Buryat ASSR, might take over that territory.

Implications for the USA and its Western allies

For the West, the implications are enormous. It placed great store in the stability of the Soviet Union as part of the hallmark of the post-war bipolar era, viewing its preservation as a mark of consistency. Unfolding events by historical necessity led to a new point where the genie could not be forced back into the bottle. The order established at the end of World War II is clearly finished. The reunification of Germany, the escape of Eastern Europe from the Soviet orbit and the fragmentation of the former Soviet Union into a number of independent states have dramatically shifted the European balance.

It is in the interest of the West to see these new states emerge as democratic systems with free market economies. The West should not seek to affect the outcome on the question of how many new states there will be—that is an internal question—but rather, the outcome of what type of states they will be. In the case of Central Asia, it is preferable for the West that secular, democratic states emerge that respect freedom of religion, rather than Islamic fundamentalist governments. This outcome can be encouraged through direct ties and expended trade, and by supporting the ideas of democratic and tolerant movements within these republics. In all of the newly emerging states, Western economic assistance offers some leverage in building new relationships.

IX. Conclusion: causes for optimism

The list of challenges to the newly-independent states seems almost insurmountable, with little light at the end of the tunnel. The road is truly full of stumbling blocks. However, there are also grounds for optimism. These states are homelands for titular nationalities seeking a better life. The Soviet years were difficult. The nationalities unwillingly paid a high price for their experience within the Union. Fettered by the central Russian bureaucracy, the other nationalities were reduced to colonial status, paying tribute and stripped of sovereignty over their own affairs. The road is now open for them to make the transition to fledgling, democratic societies.

It is clear that economic problems lie ahead: limited access to raw materials, supply shortages, problems of capital investment and all the difficulties inherent in the transition from centralized to privatized economy. This does not imply, however, that the transition cannot be made. Freed from the cumbersome Soviet centre, with hard work, rapid economic growth is possible.

There is hope that, separated from the empire, new societies will flourish that are more responsive to the cultural identities of the various nationalities. Growing national sentiment led to the formation of popular fronts, and in many of the newly independent states the current government enjoys significant genuine popular support. Presidents have been elected by popular vote. In the future, native elites ruling local governments without Russian control may successfully lead their peoples to independence and prosperity.

5. A national security policy for Russia

Sergey Rogov

I. Introduction

Since the collapse of the Soviet Union, Russia has become the main inheritor of the former's superpower role, including its seat on the UN Security Council. This inheritance may, however, involve more than just changing the name of the country; Russia may not simply continue the security policies of its predecessor. While it has taken the place of the Soviet Union and its predecessor, the Russian empire, the new Russian state is different from both of them—politically, in that it is striving to be a democracy; economically, in that it is undergoing a transition to a free market system; and geographically, in that Russia has never before had its current boundaries. The new Russia has yet to determine its identity, its character, its national interests and its place in the world. Another factor distinguishing the present from the past is the fundamental difference of today's international system, which Russia is now entering, from the bipolar system that had existed for 45 years. In a multipolar world with such centres of power as the United States, Western Europe, Japan, China and India, Russia can be at best a major player, not a superpower.

The reborn Russian state is already facing its first external affairs crisis. The agreements to establish the Commonwealth of Independent States (CIS) by 11 former Soviet republics could easily become just pieces of paper, lacking any substance. Russia could become involved in a confrontation with Ukraine or with other members of the CIS. The situation is further complicated by tremendous economic difficulties and growing social tension. Internally, as well, Russia encounters a real threat of fragmentation and dismemberment.

These factors demonstrate Russia's urgent need to establish its own national security policy as soon as possible. Russia still lacks a mechanism for coherent decision making in foreign and security policy, which results in confusion, disarray, impulsive decisions and a substantial gap between well-intended declarations and real policy.

A National Security Council of Russia should be created to develop national security strategy, to provide the president with alternative approaches to specific issues and necessary information and operational support, and to coordinate the implementation of presidential decisions by different government agencies.

II. Three circles of Russian interests

The national security interests of Russia can be envisioned as three concentric circles. The first priority of Russia should be its relations with other former Soviet republics. The greatest threat to Russia now comes from possible territorial and ethnic conflicts with those republics which have become independent states. It is vital for Russia to avoid such rivalries, to establish friendly relations and, if possible, an alliance with those states, where dozens of millions of ethnic Russians have their homes.

The second circle of Russian security interests is linked to such regions as Eastern Europe, the Middle East and the Far East, which traditionally were of strategic importance to the Soviet Union. Now Russia is separated from those regions by newly independent states. The Far East remains on the Russian border and therefore, from an economic and geopolitical point of view, developments there cannot be ignored. Some of the former Soviet republics could be drawn into the spheres of interest of such regional centres of power as China or Japan. Conflicts in those regions could force Russian involvement. The Russian hold on Siberia could be jeopardized if Russia were to come into conflict with such great neighbours as China or Japan.

The third circle includes Russian relations with the West, especially with the United States and Western Europe. Even in the case of more radical cuts in strategic nuclear arms than those envisaged by START (for example, to 75–80 per cent of current levels), Russia will retain the condition of mutual assured destruction with the United States which will give the Russian–US relationship a special character, perhaps moving from regulated rivalry to a limited partnership. Russian involvement in European and North Atlantic integration could play a decisive role for the future of democratic institutions and a market economy inside the Russian Federation itself. If Russia is not involved in this integration, its economic progress will be in doubt and its 'Euro-Asian' character might acquire more Asian colours.

Will Russia have vital global security interests apart from these three circles? It is doubtful that events in South America or Africa will have a direct impact on Russia. The main threat to Russia's security originates today from internal, not external, factors. Russia might encounter foreign threats in the future, but in the meantime Russian security may be challenged by explosive domestic problems.

This does not mean that Russia can or should unilaterally disarm. Military power remains an important factor of national security, but there is hardly a need to continue the arms race in which the Soviet Union had single-handedly opposed the rest of the world. Internationally, Russia does not need competition with major centres of power like the United States, Western Europe, China and Japan, but rather co-operation with them as reliable partners and allies.

III. Creating a defence community

Members of the CIS can and should become natural partners and allies of the Russian Federation. These nations have common economic and political problems, including the common legacy of the Soviet military machine, which still remains practically intact.

The military forces of the USSR have been under little political control since the collapse of the Soviet Union. The Soviet Army had been politically dominated by the Communist Party. After the failed coup, the Party was banned, and civilian governmental control of the military was never truly established even after the USSR was dissolved. The new independent states, including Russia, have failed to put the Soviet military under strict political control. The Defence Ministry of the USSR was formally subordinated to the Council of Heads of State of the CIS, but in fact it still acted very much as it wished. Bureaucratic interests led the Defence Ministry to try to protect its turf, limiting reform to minor cosmetic changes. The army used to act as an instrument of state policy but the Soviet state no longer exists, and the military is therefore on its own. This has brought about an untenable situation in which the military is forced to choose which political authority to support (for instance, the 14th Army in Teraspol has faced a choice between Russia, Ukraine, Moldova and the secessionist Dnestr republic) and could end up not fully supporting any of them. The army is demoralized and has lost discipline, a situation which threatens to become politically explosive. An early indication of that was the all-army meeting of officers in Moscow on 17 January 1992, during which the participants urged that an ultimatum be given to the government leaders demanding a single armed force in the CIS.

The Russian leadership probably made a major mistake when it initially refused to determine its own approach to defence issues, instead allowing the Defence Ministry to define the shape of the Allied Forces of the CIS. However, a more aggressive Russian posture would have fuelled the fears of other members of the Commonwealth, who were afraid that Russia might use the Defence Ministry to cloak its own imperial ambitions. Because of this situation, the CIS summits in Brest, Alma-Ata and Minsk failed to create a defence alliance, which could have transformed the Soviet Army into the Allied Military Forces of the Commonwealth (with some of the military transferred to the national armies of the independent states). Compromise formulas such as 'the common military and strategic space', avoiding the issue of command defence structures, were a poor substitute.

The Allied Military Forces of the CIS will need the legal basis of a common defence pact and a political structure like the political decision-making bodies of NATO. Russia must calm the fears of its potential allies by accepting the complete equality of all CIS members, with equal participation in the higher political and military co-ordinating bodies of the Commonwealth.

This approach makes it necessary to distinguish between the various Allied structures, and it is why Russia must have its own defence ministry and other military structures. In addition, the Russian Defence Ministry in the future should be headed by civilians to ensure strict political control of the Russian military.

Besides creating a defence coalition among sovereign states of the CIS, Russia should also establish bilateral security relations with its potential partners. This may be particularly necessary in the cases of the Baltic states and Ukraine. Each sovereign state has a right to build its own military forces, and an independent Ukraine cannot be blamed for doing so. However, in trying to achieve immediate military independence, Ukraine failed to take the security interests of Russia into account. Ukraine was suspicious of Russia, expecting it to make territorial claims on the Crimea and other territories and therefore thought to prepare to resist such an eventuality. Efforts to 'nationalize' the military, however, produced resistance from the mostly Russian officers. The result was a tendency towards chaos and confrontation between elements of the army and military and political institutions.

It is essential to prevent the escalation of unfriendly relations between Ukraine and Russia and between Russia and the other states where Russian forces are located as the redistribution and disposition of forces goes forward, a process that will require great skill and sensitivity.

IV. The Russian Army in transition

The nuclear disarmament of Ukraine, Belarus and Kazakhstan will make Russia the only nuclear state in the CIS. As a major nuclear power, Russia should hardly be concerned about a foreign invasion in the foreseeable future. Should it then try to maintain a military force of three or four million soldiers as the Soviet Union did?

Clearly Russia has neither the strategic need nor the economic strength to maintain such a burden. Besides, such excessive military power would be counter-productive, triggering suspicions and confrontation with close and distant neighbours. With other former Soviet republics creating their own armies, Russia must, of course, have its own military establishment. The Russian Army will include Soviet military forces on Russian soil (more than two million people), and the elements of the Soviet Army being redeployed from foreign states outside the CIS—in Germany, Poland and the Baltic states. This will place another 400 000 soldiers under Russia's jurisdiction.

Meanwhile, Belarus will follow the Ukrainians (550 000 soldiers) in nationalizing the Soviet forces on its territory (220 000). The fate of the military in Kazakhstan, Central Asia and the Transcaucasian states (660 000) is not clear, but it is a predominantly Russian force. If Russia directly claims those troops, this may bring about conflict with the states on whose territories they are deployed. The Russian Army will then be seen as a foreign occupying force, and the affected nations could demand that the troops withdraw to Russia, leaving their weapons in place.

If Russia assumes control over the bulk of the Soviet Army, it will have to redeploy more than one million soldiers and huge numbers of weapons onto Russian territory. There are no facilities for those troops in Russia, and therefore most of them will have to be demobilized. Because hundreds of thousands of officers and warrant-officers lack housing and civilian professions, such huge reductions—coming on top of what has been previously planned—might produce very serious political consequences. Russia will have to conduct a costly social rehabilitation programme to build houses and retrain former military officers. Even more expensive will be the unavoidable conversion of defence industries as a result of drastic reductions in military hardware procurement.

While remaining a formidable military power, Russia will therefore be busy trying to shrink its military legacy. These reductions can be successfully managed during a transition period, preferably in a joint effort with other members of the Commonwealth. They will also have to be tuned to the requirements of the CFE Treaty. The major security task during this period will be keeping the former Soviet military under civilian political control while simultaneously making cuts and transforming the forces of a single military into a number of allied armies.

V. Russian–US partnership

Some additional force reductions should be expected from new arms control agreements, especially in strategic armaments. Presidents Yeltsin and Bush already have agreed to ban intercontinental ballistic missiles (ICBMs) with multiple independently targetable re-entry vehicles (MIRVs). This will greatly strengthen strategic stability in relations between the two nations and will lead to a reduction to 3000–3500 strategic warheads for the USA and Russia (compared to 11 000–12 000 now).

The United States and Russia are burying the legacy of the cold war and moving to a new type of strategic relationship—from confrontation to a co-operative partnership. The two sides still have the capability to destroy each other in 30 minutes, but they will have no reason to be in conflict. Russia is not going to become an economic competitor with the United States. The geo-political interests of the two nations are not in conflict, and they may share important interests in prevention of nuclear and ballistic missile proliferation and opposition to Islamic fundamentalism. Reduced but still formidable Russian military power in the heartland of Eurasia makes Russia an important factor in US efforts to manage the multipolar balance of power, particularly when the United States itself is focusing more and more on its domestic priorities and cutting its defence expenditures.

Such co-operation should be accompanied by co-ordinated reductions in war making machines. Management of the common nuclear legacy should include joint efforts in several areas: (a) reductions in strategic nuclear arsenals to lower levels and a more stable configuration, which would allow them to retreat from launch-on-warning postures; (*b*) ensuring the safety of the nuclear infra-structure and elimination of excessive nuclear warheads; (*c*) social rehabilita-tion of the military; and (*d*) conversion of defence industries.

This agenda demands that a strategic dialogue be initiated as soon as possible to explore the possibilities for change in the substance of the US–Russian milit-ary relationship, from a regulated competition to a more co-operative model.

6. The creation of a Russian foreign policy

Mikhail E. Bezrukov

I. Introduction

One of the central elements of the collapse of the Soviet Union has been the redistribution of foreign policy responsibilities to the republics and away from the centre. Given the degree to which the members of the Commonwealth have chosen to rely on the West for assistance, not only in rebuilding their collapsed economies but also in shaping new democratic political institutions, foreign policy matters assume particular significance. This chapter first briefly outlines the course of centre–republic political history in the last days of the Soviet Union, and then describes and analyses the evolution of independent Russian foreign policy institutions and structures. It also speculates on the future of Russian foreign policy and presents some recommendations for Western action.

II. The collapse of the Soviet Union

The Gorbachev-inspired Soviet 'revolution from above' proved flawed on quite a number of principal points. While some past practices were rejected, the Soviet leaders did not renounce others. They initiated the destruction of the overly centralized totalitarian system yet simultaneously remained convinced that all parts of the mammoth Soviet state would follow the same pattern of change (another master plan) and that change would never accelerate out of the tight control of the Kremlin. The positive potential involved in republican autonomy was not understood, possibly owing to the traditional communist proclivity to suppress any independent force. The Soviet leaders saw the growing autonomy of the republics not as a means to strengthen the Union but as a menace to their omnipotence.

If the centre ultimately recognized that decentralization of power in the USSR was inevitable, it did so only because it was forced to by the republics. In the course of its endless battles with the republics, the centre lost its credentials as the driving force behind reform. It was unable to keep up with the pace of political change and eventually simply surrendered to the republican victors. Had the Soviet leadership initially chosen a more flexible policy towards the republics and not become, as it did at a certain stage, a real threat to the interests of the republics, it would have been assured the role of senior partner. As matters turned out, all parts of the disintegrating Soviet empire began to act on the assumption that they could rely only on themselves. Indeed the republics viewed suspiciously the centre's futile attempts to somehow regain influence.

What remained of the centre after the attempted August 1991 coup was not capable of playing an active role in a post-communist Commonwealth. Even the capacity of the CIS structures to perform co-ordinating functions is in doubt. CIS representatives like to talk about a new role for the remnants of the former Soviet Government, but this is sheer speculation and pipe-dreams. Reality is another matter: the republics seem ready to allow the Commonwealth a voice only in those limited spheres where they are temporarily not ready to take command.

Co-ordinating the policies of the republics on a wide variety of issues is important, but there is no centre any more that is in a position to act as co-ordinator. Major political decisions are being worked out on the republican and inter-republican levels. This is why real co-ordination of the policies of the various republics can result only from direct negotiation among them.

III. Emerging republic foreign policy

Before the abortive coup, despite spectacular pronouncements by some republican gurus, the republics asked for nothing more than a partial easing of the centre's monopoly on foreign policy. Even this slight encroachment on rights that the Soviet leadership was reluctant to share provoked aggressive resistance from all-Union Communist Party and government structures. At that time, republic representatives could claim success if they obtained access to all-Union networks of foreign policy information, or were consulted on issues directly concerning the republics.

After the coup attempt, which led to the collapse of all-Union structures of power, it became almost impossible for Gorbachev to treat republican leaders as second-rate partners. The previous arrogance of the centre began to fade. The Soviet Ministry of Foreign Affairs took the lead in promoting co-operation with its republican counterparts. The status of the newly created Council of Ministers of Foreign Affairs was upgraded, and it received additional powers.

By the end of 1991, the former Soviet republics were recognized by the world community as direct participants in international relations. The existence of two levels of Commonwealth foreign policy was accepted almost everywhere. This was only the starting point for further surrender of control of all-Union bodies under pressure from the republics. The West should be prepared to see foreign policy initiatives coming from the republics in the future.

IV. The development of independent Russian foreign policy

How ready is the Russian Federation to assume power in foreign policy matters? How have the attitudes of the Russian leaders evolved with respect to foreign policy since the first free parliamentary elections in the republic?

The system of government institutions inherited by the new Russian Federation leadership was hardly more than an empty shell. Although governmental bodies existed that were like those of a sovereign country, they were certainly not suitable for the functions traditionally associated with such institutions. In fact, they were more similar to instruments of colonial administration (i.e., the means of implementing orders which came from somewhere else).

The new government institutions of the Russian Federation have had to 'take possession' of the republic, and to an extent continue to do so. The various aspects of this process overlap and are closely linked with one another. Therefore the shaping of Russia's relations with other countries and the development of its foreign policy institutions must be analysed in the context of events in the republic and the Commonwealth at large. Tensions and conflicts between the centre and the reformers who came to power in the Russian Federation were not of a purely nationalistic nature; confrontation developed as a continuation of the political struggle over the goals and methods of *perestroika*.

The 1990 elections to the Russian Parliament gave reformers a chance to substantially improve their position (more modest gains had been made in the all-Union parliament electoral campaign of 1989). In 1990, reformers were more active and their efforts better co-ordinated. Their goal was to gain so many seats that communist hard-liners could not ignore the reformist wing. In other words, they opted for acquiring an assured veto right rather than for winning a majority in Parliament. Another important feature of the 1990 electoral campaign was that it developed as a battle primarily between the traditional 'haves' and those who saw in them an impediment to further reform. Reformers placed the task of defeating their opponents well above the need to agree among themselves on the future policies of the republic.

Before and during the 1990 electoral campaign, few among the reformers believed that their loose coalition would gain a leading position in the Russian Parliament, but that is exactly what happened. Boris Yeltsin became chairman of the republican Parliament despite fierce resistance from hard-line communists, who were joined at the final stage by Gorbachev himself. Political allies of Yeltsin moved into many important positions in the Russian Parliament. It also became evident that the old communist *nomenklatura* had lost ground in Russian Federation executive agencies, and was facing replacement by Yeltsin appointees.

When the emotions raised by the electoral clashes calmed, it became apparent that something more profound than just another confrontation between reformers and communist hard-liners had occurred. Reformers had won in the key Soviet republic, Russia—the core of the union. In fact, for decades the West had equated the terms 'Soviet empire' and 'Russian empire'. Access to potentially powerful instruments of influence opened up qualitatively new opportunities for Russian Federation reformers.

After the parliamentary elections, two interrelated goals acquired special importance for Yeltsin and his political allies: first, consolidating their power in the republic; and second, strengthening the position of the Russian Federation in the USSR. At first, relations with the outside world were not high on the agenda of the new Russian leadership. In this sense the Declaration of State

Sovereignty of the Russian Soviet Socialist Republic (adopted by the Russian Federation Parliament on 12 June 1990) is quite revealing. The issue of the republic's relation to other nations is dealt with in quite vague terms: 'For ensuring political, economic and legal guaranties of the sovereignty of the foreign countries . . . RSFSR declares its adherence to the universally recognized principles of international law and its readiness to coexist without confrontation in international, inter-republican and inter-ethnic relations while defending the interests of the peoples of Russia'.

The Russian Foreign Minister was appointed much later than were the heads of other ministries, and a young head of department in the all-Union Ministry of Foreign Affairs, Andrey Kozyrev, was named to the position. The agency he inherited—formally the Russian Federation Foreign Ministry, established in 1944—appeared quite disappointing. For decades the Russian Foreign Ministry was a purely decorative institution with only ceremonial functions. During the electoral campaign of 1990, Kozyrev's predecessor came under heavy criticism on this issue and was quite offended at accusations that he was a minister with no real function. His clumsy insistence on the positive contribution of his ministry to Soviet and republican foreign policy created amusement among the informed public and among government officials. Within the all-Union Foreign Ministry, assignment to the Russian Federation Foreign Ministry had been regarded as either honourable exile (at the minister or deputy minister level) or a means of getting rid of employees with doubtful professional skills. In 1990 the Russian Foreign Ministry team was not adequate to its new role. Although it was located in a beautiful building, the lack of space was so great that only top ministerial figures could be given offices there—additional evidence of the artificial nature of the ministry.

Initially Kozyrev chose a cautious line and, unlike many of his colleagues from the Russian Government, avoided openly challenging all-Union structures. Although rumours circulated about his loyalty to the Soviet diplomatic world he had left behind, his main reason for maintaining a low profile was that he was, at best, a general hoping to create an army. In addition, his actions and plans depended entirely on the outcome of the 'independence war' between the Russian leadership and the centre for control of Russian Federation rights and resources.

At the time many observers argued that the Russian Federation lacked its own foreign policy, a conclusion which was undoubtedly correct. Defining foreign policy goals has been and remains a serious problem for the Russian Federation. The absence of a clear set of guidelines and priorities has hindered Russian Foreign Ministry employees. It was a serious obstacle to dialogue with other countries, which were suspicious that the new Russian diplomacy was just another twist—temporary and exotic—in Soviet political life, and not a real factor in world affairs.

On the other hand, it must be recognized that this very lack of coherent foreign policy strategy is a symptom of health. At the beginning of the 20th century, the Bolsheviks presented the world with a ready set of foreign policy prescriptions to be applied universally, even before they had a clear vision of what to do in their own country. Claims of the role of world mentor remained a characteristic of Soviet leadership for decades—a tendency that did not disappear even in the second half of the 1980s when the USSR began profound domestic reforms. *Perestroika: New Thinking for Our Country and the World*, was after all the title of Gorbachev's famous book. Russian foreign policy has proved to be more down to earth, and more directly dependent on developments within the republic.

The Committee on Foreign Affairs and Foreign Economic Relations of the Russian Federation Parliament became another important source of foreign policy ideas and decisions. Professor Vladimir Lukin, a highly reputed expert on the Far East from the Soviet Academy of Sciences, was elected its first chairman, and a number of other representatives from the Soviet academic community joined the committee. In 1992, Professor Lukin became Russia's ambassador to the United States.

Among all of the bodies of the Russian Federation Parliament, the Committee on Foreign Affairs was one of the most reform-oriented. The explanation for this probably lies in the fact that, at least initially, international relations were not an important battlefield in the war between Russian Federation reformers and communist hard-liners. The latter preferred to concentrate their attention on parliamentary committees dealing with economic matters, institutional reforms, and the like. It is interesting to note that, in this respect, Russian Federation hard-liners differed radically from their counterparts in the all-Union Parliament, who tightly controlled their Foreign Affairs Committee.

The Russian Parliament Foreign Affairs Committee experienced clear difficulties even in defining its field of activity. Its members proceeded from the assumption that the Russian Federation, as a sovereign republic, should be involved in formulating Soviet foreign policy, and that it might also have interests of its own with regard to other countries, which were not necessarily identical to those of the USSR or of any of its constituent parts. How to translate this general idea into practical steps remained an open question.

The committee continuously stressed its desire to work out a foreign policy agenda for the Russian Federation, and in that spirit tried to generate appropriate policies and approaches. It also encouraged the Russian Foreign Ministry and representatives from the academic world to join the enterprise. Nevertheless moving beyond generalities proved a difficult task.

The main accomplishment of the committee during this period was establishing contacts with representatives of other countries, from legislators to business people. This dialogue began to open important channels through which information about events in the Russian Federation could flow to other nations. At the same time, it served as a limited initiation into the practical side of international politics. The majority of the members of the committee were taking their first steps as political figures, and the value of acquiring needed experience should not be overlooked. It is true that several of them had impressive academic careers, but at this point they were theoreticians rather than practitioners. For decades, Soviet foreign policy decision making and academic science had remained isolated from each other. More often than not, the former consulted the latter only to receive its 'scientific blessing' for plans already prepared inside the Central Committee of the Communist Party of the USSR.

With regard to foreign policy, both the Russian Foreign Ministry and the Russian Parliament Committee on Foreign Affairs recognized that concessions from all-Union structures would directly affect how successful the republic would be in freeing itself from Soviet dominance. Both stressed the need to share responsibility with all-Union structures and avoided insisting on the right to implement policies of their own.

The activity of the Russian Foreign Ministry and the Committee on Foreign Affairs got a strong boost when the growing political and economic autonomy of the Soviet republics resulted in direct negotiation between them. These negotiations dealt with international relations, and Russian Federation foreign policy institutions acquired additional, important responsibilities. At this point the club of Russian Federation foreign policy players enlarged, joined by the Russian Federation Parliament Sub-Committee on Inter-Republican Relations. There was, however, something more important in this switch of attention to other republics: the Russian leadership became more involved in the everyday life of Russian Federation foreign policy institutions. Earlier, the weak interest of the Russian Federation leadership (primarily Yeltsin and his closest associates) in the foreign policy sphere substantially limited the development of appropriate Russian Federation foreign policy institutions. Now 'domestic diplomacy' tied them together, upgrading the status of the Russian Foreign Ministry and the Committee on Foreign Affairs.

Teams with representatives from both the Russian Foreign Ministry and the above-mentioned parliamentary bodies represented the Russian Federation in inter-republican negotiations. The composition of the delegations was motivated at least in part by the lack of qualified negotiators; as a by-product of this co-operation, the foundation was laid for a future fruitful partnership between the legislative and executive branches on foreign policy issues.

During the winter of 1990–91, foreign policy issues took on additional importance for the leaders of the Russian Federation; these matters could no longer be seen as of secondary importance. Two factors played a role in this change. First, by the end of 1990 it became evident that the Russian Federation had made considerable gains in establishing control over its resources. However, with new opportunities came new responsibilities. Conscious of the importance of Western assistance for reform, and of the potential scope of direct economic interaction between the republic and other countries, Russian Federation reformers found additional reasons to work for the elimination of the centre's almost absolute monopoly over relations with other nations. Russia could hardly regard the centre as a reliable partner in implementing reforms within the republic. The interests of the two sides were simply not the same; their goals and reform schedules differed dramatically. Even all-Union and Russian Federation legislation was at odds on a growing number of points.

The second factor behind the increase of interest in foreign policy on the part of the Russian Federation leadership was that the conflict between the centre and the republic had entered a decisive phase, and the 'Yeltsin team' thought that the republic's ties with the outside world might serve as a shield against possible attempts from the centre to suppress reforms in the Russian Federation.

The events of 1990 made it clear that those who hoped that Yeltsin and his political allies would fail to consolidate their power in the republic had seriously miscalculated. Though Yeltsin initially lacked reliable support inside the Russian Federation Parliament, he managed to strengthen his position there, displaying exceptional parliamentary leadership talent. By December 1990, the irritation on the part of the Soviet leadership (especially among hard-liners) which had been brought on by the reformers' victory in the 1990 Russian Federation electoral campaign, began to be transformed into fear that the republic might become too autonomous and thus a strong opponent. Confronted with signs of the centre's offensive against Russian Federation reformers, Yeltsin tried to 'internationalize' the conflict by neutralizing the aggressiveness of the centre, or at least diminishing it, through the development of direct relations between the republic and the West. He expected to turn Gorbachev's most valuable asset against him—his reputation in the West as a reformist politician and guarantor that there would not be a return to the previous totalitarian practices of the USSR.

This period witnessed a rapid increase in overtures by the Russian Federation to Western political figures. Even quite exotic plans were considered. For example, an outstanding US authority on the Soviet Union, Professor Alexander Yanov, secured Yeltsin's approval of an idea to create an international non-governmental committee of world political and economic experts to provide intellectual assistance to Soviet reformers. The intended powers of this committee were very broad, in fact too broad for a sovereign nation to accept, and Yanov's initiative was very short-lived.

Events at the beginning of 1991 shed light on the inadequacies of Russian foreign policy institutions. An excessively large state bureaucracy created serious problems for efficient functioning of government agencies, and a shortage of qualified personnel created additional difficulties. Early on, the new Russian leadership realized the discrepancy between its aims and its bureaucratic possibilities, this was especially so as regards foreign policy.

Relations with other countries are an area where a reliable and efficient staff is an indispensable prerequisite to success, but when the Russian Federation entered the field of foreign relations, it did not have a strong staff except for a small group of employees from the Russian Foreign Ministry, the Russian Federation Parliament and some other Russian Federation government agencies. The staff was strengthened by the addition of academics and employees from other non-governmental organizations, but this was not adequate for the creation and implementation of a coherent foreign policy. Not surprisingly, many of the initial Russian Federation foreign policy measures showed signs of improvisation and an absence of detailed analysis of their possible consequences. This amateurish style was perceived negatively by those foreign governments that were closely observing developments inside the USSR. Almost a year after the Russian Federation launched its first diplomatic offensive the republic's foreign policy mechanism was still in a formative stage, but with a staff of almost 300 in the Russian Foreign Ministry. The staffs of the presidential services and the Russian Federation Parliament had become much more experienced and sophisticated; nevertheless, the republic was still dependent on the remnants of all-Union structures in the area of foreign policy.

The weakness of the bureaucratic structures of Russian Federation foreign policy was as a hallmark of almost all Russian Federation official agencies. 'Russia does not have at its disposal the necessary set of government instruments for an independent economic policy, and the mechanism of inter-republican co-ordination of policies is still not very efficient', complained one of the new Russian Federation Vice-Premiers, Egor Gaidar. For economic matters, a solution to the problem was soon found: the Russian Federation stopped financing a majority of the all-Union ministries and state committees, and nationalized the lion's share of the all-Union property on its territory. This led to a rapid influx of qualified all-Union bureaucrats into Russian Federation institutions.

It was much more difficult to quickly address foreign policy. Elimination of all-Union economic bureaucracies had been preceded by a prolonged period of establishing control by the republic, a process which had both its successes and its failures. However, the final outcome proved to be sufficiently encouraging for the Russian Federation to opt for full independence in the economic sphere. While the all-Union economic bureaucracy began to surrender some control well in advance of the abortive Moscow coup of 1991, in the foreign policy domain redistribution of competence between the centre and the Russian Federation was resisted until almost nothing remained of the former USSR.

By the end of 1991, Russian foreign policy had undergone significant change. With the all-Union centre rapidly losing power and purpose, the leaders of the republic were able to approach international relations more in terms of the national interest of the Russian Federation than in terms of rivalry with the 'Gorbachev team'.

V. Western policies towards centre–republic relations

For the USA the abortive August 1991 coup solved the painful dilemma of whether or not to develop relations with the new Russian leadership and openly challenge the traditional Soviet structure. It is ironic that the USA needed a plausible excuse to refocus its attention from the Soviet central leadership to the republics. By the summer of 1991 it was apparent that Gorbachev was losing initiative inside the USSR and that republican centres of power were quickly moving to the fore. In this sense, the escape of the Soviet President from the hands of high-level communist plotters with the help of the Russians was a blessing in disguise for George Bush. Stretching out his hand to Russian reformers in defence of the legitimate Soviet head of state, the US President was on comfortable moral ground (well protected against possible accusation of duplicity or betrayal of previous sympathies), while simultaneously taking an important step towards the Russian Federation.

During the last few months of Soviet power, the protracted 'Gorbymania' in Washington caused headaches for many Russian Federation political figures. President Bush seemed to ignore the rapid redistribution of political roles within the Soviet Union. His playing into Gorbachev's hands was explained in a variety of ways. It was claimed that Bush was attempting to avoid making strategic decisions and instead preferred a reactive policy of only taking small steps. Others accused him of being captive to his personal ties with the 'founder of *perestroika*' and spoke of his unwillingness to face change. For reform-minded Russian politicians fighting for the liberation of their republic from the all-permeating control of the Soviet imperial centre, there were plenty of reasons to believe that positive US responses to their activities were too weak and too slow.

In 1991 the conflict between Russian reformers and the crippled Soviet empire entered a decisive phase. Yeltsin urgently needed recognition and support from the outside world, including the USA, but the United States and its closest allies were reluctant to side with him. At best only moderate growth in their attention to the republic could be observed. The basis of US–Russian relations developed mainly via non-governmental channels, such as representatives of the scientific and business communities. At the official level, however, Washington continued to keep its distance. Real signs of softening of this intransigent position appeared only after Boris Yeltsin defeated the desperate offensive of hard-line communists inside the Russian Parliament, which was launched in the early months of 1991. This offensive was intended to paralyse Yeltsin, or even oust him. Instead, it opened the way for his presidency.

The cautious US attitude to the Russian Federation was not without logic. The USA had a stake in continuing dialogue with the Soviet Union. Gorbachev had proved the sincerity of his attempts to end the cold war on many occasions, and his far-reaching reforms promised to diminish substantially previous Soviet aggressiveness towards other members of the world community. Also the size of the Soviet debt to the West was considerable and continuing to grow.

Although they approved of the general direction of changes in the USSR, the United States and other Western nations could not, of course, ignore the fact that these very changes undermined internal order in the Soviet Union and eroded the position of the Soviet leader. However, as long as *perestroika* continued, they did their best to avoid actions that could additionally complicate Gorbachev's position. Confronted with an increasing decentralization of power in the USSR and the growing autonomy of republican leaders, the USA and other Western nations persisted in their resolution not to go over the head of the Soviet President. The only possible exceptions involved the three Baltic republics, but even there considerable restraint was displayed.

The US preference for Gorbachev in the war between all-Union structures and the republics was motivated to a considerable extent by what appeared to be the absence of republican centres of influence. For an extended period of time, the insistence of Soviet republics on sovereign rights and the desire to ease the dominance of the centre were regarded as nothing more than devitalizing factors, threatening the Soviet revolution from above. Western policy makers and observers had serious doubts about the ability of new republican leaders to perform the additional functions of which they claimed themselves capable. Moreover, since Gorbachev showed extreme sensitivity to the republics' 'rebellions' against his rule, the West had to appear even more deaf to their overtures.

A powerful anti-Yeltsin propaganda campaign, supported and directed from the top of the Soviet Olympus, was also a factor that negatively affected Western attitudes towards the new Russian Federation leaders. Rumours about Yeltsin's 'populism', 'ambitions' and, of course, his personal habits were readily accepted in the West. Yeltsin faced the sophisticated Soviet communist propaganda machine at a time when he was still not well known in the West and lacked many of the necessary tools to promote a positive image beyond the frontiers of the USSR.

If the West were to play a constructive role and influence events after the collapse of the Soviet empire, it could lose no time in developing formal relations with the sovereign republics. Two considerations motivated this. First, this would be the most reliable way to expose new republican leaders to the world of international politics, since they lacked such experience and needed to learn how to become responsible participants in international affairs. Second, the absence of formal recognition rendered useless, or largely ineffective, Western attempts to influence republican policies.

A major question that Western nations had to answer was: How can the 'great Soviet divorce' be made less detrimental to world security and stability? There was a risk of becoming a hostage to the conflicting demands of the remnants of the former Soviet Union (e.g., with respect to the future of the Soviet nuclear arsenal), instead of a Western agenda and priorities, and choosing appropriate areas for Western involvement. The expansion of the number of partners on the territory of the former Soviet Union would be very expensive for the West, of course, and would mean becoming more involved in current and future disputes between the republics. However, the price of not choosing such a policy would be even higher.

It was frequently asserted that the network of agreements between the Soviet Union and the rest of the world could not be translated onto the republican level. Gorbachev often used this argument in trying to defend his position as Soviet leader. Such a profound change was a challenge to the imagination, but methods were found to deal with the new situation. The 1992 Lisbon protocols to the START Treaty, for example, converted a Soviet–US treaty to a treaty that included Belarus, Kazakhstan, Russia and Ukraine. Even the most ingenious

Western schemes cannot guarantee that events will proceed as planned, but the feeling that they are moving in the desired direction is important for success.

Given its potential, the Russian Federation is certain to fill the vacuum left by Gorbachev's departure. The extent to which its foreign policies may differ from those of the Soviet Union is an important question for the West. For decades, the USSR was a focus of concern for other nations. It not only professed beliefs incompatible with Western values, it behaved as an aggressive bully towards the rest of the world. Though it displayed flexibility from time to time with strong competitors, this was hardly more than tactical manœuvring, and certainly not a real change in strategy. The world community had to keep a keen eye on the second nuclear superpower, which allocated huge resources for foreign policy.

Many Western political figures and analysts feel uneasy about a new nuclear superpower without unified leadership. This assumption evokes gloomy scenarios of a collapse of the system of international security that in the past ensured peace for the industrially developed nations of the world, and pictures have been painted of a sudden disruption of the existing economic ties between the former Soviet republics and other members of the world community. The Soviet Union was never an easy partner, but its disappearance seems to be an invitation to a dangerous uncertainty.

Disintegration of the Soviet empire is already a fact of life. Peace and stability now depend on the degree to which the republics, and those inter-republican structures which have not been imposed from above, are able to assume full power in a quick and orderly manner. Impetuosity here could no doubt prove highly unproductive; however, delay is also fraught with the most serious consequences.

VI. The future of Russian foreign policy

It is difficult at this stage to predict future developments in Russia, or how Russia will act in the international arena. The republic is still an enigma to many outside it, and probably to a considerable portion of its own citizens. Too many parameters are undergoing simultaneous change. Nevertheless, quite a few tendencies seem clear enough to permit one very important observation: the Russian Federation will not become a communist nuclear superpower that merely replaces the Soviet Union as we have known it. Gorbachev's insistent attempts to marry the communist past of the Soviet Union to a future of market economy and democracy could not be realized. This became increasingly evident to many Soviet citizens during the last two years of the Soviet Union's existence.

Soviet plans to modernize a totalitarian society by dismantling its mechanisms for coercion and introducing greater personal freedom also failed. Instead of giving communism a new life, they led to its funeral knell. It became apparent that the totalitarian society could survive only if repressions and limitations also continued to exist. Their elimination led to rapid collapse of the whole system. Without desiring it, Gorbachev started a chain reaction that was soon out of his control and which quickly reached the point of no return. The speed with which the communist ideology and all of its values and dogmas died is amazing; it is easy to suppose that changes of such magnitude would require decades.

Today there are still those who think that it may take the Russian Federation many years to rid itself of its communist legacy, but communism is already dead. Many of those in Russia who feel nostalgia for the Brezhnev period of state socialism regret, in fact, the sharp decline in their living standard and the loss of confidence about their own future. They do not really believe that communist ideology offers a solution to Russia's problems. They want the return not of communism, but of the safety belt to which they were accustomed. Their motto might be: 'Return the previous level of well-being, however low it was, but leave with us our new opportunities!' During the *perestroika* years, even former Communist Party *apparatchiks* changed from ideological priests to opportunists who tried to use the transformation of society for personal gain.

Russia's main task now is not liberation from communist ideology—this has been accomplished—but escape from the material and intellectual ruins of communism. Simultaneously, Russia must learn to survive in the new environment of an immature market economy. The end of communism in Russia demands radical revision of the goals of Russian society, both domestic and foreign.

A major change in priorities is a serious challenge to any nation, even one with sufficient resources at its disposal. For societies, as for individuals, drastic departures from firmly established practices are usually very painful. It is hardly possible to be adequately prepared for such strains. The situation in which Russia finds itself is not enviable. The crisis experienced by the republic deepens every day.

The Russian Federation leadership stresses its aim of building a Western society and rapidly integrating into the world of market economies. The basic dilemma, however, is to get from the gloomy present to that bright future. Today the Russian Federation must solve a very complicated problem: how to lay a new foundation for Russian society and for relations with the outside world while preventing the burial of the country under the ruins of the totalitarian pyramid created by Lenin, Stalin and their followers.

In many cases, the leaders of the Russian Federation have to deal with problems which appear insoluble, at least for the moment. One example of such a problem is the fate of the Soviet nuclear arsenal. Nuclear weapons as a sword directed against 'capitalist enemies' have lost their *raison d'être*, but remain an unbearable burden for the country. There are plenty of reasons to reduce the number of nuclear weapons, but this demands resources which do not exist. To make matters worse, the armed forces and the entire Soviet military–industrial complex have proved extremely vulnerable to economic disruption and other consequences of the disintegration of the Soviet Union, which may have very serious political and security consequences. Yet another detail should be added to this already troubling picture: the once strictly centralized control over the armed forces is eroding, and there are well-founded doubts as to who is in charge of the military. The example of the nuclear issue challenges the imagination, but it is only one among many.

VII. Recommendations for the West

For decades the West looked with anxiety at the Soviet Union and dreamed of being spared such a dangerous neighbour. This protracted conflict finally reached a critical point, and a conglomerate of new states has emerged from the ruins of the USSR. The outcome of the process depends primarily on the choices made by the republican leaders, their abilities and preferences—and on them alone. Nevertheless, the West can ease their tremendous burden and increase their chances of joining the free world. It is quite possible that the baggage they have inherited is too heavy to be carried alone.

Aggressive communism was for too long a major threat to the prosperity and security of the world. Failure to assist in reforming the 'evil empire' may be no less dangerous. Present-day Russia may be compared to a sick person who has just shown signs of recovery and who desperately requires assistance to convalesce. The extent to which this assistance is provided will be decisive for the future of the world community. Assistance from the West—intellectual and material—could take various forms. There is one sphere, however, where it is especially important now: Western nations should become involved as active intermediaries in the process of the redistribution of responsibilities among the former Soviet republics.

Some political figures and analysts point out, quite justifiably, that the Soviet republics are too interdependent and that attempts to divide the 'Soviet pie' may not achieve success. It is true that such an undertaking is very risky. The boundaries between the republics were never real; nevertheless, the partition of the former Soviet Union must proceed. No government can act successfully unless it knows what it governs, and postponing such clarification would only preserve the uncertainty of the republican governments about their responsibilities, which might further aggravate an already chaotic situation. Drawing boundaries between the republics is high on the agenda of republican governments, especially the Russian Federation, since this is an issue of particular importance to it.

The neighbours of the Russian Federation often profess the principle 'What is mine is mine, and what is not mine is negotiable'. Still this notion does not negate the need for co-operation between the republics. Common undertakings will bring about the desired results only if disputes can be settled. The West has sufficient leverage to influence decisively the final outcome of the current conflict of republican interests. Its success in this area will have a critical impact on all of its other initiatives which relate to the republics.

7. Issues and images: Washington and Moscow in great power politics

David Kaiser

I. Introduction

When this essay was begun in 1990, the changes inaugurated by Mikhail Gorbachev in 1985 seemed to have reached a climax. The pace of change has, however, continued to accelerate since then, and the original topic of this chapter—the relations between the Soviet Union and the United States—has become, literally, a matter of purely historical interest. Several centuries of Russian expansion have been reversed, communism has given way to free markets and four independent republics have taken custody of the old Soviet nuclear arsenal. Yet despite these unprecedented changes, which threaten to plunge the territory of the old Soviet empire into chaos such as it has not known since 1918–21, history still offers some idea of what to expect from the future, and how it will differ from what was known for so long. A look at the past provides both a sense of the limitations of cold war diplomacy and some more hopeful precedents for the multilateral world which is emerging.

We must first try to clear up some of the confusion over the meaning of US–Soviet relations that persisted throughout the cold war. As a few unusually perceptive figures such as George Kennan and Adam Ulam have pointed out, both the potential dangers and benefits of US–Soviet relations have been chronically exaggerated, certainly in the United States and probably in the Soviet Union as well. The widespread confusion today within the USA about the impact of the end of the Soviet Union reflects this long-standing problem. Having assumed for decades that Soviet communism was the source of much if not all of the evil in the world, the USA is bemused to find that its collapse clearly does not mean that we are now destined to live happily ever after. Meanwhile, some observers are arguing that a multipolar world—and in particular a multipolar Europe—will bring back the balance-of-power days of the 18th and 19th centuries, and increase the danger of war. Such a view looks at only one side of European international relations before 1914, and ignores a great many new possibilities for diplomacy.

One fundamental distinction between two aspects of US–Soviet relations provides assistance to understand both the past and the future. Initially, the Moscow–Washington relationship can be reduced to a series of specific diplomatic issues between the two capitals: arguments over frontiers and occupation rights, trade relations, arms control and, somewhat more broadly, competition for influence in several parts of the world. A brief look at the cold war era shows that the fabric of US–Soviet relations, in this sense, was much thinner than is generally supposed. Much of the behaviour of both Moscow and Washington during the cold war period, however, must be explained in a different way. Many aspects of the confrontation between the two governments—including much of the arms race—did not grow directly from specific diplomatic issues between them, but rather from the ways in which they perceived one another. In many areas of politics, diplomacy and defence, it is the mutual images of the two countries rather than their actual behaviour that have had such an extraordinary influence. Their view of one another as aggressive, antagonistic and continually threatening the world balance of power led them to view many local conflicts as problems in US–Soviet relations.

The changes of the past few years altered both the substance and the imagery of US–Soviet relations fundamentally before finally bringing the Soviet Union to an end. Some of the most difficult issues between the two states disappeared, and the images which they maintained of one another for so long became obsolete. Both these changes posed significant problems for both governments, all the more so because they had become so accustomed to the earlier pattern, and the collapse of the Union into its component parts poses far bigger challenges. History suggests, however, that it also creates important new opportunities.

Thus the dissolution of the two-bloc system in Europe need not lead, as some have suggested, to the recurrence of European military rivalries, but could instead mark the beginning of a new era of successful multilateral diplomacy similar to the years 1871–1914. The end of the cold war has already opened up new opportunities for multilateral initiatives to deal with crises in the developing countries, most notably during the Persian Gulf War, and the United States can now treat regional conflicts and leftist insurgencies closer to home in a more realistic spirit. Both Washington and Moscow can also expand their arms control efforts. Recent developments have also revived some very serious, long-standing European problems, such as nationality conflicts in eastern and south-eastern Europe, and these demand new kinds of solutions. In short, the end of the cold war has opened up a host of new diplomatic issues, some of whose roots go back at least a century. Before analysing them more carefully, however, another look should be taken at the more recent past.

II. Issues and images, 1945–89

Having won World War II together, the USA and the USSR rapidly became embroiled in controversies and disputes over the future of defeated nations and occupied territories. Some of these disputes became very serious, and their conflict eventually extended to every part of the globe. Twice—over Germany in 1958–61 and in Cuba in 1962—real issues brought them near the brink of war, but for most of the cold war period, real issues played less of a role in their antagonism than mutual images, and how they chose to see each other was more influential than what they actually wanted from each other.

The climate of US–Soviet relations during the cold war shows the influence of the atmosphere of World War II, from which the United States and the Soviet Union emerged as the world's most powerful nations. The governments that fought that war—like nearly every 20th century wartime government—claimed to be fighting evil, and told their people that their victory would mean the triumph of good. The idea that wartime allies might have irreconcilable aims had no place in this vision. Thus the Government of the United States (and, one might note, the British Government as well) found it more convenient during the war to overlook the true character of the Soviet Union and to assume, publicly and in many cases privately, that their governments could agree on the shape of the post-war order in Europe and Asia.[1] Soviet actions in the last months of the war, especially in Eastern Europe, thus came as a serious shock, and Soviet behaviour in the new United Nations was also a major disappointment. Yet even in the critical first few years of the post-war era, many sources of anger did not become lasting diplomatic problems. The United States recognized the Soviet-imposed, communist regimes in Eastern Europe within a relatively short time after the war. The USSR defused a minor crisis over its prolonged occupation of northern Iran in early 1946 by withdrawing. And although the USA never gave *de jure* recognition to the Soviet incorporation of the Baltic states, it did not specifically demand plebiscites in those regions, or in any way attempt to force Moscow to surrender sovereignty.

Serious issues did develop over Germany, where four-power co-operation on occupation policy faltered in 1946 and definitely broke down in 1947, when the UK and the USA decided to merge their zones and administer them in light of their own political and economic ends. The differences between Washington and Moscow became truly dangerous in 1948–49. First, the USSR cut off land access to West Berlin, apparently in an attempt to reopen talks on a common occupation policy, for the better part of a year. Then came the formation of the Federal Republic of Germany and the German Democratic Republic, neither of which was recognized by all the occupying powers. The Constitution of the FRG, moreover, challenged not only the legitimacy of the GDR, but also the loss of all territory east of the Oder–Neisse line to Poland and the USSR. The United States endorsed that position, thereby making a partial break with the original Potsdam agreement on Germany. Thus was born the real diplomatic and military conflict in Europe that persisted for exactly 40 years, from 1949 through 1989.

The US–Soviet argument over Germany was not simply an argument over ideology, but a dispute over the legitimacy of governments and borders.

---

[1] See Gaddis, J. L., *The United States and the Origins of the Cold War 1941–1947* (Columbia University Press: New York, 1972), pp. 32–62. Regarding the British case, it is interesting to recall that the Ministry of Information, in 1944, advised against the publication of George Orwell's *Animal Farm* on the grounds that it would damage Anglo-Russian relations; see Crick, B., *George Orwell* (Little, Brown: Boston, Mass., 1980), pp. 312–13.

Because Moscow in 1950 would not accept the legitimacy of the FRG—which, given the West German Basic Law, it could hardly be expected to do—it was easy to believe, especially after the North Korean attack on South Korea, that the USSR might attack the FRG as well. German rearmament and the strengthening of NATO were the result. The USSR tried more than once to reopen talks on Germany. However, the US and West German Governments preferred the existing situation—which allowed the FRG to believe that it would eventually secure reunification, and perhaps its lost territories, on its own terms—to either reunification, which Stalin proposed in 1952, or mutual recognition of East and West Germany, which Khrushchev demanded in 1958. Things became more serious in the years 1958–62, when Khrushchev threatened to turn control of the access routes to West Berlin over to the GDR, possibly leaving the Western powers with a choice between withdrawal and war. Only after 1969, when Willy Brandt began to abandon Konrad Adenauer's policy of non-recognition of the GDR and its frontiers, did the tension definitely ease. Brandt's policies enabled Moscow, Washington, London and Paris to reach a new agreement on access to West Berlin in 1972. Finally, in 1975, Washington, Moscow and all the European states joined in recognizing the existing frontiers of Europe in the Helsinki Final Act, while also acknowledging that they might peacefully be changed. This, however, was only a political document, not a treaty having the force of law, and by that time the military confrontation in Central Europe had long since developed a life of its own. Still, the real issue that had divided the USA and the USSR for so long—the frontiers and the two governments of Germany—had virtually ceased to exist.

Curiously enough, although Europe from the late 1940s until 1989 was clearly divided into Soviet and US spheres of influence, European concerns—and especially German concerns—played a critical role in bringing about, maintaining and eventually overcoming the division of Europe. The division of Germany was a provisional, medium-term solution to the German problem, and the NATO and Warsaw Pact forces that faced each other along the border between East and West Germany enforced that solution. In order for Europe to put World War II behind it, two major changes had to occur: the FRG had to accept the Oder–Neisse line, and the USSR had to accept the loss of the GDR. The first change took two decades to accomplish, and the second followed another two decades later.

The collapse of the Warsaw Pact settled the German question, but it has rapidly opened up other issues as well. As shown below in the discussion of the future, Moscow and Washington both have a role to play in these issues, but their role must inevitably be somewhat less central.

Nuclear weapons and their consequences created the second major set of issues between the USA and the USSR. As early as 1946 the USA proposed the international control of those weapons in the United States, only to have the

USSR reject the plan.[2] Proposals for arms control and the control of nuclear tests began in the mid-1950s, but had very limited success. Then, in 1962, Khrushchev brought the two countries to the brink of war by introducing intermediate-range nuclear missiles into Cuba only to withdraw them in return for a public US promise not to invade Cuba and secret assurances that US missiles in Turkey would also be withdrawn. The Partial Test Ban Treaty followed less than a year later.

With the development of effective spy satellites, verifiable arms control agreements became possible by the late 1960s, and in the early 1970s strategic arms control established a secure and prominent position on the US–Soviet agenda. The history of SALT I, SALT II, and the INF Treaty is too well known to require repetition. Only the last of these treaties resulted in a real reduction in nuclear delivery vehicles, and both SALT agreements, of course, aroused considerable controversy in the United States. However, despite its limited success, arms control was the most active aspect of US–Soviet relations during the past 20 years. Even though no binding agreement on strategic arms had been reached and ratified during the two decades since 1972, both capitals had accepted the principle that their strategic nuclear arsenals should be regulated by treaty.

The 1991 US–Soviet START Treaty provided for more reductions in sophisticated strategic weaponry than did the two SALT treaties, but like them it contained loopholes that could make any overall reduction in warheads less impressive than some descriptions of it suggest. It required significant reductions in land-based and submarine-based launchers and warheads, with cuts in Soviet land-based forces reaching 40 per cent—a highly significant achievement. At the same time, it allowed for increases in air-launched and sea-launched cruise missiles, increases in Soviet bomber-delivered warheads, and only small reductions in US nuclear bomber payloads. Increases in these latter types of forces have encountered more significant restraints from budget problems than from the Treaty. However, the conclusion of the Treaty created further opportunities for US–Soviet initiatives in arms control, despite the end of the bipolar era. These opportunities were exploited in the Bush–Yeltsin agreement to eliminate MIRVed intercontinental ballistic missiles by the year 2003 and to reduce the number of nuclear warheads to 3000–3500. Still deeper cuts seem warranted.

The long US–Soviet competition for influence in the developing countries occasionally led to talks between the two states, although both sides more frequently simply reacted to what the other was doing, or to their image of the other's role, rather than actually trying to engage the other party in a settlement of ongoing disputes. The United States, as already noted, did persuade the Soviet Union to withdraw from northern Iran in 1946, and the two countries cooperated in negotiating the neutralization of Laos in 1962, although that agree-

---

2 Bundy, McG., *Danger and Survival* (Random House: New York, 1988) suggests that a private approach to the Soviet Government might have been more effective, but it seems quite doubtful that Stalin would have agreed to forgo Soviet atomic development under any circumstances.

ment was never satisfactorily implemented. In 1977 the two governments issued a common declaration on the Arab–Israeli conflict, but Egyptian President Anwar Sadat's sudden decision to visit Jerusalem left that initiative behind. The Nixon Administration also made repeated attempts to enlist the Soviet Union's help in settling the Viet Nam War, apparently with some limited success.[3] More often, the two sides have simply reacted to one another's behaviour, rather than attempt to engage each other in a real discussion.

Economic relations and cultural and scientific contacts between the United States and the Soviet Union also had a very mixed record in the cold war era. Trade relations got off to a bad start when the two countries failed to agree to a settlement of the USSR's wartime Lend Lease debt, and Stalin's decision to refuse Marshall Plan aid in 1947 put an end to any chance for extensive economic contacts. Much later, in the early 1970s, the Nixon and Brezhnev governments arranged large-scale Soviet grain purchases and tried to establish most favored nation (MFN) trade status between the two countries, but the Jackson–Vanik amendment made this impossible. Scientific contacts also increased during the 1970s, but this process—like US grain sales—came to an end with the Soviet invasion of Afghanistan. The Reagan Administration resumed grain sales, but made other attempts to keep Western technology out of the USSR.

On the whole, direct diplomacy between Moscow and Washington accomplished surprisingly little during the past 45 years. A long struggle over the status of Germany was resolved more by changes within East and West Germany than by the superpowers themselves. The record also includes a long, but only rarely successful series of negotiations on arms control, a few rare moments of co-operation to try to solve conflicts in developing countries and some intermittent attempts to increase trade. The mutual images of the two countries, indeed, have had more influence upon their policies than any actual diplomatic exchanges between them.

Those images probably had three main sources: the very real ideological conflict between the two countries, each of which regarded itself as the model for the rest of the world; the USSR's imposition of communism in Eastern Europe after World War II; and certain habits of thought developed during that war which survived into the post-war period. As the wartime alliance broke down, both sides immediately created an image of the other that closely resembled their wartime image of Nazi Germany. In the USA, the USSR emerged as a new totalitarian threat, comparable in ambition and ruthlessness to Hitler's Germany, while in the USSR, the USA quickly became the new leader of the hostile forces of imperialism. Each argued intermittently that the other was planning its own destruction. These images had profound effects on the defence and foreign policies of the two nations.

Thus the nuclear arms race that began in earnest after the Soviet detonation of an atomic bomb in late 1949 owed less to the persistence of specific

---

[3] They may have contributed to the North Vietnamese agreement in the late summer of 1972 to allow Nguyen Van Thieu to remain in power, but they did not succeed in securing a withdrawal of North Vietnamese forces from the south.

diplomatic conflicts than to the generalized US perception that the USSR, owing to its very nature, would naturally choose to destroy the USA with nuclear weapons if it could get away with it. Many important policy makers shared this view well into the 1980s, even though other very important Americans—including Dwight Eisenhower—rejected it in private. In fact it was the USA that first acquired the capability to destroy the USSR with strategic nuclear weapons, but the USSR in the 1960s apparently decided to match that capability. Although the specific European questions that divided the two powers were largely resolved during the 1970s, the arms race had acquired a momentum of its own by then, fuelled by the largely unsupported belief that either side could profit by destroying the other.[4] Beginning in the 1950s, the perceived Soviet military threat to Western Europe led to the deployment of tactical nuclear weapons, and later to the deployment of vast conventional armies in Central Europe as well—even though there is no evidence that either side ever seriously contemplated an attack.

The image of a life-threatening, imperialistic adversary helped both Washington and Moscow form larger alliances. Several treatments of the origins of the cold war now suggest that Washington in 1947 was far more worried about the economic state of Western Europe than about possible Soviet aggression, but anti-communism proved to be the best way to win congressional support for the Marshall Plan.[5] The perception of a Soviet military threat enabled the West to integrate the rearmament of the FRG into the defence of the West. Meanwhile, the supposed danger of imperialist aggression—led by West German *revanchism*—was the ideological glue that held the Warsaw Pact together from 1955 until 1990, and provided the excuse for Soviet intervention in Hungary in 1956 and Czechoslovakia in 1968. The Western alliance, of course, was built upon a very real basis of mutual interest while the Warsaw Pact was an alliance of ruling oligarchies rather than peoples, but in both cases the image of the adversary helped create and maintain the alliance.

The US image of the Soviet Union as the leader of an expanding communist bloc also had an enormous influence on US foreign policy in many developing countries. The Chinese civil war, the North Korean attack on South Korea, the Viet Minh revolt in Indo-China, the advent of the Castro regime in Cuba, the Arbenz regime in Guatemala, the Sandinistas in Nicaragua and numerous other communist movements around the world were all treated to some extent as Soviet-inspired or Soviet-directed events. As late as the Reagan Administration, high officials were suggesting that the USSR bore direct or indirect responsibility for virtually every threat to US interests around the world. Such views led to dozens of US political and military interventions in response, with varying degrees of success. The US anti-Soviet strategy became more flexible in

---

[4] George Kennan had questioned whether the destruction of the Soviet Union would benefit the United States as early as 1951, but such questions were very rare. See Kennan, G., *Memoirs, 1950–1963* (Little, Brown: Boston, Mass., 1972), pp. 94–97.

[5] See Gimbel, J., *The Origins of the Marshall Plan* (Stanford University Press: Stanford, Calif., 1976); and Freeland, R., *The Truman Doctrine and the Origins of McCarthyism* (New York University Press: New York, 1970).

1971–72, when President Richard Nixon's visit to China showed that even a communist country could be a diplomatic asset against the Soviet Union. Similarly, the USSR regarded its allies' triumphs as signs of the eventual victory of world socialism, and ultimately attracted some non-communist clients in South Asia and the Middle East—including Afghanistan, where it decided to intervene militarily on behalf of a client. As long as Moscow and Washington saw themselves locked in a world-wide struggle, they had a ready-made excuse to jump into any local conflict, however dubious its strategic importance.

These negative images led mostly to military buildup and proxy confrontations, but they had another countervailing effect as well. Because of the belief that US–Soviet hostility was the root of all evil, high-level US–Soviet contacts inevitably raised hopes for world peace. Although summits rarely resulted in substantial agreements (the 1972 Moscow summit meeting was the major exception), they were such successful media events that no US President after Harry Truman managed to resist them.[6] Even in the Eisenhower and Kennedy years, when serious differences of policy over Germany were bound to make any real settlement impossible, hopes soared in preparation for summits in 1955, 1959, 1960 and 1961. The spectacle of a meeting between the leaders of the two opposing camps often obscured how little bargaining room they had.

Summitry, to be sure, had its dangers, especially in US politics. The supposed betrayal of Yalta was part of the conservative mythology of the cold war, and Presidents Richard Nixon and Gerald Ford suffered among conservatives in the 1972–76 period when they appeared to endorse the belief that frequent summits and agreements could actually change Soviet behaviour. Nixon had invited such criticism at the 1972 Moscow summit, when the USA and the USSR jointly endorsed Basic Principles of Relations between the two countries and promised, among other things, to eschew 'unilateral advantage at the expense of the other, directly or indirectly', and to renounce claims 'to any special rights or advantages in world affairs'. In general, however, summits benefited US presidents politically throughout this period. 'There is much that divides us', Ronald Reagan reportedly told Mikhail Gorbachev in Geneva in 1985, 'but I believe the world breathes easier because we are talking'. Larry Speakes' later admission that he fabricated this quote only underlines that such a statement was precisely what the situation called for.

In short, while progress on bilateral US–Soviet issues has been intermittent at best, the two countries' images of one another have determined most of their military posture and much of their foreign policy. And in the new era which lies ahead, the loss of those mutual images may also turn out to be at least as significant as any changes in bilateral relations. Initially, this change will be

---

[6] After meeting Stalin at Potsdam in 1945, Truman showed no interest in any further summit meetings. Presidents Eisenhower, Kennedy, Johnson, Nixon, Ford, Carter, Reagan and Bush have all met with a Soviet leader at least once. In addition to the 1972 summit, several other high-level meetings have been the occasion of signing new agreements, but not of negotiating them.

disorienting, but in the long run it offers much greater hopes of arriving at more sensible positions on a variety of issues.

III. Issues and images, 1991 and beyond

The events of the past few years have clearly made the cold war paradigm of international relations obsolete. The USSR in 1989–90 changed its foreign policy in ways that made the image of an aggressive, expansionist state untenable. The initial reaction to Gorbachev's domestic reforms suggests that they alone would not have had this result. Many conservative commentators during the late 1980s suggested that Gorbachev was simply trying to make the Soviet Union a more competitive superpower and a more dangerous enemy. However, the Soviet withdrawal from Afghanistan and events in Eastern Europe—including the fall of communist governments throughout the region, agreement to the unification of East and West Germany, the dissolution of the Warsaw Pact and agreement in principle to withdraw Soviet troops from the region—undid most of the Soviet expansion of the past 45 years and clearly signalled an entirely new era. Gorbachev's rightward turn during the winter of 1990–91 tarnished his image, but Moscow's co-operation with the US-led coalition during the Gulf War confirmed that a major change in Soviet foreign policy had occurred. This change—a very real change, as well as a perceptual one—enabled the two sides and their allies to resolve many of the critical issues of the cold war. The USSR accepted German reunification on Western terms, and reached an agreement on mutual (and quite unbalanced) withdrawal of forces from Germany. It agreed in principle to withdraw all forces from Germany by 1994.

This, however, has turned out to be only the first stage of Soviet retreat. In 1991, the disintegration of the Soviet Union moved from the realm of possibility to the realm of fact. The independence of the Baltic states rolled the Soviet frontier there back to the 1939 border, and the failed coup in August 1991 led within just a few months to the total eclipse of the Soviet Union and the independence of all the constituent republics. While some new federation may yet emerge, the whole idea of 'US–Soviet relations' has become obsolete.

Both the rest of Europe and the United States had very good reasons for discouraging the complete breakup of the Soviet Union. Western governments obviously would have found it easier to reach mutually beneficial agreements with a single Soviet Government than with numerous successor states, four of whom possess nuclear weapons. Now, as the old union disintegrates, the Western nations should do whatever they can—which may not be nearly enough—to make the process as peaceful as possible. Meanwhile, some opportunities for mutually beneficial agreements with Belarus, Russia and Ukraine will certainly remain.

Multilateral diplomacy and regional conflicts

As many observers have pointed out, the end of the cold war has now recreated a truly multilateral world, diplomatically and militarily. What will the new world be like? Some observers have jumped to the conclusion that the end of the cold war in Europe will lead rapidly to the creation of new, shifting alliances and, quite possibly, new military conflicts such as Europe experienced in previous centuries.[7] But history shows that this is hardly the only possibility, and recent events suggest that it is not the most likely one. The example of the Gulf War suggests that instead a new era of effective multilateral diplomacy may be dawning, such as characterized great-power relations in the late 19th and early 20th centuries. Such an environment lacks the stability—not to say the paralysing inertia—of the cold war period, but it can also be much more productive diplomatically.

The catastrophe of World War I has tended to discredit the entire system of international politics that had grown up in late 19th century Europe, and to obscure its remarkable achievements. From 1871 through 1914 the European great powers not only remained at peace with one another, but also settled an enormous number of controversies with impressive ease. The issues they dealt with fell into two major categories: questions arising from their territorial, political and economic expansion in Africa and Asia, and emerging nationality conflicts in south-eastern Europe.

With respect to imperialism, the British, French, Germans, Italians and Russians reached numerous agreements delimiting their territorial possessions in Africa and, later, their spheres of influence in China, Turkey and other parts of the Middle East. Only occasionally did disputes over such issues seem to threaten war, such as in 1898 at Fashoda and 1911 over Morocco, but even these crises were eventually resolved peacefully. Until 1914, the only wars arising out of imperialism involved non-European powers, including the Boers, the Japanese and the United States. In 1900, in China, all the powers combined to put down the Boxer rebellion. Meanwhile, individual states managed to win recognition of their special role in certain areas of the world, such as the British in Egypt and the United States in the Caribbean.

Russia and the United States played important roles in this process, although their interests did not extend quite as broadly as those of Britain, France or even Germany. Neither took any part in the scramble for Africa, although both participated in the 1906 Algeciras Conference on Morocco, and Russia had virtually nothing to do with Latin America. But they dealt with one another quite frequently over Asia, most notably in connection with the Russo-Japanese War, which the Government of the United States helped bring to a close. The USA was not called upon to play this role because it was the most directly interested third party—both Britain and Germany had more important interests in North China—but because its freedom from European alliances gave it more

---

[7] Mearsheimer, J. J., 'Back to the future: instability in Europe after the cold war', *International Security*, vol. 15, no. 1 (summer 1990), pp. 5–56.

chance of success. Russian expansion southwards into Afghanistan, Iran, Tibet and Turkey brought Moscow into frequent conflict with London in the late 19th century, but the tsarist government finally reached a settlement of most of these conflicts in 1907. Meanwhile, attempts to extend US political influence in the Caribbean led to some diplomatic conflicts with Britain and Germany and to war with Spain, but Russia was not involved in these crises. Russia and the United States were two expanding powers whose geographical extent involved them in a number of crises in the less-developed world, but other powers were always involved in these crises as well, and Russian–US relations never played a central role in international politics.

Today any renewed co-operation among the world's great industrial powers to protect their interests in the developing countries must take account of a very different context. The age of formal imperialism is over, and many developing countries will resist any attempt to re-establish spheres of influence. Any industrial nations seeking to intervene in these countries will almost certainly need the support of some local powers as well. And some especially difficult problems, led by the Arab–Israeli conflict, will not be solved until the parties involved change some of their objectives. Yet the example of the Gulf War shows what multilateral co-operation can achieve, given the proper circumstances. The spectre of a heavily armed and aggressive state that threatened both its neighbours and the interests of the leading industrial powers enabled the United States to organize a multilateral coalition supported by the Soviet Union. In some ways the Gulf War was reminiscent of the late 19th century, since in addition to defending the territorial integrity of Kuwait, the United States and its industrial allies were making it quite clear that no hostile power would be allowed to threaten their oil supplies. Yet at the same time, the Western powers went to enormous lengths to avoid offending their local allies, led by Saudi Arabia and Egypt, and so far their victory has not led to any substantial anti-US or anti-Western backlash in the developing countries.

Meanwhile, the eclipse of the image of a world-wide Soviet threat could help the USA approach many regional issues in a much more flexible and realistic spirit. Washington can estimate the dangers of the El Salvadorean guerrillas, Castro's Cuba, the Qadhafi regime in Libya or the Government of Viet Nam much more accurately if it abandons the tendency to regard them as 'Soviet surrogates'. Indeed, at the time of writing, the Salvadorean Government and the guerrillas appear to have reached a settlement on terms which would have been most unlikely to be acceptable to the USA just a few years ago, and Washington seems to be considering the normalization of relations with Viet Nam. The US Government may also find it easier to encourage local initiatives to solve regional problems now that it no longer seems necessary to regard them as episodes in a larger US–Soviet struggle. It will not always be easy, however, for Washington to adopt a more flexible perspective, and some regional conflicts will be extremely intractable anyway. The Panama invasion also suggests that the United States will find other reasons for intervening, at least in its own hemisphere, just as it did in the first half of the 20th century. And the United

States will face new competitors at least for political influence in various parts of the world—Mexico and Venezuela in Central America, India in South Asia and France in much of Africa and the Middle East. In this sense, too, the new international environment recalls the era before 1914.

The revival of nationalism

Nationality conflicts were the second major preoccupation of the pre-1914 European concert, and this subject obviously has even more powerful implications for the immediate future. During the 19th century, several European governments began to encourage the national aspirations of some of the Christian subjects of the Ottoman empire. The Greeks and Serbs managed to create small states in the first half of the 19th century, and the Congresses of Paris (1856) and Berlin (1878) led to the creation of Bulgaria and Romania as well. Various combinations of European powers also interceded to secure better treatment of the Armenians and the Macedonians, although not always with much success. In 1912–13, after the Balkan states attacked Turkey, the five great European powers (Austria-Hungary, Britain, France, Germany and Russia) tried to control the territorial changes that resulted so as not to threaten any of their vital interests. Russia played a critical role in all these crises, sometimes (1874–78) trying to turn them decisively to its own advantage, and sometimes (1912–13) co-operating fully with other powers to maintain European peace. Moscow also co-operated with Berlin, and to a lesser extent Vienna, to continue the partition of Poland and prevent Polish nationalism from winning any major victories in any of the three eastern empires.

Diplomatic attempts to control nationality conflicts broke down spectacularly, however, in 1914, when Austria-Hungary decided to crush Serbia after the assassination of Archduke Francis Ferdinand, and thereby helped unleash World War I. While Russia did not instigate the assassination or actively promote the conflict, Moscow would not allow Vienna simply to crush the Serbs and destroy the regional balance of power. This episode also highlights the limitations of the great powers' efforts on behalf of subject nationalities before 1914: they did not extend to subjects of the great powers themselves. No great-power government before 1914 undertook any initiative on behalf of any of the minorities living within Austria-Hungary, or the Poles living in Germany and Russia, or the much-persecuted Russian Jews or the French of Alsace-Lorraine. After World War I, several new states in eastern and south-eastern Europe had to sign minorities treaties pledging equal treatment of their minority citizens, but the League of Nations never managed to enforce these obligations very effectively. Minorities suffered new persecution in the interwar period, and many suffered extermination or expulsion during World War II.

The deaths and population transfers of World War II substantially reduced the total minority population of Europe, but did not eliminate it. Meanwhile, communist rule provided at least a theoretical foundation for the government of subject nationalities, and prevented conflicts from coming to the surface. The collapse of communism unleashed the Serbo-Croat conflict in Yugoslavia with frightening speed and intensity, leading to civil war and attempts to break up the country. With other similar conflicts likely to escalate in Romania and various parts of the former Soviet Union, Europe desperately needs a new mechanism both to mediate disputes and to assure minorities the fundamental rights which they are guaranteed under the Helsinki accords of 1975.

In the years before 1914, a series of local nationalities crises eventually led to a European war. Today the nations of Central and Western Europe do not seem likely to be drawn into a war over conflicts in eastern and south-eastern Europe, but Europe needs an international framework to secure fair and equal treatment of minorities and head off a series of local catastrophes. This will be very difficult to achieve, but no other solution seems very likely to work. Moving frontiers or creating new sovereignties in Yugoslavia or Romania will not solve the problem because many areas still contain mixed populations, as the conflict in Croatia shows. In the former Soviet Union, Russian minorities in non-Russian republics may become sources of conflict between them and Russia. Worst of all, changes in the frontiers established by World War II might, in time, set off an uncontrollable process. Now that the Baltic states have secured their independence, Moldovans may claim that since their incorporation in the USSR also resulted from the 1939 Nazi–Soviet Pact, they should once again become part of Romania. This in turn could encourage the Magyar minority in Romania to demand incorporation into Hungary—and so on. Even reunited Germany's acceptance of its frontiers could be threatened if enough changes took place in the East.

Having written at length about the catastrophic effects of nationalism upon European life during the first half of the 20th century,[8] this writer views the emergence of so many new independent states—each with its own national minorities—with more fear than enthusiasm. Europe still lacks any formal mechanism for assuring minority rights, and even the Western European states are apparently becoming more intolerant of minorities, not less. Since 1957 the states of Europe have been gradually moving towards the eclipse of national sovereignty within the European Community, but the community members are still struggling separately with related problems of immigration, foreign workers and minority rights. The community, to its credit, has taken the lead in trying to mediate the war in the former Yugoslovaia, but even if it succeeds, the problem of long-term guarantees for European minorities will remain. Several East European countries clearly hope to join the EC, and may eventually do so, but many serious nationality conflicts will break out before the enlargement of the EC takes place.

In the short run, the Helsinki framework offers the best opportunity to create some kind of common European citizenship, with some mechanism for enforce-

[8] Kaiser, D., *Politics and War: European Conflict from Philip II to Hitler* (Harvard University Press: Cambridge, Mass., 1990), pp. 307–409.

ment of minority rights. Only such a framework could cope with emerging problems in the former Soviet Union and among the peoples of Eastern Europe. The EC, the Russian leadership and the United States could all encourage this process, just as the major European powers 100 years ago tried to do something for the subjects of the Ottoman empire. Whether they can find a way to deal with newly reawakened, centuries-old hatreds, remains to be seen. A broader emerging problem involves the future relationship of Western, Central and Eastern Europe. The European Community will apparently eventually add new members from the East—how many, how fast and on what terms? Eastern Europe has lagged far behind Western Europe throughout the 20th century, and the question of how to begin closing this gap has critical implications for Eastern Europe and the former Soviet Union.

New issues in arms control

Other issues offer opportunities for multilateral European agreement. Belarus, Russia, Ukraine and all the European states urgently require a permanent framework for conventional arms control within Europe—a problem for which historical precedents offer no clear solution. For most of the 19th century the European states fully accepted the possibility of European war, although diplomacy made it a relatively infrequent occurrence. The catastrophe of World War I led to a more intensive search for ways to make such a conflict impossible. The Paris peace treaties of 1919 disarmed the defeated states of Austria, Bulgaria, Germany and Hungary, and called for further steps towards general disarmament. Unfortunately, the conference designed to achieve this did not convene until 1932, and the advent of Adolf Hitler eventually made it impossible for it to achieve its goals. After World War II, Europe was divided into two opposing security systems.

The further limitation of conventional forces within Europe will pose many complex problems, just as it did in 1932, partly because several European powers, including Britain, France, and Russia, will want to retain forces for employment outside of Europe. Yet Europe needs a lasting security structure to replace the frozen, nuclear-enforced equilibrium between NATO and the Warsaw Pact. The US Government, which still has large conventional forces in Europe, obviously has a role to play in this process as well. Any lasting structure will probably have to include some mixture of arms limitation and confidence-building measures. It will also require a broad consensus on the kinds of conflict that are likely to arise in Europe and the diplomatic means that will be used to resolve them.

While Washington and Moscow will now become two among many important players in issues which affect Europe and the developing countries, some bilateral issues between Russia and the United States will remain important. Strategic arms control still offers very important possibilities for Russian–US relations. In strategic weaponry the USA and Russia are still in a class by themselves, and in this area at least the other nuclear-armed republics will probably be willing to follow Moscow's lead. Their preponderance in long-range nuclear forces makes them the critical players in any strategic arms talks and also gives them considerable leverage, if they can agree to try to use it, to try to restrict, reduce or prevent the development of strategic forces in other countries. Given the constraints on the US military budget and the renewed emphasis on conventional forces that will likely result from the Gulf War, it would probably benefit the US Government, as well as the Russian one, to accept even deeper cuts in nuclear weapon systems and to dismantle the warheads themselves. Russian President Boris Yeltsin seems prepared to go much further and move towards the abolition of strategic weapons. Meanwhile, the emerging danger that Russian nuclear scientists may sell their services to nations aspiring to acquire nuclear weapons also increases the need for new agreements on proliferation.

For quite a long time, Russia and the other new republics will be preoccupied with their internal situation, but if Russia can stabilize its economy, both Moscow and Washington will find themselves in a strong position to push for multilateral arms control. The two governments clearly share an interest in checking the spread of ballistic missiles and chemical, biological and nuclear weapons, and could take the lead in promoting the reduction or elimination of any or all of these types of weapon. Washington might also finally decide to push for a comprehensive nuclear test ban. Of all the major issues in contemporary international politics, these remain those for which the two governments can most easily try to define the terms of any new discussions. Time, however, is short. The production of various types of sophisticated weaponry is proliferating rapidly, and it will become harder and harder for the United States and Russia to use their roles as the world's largest arms producers as leverage.

Economically US–Soviet relations seemed to have made progress during the past two years of the Soviet Union's life, as Washington finally prepared to grant the USSR MFN status, but the breakup of the USSR and the catastrophic state of the new republics' economies do not hold out much hope of dramatic, mutually beneficial increases in trade during the next few years. The wisdom of US economic help to Russia and the other republics has become a political issue, and the US budget deficit will probably militate against any substantial commitment to help the USSR on domestic grounds alone. If Moscow opens up its economy to Western aid and investment, it will probably seek multilateral help rather than rely on any one power, and the USA has less help to provide than some of its competitors.

The failure of the August 1991 coup and the breakup of the Soviet Union has ensured that the image of an aggressive, totalitarian power threatening the survival of the USA and world-wide US interests will disappear. That, in turn, will have profound and uncertain effects upon US defence and foreign policy.

Before the Gulf War, the collapse of the Warsaw Pact had clearly created a major crisis in US military planning. The war in Central Europe for which the Army, Navy and Air Force had prepared so carefully for so long had been consigned to the ash-heap of history. Many had immediately questioned US needs for many types of forces, including armoured forces. The Gulf War briefly renewed interest in a strong US military, but while the utility of military force was substantially confirmed, the actual uses for which it is likely to be needed in the next few decades remain very hard to predict. US requirements for strategic weapons seem equally murky.

New thinking for a new world?

Largely because the USA has viewed foreign policy in such simplistic terms for so long, it will have difficulty developing an explanation of international conflict that does not postulate a world-wide struggle between good (the USA and its friends) and evil (the Soviet Union and its satellites, clients or ideological allies.) Yet this challenge should be welcomed precisely because it could enable the USA to develop foreign policies more firmly grounded in reality. The old view of US–Soviet relations reflected a US passion for ideological simplicity and served the interests of some powerful institutions, but the policies it encouraged had major flaws. It assumed, most doubtfully, that the USSR intended both a conventional attack on Western Europe and a strategic nuclear attack on the United States as soon the balance of forces tipped in their favour. It assigned the ultimate responsibility for all Marxist-Leninist revolutionary movements to Moscow, rather than trying to understand the appeal of Marxist-Leninist revolutionary doctrines in many developing countries. It also led to the belief that the rest of the non-communist, industrialized world owed the USA a special debt for its leading role in the containment of communism.

The eclipse of the Soviet Union will initially create more confusion in foreign policy. In the midst of a conflict-ridden world, the USA must suddenly abandon the test according to which it has chosen to intervene in a wide variety of conflicts: the involvement of communists, and, by a logical extension, of the Soviet Union. Less than 10 years ago, President Reagan was still characterizing the Soviet Union as 'the focus of evil in the modern world', and high officials of his Administration blamed the USSR for conflicts as far-flung as the guerrilla war in El Salvador and the Syrian occupation of Lebanon. Changes in the foreign policy of the Soviet Union did not decrease US willingness to intervene in overseas conflicts, as the invasion of Panama and the Gulf War revealed in striking fashion, but the lack of a clear enemy has made the justification of such interventions more difficult. In the Gulf War, in which all the major local powers co-operated with the entire permanent membership of the UN Security Council to punish an aggressor, President Bush could easily speak of a 'new world order', but the meaning of that phrase will become much less clear in any crisis in which leading powers find themselves on opposite sides. The controversy over US post-war behaviour in the Gulf, including many attacks on President Bush for failure to support revolts against Saddam Hussein, suggests that there is no new consensus on the long-range goals of US foreign policy. Perhaps a new general rule should be established, or perhaps the wisdom will be found to analyse each crisis on its own merits, and base any decision to intervene simply on the limited, specific purpose which intervention might serve in that specific case.

The new international environment also poses some important institutional challenges to US foreign policy. The focus on East–West conflict, with the President of the United States identified as the 'leader of the Free World', increased interest in high-level diplomacy, summits and the climate of relations between the United States and the Soviet Union. The new environment opens up numerous opportunities for multilateral diplomacy, but such diplomacy is both more complex and more difficult to exploit politically than summitry. The European governments of the late 19th and early 20th centuries accomplished so much partly because they delegated authority to ambassadors so willingly. Occasionally foreign ministers or heads of government met at a congress to settle important issues, but many questions were settled by conferences of the ambassadors to one major European power, working together with the foreign minister of the host country. Since World War II, Washington in particular has been much less willing to delegate real authority to representatives in the field, and a long negotiation in a distant foreign capital can never achieve the same media prominence as a US–Soviet summit or a one- or two-week shuttle among various capitals by the Secretary of State. And as agreements include more and more parties, they will also involve more compromises, with fewer opportunities to present them as clear-cut victories for the United States. US ability to contribute to the new international environment will depend largely on an increased capacity to see diplomacy as something less than a simple struggle between good and evil.

The end of the cold war will not create a world without conflict, or lead rapidly to the world-wide triumph of Western democracy. It can open up new opportunities for broad-based co-operation to solve regional conflicts, as the Gulf War and the opening of Middle East peace talks have shown. It increases the need for a multilateral framework to assure minority rights in much of Europe and the former Soviet Union, in which the United States could perhaps be a peripheral player, or at least a helpful influence. But summits between US and Russian leaders, if they occur at all, will lose their special aura. The best way for Moscow and Washington to retain some special status is probably to try to keep arms control at the forefront of the international agenda, and to use their status as the world's most heavily armed powers to push for general reductions. But with respect to many issues, Washington and Moscow can expect other nations to emerge from the enormous shadows the superpowers have cast during the past 45 years. What is probably coming to an end in the last decade of the 20th century is not merely the Soviet bloc or the Leninist system in Russia, but the long era, originally identified by Tocqueville, in which the Russians and the Americans seemed 'marked out by the will of Heaven to sway the destinies of half the globe'.

Part III
Military power and international stability

8. Theatre forces in the Commonwealth of Independent States

Edward B. Atkeson

I. Introduction

The Soviet Union entered the final decade of the 20th century in a high state of flux. Changes seemed to be occurring at an ever increasing pace. The entire fabric of the dying empire was engulfed in processes which created profound dislocations of historic patterns in political, economic, social and military life. The phenomenon was of such scope as to threaten most observers with a bad case of cognitive overload. In such an environment, forecasts for the morrow seem difficult enough; forecasts for the close of the decade may seem to border on the foolhardy.

Nevertheless, policy makers of both East and West must deal with conditions as they are, not as they might wish them to be. Moreover, their plans for the future must be based upon some estimate of future conditions—the milieu in which they hope their policies will blossom. Accordingly, those concerned with international security matters cannot abstain from making forecasts, however difficult such tasks may seem at the moment.

This chapter attempts to look ahead to the close of the century and to shape suppositions regarding the nature and principal dimensions of the armed forces which may replace those currently deployed in the region of the former USSR. It examines the political–military environment as it may be perceived by the heirs of the Red Army and assesses the possible impact of a decade or more of political turmoil and *perestroika* on the armed forces.

There is no assurance at this writing that there will be a coherent set of theatre forces concerned with the protection of the Eurasian continent in the sense that Soviet forces have been in the past. Indeed, Dr Georgiy Arbatov, Director of the Moscow-based Institute of the USA and Canada, has ventured the opinion that, except for central control of strategic nuclear forces, there probably will not.[1] On the other hand, it seems reasonable that some of the smaller republics of the former union might find convenience or cause to co-operate with the Russian state in other types of military endeavour, and that some form of unified command structure would either endure or evolve.

With this background, the chapter identifies certain implications of the setting which may impact thinking regarding the force structure of the Common-

---

[1] Remarks by Georgiy Arbatov, Director of the Institute of USA and Canada, Russian Academy of Sciences, at the Center for Naval Analyses, Alexandria, Va., 21 Feb. 1992.

wealth of Independent States (CIS) and suggests alternative ways in which a co-operative or integrated effort may develop. Finally, it provides illustrative models of theatre force structure to illuminate three possible patterns which could emerge.

II. The political–military environment

Any assessment of the future political–military environment surrounding the CIS will be affected by the nature of the surviving regime or regimes. Further, certain aspects of regional security are likely to influence analytical judgements, regardless of the form of union (or lack of union) the CIS may take. Both of these factors are considered here.

Europe

The dissolution of the Warsaw Pact and the subsequent Soviet ratification of the German unification treaty[2] exemplify the asymmetry of the emerging Eastern and Western security regimes. Whereas the Warsaw Pact is dead, NATO lives on, albeit in a looser, less purposeful atmosphere, but crowned with success and pleased with its record. German unification has emerged as an important symbol of the strength and wisdom of the Western alliance.

Nevertheless, shadows remain. The spectre of nuclear conflict has not entirely departed the scene. The 1987 Treaty between the USA and the USSR on elimination of their intermediate- and shorter-range nuclear missiles (the INF Treaty) abolished theatre nuclear missiles with ranges over 500 km, and both Washington and Moscow have declared their intent to eliminate shorter-range systems in Europe. The USSR long called for the elimination of all nuclear weapons by the year 2000, but that objective was sceptically received in the West. Strong Western belief in the stabilizing influence of nuclear weapons has tended to cool enthusiasm for total nuclear disarmament. Moreover, there are signs that some analysts on the Russian side are having second thoughts about the matter, too.[3] In any event, the heirs to the Soviet Army and three of the four major Western powers are likely to continue to maintain nuclear weapons in Europe, or in its immediate vicinity, at the end of the decade. It should be noted, however, that Moscow was able to wring an important military benefit from the German unification treaty (besides the reduction of the Bundeswehr to 375 000 men) in the permanent German renunciation of nuclear arms.

Also on the positive side, from the CIS point of view, is the absence of major outstanding issues of contention between Bonn (or Berlin) and the 'Centre' in Moscow. The Oder–Neisse border appears to enjoy broad acceptance, and the

---

[2] Treaty on the Final Settlement with Respect to Germany, Moscow, 12 Sep. 1990.

[3] Remarks by Alexey Arbatov, Institute of USA and Canada, Russian Academy of Sciences, at a workshop on US–Soviet Co-operative Security, Carnegie Mellon University, Pittsburgh, Pa., 22 Apr. 1991.

FRG has agreed to build two million square meters of housing for military families returning to the CIS.[4] Assuming that the Russian Federation fulfils pledges to remove forces from German and Polish soil by 1994, security issues between the Federal Republic and the CIS in the year 2000 should be manageable. If, on the other hand, the troop presence were to drag on, the matter could become rather more awkward.

Of special significance to the political–military environment in Europe is the 1990 Treaty on Conventional Forces in Europe (CFE). The Treaty has never been popular within the CIS military, in part because it affects Commonwealth forces on their own territories while not affecting US forces on theirs, and in part because it limits tactical forces in Central Europe, where the Soviet Union enjoyed a traditional advantage, without affecting naval forces, a Western strength. Besides, most senior officers have considered it an imposition by the liberal Foreign Ministry, under Eduard Shevardnadze, for which they harboured little regard. The military demonstrated its dissatisfaction through such actions as reassigning a number of motorized rifle divisions to naval coastal defence duty (thus arguably placing them outside the Treaty limits) and transferring large quantities of weapons east of the Ural Mountains rather than destroying them. These problems raised questions about the ultimate fate of the Treaty; however, Soviet military leaders expressed some praise for the Treaty, pointing out that it permitted the USSR (now, presumably, the combined republics) to maintain 'the highest national arms levels' in Europe of the 22 signatories.[5]

Exactly how the Treaty provisions may play out is a matter of conjecture. The great dislocations which have occurred in the former empire since the attempted coup of 1991 have reduced consideration of CFE restrictions to low priority. While most authorities express support for the matter in principle, there is little machinery for implementation of the provisions and as yet no formal recognition of their legal application.[6]

As discussed elsewhere in this volume, the promise of a broadly based security regime for the European region is likely to provide appropriate organization and procedures for addressing security disputes. An institutionalized Conference on Security and Co-operation in Europe (CSCE) should be as suitable for discussion of major power differences as for those involving lesser powers. Further, the continued existence of NATO should provide Germany with confidence that it would not have to deal with major elements of the former Soviet Union alone, thus dampening any inclination on its part to look to its own resources in the military sphere for security assurance. This factor may serve to reassure the newly independent eastern republics as well.

[4] Moscow, TASS International Radio Service, 2 Jan. 1991, in Foreign Broadcast Information Service, *Daily Report–Soviet Union (FBIS-SOV)*, FBIS-SOV-91-002, 3 Jan. 1991, p. 49.
[5] For a summary of the Treaty, see International Institute of Strategic Studies, 'Documentation', *Survival*, Nov./Dec. 1990, pp. 562–63. For General Moyseyev's remarks, see Fisher, M., 'Deadlock eases on treaty cutting European forces', *Washington Post*, 13 Apr. 1991, p. 13.
[6] Twigg, J., 'The implications for Soviet defence and arms control policies of the devolution of power from the center to the republics', Unpublished conference report, Wolfson College, Oxford University, 10–11 Dec. 1991, p. 21.

By the year 2000 the Baltic Sea basin could become an international nuclear-free zone. This is the apparent desire of the littoral states. The USSR removed all known nuclear missile submarines from the waters, and both Presidents Bush and Gorbachev pledged the removal of tactical nuclear weapons from naval ships. If Russia is willing to subscribe to an adequate verification regime, the Western powers may be persuaded to agree. The principal difficulties in the negotiation of a treaty on the matter would seem to lie in the proximity of other Russian air and possibly nuclear-capable air defence missile forces in the former North-west Theatre of Military Operations (TVD).

Unfortunately, there is some likelihood that small power disputes in Europe, both domestic and international, will continue and perhaps grow in the current decade. The CSCE may be able to mitigate the strife in some cases, but there are numerous instances where political boundaries do not follow demographic patterns. Often, ethnic minorities perceive discriminatory treatment by majority groups and national sensitivities are rubbed raw. Problems of this sort can be quite destabilizing, at least within a local context, and have been known to expand beyond reasonable proportions. Russian identification with the causes of foreign Slavic peoples, for example, has led Moscow into trouble before.

The single greatest military threat to Russia and possibly to some of its sister republics in the year 2000 will likely continue to be posed by the US strategic nuclear striking forces. British and French nuclear forces are likely to remain, if somewhat reduced in size. The Chinese nuclear threat, on the other hand, may become more important as an independent factor. It may well develop both in size and sophistication over the years. An important point here, however, is that the former Soviet theatre forces are likely to have somewhat greater opportunity for countering Chinese strategic forces than those of the West. Western nuclear bases and operational areas tend to lie at greater ranges, and the higher level of sophistication of Western weapon systems is likely to continue to make them more difficult to attack or otherwise counter by theatre forces.

The eastern frontier

Other aspects of the Chinese threat are also noteworthy. An article in the journal of the Chinese Academy of Military Economics has called for large increases in funding for the People's Liberation Army in coming years. By the year 2000, increases could total 250 per cent (from $6.16 to $15.5 billion). Generally speaking, the forces are expected to be smaller, but more modern and professional.[7]

The Chinese have largely replaced their traditional Maoist concept of defensive 'peoples' war' with a strategic notion of 'rapid response', placing greater emphasis on offensive operations and on the projection of military power

---

[7] 'Chinese Army urges big buildup', *Atlanta Journal Constitution*, 13 Dec. 1990, p. D4. Chinese Finance Minister Wang Bingqian lent some credence to the report on 26 Mar. 1991, when he announced that military spending would rise another 12% in the current year, to about $6.25 billion. This is on top of a 15% increase in 1990. *New York Times International*, 27 Mar. 1991, p. A3.

beyond national borders. However, it does not appear at this juncture that the CIS is a prominent target of Chinese concern. Rather, while the Russian threat may be theoretically the most dangerous, local limited conflicts in the south, particularly around the Spratly Islands, are believed to be more likely.[8] Russo-Chinese relations have improved to the point that the Chinese have been probing possibilities of procurement of Russian fighter aircraft in return for economic assistance.[9] Before his expulsion in the wake of the attempted coup against President Gorbachev, former Minister of Defence Marshal Dmitri Yazov characterized relations between the USSR and China as 'normal', and he drew attention to the fact that Soviet infantry units on the border had been replaced with fixed machine-gun and artillery divisions which have no offensive capability.[10]

Some Russian writers have speculated beyond 'normalcy' to suggest resumption of military co-operation between the two powers. In March 1991 Rear Admiral Vladimir Z. Khuzhokov wrote that Gorbachev 'established the beginning of the [co-operative] process' during his 1989 visit to Beijing. Western analysts who suspect that Gorbachev may have signed a secret agreement with the Chinese were given encouragement in early 1991 when an unattributed editorial in *Pravda* commented that 'relations are only beginning to bear fruit . . . each of the two neighbouring peoples have sensed that they have a reliable secure rear'.[11]

It is possible, of course, before the end of the century, that the direction of Chinese strategic focus could shift back towards the north, as it has in the past. (Some observers may note that Russia has indicated that it does not plan to remove some nuclear missile systems from the Far East border as quickly as it does in Europe.)[12] If such a shift were to occur, the revised Beijing military doctrine might be perceived as more threatening by Russia, and fears could increase regarding the overall strategic situation.

Russian conflict with Japan is highly unlikely for many years. Japan is not a nuclear power, nor does it maintain forces of sufficient size or quality for aggressive action. On the other hand, it is an important economic and political power, and it enjoys the protection of the US nuclear umbrella. Moscow has had difficulty in normalizing relations with Japan, primarily because of a continuing territorial dispute over a number of islands. The problem is a difficult one because concession could open the Sea of Okhotsk to hostile (Western) submarine operations, and major concessions could be interpreted as admission of error since 1945. However the issue is resolved, unless there is a radical

[8] DuBois, J. V., 'New directions in Chinese strategy', *International Defense Review*, Nov. 1989, pp. 1483–88.
[9] WTOP radio news, Washington, DC, 10 a.m., 14 Mar. 1991.
[10] 'Yazov interviewed on Gulf, Pact, China', Moscow International Radio Service, 0100 GMT, 27 Feb. 1991(in Mandarin), in FBIS-SOV-91-041, 1 Mar. 1991, pp. 51–52.
[11] Foreign Systems Research Center, Science Applications International Corporation, 'Soviet and Eastern European notes', *Newsletter*, no. 8 (14 June 1991), p. 4.
[12] According to Japanese KYODO broadcast, 1450 GMT, 15 Oct. 1991, the Soviet Ambassador to China, Nikolay Solovyev, said that removal of Soviet nuclear arms from the Far East frontier would not occur until after they were removed in Europe. FBIS-SOV-91-201, 15 Oct. 1991, pp. 2–3.

change in Japan's attitude towards military affairs, Japan is not likely to loom as a particularly important factor in the shaping of theatre forces of the CIS in the time-frame under consideration here.

The southern front

Military planners concerned with the security of the southern borders of the CIS must consider that by the year 2000 both India and Pakistan could have substantial nuclear forces, including both surface-to-surface missiles (SSM) and aircraft with in-flight refuelling capability. While the Indian force is likely to be greater, there is no apparent reason why Moscow's traditionally warm relations with Delhi should change any time soon. Further, the Soviet withdrawal from Afghanistan has greatly diminished the likelihood of conflict with Pakistan; thus the subcontinent is not likely to figure prominently in CIS security calculations in the time-frame of concern.[13]

Iran and Iraq, on the other hand, are perennial sources of potential trouble in the Southern TVD. The Persian Gulf War has tended to redistribute the balance of power in the area, perhaps to the detriment of CIS security. The impact of overtures by Iran and Turkey for closer ties with Islamic republics will be carefully watched in Moscow and Kiev, and in some of the other capitals. In addition, the continued presence of US forces in the Persian Gulf region in the wake of the 1991 conflict is bound to be a focus of interest among Commonwealth security analysts.

III. The impact of *perestroika* on CIS theatre forces

The initial thrust of CIS military reform was developed during the final stages of the Soviet period in the late 1980s, in conjunction with the promulgation of the new, defensive doctrine for the Warsaw Pact. There was widespread recognition of existing systemic problems within the armed forces, and others developed as *glasnost* loosened the tongues and heightened the political aspirations of the people at home.

Traditional problems within the military included: hazing (*dedovshchina*) and other mistreatment of young conscripts, particularly of non-Russian minorities; insufficient incentives for good service or recognition for combat service in Afghanistan; low morale and discipline; inflexible training; meaningless political lectures; loose control over arms and other property; low pay; and inadequate housing for military families. The housing problem has been greatly exacerbated by the withdrawal of forces from the forward area in Europe and

---

[13] There are indications that Pakistan is seeking the nuclear-capable, M-11 SSM from China. The limited range of the weapon (290 km.) would limit its effectiveness against the former USSR. The range could be extended somewhat by reducing the payload. See Fialka, J. J., 'Pakistan seeks Chinese missile, US believes', *Wall Street Journal*, 5 Apr. 1991, p. 16; and Hull, A., 'The role of ballistic missiles in Third World defence strategies', *Jane's Intelligence Review*, Oct. 1991, p. 468.

their restationing in the Commonwealth. As of the end of February 1991, 180 000 officers and warrant officers were without housing.[14]

As the Army attempted to come to grips with these issues, much greater ones developed as part of the larger stresses on the overall society, particularly the emergence of national separatist sentiment. Desertion and conscription avoidance increased and media coverage of military affairs strung much of the military's dirty laundry out in public view. Draft dodging in late 1990 reached 79.2 per cent in the Baltic states and 90 per cent in Georgia. Nation-wide it was 21.2 per cent.[15] The spring of 1991 reflected further deterioration in most republics, but a return to full compliance with the law in three: Russia, Belarus and Azerbaijan.[16]

Mistreatment of ethnic minorities has tended to increase as tensions have risen around the country. In January 1990 the Main Military Procurator stated that every fifth crime in the armed forces, and possibly as many as 70 per cent of gross violations of discipline, were ethnically connected.[17] The number of suicides in the services rose to alarming proportions, variously reported at 25–50 per cent of all fatalities.[18] Military families stationed in separatist republics were subjected to much scorn and verbal abuse. Further, the necessity to employ regular troop units in the suppression of demonstrations and riots in many areas around the country placed additional psychological burdens on the Army.

In reaction to these developments some military personnel banded together to form a union, *Schit* (Shield) to protect their interests. The organization claimed 10 000 members, most of them secret.[19] Other servicemen wrote articles and ran for election to councils, including at the highest level, the Chamber of Deputies and the Supreme Soviet of the USSR. Within the latter two bodies, for the first time, special committees were established to oversee and to rule on military affairs. The result was the development of a discordant din, with voices from these organizations often clashing with that of the Ministry of Defence. To further confuse the matter, President Gorbachev weighed in, personally, with suggestions which seemed in most respects to favour and encourage the reformists. 'Perhaps the time has come', he said, 'to move toward a voluntary professional army'. He went on to remark that the it might be desirable to re-examine the basic structure of the armed forces, composed of the five traditional services. He also said that the Government was considering the creation of

[14] 'Deputy defence minister on Army, Navy Day', Moscow Central Television, 1st Program Network, 1046 GMT 23 Feb. 1991, interview with Army General Konstantin A. Kochetov, First Deputy Minister of Defence (in Russian), in FBIS-SOV-91-037, 25 Feb. 1991, p. 64.

[15] Kuznetsov, S., 'For whom the paratroopers are looking', *Selskaya Zhizn*, 12 Jan. 1991, p. 6, in FBIS-SOV-91-012,17 Jan. 1991, p. 54.

[16] Dick, C. J., *The Current State of the Soviet Military* (Soviet Studies Research Centre, Royal Military Academy (RMA): Sandhurst, UK, Dec. 1991), table 1.

[17] Borodin, N., 'From a demonstration to the Voyenkomat', *Soyuz*, 22–28 Jan. 1990, in Joint Publications Research Service–USSR Military Affairs (JPRS-UMA), JPRS-UMA-90-006, 20 Mar. 1990, p. 85.

[18] The 25% figure appeared in a Polish source: Pogrebenkov, V., 'Specially for *Polska Zbrojna*' (Poland), 24 Oct. 1990, p. 3, in FBIS-SOV-90-213, 2 Nov. 1990, p. 58. The 50% figure appeared in Kharlamor, A., 'Killed in peacetime', *Kuranty*, no. 6, reprinted in IAN press release, Moscow, 24 Apr. 1991, in FBIS-SOV-91-080, 25 Apr. 1991, p. 47.

[19] Klebnikov, P., 'The soldier's shield', *Forbes*, 29 Oct. 1990, p. 84.

separate military units for the republics, but he seemed ambivalent on this. He made it clear that he disapproved of the creation of fully independent territorial armies which might not be responsive—and which might even constitute a threat—to the central government.[20]

While many issues surfaced in the debate, three seemed dominant: (a) abolition of conscription in favour of a volunteer armed force; (b) limitations on the mandatory assignment of military personnel outside their home republics ('extra-territoriality'); and (c) reductions in the size of the forces. Under the leadership of Marshal Yazov the Ministry of Defence (MOD) was generally opposed to the first two proposals and considerably more conservative than most other interested groups and agencies with respect to the third.

Both Presidents Gorbachev and Yeltsin expressed the view that the internal and external threats which they envisaged in the future could be dealt with by far more modest forces than had traditionally been maintained in the structure. Yeltsin indicated a preference for a national military establishment of about 1.5 million men, substantially less than the 2.5 million suggested by the Defence Ministry in Marshal Yazov's time.[21] How realistic either of these figures might be depends to some extent upon which forces are included. In the wake of the attempted coup of 19–21 August 1991, the 240 000 man border guard and possibly as many as 35 000 other KGB troops were transferred to MOD control. In addition, an airborne division and two Ground Forces divisions, which had been 'chopped' to KGB control, apparently for use in just such operations as the coup, were returned to the MOD.[22] On the other hand, the ministry sought with varying degrees of success to unload unwanted, non-combatant organizations such as construction and railway troops and, indeed, the border guard. Nevertheless, the great social and political changes of more recent months are likely to have a more definitive impact in the longer term. The nature of the evolving political structure and the internal and intra-republic pressures on the various components of the CIS are bound to dominate as matters unfold.

More cogent than the size of the forces has been the question of their sub–ordination. President Yeltsin's Deputy Defence Minister, former Army major, Vladimir Lopatin, began pressing for a dual-command structure between the central government and the republics in 1989. He feared then that if some such move were not made the republics would establish their own armies—as, indeed, a number have chosen to do. Yeltsin threw his weight behind the Lopatin plan whereby the nation's general-purpose troops would be grouped in two tiers. The first tier would be composed of troops, largely based in Russia and maintained in a high state of readiness, comparable to the international rapid-reaction force now under development by NATO. The second tier would

[20] Keller, B., 'Gorbachev vows to reorganize military', *New York Times International*, 18 Aug. 1990.

[21] 'Soviet turmoil: the Boris and Mikhail show', *New York Times*, 7 Sep. 1991, p. 6.

[22] *Komsomolkaya Pravda*, 27 Aug. 1991, p. 3, in FBIS-SOV-91-166, 27 Aug. 1991, p. 60.

be made up of territorial defence troops under the control of the interior ministries of the constituent republics.[23]

However responsive the proposal might have been to some problems, it was
strongly opposed by the former Chief of the General Staff, General Vladimir
Lobov. The interesting point was the novelty of the general's argument. Far
from opposing the plan, as his more conservative predecessors might have
done, on grounds of devolution of power from the centre, he attacked it for a
very practical reason. With some degree of prescience, he said: 'They [the
troops] can only be united! . . . I will say this bluntly: the more individual
armed forces there are, the more real the danger of confrontation between the
republics. Imagine for just a second if Azerbaijan and Armenia had their own
armies today . . .'.[24]

The Defence Ministry information chief, Lieutenant General Valeriy
Manilov, told Moscow Radio on 20 September 1991, that the Soviet Defence
Ministry envisaged only small, lightly armed guard units operating under the
direct control of the republic defence ministries. These troops, which would
protect important facilities and Government officials, might not number more
than 5000 in each republic.[25]

Subsequent announcements from republican sources indicated that a number
of republics expected to maintain substantially larger indigenous formations. In
October 1991, Russian Vice President Alexander V. Rutskoi announced that a
national guard for that the Russian Federation would be raised over a period of
years to a strength of 66 000.[26] In Ukraine, where leaders initially spoke of an
army of 450 000 troops, more sober reflection brought the figures down into the
200 000–250 000 range.[27] Moldova announced plans for a professional force of
12 000–15 000 men, and Belarus is expected to seek a home army of about
90 000 troops.[28]

Whatever the subordination of the troops, the size of the force, or forces, is
likely to be a constraining factor on technical sophistication. This point has
been brought out by analysts arguing that smaller, more technically skilled military forces would be more effective than would the continuation of large, mass
armies. Less likely a limiting factor, in view of the great economic dislocations
in the republics, but nevertheless important, is the availability of readily trainable talent. A 1989 study by Dr Murray Feshbach of Georgetown University
indicated that the shift in the proportion of draft age males (18–21 years) in the
former Soviet Union coming from the seven republics of Transcaucasus and
Central Asia in the last decade jumped from 28 per cent to 37 per cent (a

[23] Adams, P., 'Republics' military birth may entail common security', *Defense News*, 2 Sep. 1991, p. 14.

[24] *Pravda*, 9 Sep. 1991, pp. 1–2, in FBIS-SOV-91-174, 9 Sep. 1991, p. 42.

[25] Moscow Radio, 0000 GMT, 20 Sep. 1991, in FBIS-SOV-91-184, 23 Sep. 1991, p. 48.

[26] Buldkov, V. and Morozov, R., interview with Alexander V. Rutskoi, *Argumenti i Fakti*, no. 40 (Oct. 1991), p. 2.

[27] Kramer, M., 'Army won't be a loose cannon', *Los Angeles Times*, 4 Dec. 1991, p. B5; and 'Ukraine outlines new doctrine', *Jane's Defence Weekly*, 15 Feb. 1992.

[28] Atlantic Council of the United States, 'Russia and the Commonwealth states: changes in security policies, 11 Nov. 1991–24 Jan. 1992', *Bulletin*, vol. 3, no. 1 (24 Jan. 1992).

development which had not previously been expected before the year 2000).[29] More recent data reflect an increase in the proportion of recruits from the Central Asian states alone in 1991 to 40 per cent of all inductees.[30] While fertility trends throughout the CIS are currently on the increase, the number of women of child-bearing age in the Slavic areas is expected to drop precipitously in the 1990s as a result of decreases in fertility rates in those areas in the early 1970s.

Some 90 per cent of rural youths from Central Asia either speak no Russian or speak it very poorly.[31] In the past these lads could be assigned to non-technical tasks in the combat arms or to labour units in the construction and railway branches. If the CIS were to adopt the Lopatin plan, or something like it, the burden of training sufficient soldiers to fill the increasing number of complicated and sensitive duties could become more taxing.

As long as conscription remains, the matter will probably be affected by a law exempting or deferring the call-up of university students for service. According to Viktor A. Sadovnich, First Vice Chancellor of Lomonosov Moscow State University, hundreds of thousands of students have been affected since 1989 when the law was first promulgated.[32] The nationalities most keenly affected have been those with the highest proportion of secondary school education and youths with the greatest potential skills for handling sophisticated weaponry. Clearly, these are the Slavs.

On the other hand, the abandonment by the CIS of all efforts to maintain any sort of centralized theatre force may produce even more dramatic results. Depending upon the willingness of the Slavs to serve, the forces of Belarus, Russia and Ukraine could emerge as not only larger, but also more competent than those of the other republics.

The Interior Ministry (MVD) was first to move towards a limited experiment with 'contract' recruits. Soldiers on contract receive a small wage while they serve for an additional year beyond their obligated period. The Navy attempted to conduct a similar programme on an experimental basis in 1991, but the necessary funds were not approved.[33] Prior to the collapse of the central regime, a Defence Ministry reform proposal provided that after 1996, conscripts might have three choices: (*a*) 18 months normal service, as opposed to the current two years; (*b*) 2–3 years contract service; or (*c*) longer 'alternative' service in construction or other support organizations.[34] Regarding home stationing, in accordance with a decision of mid-1990, the residual Defence Ministry might

[29] Feshbach, M., 'Demographic trends in the Soviet Union: serious implications for the Soviet military', *NATO Review*, Oct. 1989, pp. 11–12.

[30] 'Army without a country, countries without an army', *The Economist*, 25 Jan. 1992, p. 44.

[31] Feshbach (note 29).

[32] 'The army reduction and the students', *Literaturnaya Gazeta*, 5 Apr. 1989, p. 13, in FBIS-SOV-89-072,17 Apr. 1989, p. 107.

[33] Foye, S., 'The Gulf war and the Soviet defense debate', Radio Free Europe/Radio Liberty Research Institute, *Report on the USSR*, 15 Mar. 1991, p. 5.

[34] Zaloga, S. J., 'Soviets draft reform plan', *Armed Forces Journal International*, Feb. 1991, p. 16.

assign 20–25 per cent of troops to posts within their home republics.[35] In practice, the proportion appears to be expanding.

Defence costs are expected to increase from their current levels because of the higher anticipated cost of contract personnel, requirements for more sophisticated equipment, the cost of destruction of old and treaty-limited equipment and decontrol of the cost of raw material and research and development. Even by the mid-1990s, artillery is expected to increase in cost by 40 per cent, tanks by 50 per cent and aircraft by 60–70 per cent. Average defence expenditures in mid-decade may approach 200 per cent of current levels.[36] Moreover, as Russia has gained better understanding of the cost of its inefficient defence plants and programmes, it has had to adjust defence budget figures to better reflect true costs. Shortly before the abolition of the union, the chief of the Gosplan Research Economics Institute announced that the official 78 billion rouble defence budget for 1990 could be barely more than half of the real budget due to omission of items carried elsewhere in national accounts and to hidden subsidies.[37] Conceivably, defence budget figures could double again—or quadruple—by the end of the decade as further accounting discrepancies emerge.

With respect to the career officer corps, the impact of *perestroika* could take a different form. While pay and standards of living are important, a US visitor to the V. I. Lenin Military Political Academy in Moscow in 1990 came away with an overriding impression of an officer corps eagerly seeking to establish a more professional identity. He reported that the officers seemed not only to understand the notion of depoliticizing their profession, but also to welcome it. The point may be particularly telling, coming from political officers.[38]

IV. Development of CIS operational thinking in the 1990s

Most operational thinking in the CIS is based upon assumptions of the survival of a coherent, dominantly Russian, political entity with responsibility for the defence of a Eurasian heartland. While it was developed with the 1985 borders of the USSR in mind, the concept appears generally applicable to a substantially smaller state, or coalition of states, including one consisting exclusively of the Russian Federation.

At the highest levels of theatre command, the Soviet Union and its CIS successors have professed a commitment to the avoidance of war. The Chernobyl disaster, it was argued, demonstrated the danger of widespread damage to an area, even if only conventional arms are employed. The large number of nuclear power plants now in use in Europe was noted with particular mention of

---

[35] Kulikov, V., 'Who profits by making the army fall out with the people?', *Partiynaya zhizn*, no. 13 (July 1990), pp. 13–15, in FBIS-SOV-90-144A, 26 July 1990, p. 10.

[36] Zaloga (note 34), p. 16.

[37] 'Red hot news', *Armed Forces Journal International*, June 1991, p. 28.

[38] Moskos, C., 'Inside a Soviet war college', *Army Times*, 5 Mar. 1990, p. 12.

how the plants might be damaged in a conflict.[39] However, the extent to which this argument affects CIS strategic and operational thinking is not clear.

Beyond this, Russian planners foresee retention of a strategic (theatre) capability for defence. Ostensibly, the defence would be sufficient to afford the political leadership the opportunity to terminate any crisis before it erupted into a major conflict.[40] Failing that, theatre forces would be prepared to mount a counter-offensive of decisive proportions. They anticipate the use of long-range fire as a 'stabilizing factor' on the battlefield to facilitate manoeuvre. The manoeuvre, they suggest, may be accomplished as much by fire as by physical movement of troops.

The timing of the counter-offensive has been a matter of extensive debate. Early in the development of the concept, some writers cited the Battles of Stalingrad and Kursk as models, in which counter-offensive forces were restrained until a critical juncture in the action before they were committed. Then some authors indicated an interest in a reduction in the planned reaction time. In January 1991, Major General (ret.) Ivan N. Vorobyev, a prominent theoretician, condemned as 'untenable' the notion that 'at the outset of aggression, the main form of military doctrine will be defence'. Much better, he argued, would be something closer to 'an adequate reaction'—apparently a concept not far removed from the Western notion of flexible response.[41]

Vorobyev is so well known that it is difficult to imagine that his views are not representative of others far more senior and still in positions of importance on the General Staff. His article may well have been a stalking horse for a significant pocket of disgruntled generals who preferred not to weigh in personally on the issue. Further, the article may have been intended to open the entire matter of defensive doctrine for re-examination and debate, rather than simply to register a dissenting opinion.

A hint that there was more to be heard was given by retired Marshal of Armoured Troops Oleg A. Losik in a long article in *Krasnaya Zvezda* two months later: 'we must not perceive our rejection of the first use of military operations as consenting in advance to giving the initiative to the other side', he wrote. Further, arguing that the defensive doctrine should not impinge too sharply upon the design of tactical units, he said, 'the combat composition of our combined arms formations (apparently including army and front level) must also be universal, i.e. suitable for both defensive and offensive operations'.[42] Clearly the marshal thought that the military leadership should take a very broad view of the 'defensive' doctrine.

The other major question regarding Soviet thinking about a counter-offensive—the depth to which it might have been pursued—similarly remains

[39] From private discussions by the author with Soviet general officers in Moscow on 23–24 Jan. 1989.

[40] Interview with Marshal of the Soviet Union Sergey F. Akhromeyev, 'Our military doctrine', *Agitator Armii I Flota*, no. 24 (1989), in FBIS-SOV-90-021, 31 Jan. 1990, p. 115.

[41] Vorobyev, I., *Krasnaya Zvezda*, 26 Jan. 1991, in Foreign Systems Research Center, Science Applications International Corporation, *Soviet and Eastern European Notes*, 21 Feb. 1991, p. 1.

[42] Losik, O., 'Military reform: polemical notes—where the limits of reasonable sufficiency are', *Kraznaya Zvezda*, 5 Mar. 1991, pp. 1–2, in FBIS-SOV-91-045, 7 Mar. 1991, pp. 57–58.

an open question. On 1 January 1990 General Mikhail Moiseyev, then Chief of the General Staff, wrote: 'With respect to subsequent operations of the USSR Armed Forces, including on the aggressor's territory after repulsing his invasion, everything will depend on the scale and direction of aggression, the nature of military operations, and the means and methods of warfare being used'.[43] This seemed remarkably similar to the writings of some Soviet military thinkers of a decade or more ago. Many of them had in mind an offensive which would carry Soviet banners to the English Channel.

Up to the time of the attempted coup in August 1991, it appeared that a strong current for revision of the doctrine might be developing. Not surprisingly this trend was viewed in the West with some concern. The subsequent expulsion of Marshal Yazov and General Moiseyev in the wake of the coup, however, appears to have cleared the air, and the doctrine continues to have currency. If anything, the trend since August 1991 seems to be in the opposite direction. In late October 1991, Army General Konstantin I. Kobets, chairman of the State Council committee on military reform, commented: 'our military doctrine must change. I think it will be aimed at preventing wars on any scale. That is what I would provisionally call it: "a doctrine for the prevention of wars"'.[44]

Even before the adoption of a defensive military doctrine, Soviet writers on tactical and operational matters began to express a view of a 'levelling', or rough equality of offensive and defensive operations under the impact of new high-technology weaponry. Whereas offensive operations had been traditionally viewed as the principal means for gaining the initiative and for achieving decisive results, some writers ventured the idea that a transformation was in the offing. With long-range reconnaissance and strike systems, they argued, it might soon be possible for units on the defence to reach out and engage the opponent while he was still on the approach march. Further, they wrote, rather than having to manoeuvre to engage the enemy, the defender might be able to remain in a well-prepared and well-concealed position, engaging the attacker by fire. The thrust of these writings would seem to facilitate the development of a new operational art in accordance with the defensive doctrine.[45]

In 1987 the Soviet Union issued a new tactical manual, *Taktika*, providing a reasonably coherent picture of future battle as the USSR imagined it.[46] According to this document, the strategic (theatre) objectives in the initial period of war would be to inflict severe losses on the enemy, to halt his advance and to create conditions necessary for a counter-offensive.

---

[43] Moiseyev, M., *Military Herald*, 1 Jan. 1990.

[44] *Izvestia*, Union edn, 21 Oct. 1991, p. 2, in FBIS-SOV-91-204, 22 Oct. 1991, p. 44.

[45] For example, see Koziej, S., 'Anticipated directions for change in tactics of ground troops', *Ground Forces Review* (Poland), Sep. 1986, p. 4, cited in Petersen P. A. and Trulac, III, N., *A New Soviet Military Doctrine: Origins and Implications*, document C68 (Soviet Studies Research Centre, RMA: Sandhurst, UK, summer 1988), p. 20.

[46] Reznichenko, V. G., *Taktika* (Moscow: Voyenizdat, 1987). For an excellent analysis of this manual, see Grau, L. W., 'Soviet nonlinear combat in future conflict', *Military Review*, Dec. 1990, pp. 18–28.

The action at lower levels, said the manual, would incorporate high-tempo, high-intensity operations over large areas and in new realms (to include space). Tactical operations, it said, would be characterized by fragmented (*ochagovyy*) combat—battle undertaken by units with open flanks and discontinuous lines. The concepts appear compatible with others familiar to Western observers. Nuclear operations would be avoided. Instead, new conventional weapon systems with high accuracy and lethality would have the same practical military effect as might have been expected from nuclear weapons in the past.[47]

The authors of the manual described small units of brigade, regiment and independent battalion size fighting separate meeting engagements, using speed, hasty obstacles (such as scatter mines) and long-range fires to cover their flanks. The units would be composed of versatile, combined arms teams, rather than troops of a single branch, in order to ensure a maximum range of possible operations. A particularly novel concept suggested by the writers was the employment of infantry fighting vehicles, separate from their associated rifle squads, in teams referred to as *bronegruppa*. These organizations would constitute light armoured groups which might be directed along separate axes of operations. However, it was not expected that the vehicles would normally be used against enemy tanks because of their vulnerability to high-velocity gunfire. It would appear that the new 20 ton BMP-3 infantry fighting vehicle, with its heavy armament (100-mm gun, 30-mm coaxial gun and AT-10 guided missile) and advanced fire-control equipment, was designed with just such missions in mind.[48]

It is apparent that the thinking of the former Chief of the General Staff, Marshal Nikolai V. Ogarkov, continued to have a grip on Soviet military art. Especially notable is the retention of his ideas regarding high-technology reconnaissance strike complexes (RUK). The marshal conceived these groupings as a principal way of harnessing emerging technologies having to do with real-time surveillance reporting systems; rapid data-handling capabilities; smart, precision-guided missiles; and conventional warheads of increased lethality.[49] The demonstration of US progress in these fields in connection with Operation Desert Storm undoubtedly spurred Soviet interest. The USSR also discussed a shorter-range, tactical version of the RUK concept, dubbed 'reconnaissance fire complex (ROK)', incorporating the fires of tube artillery. Both systems have as a principal objective the timely location and destruction of like systems on the other side.[50]

[47] For example, see Atkeson, E. B., *Soviet Theater Forces at the Crossroads*, Land Warfare Paper no. 1 (Institute of Land Warfare, Association of the US Army: Arlington, Va., 1989), pp. 7–9.

[48] 'Red hot news', *Armed Forces Journal International*, May 1991, p. 18. Also see Szulz, T., 'Infantry fighting vehicle 3', *Zolnierz Polskiv* (Poland), 2 Sep. 1990, p. 15, document no. 00468, trans. (Soviet Studies Research Centre, RMA: Sandhurst, UK, 1990).

[49] For a discussion of Marshal Ogarkov's operational concepts, see Atkeson, E. B., 'World War III, Soviet style', *The Final Argument of Kings: Reflections on the Art of War* (HERO Books: Fairfax, Va., 1988), pp. 183–89.

[50] Reznichenko (note 46), p. 24, cited in Grau, L. W., 'Soviet nonlinear combat in future conflict', *Military Review*, Dec. 1990, p. 23.

In the defence, the USSR foresaw a shift of emphasis in its tactics from a focus on terrain to a focus on weapon systems. The objective of such systems was described as the development of a capability to reach out and engage advancing enemy forces early in the evolution of the campaign. This was envisaged as enhancing the role of conventional artillery. Traditional normative-based fire techniques may become less important as longer-range, precision projectiles are developed. Multiple-rocket launchers are expected to be used for delivery of fuel-air mixture weapons, scatterable mines and anti-tank guided missiles.

The USSR entertained a lively debate regarding the viability of armour-heavy forces. The chief of the Tank Department of the Malinovskiy Military Academy of Tank Troops remarked in an interview with the editors of the military journal, *Voyennyy Vestnik*, that strong 'anti-tank' sentiments had arisen among his colleagues in the wake of the 1973 Arab–Israeli War when, he said, both sides 'lost about 30 per cent of their tank inventory'. He described the experts, as 'stunned', at least for a time, apparently until they could marshal their thoughts and counter-arguments. The issue came up again, he went on, after the Israeli invasion of Lebanon in 1982, but again was argued down. The department chief explained the Soviet attitude with these words: 'a thorough analysis of the situation at hand and of the forecasts of [tank] development in the foreseeable future leads to the opinion that there are not yet any alternatives to tanks. . . . there is no other weapon in the entire ground forces weapon inventory that is capable of performing such a broad range of combat missions under difficult conditions'.[51]

The interviewee, however, faulted Soviet tank designers for pursuing a number of different models in the development of the second post-World War II generation of tanks (the T-64, the T-72 and the T-80). He forecast that future Soviet tanks would have much higher levels of standardization, saying, 'We cannot allow what happened with the second generation of tanks to be repeated'.[52]

In mid-1991, Soviet CFE Treaty negotiators released an unprecedented quantity of data regarding the combat effectiveness of Soviet and Western military equipment and units. Included with the data were references to a new type of combined arms organization designed for northern and southern frontier areas. The new units would be smaller than equivalent units in the central area and less heavily equipped. While 'southern' units would be somewhat more powerful than 'northern' units, neither type would have much more combat potential than half of that of a regular motorized rifle division.[53]

On 17 October 1991, *Krasnaya Zvezda* disclosed that the Soviet Ground Forces (soon to be redesignated Ground Defence Troops) would switch from

[51] Safonov, B. S., 'The tank remains in service', interview, *Voyennyy Vestnik*, Dec. 1989, pp. 21–24; trans. in *Military Technology*, Soviet Press Selected Translations (US Air Force Intelligence Agency: Washington, DC, 1990), p. 63.

[52] Safonov (note 51).

[53] Zaloga, S., 'Soviets denigrate their own capabilities', *Armed Forces Journal International*, July 1991, pp. 18–20.

their traditional organization based on field armies to a new one based on corps and combined arms brigades. Whether the brigades, with strengths of 2500 to 3000 men, equate to the northern and southern units previously mentioned is not completely clear.[54]

Apparently behind this report was an initiative of the Army Reform Commission of the General Staff proposing the transformation of the Army into a much smaller, all-volunteer force with capabilities for only very specialized operations beyond the borders of the CIS. Under the proposal, theatre forces would be organized into two regional commands, 'East' for Asia, and 'West' for Europe. A third command, composed of two corps-size elements, would form a rapid-reaction force under central control. The third force would have organic airlift for deployment on international missions.[55]

Reportedly, the western command would have three corps, including a rapid-reaction corps for regional employment. There would be no front level command. Instead, senior echelons would be tailored for compatibility with NATO, presumably in consultation with NATO officials. The eastern and western commands would total about 1.2 million troops, while the size of the rapid-reaction force has not been disclosed, and may not have yet been determined. National participation in the organization, if approved, would be expected from Belarus, Kazakhstan, Russia and Ukraine, with each also providing a number of local brigades for support. Kazakhstan and Ukraine would each provide three brigades; another two or three Russian brigades would be stationed in the Far East. Belarus' contribution is not clear.

The theatre forces structure would be directed by a military–political leadership composed of representatives of the four republics involved. Major inter-republic staff sections supervising the forces would deal with operations, reconnaissance, and recruitment and reserve affairs. These elements would report to the Chief of the General Staff who would be appointed for a two-year term. Exactly how the three staff elements might relate to other divisions of the General Staff has yet to be clarified.

Also requiring some explanation is the larger question of how the modest force structure described might exceed one million men. Composed of units of no more than brigade size, the corps would be unlikely to contain more than 50 000 troops each. Hence, the three-corps structure for the western command might not account for more than 150 000 men. The explanation may lie in the nature of the responsibilities envisaged for the regional commanders. If they were to have administrative jurisdiction over all theatre elements—ground, air and air defence, plus logistics and training—the figures might converge. If this were the case, it would seem unlikely that the regional command headquarters would be able to deal with much in the way of operational responsibilities, considering the heavy administrative load.

[54] *Kraznaya Zvezda*, 1st edn, 17 Oct. 1991, p. 3, in FBIS-SOV-91-202, 18 Oct. 1991, p. 34.
[55] Plugge, M., 'Soviet armed forces plan operations alongside NATO', *International Defense Review*, Oct. 1991, p. 1316.

This may indicate that the Army Reform Commission envisages a substantially different type of theatre force than has been the norm in the past. Instead of a huge armed juggernaut under the operational control of offensively oriented 'strategic directions' or regional high commands, the proposal seems to call for a modest posture under the administration of headquarters unlikely to be prepared to go anywhere. With no front level of command, the General Staff would be obliged to direct the operations of units which Russia has traditionally considered to be of little more than tactical significance. In this light, the concept of compatibility with NATO makes a great deal more sense.

In effect, the Commission appears to be proposing a posture for the forces for a deal with NATO under which the international command system might exercise control, presumably in return for the security inherent in membership in or association with the alliance. The concept is revolutionary, to say the least, but then so is almost everything else going on in the former USSR. The overall picture which emerges is one of a manageable defence structure compatible with both a defensive doctrine and with the share of resources likely to be available on a sustained basis. It also appears operationally compatible with the lone surviving military alliance structure offering its constituency a high degree of security in turbulent times.

The NATO connection, of course, must remain conjectural for some period of time. As much as the West may desire to encourage CIS movement along the path it seems to favour at the moment, it is quite unlikely that NATO would wish to extend its responsibilities into the vast Eurasian land mass. Certainly there would be little enthusiasm for undertaking any commitment as exotic as a guarantee of the Sino-Russian or Russo-Japanese frontiers.

Nevertheless, it may be concluded that the Commission did its work well. The burden now lies with the political and military leadership to recognize the tool it has for correcting the enormous historical imbalance between forces and resources inherited from the Soviet era and to make the changes prescribed.

In any event, whatever success Russia and its former countrymen may have in building an inter-republican army to survive the decade, it is bound to be far smaller and better tailored for dealing with a far different external milieu than could have been imagined before. Whatever the organizational path, the transition will take time to implement. Many decisions regarding training, equipment, combat service support and the whole breadth of implementation within the overall structure remain to be addressed. How realistic it is to expect complete realignment of the forces by the end of the decade is a significant question considering the great trials through which the CIS has yet to progress.

As noted above, there are indications that nuclear doctrine is being re-examined. At least some analysts are beginning to see a new political–military utility for nuclear weapons, principally as a deterrent against hostile powers seeking to take advantage of current dysfunctions in the former USSR.[56] While it is not apparent how widespread the thinking may be, the development cannot

---

[56] Arbatov (note 3).

be ignored because of the ramifications of a CIS reversion to reliance on nuclear weapons, following the Soviet path of the 1950s and 1960s.

Reportedly, there are two important schools of thought on the matter. One assumes that the weapons will never be used and virtually ignores their existence in its analysis of future conflict. The other holds that the weapons are a continuing reality and must be factored into all military calculations of relative power and operational practices. The latter group allegedly has recently enjoyed a measure of prominence as a result of the adoption of defensive doctrine. For the strategic defence, this group has argued, nuclear weapons have a special utility for deterrence and, in the final analysis, for defence—witness, for example, the posture and attitude of NATO virtually since its inception. For the offence, on the other hand, the weapons represent an incalculable factor, upsetting rational assessment of likely battle outcomes and therefore rendering them unattractive tools for aggression. These truths, the adherents contend, are likely to make CIS theatre forces, in their defensive posture, more reliant on nuclear weapons than was the case in the past.[57]

The notion appears to be somewhat immature at present. There is no indication, for example, that the CIS has any intention of altering its well-defined policy of no-first-use of nuclear weapons. Nevertheless, it suggests the possibility of a future quite different from recent years in which many aspects of Western security attitudes towards the weapons might be adopted by Moscow.

The future suggested would be one in which the number of nuclear weapons might be substantially smaller than at present and perhaps deployed well to the rear of the western frontier—perhaps beyond the Urals. There would be no concept for offensive use, but long-range delivery systems might be employed to ensure that the centre of destruction was not located on the soil of the former Soviet Union. These would include aircraft delivered air-to-surface systems of about 400-km range. Targeting would be highly selective, focusing on enemy command and control centres, nuclear delivery means and some key transportation centres.

V. The impact of the Persian Gulf War on military thinking in the CIS

As in the West, but perhaps even more keenly because of its view of war as a historically based science, the USSR regularly studied armed conflicts for clues about the future. The 1991 Persian Gulf War was no exception. Soviet staffs carefully dissected the actions of both sides, even while some of their spokes-

---

[57] Arbatov (note 3). A slightly different description of new thinking in the CIS about nuclear weapons was given by Dr Andrey A. Kokoshin at the Center for Naval Analysis in Dec. 1991. He wrote, 'some Soviet experts have reconsidered the role of nuclear weapons in ensuring USSR security. These experts feel that nuclear weapons will become more important because they are relatively cheap and could ensure a rather comprehensive defense. Many Soviet experts, therefore, are very interested in French military doctrine'. See Kokoshin, A. A., *The Evolving International Security System: A View from Moscow*, CNA Occasional Paper (Center for Naval Analysis: Alexandria, Va., Dec. 1991), p. 21.

men attempted to minimize the impact of unfavourable reflections on Soviet equipment and procedures.

Foremost among conclusions developed by the Soviet staffs was a recognition of the major contributions of high-technology weaponry, particularly that employed by aerial attack and air defence forces, in the form of long-range missile and anti-missile systems. In a February 1991 interview, General Moiseyev, Chief of the General Staff, remarked, 'The Persian Gulf has to all intents and purposes, become a kind of testing ground for state-of-the-art technology and weapons which are or will become standard equipment for NATO's combined arms forces in the near future'.[58]

Defence Minister Marshal Dmitri Yazov agreed. He revealed that the Soviet military leadership had internalized observations of the air campaign when he remarked that a thorough review of Soviet air defences had been undertaken as a result.[59]

In addition, other observers stressed a newly perceived imbalance of power between East and West resulting from the war. In May 1991, Major M. Pogorelyy, writing in the military paper, *Krasnaya Zvezda*, reflected a growing concern among conservatives for the strategic advantage which the victory may have afforded the USA. He wrote:

jingoistic attitudes spawned by the victory are on the rise in America, whereas, on the other hand, the brakes of the Vietnam syndrome, which to a considerable degree restrained the United States from becoming involved in large-scale military actions, are gone. . . . the Pentagon is concerned with . . . setting up weapons and combat *matériel* depots for at a minimum, one division of its ground forces on the territory of Saudi Arabia, an airbase for one or two aviation wings, and other installations for the deployment of American troops. [60]

General Lobov, General Moiseyev's successor, echoed concerns of this sort when he observed that the presence of allied troops in the Middle East created a 'single arc' of NATO-associated forces through Turkey to the Persian Gulf, sharply altering the strategic balance in the region.[61]

In May 1991 Lieutenant General Sergey A. Bogdanov, Chief of the USSR Armed Forces Research Centre, provided a glimpse of some of the impressions within his organization. The first was that the coalition forces had attained operational–tactical surprise by the use of 'disinformation' (apparently referring to electronic jamming and deception techniques) in connection with the offensive air operation. This, he said, paralysed the Iraqi troop and weapon control systems. His second point was the importance of coalition space-based reconnaissance, communications and navigation systems. The Iraqi lack of countermeasures in this area, he said, enabled the coalition to use these assets under

[58] Thurman, M. R., Speech to the annual meeting of the Army and Air Force Mutual Aid Association, Ft Myer, Va., 9 Apr. 1991.

[59] Radio Free Europe/Radio Liberty, *Daily Analyses*, 1 Mar. 1991.

[60] Pogorelyy, M., 'The world today: problems and judgements', *Krasnaya Zvezda*, 31 May 1991, 1st edn, p. 3, in FBIS-SOV-91-109, 6 June 1991, p. 32.

[61] Dahlburg, J.-T., 'Soviets see power shift in Gulf area', *Los Angeles Times*, 31 May 1991, p. 1.

'testbed' (ideal, laboratory) conditions. Third, he said, coalition ground forces determined the ultimate victory. While future localized conflicts in separate theatres of military operations will be prosecuted using non-standard techniques and modern aircraft will enjoy great manoeuvrability and long-range strike capabilities, the services of all branches of the armed forces will be important.

Stealth technology received favourable comments by the general, as did high-accuracy aircraft weapons, air transport and army aircraft. In his view no single element was of much greater importance than the others. Noting that many Iraqi ground forces offered little resistance to the ground assault, the general praised the performance of the professional servicemen on the other side. He tempered his remarks, however, with the comment that 'the results of that war do not contain any arguments in favor of our army's full switch to professional manning'.[62]

A number of Soviet writers raised questions about the quality of Soviet equipment and the real feasibility of the new defensive doctrine. These points were seized upon by both liberal reformers and conservative groups to bolster arguments against 'wasteful spending on large, obsolete forces', on the one hand, and in favour of greater overall defence investment, on the other.

An extremist view was presented by Major General Vladimir I. Slipchenko at the National Defense University in Washington, DC, in March 1991. General Slipchenko argued that warfare has shifted from a reliance on ground forces to a reliance on air-delivered weapons. In his view the Persian Gulf War clearly demonstrated that victory could be achieved by air forces alone. Further, he argued, the 1990 draft military doctrine was 'extremely dangerous' for the Soviet Union; the armed forces should be prepared to conduct all types of operations—not just defensive. In sum, he said, 'The defensive doctrine does not mean a defensive strategy'.[63]

In their assessments of the air action the Soviet analysts evidenced a sense of inferiority. They recognized that the coalition forces were able to mount a classic air offensive because they not only had superior technology, but also because they had high-quality technical and operational support. As the Chief of the Main Air Staff, Lt Gen. of Aviation Anatoli I. Malyukov, commented, 'There is only one conclusion [regarding such an operation]—everything must be developed comprehensively, and then, when the whole system comes into play, it will produce the corresponding results'.[64]

General Malyukov implicitly faulted the Soviet Air Force for placing too much emphasis on high-performance equipment and too little on support. He particularly cited the shortage of military airlift as a problem area inhibiting the Air Force from achieving its full potential. 'Whenever the need arises to transfer a sizeable grouping somewhere', he said, 'we usually use virtually the

---

[62] Interview with Lt Gen. S. Bogdanov, *Krasnaya Zvezda*, 17 May 1991, 1st edn, p. 2, in FBIS-SOV-91-098, 21 May 1991, pp. 65–67.

[63] Fitzgerald, M. C., 'Soviet armed forces after the Gulf War: demise of the defensive doctrine?', Radio Free Europe/Radio Liberty Institute, *Report on the USSR*, Apr. 1991, p. 3.

[64] Lt Gen. of Aviation A. Malyukov interview, *Krasnaya Zvezda*, 14 Mar. 1991, 1st edn, p. 3, in FBIS-SOV-91-053, 19 Mar. 1991, p. 50.

whole of our military transport aviation . . . [furthermore] our aircraft are getting old. . . . New aircraft are needed'.[65]

In June 1991, General Moiseyev weighed in a second time, probably as much to dispel what he thought were damaging misconceptions as to inform his audience of his views. Clearly sensing the pressure from liberals and conservatives alike, he said, 'We should not link the results of the war with the reform in the Soviet Armed Forces'. He struck back at those whom he felt were attempting to place the results of the war in 'a different, unrealistic light' for their own purposes. The trouble with such 'deliberate and propagandistic action,' he argued, was that 'it aims to provoke a public opinion that we are not powerful enough, that our army has lost its previous might, that we can be ignored, and that the time has come [when foreigners may choose] to dictate [their] will to us'.[66]

For the most part, military leaders in the CIS appear to be accepting the lessons of the war as confirmation of their instincts regarding the role of technology on the future battlefield. While the arguments of Marshal Ogarkov for heavy investment in high-technology weaponry—especially deep-surveillance and deep-strike systems—may have appalled his superiors in the early 1980s, Ogarkov may be enjoying some sense of exoneration in the wake of the war. His proposals may be even less feasible today than a decade ago from a fiscal point of view, but he clearly laid out the basic parameters of successful modern warfare. Indeed, whatever his intentions might have been, there is reason to believe that it was his clarity of vision and description of requirements which eventually convinced the leadership that the USSR could no longer compete with the West in the military field.

VI. Implications of CIS operational thinking on force structure in the year 2000

This review of Soviet and more recent CIS operational lessons and thinking highlights some likely new and some renewed emphasis on certain capabilities of CIS theatre forces in the coming decade. This, together with the bounds established through *perestroika* and the military reorganization effort, has implications for the force structure which may take form by the end of the century.

It is quite clear that tactical-level CIS planners envisage substantially smaller and more professional forces, manoeuvring with greater independence over longer distances than has been the norm in the past. It is apparent that they also envisage the forces having a better balance of capabilities, for both offensive and defensive operations, than provided for in their earlier tables of organization and equipment (TO&E). It is likely, for example, that they view the new corps and brigade structure as more nimble than that of the armies and divisions of the past. With more competent, professional soldiers anticipated to man the

---

[65] Malyukov (note 64).
[66] 'Moiseyev on results of Gulf war, armed forces', TASS, Moscow Radio, 2145 GMT, 6 June 1991 (in English), in FBIS-SOV-91-110, 7 June 1991, pp. 51–52.

new units, they probably expect to attain a higher return on investment, in terms of combat effectiveness and operational flexibility, than they have had from the traditional structure.

In this context, the emergence of the *bronegruppa* concept would appear to be a manifestation of interest in obtaining maximum combat potential from a given level of force. The restrictions of the CFE accords on *matériel* densities in the Atlantic-to-the-Urals (ATTU) region probably prompted the Soviet Union to experiment with new operational techniques for achieving additional manoeuvre elements. While the CFE Treaty may diminish in importance as CIS forces are reduced, the motivation for obtaining the highest possible combat potential within the new force posture may actually increase. The last thing which CIS planners would wish would be to encourage any potential adversary to take advantage of the lower troop densities expected in the future.

It should also be noted that the heirs of the Soviet Union expect their forces to rely heavily on longer-range, highly accurate fire for engagement of the enemy in the early stages of battle development, and on new systems for target location, data compilation and fire control. Notably, they evidenced a fresh interest in the formation of heavy artillery 'high powered' brigades and divisions in the late 1980s.[67] These organizations have impressive range and ordnance payload capabilities. CIS planners may be expected to seek to provide greatly improved target-acquisition systems and 'smart' shells for these weapons in the future. While the military doctrine is defensive, it appears that there is still a strong school favouring a relatively short period of defensive operations before the counter-offensive might be launched. This would imply that most units in the diminished central forces must maintain a versatility for a wider range of activities than may have been anticipated when the doctrine was first promulgated. If there are to be many 'defensive' units, such as machine-gun/artillery divisions, they are likely to be maintained at a lower state of readiness. Since they do not have large quantities of mobile equipment, they are not likely to impact heavily on the force limitations of arms control and confidence-building agreements. Presumably, these units would be brought up to combat preparedness during a period of international tension, or, in case of surprise attack, during the initial stages of the defensive operations.

It is also likely that additional reserve forces will exist which will have high offensive capability. Presumably, these forces would be brought up to strength and increased in readiness during the initial, defensive stages of a conflict and would participate in the general counter-offensive. Since much of the equipment for these units is likely to be treaty restricted, a system may be devised for bringing forward major items of equipment to the units from stores outside the ATTU region, rather than having the personnel assemble at the location of the equipment as has been the traditional pattern.

The two schools of thought regarding reliance on nuclear weapons described above may represent the thinking principally of the professional military leader-

---

[67] 'Soviets revive heavy artillery formations', *Jane's Defence Weekly*, 19 Mar. 1988, p. 534.

ship, on the one hand, and the civilian *institutchiki* of the Academy of Sciences, on the other. Whatever the merits of the arguments of the two sides, the matter smacks of a struggle for control of policy formulation. An overt turn towards reliance on theatre nuclear weapons for deterrence, coupled with a renunciation of the no-first-use doctrine might reveal more about the relative influence of the respective groups than about the actual behaviour of the Russian leadership in time of crisis or conflict.

The other principal issue relating to nuclear weapons is that of control authority. Some voices in republican councils have evidenced aspirations for devolution of control of the weapons to the republics in which they are located. Others are less ambitious, seeking only approval authority for matters pertaining to their maintenance and use. In October 1991, for example, the independence-minded Ukrainian Parliament accepted the principle of central Soviet control, but demanded the right of veto over employment.[68] The Russian Government has chosen not to challenge the move for fear of precipitating further discord. A policy of central control with republican right of veto could become the *de facto* model even among nominally equal republican states.

Finally, it is clear that the Soviet Union was impressed with the impact of high-technology weaponry and with requirements for high-speed command and control on the modern battlefield. If nothing else drives its successors towards a smaller force structure, the cost of such features may do so. The larger the forces they seek to maintain, the less capable the forces are likely to be in coping with Western class opponents. While one cannot discount CIS interest in embracing a mix of high- and low-capability forces, the traditional Soviet (and Russian) reliance on mass as a qualitative factor in military affairs may not survive the century.

VII. CIS force structure options in the year 2000

There is a broad range of possible force structures for the Eurasian Commonwealth in the year 2000—if, indeed the Commonwealth survives. Everything will depend upon the political turn of events in the intervening decade. The foregoing discussion has given some indicators of how central planners may view their force development tasks, but in the final analysis the armed forces must adjust themselves to the fortunes of the country—not the other way around. This section describes three options, based upon different assumptions regarding the evolution of the political structure. All are drawn against the common strategic background and thread of professional military thought described above, and yet they are quite different. The point of greatest coincidence is that no forces are stationed outside the borders of the USSR (as formerly constituted). It may be noted in some cases that equipment totals exceed CFE allowances for active units. In these cases some of the units may be unmanned,

---

[68] Popeski, R., 'Ukraine accepts central control of nuclear arms, but wants veto', *Washington Times*, 25 Oct. 1991, p. A8.

with the equipment placed in storage, or the units may be issued less than their tables of organization (TO) would allow.

Option 1, the base case, assumes that whatever the political unity, or lack of it, there will emerge before the turn of the century an acceptance of a coherent military establishment for defence of most of the region previously occupied by the Soviet Union. Further, the case assumes that the structure of the forces will generally conform with the MOD proposal of February 1991 as modified by Marshal Shaposhnikov and General Lobov in the aftermath of the failed coup. Option 2 assumes that the Commonwealth will play little part in the determination of the strength or structure of conventional theatre forces. Instead, the republics will shape their forces according to their individual perceptions of need and ability, limited solely by the agreement signed in Tashkent in May 1992 governing the allocation of arms limitations under the CFE Treaty.[69]

Option 3, a special case, derives from the proposal of the General Staff Army Reform Commission for creation of a modest, centrally controlled force in the Slavic republics and Kazakhstan, with provision for integration or co-ordination with NATO. It assumes that the two republics of greatest strategic and economic importance, Russia and Ukraine (along with Belarus and Kazakhstan), will continue to co-operate on major defence issues, but it leaves many matters of local and internal security under the jurisdiction of individual republics.[70] Not addressed in this chapter, but highly pertinent to the relationship is the matter of control of the Black Sea Fleet. All three cases assume that a rational division of fleet elements will take place, particularly with those units capable of making a significant contribution to air defence remaining under Russian control.

It is possible, of course, that the infant Commonwealth could suffer a coup or other reverse which would lead to the imposition of a regressive, inwardly looking government with little concern for human rights or good relations with the West. Alternatively, the country could deteriorate into a state of chaos, with no recognizable order emerging before the end of the decade. These cases are less interesting from an analytical point of view. The forces which might develop under a totalitarian regime are a historic reality and require little imagination. On the other hand, it is virtually impossible to credibly forecast any sort of useful military patterns or practices for a chaotic milieu. Accordingly, this examination is restricted to the three cases described.

Option 1: the base case

This case is an extension of trends in Soviet force structure development springing from the fundamental change in military doctrine in the late 1980s. It takes into consideration the reorganization of ground forces announced in Vienna in October 1991 and earlier announcements regarding the creation of 'defensive' units with limited mobility. It also takes into consideration the im-

---

[69] Erlanger, S., 'Yeltsin angrily assails his critics and Gorbachev', *New York Times*, 16 May 1992, p. 4.
[70] Russia and Ukraine account for over 90% of the military industries in the former Soviet Union.

pact of the INF and CFE Treaties and the desire of the Soviet military leadership to modernize the forces according to the mainstream of thinking described above. Further, it assumes that the CIS will retain additional armoured combat vehicles for protection of Strategic Deterrent Forces (SDF) facilities containing nuclear weapons. (SDF is the new service combining the Strategic Rocket Forces and the Troops of Air Defence.) The exception to CFE limits seems prudent in view of the possibility of prolonged civil turbulence in the country.[71]

Theatre forces are assigned to republics, or groups of republics, rather than by the traditional pattern of military districts. Senior CIS officials have lost confidence in the utility of the districts in recent years as republican authorities have become more assertive. Accordingly, the districts have been recast to coincide with republican borders to facilitate co-ordination between host republic governments and military organizations operating in their areas of jurisdiction. Regional fronts are identified for operational planning and direction of the forces assigned. Theatres of military operation (TVD) may be designated for planning, but the fronts receive instructions directly from the General Staff with no intervening headquarters.

The Ground Defence Troops (GDT) have been restructured, with the majority of them organized as brigades and corps rather than as divisions and armies. These lighter elements are located primarily in the north-west, south-west and southern TVDs for maximum flexibility. The ground forces in Belarus retain a more traditional configuration, but reflect the early (defensive) organizational patterns seen in the Western Group of Forces (eastern Germany) in which a tank regiment was replaced by a motorized rifle regiment in each division. The structure includes five airborne divisions. Airborne troops have proven highly ready tools of civil control for the Government, and, of course, would provide forces for early counter-offensive operations in an international conflict. On the other hand, the formerly Soviet airborne forces, trained and equipped with light armoured vehicles and dependent upon the airlift capabilities of the current CIS Air Forces, have not had the strategic reach of comparable US troops—hence, they have tended to be somewhat less threatening to all but their closest neighbours.

This projection assumes that CIS Military Air Transport (VTA) will be modestly reinforced so that it will have a capability of providing sufficient airlift for the simultaneous movement of the combat elements of two airborne divisions to a range of approximately 1000 km.[72] It should be noted, however, that the principal purpose of the reinforcement would not be for extending offensive airborne operations, but to facilitate the rapid redeployment of light

---

[71] Besides the armoured combat vehicles for the Strategic Rocket Forces, the Soviets asked for exceptions for 933 tanks, 1743 ACVs, and 1080 artillery pieces for coastal defence and naval infantry organizations. See 'Resolution of the arms impasse', *New York Times*, 9 Apr. 1991, p. 24. The case for ACVs for the SDF appears more meritorious than the others. For the absorbtion of air defence into SDF, see 'Russian reports', *Armed Forces Journal International*, Feb. 1992, p. 27.

[72] Except for current fuel shortages, VTA capabilities include the simultaneous lift of one airborne division to a range of 1610 km., or two divisions to a range of 480 km.; see Isby, D. C., *Weapons and Tactics of the Soviet Army* (Jane's: London, 1981), p. 291.

forces to meet unanticipated emergencies around the Eurasian land mass in an era of diminished overall military capability.

Long-range fire support (for RUK and ROK groupings) is provided through the allocation of artillery divisions, composed of heavy artillery and rocket brigades (aggregating some 430 pieces), to most fronts. With the exception of the Far East, this is done at the expense of ground divisions in order to remain within overall CFE restrictions (13 700 pieces for 'sufficiency').

Table 8.1 below provides a typical composition and deployment (by front and republic) of theatre forces under this option. Notable is the provision of a number of semi-static defensive 'machine-gun/artillery' divisions in the central western and Far East fronts. This, together with the replacement of a tank regiment with a motorized rifle regiment in the ground manoeuvre divisions, greatly reduces the number of tanks. Only through the provision of an independent tank regiment for most armies and corps (with additional regiments in the central reserve) does the tank count begin to approach the number authorized under the CFE Treaty.

A likely development would be the stationing of quantities of equipment at one or more training centres in the interior of the country. CIS military officials have long admired the US National Training Center at Fort Irwin, California. A move on their part to replicate the US facility could enhance the quality of training in their ground forces and provide a pool of equipment for issue to units with shortages in time of emergency. As many as 1000 tanks might be distributed to training centres and to local garrisons for training purposes in order to reduce wear and tear on unit equipment. The location of major training centres east of the Urals, of course, would avoid inclusion of much of the training equipment in Treaty-related weapon counts. Another 500 tanks might serve as maintenance float (replacements for tanks undergoing rear echelon repair or modification).

The CFE Treaty impacts the number of manoeuvre divisions and brigades in the ATTU region primarily through its restriction on armoured combat vehicles (ACV—three specific types of armoured vehicles, other than tanks). Table 8.1 makes no allowance for heavy equipment in the hands of border guard and MVD interior troops (the KGB has been disestablished).[73] Requirements for these forces would have to be met within CFE limitations. Some ground force units in the ATTU region might have to go without their full allowances if the security forces were to be given high priority.

CIS frontal air forces follow traditional patterns with a helicopter regiment in support of each field army and an air army in support of most fronts. The frontal air armies are composed of various types of regiments for reconnaissance, electronic warfare and interdictive ground attack missions. Most close air support is provided by attack helicopter units organic to the ground armies, corps, divisions and brigades. Owing to Soviet impressions of the effectiveness of US attack helicopters in the Persian Gulf War, these weapons are now more

---

[73] *Pravda*, 25 Oct. 1991, p. 6, in FBIS-SOV-91-207, 25 Oct. 1991, p. 13.

Table 8.1. CIS peacetime order of battle: option 1, base case[a]

Front	Tank	Artillery	Armoured combat vehicles	Helicopter	Aircraft
Northern front					
North-west Russia					
2 Corps		100		80	
7 Combined arms brigades	350	350	1400	70	
1 Independent tank regiment	150				
1 Artillery division		430	85		
1 Tactical air army					300
North-west air defence sector					400
Belarus front					
Belarus					
1 Tank army		100		50	
1 Combined arms army		100		50	
3 Tank divisions	750	630	1206	60	
3 Motorized rifle divisions	450	648	1911	60	
2 Machine-gun/artillery divisions	80	500	400	30	
2 Combined arms brigades	100	100	400	20	
1 Artillery division		430	85		
2 Independent tank regiments	300				
1 Tactical air army					400
1 Airborne division (VGK control)		85	350		
Belarus air defence sector					400
South-west front					
Ukraine, Moldova					
6 Corps		300		240	
24 Combined arms brigades	1440	1200	6000	240	
4 Independent tank regiments	600				
1 Artillery division		430	85		
1 Tactical air army					350
1 Airborne division (VGK control)		85	350		
South-western air defence sector					400
Southern front					
Southern Russia, Georgia, Armenia and Azerbaijan					
5 Corps		250		200	
18 Combined arms brigades	1080	900	4500	180	
3 Independent tank regiments	450				
1 Artillery division		430	85		
1 Tactical air army					400
1 Airborne division (VGK control)		85	350		
Southern air defence sector					400
Central reserve					
European Russia					
2 Corps		100		80	
9 Combined arms brigades	540	450	2250	90	
1 Artillery division		430	85		
4 Independent tank regiments	600				

Front	Tank	Artillery	Armoured combat vehicles	Helicopter	Aircraft
1 Tactical air army					300
2 Strategic air armies (VGK control)					700
1 Airborne division (VGK control)		85	350		
Central air defence sector					300
South-central front					
Kazakhstan, Uzbekistan, Turkmenistan, Kyrgyzstan and Tajikistan					
6 Corps		300		240	
28 Combined arms brigades	1680	1400	7000	280	
2 Artillery divisions		860	170		
3 Independent tank regiments	450		255		
1 Tactical air army					300
South-central air defence sector					300
Far East front					
Far Eastern Russia					
2 Combined arms army		200		100	
4 Corps		200		120	
2 Tank divisions	500	420	804	40	
6 Motorized rifle divisions	900	1296	3822	120	
10 machine-gun/artillery divisions	160	1000	800	60	
16 Combined arms brigades	960	800	4000	360	
3 Artillery divisions		1290	255	30	
5 Independent tank regiments	750				
3 Tactical air armies					900
1 Strategic air army (VGK control)					400
1 Airborne division (VGK control)		85	350		
Far East air defence sector					700
Total authorized in ATTU region under CFE Treaty	**13 300**	**13 700**	**20 000**	**1500**	**5150**
Attached to strategic deterrent forces			**1701**		
Total theatre forces in ATTU under option 1	**6890**	**8218**	**19 892**	**1450**	**4350**

^a For assumed equipment standards, see table 8.5.

VGK = Supreme High Command

Source: Data derived from *Krasnaya Zvezda*, 17 Oct. 1991, p. 3, in FBIS-SOV-91-202, 18 Oct. 1991, p. 34. Other data derived from US Department of the Army, *The Soviet Army: Troops, Organization and Equipment*, FM 100-2-3, 16 July 1984, and Karber, P. A., 'The Gorbachev unilateral reductions and the restructuring of Soviet/Warsaw Pact Forces', testimony before the House Armed Services Committee, 13 Sep. 1989, and Plugge, M., 'Soviet Armed Forces plan for joint operations alongside NATO', *International Defense Review*, Oct. 1991, p. 1316, and estimates by author.

plentiful in the CIS structure than they were in the Soviet Union. Additional air armies operate under Supreme High Command (VGK) control for strategic theatre strike tasks. Air defence aircraft are grouped under Strategic Deterrent Forces control in peacetime. Some regiments would be expected to pass to control of the fronts in time of war.

Some Western writers have speculated that the CIS may merge air defence aircraft (now part of SDF) with those of the air force. While this is a possibility, it should be noted that such an alignment was attempted in the mid-1980s and found unsatisfactory considering the growing sophistication of the US manned bomber and cruise-missile threat.[74]

Option 2: separate national forces

Option 2 assumes that the various republics will pursue the development of independent theatre forces. While a central General Staff may exist for operational co-ordination of forces in time of emergency, its influence over the size and consistency of the forces will be little more than advisory. The principal determinants of these aspects of the forces will be shaped in the capitals of the republics, subject only to the restrictions of the CFE Treaty and the inter-republican agreement of Tashkent of May 1992 allocating equipment ceilings among the seven republics involved.[75]

The relative size of the national forces may be expected to generally follow demographic distribution patterns, tempered by special factors, such as the nature of the terrain, access to the sea, the national economy, perceived threats posed by other republics and third parties, and the possession or non-possession of nuclear weapons. Considering these factors, it would not be surprising to see the national forces aligning something like that outlined in table 8.2 below for a total of approximately 2.2 million troops in the year 2000.

Option 2 considers that all former Soviet troops have been withdrawn from the Baltic states and that Estonia, Latvia and Lithuania are independently responsible for their own defence. It is possible that Russia, or the CIS, if it exists, will have concluded long-term treaties with the Baltic states and with Ukraine for use of naval bases and facilities on the Baltic and Black Seas. Some naval units will have been transferred to the littoral states as part of the agreements. A broad multilateral treaty may have been signed providing for periodic consultation among the chiefs of services of the 12 states listed in table 8.2. Under the terms of the treaty, Russia (or the CIS) will provide military assistance to the other states, particularly in the area of air and coastal defence.

The force reflects a common origin in many respects, particularly at the small unit level. At higher levels, however, the structures are more likely to reflect the particular circumstances surrounding their locations and the individual thinking of the national staffs. Some republics may adhere to division and army formations, while others are likely to switch to brigades and corps. Still others may be hybrids.

[74] See, for example, Collins, B. J., 'Soviet military reform restructuring aerospace forces', *International Defense Review*, June 1991, pp. 561–64.
[75] 'Central CFE levels fixed', *Jane's Defence Weekly*, 6 June 1992, p. 966.

Table 8.2. Alignment of national forces

Republic	Per cent of population	Armed forces strength in the year 2000
Russia	54	1 500 000
Ukraine	19	200 000
Kazakhstan	6	125 000
Uzbekistan	6	90 000
Belarus	4	90 000
Azerbaijan	2	35 000
Georgia	2	20 000
Moldova	2	15 000
Tajikistan	2	30 000
Armenia	1	20 000
Kyrgyzstan	1	15 000
Turkistan	1	15 000

Source: Unpublished paper by Warner, III, E., *Recent Defense Policy Developments in the Former Soviet Union* (RAND Corporation: Santa Monica, Calif., 6 Apr. 1992); and estimates by the author.

It is assumed in this case that the national armed forces are composed primarily of contract and extended service personnel. In Russia, and in perhaps one or two of the other republics, particularly where territorial or ethnic problems may persist, there may be some short-term (6 to 18 months) conscripts, serving in so far as possible near their home towns. Russian soldiers posted to distant stations are paid an additional allowance. The forces are depoliticized, with some former political cadre retained as morale, training and welfare officers responsible to their immediate commanders. All nuclear weapons have been withdrawn to central storage facilities in Russia. All MVD forces are under the control of their separate republics and largely stripped of heavy equipment countable under the CFE Treaty.

As depicted in table 8.3 below, the Russian ground forces are dominant, composed of some 12 corps and 56 tank and mechanized brigades and regiments in the ATTU area. In addition, there are 3 airborne and 4 artillery divisions west of the Urals. Siberian forces (not listed in the table) may approximate up to 50 per cent of the strength deployed in the western part of the country. Tactical air armies and air defence sectors provide support and protection to each of the regional *fronts*. The preponderance of power is concentrated in the heartland around Moscow in accordance with the defensive doctrine. The structure exceeds the allowance for armoured combat vehicles and is short in artillery. In order to better accommodate the CFE restrictions, Russia may wish to field fewer brigades than listed in the table, perhaps with a larger authorization for artillery in each.

There is some evidence that Ukrainian forces will be different, perhaps

Table 8.3. CIS forces in ATTU in the year 2000: option 2, separate national forces[a]

Front	Tank	Artillery	Armoured combat vehicles	Helicopter	Air-craft
Russia					
North-west front					
3 Corps				120	
10 Northern combined arms brigades	500	500	2000		
4 Independent tank regiments	600				
1 Artillery division		430	85		
1 Airborne division (central control)		85	350		
1 Tactical air army				100	300
2 Air defence sectors					800
Central front and central reserve					
6 Corps				240	
22 Standard combined arms brigades	1760	1760	5500		
6 Independent tank regiments	900				
2 Artillery divisions		860	170		
2 Airborne divisions (central control)		170	700		
2 Tactical air armies				200	400
2 Air defence sectors					800
South-west front					
3 Corps				120	
10 Southern combined arms brigades	600	500	2500		
4 Independent tank regiments	600				
1 Artillery division		430	85		
1 Airborne division (central control)		85	350		
1 Tactical air army				100	350
2 Air defence sectors					800
Total equipment allowed	**6400**	**6415**	**19 984**	**890**	**3450**
Permitted in active units	**4975**	**5105**	**10 525**	**890**	**3450**
Total equipment identified	**4960**	**4820**	**11 740**	**890**	**3450**
Ukraine					
4 Corps					
8 Motorized rifle divisions	1760	1616	4608		
7 Tank brigades	875	735	1407		
7 Artillery brigades		700	280		
3 Army aviation brigades				330	
1 Airborne division		85	350		
Combined tactical air/air defence command					1090
Total equipment allowed	**4080**	**4040**	**5050**	**330**	**1090**
Permitted in active units	**3130**	**3240**	**4350**	**330**	**1090**
Total equipment identified	**2635**	**3136**	**6645**	**330**	**1090**

Front	Tank	Artillery	Armoured combat vehicles	Helicopter	Air-craft
Belarus					
1 Tank army				40	
1 Combined arms army				40	
2 Tank divisions	500	420	804		
2 Motorized rifle divisions	300	432	1274		
1 Combined arms brigade	80	80	250		
4 Independent tank regiments	600				
4 Artillery brigades		400	160		
Combined tactical air/air defence command					260
Total equipment allowed	**2600**	**1615**	**4320**	**80**	**260**
Permitted in active units	**1525**	**1375**	**2600**	**80**	**260**
Total equipment identified	**1480**	**1332**	**2488**	**80**	**260**
Armenia, Azerbaijan and Georgia (each)					
1 Corps				40	
2 Combined arms brigades	160	160	300		
1 Independent tank battalion	40				
1 Artillery brigade		100	40		
Combined tactical air/air defence command				10	100
Total equipment allowed	**220**	**285**	**366**	**50**	**100**
Total equipment identified	**200**	**260**	**340**	**50**	**100**
(No separate limits for active units)					
Moldova					
1 Corps				40	
2 Combined arms brigades	160	160	300		
1 Independent tank battalion	40				
1 Artillery brigade		100	40		
Combined tactical air/air defence command				10	100
Total equipment allowed	**210**	**250**	**350**	**50**	**100**
Total equipment identified	**200**	**260**	**340**	**50**	**100**
(No separate limits for active units)					

[a] For assumed equipment standards, see table 8.5.

Source: Data derived from *Krasnaya Zvezda*, 17 Oct. 1991, p. 3, in FBIS-SOV-91-202, 18 Oct. 1991, p. 34. Other data derived from US Department of the Army, *The Soviet Army: Troops, Organization and Equipment*, FM 100-2-3, 16 July 1984, and Karber, P. A., 'The Gorbachev unilateral reductions and the restructuring of Soviet/Warsaw Pact Forces', testimony before the House Armed Services Committee, 13 Sep. 1989, and Plugge, M., 'Soviet Armed Forces plan for joint operations alongside NATO', *International Defense Review*, Oct. 1991, p. 1316, and estimates by author.

structured around a mixture of traditional motorized rifle divisions, supplemented with tank and artillery brigades, with corps headquarters for operational control.[76] The structure under discussion, and outlined in table 8.3, falls substantially short of the permissible number of tanks under the CFE and Tashkent accords, but it has far too many armoured combat vehicles. The Ukrainian High Command may be considering adoption of tables of organization for the tank brigades which would bring the force structure into closer agreement with the weapon authorizations. Under this formulation all combat aircraft are assigned to three multi-mission groups (Kiev, L'vov and Odessa) under a central air command. Fighter regiments assigned to the groups provide air defence for both the field forces and the country as a whole. Surface-to air missile units are also under central (Air Force) control.[77]

Belarus is depicted as using a traditional structure of divisions and armies, but is also has a combined arms brigade and 4 independent tank regiments. As in the case of Ukraine, tactical air and air defence aircraft are assigned to an integrated tactical air and air defence command.

The smaller republics, Armenia, Azerbaijan and Georgia, have equal authorizations of *matériel*: 220 tanks, 285 artillery pieces, 366 armoured personnel carriers, 50 attack helicopters and 100 combat aircraft. Table 8.3 depicts a typical distribution of these assets in a two-brigade corps, with an independent tank regiment and a separate artillery brigade. Moldovan equipment authorizations are only slightly smaller than those of the aforementioned states and are similarly portrayed.

Option 3: the NATO integrable force

Option 3 provides for modest theatre forces designed both for independent defensive operations and for operations as part of, or in co-operation with, a major NATO command. The forces are composed entirely of volunteers; there is no conscription. The ground contingent is structured primarily into brigades and corps (five brigades to a corps), with the exception of the airborne and artillery divisions and independent tank regiments. The airborne divisions retain the tactical mobility and striking power of their Soviet forerunners, but have half the manpower of a Western counterpart. The artillery divisions are generally comparable to corps artillery brigades in the West, and the tank regiments provide offensive punch for counterattacks.

In addition to the five brigades in each corps, the eastern and western regional commands have a number of independent brigades of limited mobility. These are designed for supportive roles within their home districts (national borders), but are subordinate to central authority. In addition, the various republics have their own national guard which may receive technical assistance and instruction

---

[76] 'Ukraine outlines new doctrine', *Jane's Defence Weekly*, 15 Feb. 1992, p. 215.
[77] See note 76.

Table 8.4. CIS peacetime order of battle: option 3, NATO-compatible forces[a]

Front	Tank	Artillery	Armoured combat vehicles	Helicopter	Air-craft
Western command					
2 Corps		100		160	
5 'Northern' combined arms brigades	250	250	1000	50	
5 'Southern' combined arms brigades	300	250	1500	50	
2 Artillery divisions		860	170		
4 Independent tank regiments	600				
1 Rapid-reaction corps		50		160	
1 Airborne division		85	350		
1 'Northern' combined arms brigade	50	50	200	25	
3 'Southern' combined arms brigades	180	150	750	75	
1 Artillery division		430	85		
2 Independent tank regiments	300				
8 Independent (national) combined arms brigades	320	480	1200	200	
3 Tactical air corps					900
2 Strategic (theatre) air corps					600
Supreme High Command (VGK) rapid-reaction forces					
2 Corps		100		320	
3 Airborne divisions		255	1050		
2 'Northern' combined arms brigades	100	100	400	50	
5 'Southern' combined arms brigades	300	250	1250	125	
2 Artillery divisions		860	170		
4 Independent tank regiments	600				
Total CIS forces in ATTU under this option	**2470**	**3505**	**6740**	**955**	**1500**

[a] Eastern command (east of the Ural Mountains) is the same as western command. The VGK rapid-reaction force has 1 corps on each side of the Urals. The western corps has 2 airborne divisions. Air defence aircraft (1200 in ATTU) are assigned to Strategic Deterrent Forces. For assumed equipment standards, see table 8.5.

Source: Data derived from *Krasnaya Zvezda*, 17 Oct. 1991, p. 3, in FBIS-SOV-91-202, 18 Oct. 1991, p. 34. Other data derived from US Department of the Army, *The Soviet Army: Troops, Organization and Equipment*, FM 100-2-3, 16 July 1984, and Karber, P. A., 'The Gorbachev unilateral reductions and the restructuring of Soviet/Warsaw Pact Forces', testimony before the House Armed Services Committee, 13 Sep. 1989, and Plugge, M., 'Soviet Armed Forces plan for joint operations alongside NATO', *International Defense Review*, Oct. 1991, p. 1316, and estimates by author.

from CIS forces, but remain under republic authority unless otherwise ordered by their respective governments.

The attack helicopter strength of both the brigades and their parent corps is substantially larger than under the other two options. For those corps designated as rapid-reaction units, the helicopter count is four times that of a corps head-quarters in options 1 and 2. Also, for the rapid-reaction force (an organization of two corps directly subordinate to the Supreme High Command) organic air-lift is provided capable of lifting the combat elements of two airborne divisions to a range of 1000 km.

Each corps of the eastern and western commands has a tactical air corps of approximately 300 aircraft available for direct support. Using NATO practice as a model, the ground corps would be 'chopped' to a designated regional command (cf., Allied Forces Central Europe, AFCENT) while the air corps would be attached to a corresponding air command (cf., Air Forces Central Europe, AIRCENT).[78] The eastern and western commands are not operational head-quarters, but have administrative responsibility for all centrally controlled ground, air and air defence units in their respective regions. In peacetime the units remain under the operational control of the General Staff and may be otherwise assigned or grouped in wartime. With no large military threat to the CIS in view, the arrangement is adequate for the foreseeable future. Table 8.4 above depicts the forces under this option.

VIII. Mobilization

CIS capabilities for rapid theatre force expansion are likely to be moderately to severely reduced under many of the scenarios currently under public discussion. Efforts towards elimination or reduction of conscription and professionalization of the Armed Forces would likely impact the number of young men trained for military duty. Further, if the Slavic states do not attach great importance to mil-itary service, they might reduce manpower pools containing some of the best educated and most trainable talent in the country. Most troublesome of all may be the lack of standardization which could develop among the forces of the various republics if they are not subject to some form of central planning and standards of readiness.

In addition to these factors, CIS planners must consider that under some scenarios the CFE Treaty might create imbalances in the distribution of war *matériel* inimical to rapid mobilization. The equipment inventories authorized under the Treaty might not fit very well with the modified tables of organiza-tion and equipment assumed to be adopted in this study. Clearly, the forces depicted would be highly dependent upon reinforcements and equipment to be brought forward from the interior.

This dependency is remarkable for the likely inversion in mobilization pro-cedures which it would cause, in comparison to those which were traditionally

[78] Under the 1992 NATO reorganization, the headquarters of Northern and Central Army Groups and 2nd and 4th Allied Tactical Air Forces will be abolished. Ground forces in the central region will be sub-ordinated to AFCENT Headquarters and air forces to AIRCENT Headquarters. See 'Defense planning committee communiqué', *NATO Review*, Feb. 1992, p. 31; and 'The JDW interview' (with Lt Gen. Jorg Kuebart, Chief of Staff, Luftwaffe), *Jane's Defence Weekly*, 29 Feb. 1992, p. 368.

Table 8.5. CIS peacetime order of battle: theatre forces equipment standards

Forces	Tank	Artillery	Armoured combat vehicles	Heli-copter	Air-craft
Options 1 and 3 (base case and NATO-compatible forces)					
Combined arms army		100		50	
Tank army		100		50	
Tank division	250	210	402	20	
Motorized rifle division	150	216	637	20	
Machine-gun/artillery division	40	250	200	15	
Airborne division		85	350		
Corps		50		40	
NATO-compatible corps		50		80	
Rapid-reaction corps		50		160	
'Northern' combined arms brigade	50	50	200	10	
'Southern' combined arms brigade	60	50	250	10	
Combined arms brigade in rapid-reaction corps	??	??	??	25	
Independent combined arms brigade	40	60	150	25	
Artillery division		430	85		
Independent tank regiment	150				
Tactical air corps/army					300–400
Strategic air corps/army					300–400
Option 2 (separate national forces)					
Tank army				40	
Combined arms army				40	
Corps (except Ukraine)				40	
Ukrainian motorized rifle division	220	202	576		
Airborne division		85	350		
Artillery division		430	85		
Standard combined arms brigade	80	80	250		
Small state combined arms brigade	80	80	150		
Russian 'northern' combined arms brigade	50	50	200		
Russian 'southern' combined arms brigade	60	50	250		
Ukrainian tank brigade	125	105	201		
Ukrainian artillery brigade		100	40		
Ukrainian aviation brigade				110	
Independent tank regiment	150				
Independent tank battalion	40				
Tactical air army					300–400

Source: Data derived from *Krasnaya Zvezda*, 17 Oct. 1991, p. 3, in FBIS-SOV-91-202, 18 Oct. 1991, p. 34. Other data derived from US Department of the Army, *The Soviet Army: Troops, Organization and Equipment*, FM 100-2-3, 16 July 1984, and Karber, P. A., 'The Gorbachev unilateral reductions and the restructuring of Soviet/Warsaw Pact Forces', testimony before the House Armed Services Committee, 13 Sep. 1989, and Plugge, M., 'Soviet Armed Forces plan for joint operations alongside NATO', *International Defense Review*, Oct. 1991, p. 1316, and estimates by author.

held in the USSR. Rather than the assembly of reserve personnel in the vicinity of low-strength and inactive sets of equipment, the pattern is likely to be largely one of transporting heavy equipment forward from eastern depots to assembly areas where it can be distributed to fledgling units. The logistical load on CIS transportation systems would likely be much greater than under previous arrangements.

However, just as the forces may become more dependent upon CIS transportation systems for support, it appears that the systems, particularly the railroads, have considerably less flexibility than previously supposed. In October 1989, the railroads went into virtual gridlock as a result of the Nagorno-Karabakh dispute. Rail lines were backed up to Leningrad in the north and to Poland and Czechoslovakia in the west, with loaded trains which could not move. Millions of roubles worth of perishable goods were lost. At one point the Soviet Minister of Railways reported 'there are 176 000 containers awaiting dispatch on the main lines, and 500 trains standing idle—that is 25 000 freight cars'.[79] The necessity of the former Soviet Union to operate trunk lines at 95–100 per cent of capacity in peacetime bodes ill for the ability of its successors to meet surge demands in wartime under attack.[80]

IX. A final note

It should be borne in mind that the cases presented are intended for illumination of possibilities and not as prescriptive options for CIS forces under any particular political arrangement. Chapter 9 presents a similar outline of US force structure, focusing upon that which may remain in Europe. The US and CIS force structures will have a degree of interdependence—neither will be developed in a vacuum. However, most cogent for both is likely to be the fundamental political philosophy to emerge in the East and the degree of cohesion which the various republics may achieve in their search for economic and political stability. The range of possible developments in the East is clearly wider than that in the West.

[79] 'Fact and comment: the situation on the railroads', *Izvestia*, 24 Oct. 1989, morning edn, p. 1, in FBIS-SOV-89-204, 24 Oct. 1989, p. 73.
[80] N. I. Ryzhkov, interview by *Gudok*, 3 Dec. 1989, p. 1, in FBIS-SOV-90-002, 3 Jan. 1990, p. 93.

9. US theatre forces in the year 2000

Edward B. Atkeson

I. Introduction

The most important strategic development affecting US perceptions of foreign threats and programmes for the development of US theatre forces has been the fundamental political change in the Soviet Union since the mid-1980s and the concomitant extraction of Soviet forces from forward areas, particularly in Europe. These events have been accompanied by a profound change in the US sense of threat from international communism world-wide, and hence of the polarization of the globe between communist and free world blocs. The 1990–91 Persian Gulf War served as a demonstrable watershed in which the United States was able to lead a coalition of states countering regional aggression without undue risk of superpower estrangement or wider conflict. As in Europe, the United States provided not only the leadership in the Gulf effort, but the 'glue' to hold the group together. It was US political resolve and readiness to thwart the aggression of the Baghdad regime that formed the critical nucleus around which the co-operation could be assembled. While the Arab forces operated under separate command, US intelligence, doctrine and military practices made possible the integration of the effort. Fundamental US patterns of command, control and communications (C^3) at the macro-level set the standards for all. It should be expected that this basic element of US power will underwrite any contingency in which the USA may become involved in the future.

II. Force dimensions

The factors of change in the former Soviet Union and Eastern Europe, noted above, will have a strong influence on the size and shape of US theatre forces at the end of the century. Like the theatre forces of the Commonwealth of Independent States (CIS) discussed in chapter 8, comparable US forces are likely to be substantially smaller than in recent decades, and with quite different orientation. Sharp reductions in forward troop stationing can be expected and a corresponding shift in the centre of gravity of US forces back towards the North American continent.

Moreover, the changes are not likely to prove ephemeral. Even if the CIS were to suffer a reversal of its recent political trends and to return to the Messianic, xenophobic model of the Stalinist years, the changes which have occurred are of such magnitude that it is quite unlikely that the threat to Europe in the foreseeable future would assume its former proportions. Germany is united, the

Warsaw Pact dissolved and the mass appeal of the communist movement has been substantially discredited. Estimates of the warning time which NATO might reasonably expect of an attack from the East under current conditions vary from in excess of a month to as much as two years.[1] The latter gains credibility as the former Soviet state continues to lose coherence.

NATO has mapped out a new military strategy in an effort to match its new circumstances. With Germany united and the Warsaw Pact threat dissolved, non-German NATO forces are being withdrawn. The former doctrine of forward defence is no longer relevant. Accordingly, NATO has turned to a concept of rapid buildup of defences if peace were to give way to crisis.[2] Presumably, the extended warning time would permit such action.

The fiscal year (FY) 1991 Congressional National Defense Authorization Act projected the strength of the US Armed Forces on 30 September 1995 at 1.6 million persons, representing a reduction of 363 000 troops from the 1991 authorization. By far the largest cuts will be in theatre forces, with the Army absorbing half.[3] Barring a conflict or the emergence of severe international tension, a reasonable steady state figure for US forces for the remainder of the decade would seem to fall remarkably close to that forecast by a former Soviet General Staff official: 1.5 million.[4]

As the threat to Europe has receded, threats to Western interests in other arenas have gained in relative prominence. Perennial instabilities in the Middle East, Latin America and the Far East continue to demand US strategic attention. The attention is manifest in some cases in the deployment of forces (e.g., Korea), in others with pre-positioned *matériel* (the Middle East) and in still others by the conduct of strategic exercises (globally). It may also be manifest, albeit more subtly, in the maintenance of forces capable of long-range power projection, whether or not they have occasion to deploy to the area in question. The emphasis, where physical presence is deemed necessary, will generally be on demonstrating interest and commitment rather than upon development of a capability for forward defence.[5] Nevertheless, the combination of limited

[1] A warning period in excess of one month was reported as a US intelligence view; see Starr, B., 'NATO will get "1 month warning of attack"', *Jane's Defence Weekly*, 23 Dec. 1989, p. 1366. The two-year warning period is suggested by Tritten, J. J., *America Promises to Come Back: A New National Strategy*, US Naval Post Graduate School NPS-NS-91-003, 26 Dec. 1990, p. 35. Another report, attributed to 'a senior administration official', says, 'Even our most concerned European allies say warning time would now be at least a few months. Frankly, our goal is to do better; we'd like several months to a year or more'. See Beecher, W., '"Disarmed" Soviets vex NATO planners', *Minneapolis Star-Tribune*, 4 Apr. 1991, p. 2.
[2] Hitchens, T., 'NATO eyes fast-acting command structure', *Defense News*, 1 Apr. 1991, p. 3.
[3] US House of Representatives, 101st Congress, 2nd Session, *National Defense Authorization Act for Fiscal Year 1991*, conference report to accompany HR 4739, 23 Oct. 1990 (US Government Printing Office: Washington, DC, 1990), p. 62.
[4] Twigg, J., 'The implications for Soviet defence and arms control policies of the devolution of power from the center to the republics', Unpublished conference report, Wolfson College, Oxford University, 10–11 Dec. 1991, p. 23.
[5] US Department of Defense, *1991 Joint Military Net Assessment*, Mar. 1991 (DOD: Washington, DC, 1991), p. 4-2.

presence, pre-positioned equipment and credible strategic lift[6] capabilities is expected to provide a measure of stability and deterrence of hostile initiatives.

Further, the diminished size of US forces and the prevalence of high-technology weaponry on world markets imposes certain imperatives regarding the quality of the forces. To maintain their effectiveness US forces must be of sufficient capability and dexterity to cope with potential opponents with celerity. Under the circumstances likely to surround the distribution and balance of military power in the year 2000, and with respect for the mantle of leadership which the United States has assumed in these various regions, it will be incumbent upon planners to maintain exceptionally high-quality forces to support the nation's interests and responsibilities. In addition, substantial fractions of the forces will necessarily be maintained in high states of readiness and provided with the means for expeditious long-range transport.

Secretary of the Army Michael P. Stone commented in April 1991 that he believed that the Army, even after being reduced to the 535 000 member level planned for 1995, would still be able to execute operations similar to Desert Shield and Desert Storm, but that troop withdrawals from Europe would necessitate greater dependence upon units drawn from the continental United States (CONUS), hence the buildup period might take longer to complete.[7]

III. Conceptual organization

General Colin L. Powell, Chairman of the Joint Chiefs of Staff, has described the conceptual grouping of US forces in the future according to four sets of requirements. These he labels Strategic, Atlantic, Pacific and Contingency. The Strategic Force, he says, will be designed to deter nuclear attack from abroad, as such forces have done for decades. The others will be composed of general purpose forces, tailored for the roles likely to be assigned. The grouping does not affect the existing command structure, rather it provides a convenient way for associating the forces with likely mission requirements.[8]

The Atlantic Force the Chairman described as 'heavy' and intended to operate in the European environment. He said that the USA also has interests in the Persian Gulf and South-West Asia, and that the types of forces in this grouping would be suitable for both. 'In fact', the general asserted, 'we fought a European war in the sands of Kuwait'. The forces, he contends, should be well trained for joint operations, inferring that a significant portion of them had to be air transportable.

---

[6] Strategic lift is composed of ships and long-range aircraft designed for intercontinental movement of troops and equipment. It includes both military and civilian carriers designed and designated for the task. Related, but not included, are prepositioned stocks of equipment, ashore and afloat, intended for use by troops deployed overseas in time of emergency.

[7] Speech by Secretary of the Army Michael P. W. Stone to the Land Warfare Forum, Association of the US Army, Arlington, Va., 4 Apr. 1991.

[8] Wolffe, J., 'Powell outlines plan for small, versatile force of the future', *Air Force Times*, 15 Apr. 1991, p 3.

The Pacific Force would be primarily an economy of force grouping because of the absence of a clearly defined threat. It would include maritime forces, Marines and some light Army presence. The general did not discuss the types of air forces required, but presumably they would be those appropriate for support of the surface forces specified. Finally, he said, the Contingency Forces would be available for:

the thing I never knew was going to come. [For the times] when I didn't know it was coming but here it is, we have to have forces that are not just regionally committed but are stand-alone, ready to handle an immediate contingency. Special forces, paratroopers, Marine maritime pre-positioned ships, amphibious capability out with the fleet. . . . Their beauty is they're light. They can get anywhere in the world in 24 hours to plant the American flag and say, 'don't screw with me'.[9]

Nevertheless, however much the acuity of the threat to Europe may subside in coming years, the primacy of US commitment to the security of that theatre will likely be slow to change. US political, economic and cultural interests in Europe are unparalleled outside the 50 states of the union. Accordingly, while the military dimension of US commitment may diminish, it is unlikely that Europe will be eclipsed in the view of the United States by concerns elsewhere in the world in the next decade.[10]

In addition to the perceived threats, US military commitments to Europe in the future will be coloured by doctrinal concepts governing the utility of theatre forces. The doctrine itself will be affected by emerging technologies and by perceptions of opportunities for competitive advantage which can be developed among the forces in the field. It should be noted that threat perceptions, technology and doctrine are interactive factors impacting concepts of force structure and design. Advancements in technology and doctrine, for example, may diminish the perception of threat from some quarters, just as an increase in threat may drive new initiatives in the other two areas. The following discussion examines the principal features of the matter.

IV. US military thinking about theatre warfare in the 21st century

US thinking about theatre warfare in the next century is developing under a conceptual umbrella, AirLand Battle-Future. The process is evolutionary, but the term 'revolution' appears frequently in discussions regarding advances in the related high-technology weapon systems. The advent of multi-spectra

---

[9] Wolffe (note 8).

[10] Representative Les Aspin has suggested that US conventional force structure should continue to be based on identifiable threats to US interests. However, he believes that 'the residual, post-Soviet conventional threat is not sufficient to greatly influence the size of US conventional forces'. Further, he identifies no other threat in the European theatre. This would appear to leave little justification for any forward deployed forces in Europe. See 'An approach to sizing American conventional forces for the post-Soviet era', Paper promulgated by Rep. Les Aspin, Chairman of the House Armed Services Committee, 24 Jan. 1992.

sensors, electronic microprocessors, real time data links, long-range, highly accurate missile systems and improved conventional munitions is viewed by many as having as great potential impact on armed conflict in the future as nuclear weapons have had in the years following World War II. Some analysts have begun referring to the new era of weaponry as the 'post-conventional period'.[11]

The scheme is a derivative and extension of the US Army's older doctrine, AirLand Battle. This formula was characterized as a 'maneuver doctrine' which:

seeks operational success through a disruption–destruction sequence in which larger enemy forces are first dislocated, disorganized and fragmented, and then defeated in detail. It relies on seizure of the tactical initiative and seeks through agile counter-maneuver to confront the enemy with a succession of unforeseen threats. It is directed toward wresting control from the attacker and ultimately collapsing his ability to fight.[12]

While it is envisaged that the fundamentals of the AirLand Battle doctrine will remain, greater emphasis will be placed upon selected functions and changes in how the doctrine is executed. Particularly, ground forces in a large land mass environment, such as the European continent, will be expected to be prepared to fight with smaller, more lethal elements operating at considerable distances from one another. This paucity and non-linearity of the forces will be largely the result of arms control agreements and of the high cost of modern forces.[13] As General John W. Foss, former commander of the Army's Training and Doctrine Command commented, '[Y]ou're not going to see the dense bat-tlefield we saw before. We are projecting that we will be moving [conceptually] into a non-linear battlefield somewhere in the late '90s'.[14]

The Army envisages ground commanders employing high-technology sensors to locate and track enemy forces at ranges up to 400 kilometres. When the distance between contending ground forces closes to about 100 km, US commanders will employ long-range strike systems to engage and destroy their opponents. However, war-games indicate that while massed fires can inflict heavy damage upon an opponent, they are not expected to be decisive in themselves. There will still be a requirement for a manoeuvre phase of the battle in which highly mobile forces would close with the enemy and force him to decisive engagement.[15]

[11] Comment to the author by Dr Mohammed El-Sayed Said, Director of the Center for Political and Strategic Studies, Cairo, Egypt, 30 Jan. 1992.
[12] *AirLand Battle-Future: Doctrine for a Strategic Force for the 1990s and Beyond*, Background Brief no. 9 (Association of the US Army: Arlington, Va., Feb. 1990).
[13] Silvasy, Jr, Major General S., 'AirLand Battle-Future: the tactical battlefield', *Military Review*, Feb. 1991, p. 3.
[14] Roos, J. G. and Schemmer, B. F., 'An exclusive AFJI interview with General John W. Foss, USA, Commanding General, US Army Training and Doctrine Command', *Armed Forces Journal International*, Mar. 1990, p. 63.
[15] Foss, General J. W., 'AirLand Battle-Future', *Army*, Feb. 1991, p. 23.

One writer has described the execution of the manoeuvre phase as 'a sequence wherein dispersed forces mass rapidly; conduct the fight; and redisperse to reconstitute forces'. He listed the following force implications of the new thinking:

1. The corps remains the centrepiece.
2. Greater agility is achieved for the division echelon.
3. Brigades are to be combined arms forces.
4. A simpler, service-oriented logistics system is attained.[16]

AirLand Battle-Future is particularly notable for its emphasis on the tactical initiative. It envisages retention of an offensive posture against hostile forces at lower levels, even though the overall command may be on the defensive at higher (e.g., operational) levels. It avoids meeting engagements, and seeks to pre-empt enemy preparation of hasty defensive positions. Tactical units (division and below) are expected to be relieved of much of their logistical responsibilities in order to enhance their operational agility. In this regard, the corps echelon is expected to shoulder much of the support work currently done at lower levels.[17]

US Army thinking for the future security of Europe has focused on a notion of a US ground contingent in Germany consisting of a single corps composed of two divisions and an armoured cavalry regiment. The corps would not be assigned a sector of the front for defence, as in the past, but rather an area of operations, in consonance with the idea of a non-linear battle area. Hostile forces might be detected at great distance from the forward elements of the organization by long-range reconnaissance systems, and taken under fire long before they came in contact with friendly troops. The principal combat elements would then rapidly mass at advantageous points to attack the enemy, destroy his forces and disperse again to prepare for other engagements. The precise size and composition of the force would depend upon constraints imposed by international agreement and by US security policy. General Powell has estimated that the total strength figure for all services might be as much as 150 000. General C. E. Saint, then Commander-in-Chief of the US Army in Europe, remarked in 1990 that 80 000 ground troops would be sufficient in a total force of slightly over 100 000.[18]

Whether either of these figures might still pertain in the year 2000 is a matter of conjecture. So, too, is the matter of retention of a corps structure. Other factors may become dominant as is discussed below. One such factor, of course, is the attitude of the host government as the years progress. Recent opinion polls

[16] AirLand Battle-Future: Doctrine for a Strategic Force for the 1990s and Beyond (note 12).

[17] Silvasy (note 13), p. 10. On p. 24 of his article, General Foss identified the gaining and maintaining of the initiative as critical to the success of AirLand Battle-Future, and the criticality of this feature as the most important finding of exploratory war-gaming exercises.

[18] General Powell gave his view in a speech to the Land Warfare Forum, Association of the US Army, Arlington, Va., 8 Aug. 1991; General Saint's view was reported in Gordon, M. R., 'NATO weighing new look with combined allied units', New York Times, 23 May 1990, p. A-8.

in Germany reflect a waning enthusiasm among Germans for even a limited US troop presence in their country. Respondents favouring a complete withdrawal of US forces rose to 57 per cent of those polled in 1991.[19] Further, prominent US senators have recently made reference to similar views among their constituents. Senator William Cohen of Maine described the 'prevailing view' in the United States towards NATO as 'no longer necessary, relevant or affordable', and likely to become a 'mainly European organization'. At most, he thought, the US troop figure might be 75 000. A colleague, Senator Warren Rudman, cited a figure of 60 000.[20] Neither of these latter figures would necessarily rule out retention of a corps structure for the ground element, but the manning would clearly be thin.

AirLand Battle-Future, of course, is necessarily tentative and subject to modification, at least in its details, as the evolving security structure in Europe gradually clarifies. It will be affected by agreements on conventional armed forces in Europe (CFE), by agreements on confidence-building measures (CBMs) and by the role ascribed to the Conference on Security and Co-operation in Europe (CSCE). Most importantly, as noted above, it will be impacted by unilateral national decisions in Washington and Bonn and by multilateral NATO decisions about the future of the alliance and about residual force levels in a very different Europe than that of the past four decades. Finally, it may be affected by the emergence of a more vital, activist Western European Union (WEU) with a growing sense of purpose for a role in the military area. To what extent WEU activism may reduce requirements for US forces in Europe is uncertain, but it clearly represents a fresh and important factor for consideration.[21]

An important area of difference in Europe will be the density of nuclear weapons which may be deployed in Europe and the residual political and psychological dependence which NATO states might place on them. As noted earlier, CIS forces have been withdrawn from Hungary and Czechoslovakia, and are scheduled to be out of eastern Germany in 1994. The Soviets announced the initiation of the withdrawal of their Northern Group of Forces from Poland on 9 April 1991. The movement should be complete before the middle of the decade. The departure of these forces and the dissolution of the Warsaw Pact will create a significant non-nuclear belt across the centre of the European continent, leaving little justification for continued deployment of ground-based nuclear weapons in the West. Political pressures for their removal are strong, from both sides of the Atlantic.

By the year 2000 it is estimated that, in addition to the industrialized nations, at least 15 developing nations may be capable of manufacturing ballistic missiles. Further, 8 may be able to produce nuclear warheads, and as many as 30 chemical munitions. For this reason the United States expects to have by that time in place a system for Global Protection Against Limited Strikes (GPALS).

---

[19] 'Mood shift in Germany', *International Herald Tribune*, 30 Jan. 1992, p. 1.

[20] Fisher, M., 'Europeans told of US isolationism', *Washington Post*, 10 Feb. 1992, p. A1.

[21] van Eekelen, W., 'Developing the WEU', *Defense '92* (International Defense Review: Coulsdon, Surrey, UK, 1992), pp. 35–38.

The system will provide a measure of defence against ballistic missiles for US forward deployed forces and allies.[22]

In late 1990 the Chief of Staff of the US Air Force, General Merrill A. McPeak, outlined the thrust of major programmes for his service. As his 'number one priority' he identified reorganization of the tactical forces. He pointed out that in the decade from the mid-1980s to the mid-1990s the Air Force will have shrunk by 20 per cent. It will be necessary to shift from homogeneous to composite wings, he intimated, in order to maintain force effectiveness.[23] The composite wing would have different types of aircraft assigned for different missions, including air superiority, long- and short-range land attack, reconnaissance and suppression of enemy air defences.

'The composite wing makes a lot of sense to me', McPeak said, 'especially in forward deployed locations. Wings ought to be organized around their missions [in] the way we intend to use them in wartime, so they can train together and work together in peacetime'. Wings intended primarily for logistical support might have a mix of transports and tankers, but they might also have a squadron or two of combat aircraft.

'Some [wings] can continue to be monolithic', he allowed, apparently referring primarily to those based in the United States with a primary mission of overseas reinforcement. In these units there are considerations regarding economies of scale to be taken into account. The result will be a mix in the Air Force of both composite and monolithic wings.

In anticipation of the conflict in the Persian Gulf region General McPeak remarked, 'We know that if we have to do something in Saudi Arabia today it will not be a wing of 72 PAA (primary aircraft authorized) F-16s that does it. It will be a force made up of some attackers, some defenders, some stand-off jammers, some [Wild] Weasels (anti-radar attack aircraft), some tankers, and so forth'. Subsequent events in the region were to prove him quite correct in this regard. Moreover, the vulnerabilities of the early deployed Desert Shield forces to hostile attack were evident. The necessity for a balanced tactical air capability from the outset was equally clear.[24]

More dramatic, and perhaps further reaching in its implications, has been the restructuring of the Air Force. Essentially, the Tactical and Strategic Air Commands have been combined into a single Air Combat Command (ACC), with tanker aircraft grouped with transports to form the new Air Mobility Command (AMC). As General John M. Loh, newly designated ACC commander, commented, 'In the 1980s it became increasingly apparent that while a target may be strategic or tactical, an aircraft is not. Capability is capability. The bold reorganization now underway capitalizes on this understanding'.[25] The concept

[22] Cheney, R., 'US defense strategy for an era of uncertainty', *Defense '92* (International Defense Review: Coulsdon, Surrey, UK, 1992), p. 8.

[23] Canan, J. W., 'McPeak's plan', *Air Force Magazine*, Feb. 1991, pp. 20–21.

[24] Moore, M., 'War exposed rivalries, weaknesses in military', *Washington Post*, 10 June 1991, p. A-17.

[25] Wilson, J. R., 'US Air Force reorganization', *International Defense Review*, Dec. 1991, p. 1311.

reinforces the trend towards command unification manifest in the composite wing reorganization.

One Air Force weapon programme which scored particularly startling success in the Persian Gulf conflict was the F-117A stealth fighter. Although the aircraft represented only 2.5 per cent of the air forces deployed, it was responsible for attacking 31 per cent of the targets during the first day of operations. Further, according to Air Force analyses, 8 F-117As can accomplish the same bombing tasks as 16 conventional aircraft, and without any requirement for radar and air defence suppressing aircraft to accompany them. Without the accompaniment, the F-117As could operate with only 2 supporting tankers instead of 11 for the larger conventional force. According to Air Force Secretary Donald Rice, the stealth aircraft can 'provide more combat capability from a smaller number of assets with less risk to personnel'.[26]

With respect to development programmes for the future, General McPeak said that he planned to continue the Air Force focus on one major programme in each mission area. This would include the B-2 for strategic bombing, the C-17 for airlift and the Advanced Tactical Fighter for air superiority. He also mentioned 'other important modernization programmes—the Advanced Cruise Missile, AMRAAM (advanced medium-range air-to-air missile), ICBMs, Titan IV, Joint STARS (Joint Surveillance and Target Attack Radar System) and KC-135 (tanker) re-engining'.[27]

The Air Force plans to reduce its number of tactical fighter wings through the 1990s from 36 to 26.5, largely through the purchase of additional stealth fighters and the retirement of older aircraft. Lower numbers of conventional fighters will be acquired, and many reconnaissance and radar attack aircraft will be eliminated.[28]

Air Force hopes for increasing the proportion of stealth aircraft in the total force through acquisition of large numbers of B-2 bombers appear unlikely to be realized before the year 2000. Secretary Rice told the congressional House Armed Services Committee in March 1991, that the B-2 was 'stealthier' than the F-117A and that it would fly five or six times further and deliver five or six times the number of precision munitions of the smaller aircraft. General Michael Dugan, retired former chief of staff, elaborated to the effect that Air Force plans for reduction in the size of its strategic and tactical forces had been predicated on the benefits to be derived from the stealth technology. However, subsequent budgetary pressures seem likely to delay the programme.[29]

Remarkable as the performance of the F-117A was early in the Persian Gulf War (only the F-117A was used to attack heavily defended targets in downtown Baghdad), it was soon outpaced by larger numbers of sorties by other types of aircraft. As one observer commented, 'Desert Storm has shown us that precision and stealth cannot do it alone; you need mass and persistence. We still

[26] Opall, B., 'Air Force sticks by its stealth plans', *Defense News*, 1 Apr. 1991, p. 6.
[27] Canan (note 23).
[28] Opall (note 26).
[29] Opall (note 26).

need weapons to deliver bombs *en masse'*. He went on to argue that the B-52 heavy bombers employed against the Iraqi Republican Guard could never have been replaced by F-117As because of the requirement for high-ordnance tonnage against targets of that type.[30]

V. The nature of US theatre forces in the year 2000

The variety and complexity of the weaponry of theatre forces is a constantly expanding spiral, harnessing new technologies and physical principles and integrating them into the calculus of war. For each new weapon there rapidly emerges a counter-weapon, with requisite functions being performed in novel ways on the ground, in the air or in space. Each system requires sensors or sensor data, fed through high-speed communications systems, for the acquisition and identification of potential targets and for post-strike assessment of damage inflicted. As counter-weapons emerge, counter-suppressants are devised to neutralize or destroy them. The entire process is a constantly shifting kaleidoscope of capabilities in ascendancy or remission. While it is not the purpose of this chapter to provide a comprehensive digest of weapon developments of the future, it is instructive to review a few of the more important weapon programmes in their early stages in order to gain some insight into the likely nature of future theatre war. Such insight may afford a rudimentary understanding of the possible risks and costs involved.

The US Army has fostered a comprehensive armoured systems modernization programme for the development of the next generation of heavy weapon systems. The first of over 6000 planned acquisitions is scheduled for late in the current decade, but most will not be fielded until 2004 or 2005. Four essential elements of the Army's combined arms team are earmarked to be built on a common heavy vehicular chassis, and two on a medium chassis. The four heavyweights are the next generation tank (often referred to as 'Block III' main battle tank), the advanced field artillery system (AFAS), the future infantry fighting vehicle (FIFV) and a combat mobility vehicle (CMV—essentially, an armoured mine clearing machine). The two middle weights are a 'line-of-sight antitank vehicle' (LOSAT) and a 'future armored rearm vehicle-artillery' (FARV-A).[31]

Notably, all six weapons are intended to fulfil their roles in context with a combined arms threat of the type recently posed by Soviet and Iraqi forces. In spite of the current disarray of forces and defence industries in the new Commonwealth of Independent States, the troop units and weapons systems of that bloc remain a benchmark for US Army planning. The CIS armaments industrial

[30] Opall (note 26), p. 29.

[31] Ludvigsen, E. C., 'Armor's future from one, many', *Army*, May 1991, pp. 32–42. Colonel Daniel Kaufman, Professor and Head of the Social Sciences Department at the US Military Academy, has expressed doubt about the Armor Modernization Program. He believes that the Army may forgo the programme in favour of improvements in communications and logistics. See Kaufman, D., 'The Army in transition', Defense and Arms Control Studies Program, Center for International Studies Massachusetts Institute of Technology, 24 Sep. 1991.

base remains the largest in the world, and it is likely to remain a major source of armoured equipment, not only for indigenous forces, but also for ambitious regimes in developing countries .

The Block III tank is expected to have a 50 per cent more powerful gun than the current generation, perhaps using electrothermal energy rather than powder for propellant. The larger 140-mm calibre of the gun will necessitate an automatic loader, but reduce the size of the crew from four men (as on the Abrams M1A2) to three. Frontal protection will be at least 35 per cent greater than the Abrams, but the vehicle is expected to be lighter due to savings connected with the crew reduction. Armour will be of modular, bolt-on type to enable upgrading in the future, whenever new designs of armour might become available. The removable armour arrangement might also permit more expeditious strategic deployment of the vehicles by permitting them to be shipped in a stripped-down configuration when the potential hostile force appears to be of only modest proportions.[32]

The AFAS self-propelled field gun is expected to have a greatly increased range over current artillery—up to 40 km—and a 300 per cent increase in rate of fire, possibly using a liquid propellant rather than powder. It will have greatly improved armour against hostile counter-battery fire and be able to operate independently, without a fire direction centre. Its firing options will be so flexible that it will be able to fire as many as four rounds at differing elevations in such a manner that they will all arrive at the target at the same time, achieving maximum surprise.[33]

The FIFV will have the same degree of armour protection as the tank, permitting it to travel wherever the tank may go. This will permit the infantry to remain mounted until they have overrun assigned objectives. The main armament of the vehicle will consist of an automatic gun in the 30-mm to 60-mm range and an antitank missile system. In addition, the vehicle will have a centrally controlled hostiles proximity suppression system for dealing with enemy infantry in the immediate vicinity. The FIFV will have a 70 per cent greater cruising range than the current Bradley IFV and one-third greater cross-country speed. Vehicular electronics will improve fire control while permitting a reduction of one man in the size of the crew. The first FIFV is scheduled to be produced in 2005, with a planned (perhaps ambitious) purchase of 1321 units over the life of the system.[34]

The CMV, which may also begin to appear in 2005, will be designed to provide the first real capability for mine removal at speeds commensurate with armoured attack. AirLand Battle-Future envisages very rapid concentration of forces and virtually immediate offensive action. The CMV is intended to give armoured forces the practical capability for fulfilling the doctrine.[35]

[32] Ludvigsen (note 31).
[33] Ludvigsen (note 31).
[34] Ludvigsen (note 31).
[35] Ludvigsen (note 31).

The LOSAT, which began as the highest priority item in the family of systems under development, may be postponed. The intent has been to provide a replacement for the current improved TOW (tube-launched, optically tracked, wire-guided) antitank missile vehicle (M901), but fiscal constraints may intervene.[36] Scheduled for deployment in 1998, the LOSAT will employ a laser-guided kinetic energy weapon with terminal ballistics comparable to that of a tank gun. The missile will have a time of flight of only two or three seconds, minimizing enemy countermeasures, and an ability for multiple target tracking.[37]

Finally, the FARV-A is planned for deployment with the AFAS in 2004. It will provide automated ammunition resupply through a quick disconnect port that protects the entire operation from hostile artillery and small arms fire and nuclear, biological and chemical (NBC) contamination. A remarkable feature of the system will be its ability to electrically 'read' each round of ammunition, establish its exact weight, its production lot, and so on and provide that information to the AFAS computer for the preparation of firing orders.[38]

The armoured systems modernization programme represents but one such effort currently underway, shaping the Army of the 21st century. It is of special importance, however, inasmuch as it impacts the principal combat arms, honing them in accordance with the vision established by AirLand Battle-Future doctrine. It also sets the standards for commonality of systems protection and performance, affording maximum opportunity for integration of the arms on the conceptual battlefield. Undoubtedly, much will change in the plans as currently written, but the fundamental direction has been set. The ground forces of the 2000s will be a highly sophisticated, automated, protected, versatile team.

The principal combat aircraft envisaged for the next decade is the Advanced Tactical Fighter (ATF, also called F-22), of which the Air Force anticipates acquiring 750. The aircraft will employ a new generation of low observable technologies making it 1000 times more difficult to detect than the current F-15 fighter. It will have twice the range of the F-15 and cruise at one and one-half times the speed of sound. It will be more manoeuvrable than present day fighters and will contain a substantially enhanced suite of avionics. Its sensor devices will afford it an ability to detect hostile aircraft and to launch air-to-air missiles before it is detected itself.[39]

Finally, it should be borne in mind that the integrative networks which tie the various battlefield players together may constitute the most critical element of all. High-technology weaponry tends to be far more dependent on other systems than most weapons of the past. Long-range strike systems are no better than the sensors which find the targets, the computers which determine the targeting data and the communications networks which link the various components.

---

[36] Association of the US Army, *Washington Update*, Feb. 1992, p. 2.

[37] Ludvigsen (note 31).

[38] Ludvigsen (note 31).

[39] Gellman, B., 'Zeroing in on America's 21st century fighter jet, *Washington Post, 21* Apr. 1991, p. 1.

These elements are all likely to undergo substantial, if less visible, development as the decade advances.

VI. The view from NATO

To the extent that the views of the NATO Secretary-General Manfred Wörner reflect those of the European members, the continued active involvement of the United States, however diminished its force representation, is an essential element of the vitality of the alliance. Writing in December 1991 Wörner said:

Of course, the North American military commitment can and is being reduced—indeed by as much as 50 per cent for the United States—but it should still be militarily meaningful. Without a North American commitment, European nations would lack the element of reassurance that has allowed them to integrate and overcome historical animosities. In the words of one commentator, the United States remains Europe's 'pacifier'.[40]

With much of the cogency of the traditional threat alleviated, the necessity for NATO to place heavy reliance on resort to nuclear escalation as a prominent element of its deterrent strategy has diminished as well. Nevertheless, Europe will remain a centre of great importance to the world, and policy makers may choose to underscore the point with persuasive evidence of continued US commitment to regional security. However well US military presence and political reassurance may serve the purpose, the retention of some theatre nuclear capability seems likely. Without short-range ground-based systems, and without intermediate-range nuclear forces (INF), the USA must look to air- and sea-based systems to provide the residual theatre nuclear capability. Addressing the air element, the former Supreme Allied Commander, Europe (SACEUR), General John Galvin, punctuated his remarks to the US Senate Armed Services Committee in March 1991, by saying, 'It is essential for the [NATO] alliance to retain a reliable, effective, dual-capable [nuclear and non-nuclear] aircraft force, armed with modern delivery systems'.[41]

Clearly an issue which has required close examination is the one regarding the possible abolition of national corps within the NATO structure. As is evident from the discussion above, the notion has run at cross purposes with US Army thinking in context with AirLand Battle-Future. The United States has been generally supportive of a German initiative which will create multinational organizations in place of the current pattern of national corps. Defense Secretary Richard Cheney described a typical multinational corps as one made up of a British division, a US division and a German division.[42] Further, the USA participated in the NATO summit meeting in London in July 1990 and concurred in the London Declaration on a Transformed North Atlantic Alliance,

[40] Wörner, M., 'NATO transformed: the significance of the Rome summit', *NATO Review*, Dec. 1991, pp. 7–8.
[41] Hitchens, T., 'Stand-off capability key to NATO nuclear plans', *Defense News*, 18 Mar. 1991, p. 11.
[42] Gordon (note 18).

an instrument of that meeting. In part the document said that NATO 'will rely increasingly on multinational corps made up of national units'.[43]

Such an arrangement would have a number of advantages. Most importantly, it would lower the visibility of foreign forces on German soil, and it would continue the subordination of German forces to international authority without encroaching on German sovereignty by 'particularizing' the manner in which their troops were controlled. It might also facilitate the deployment of certain German contingents to other countries where they might otherwise be less welcome. Secretary Cheney expressed the heart of the matter with his comment that we face a 'set of circumstances in which we will have to be more sensitive than we've had to be in the past about how host nations look at the troop presence of NATO forces in their areas'. In addition, he pointed out that, in an era of greater emphasis on political matters in Europe, the multinational units would provide 'one more way to give a political dimension to our military arrangements'.[44]

A key element of the newly evolving NATO military strategy is the formation of a corps-size rapid-reaction force. The only such force available in the past to the SACEUR has been the Allied Command Europe (ACE) Mobile Force, traditionally a brigade-size formation assembled from different national units. The ACE Mobile Force has provided an essentially politico-military instrument for demonstrating the solidarity of NATO in the event of hostile pressure or threat to a particular sector of the defensive perimeter. The concept has had particular relevance for the northern and southern flanks (Norway and Turkey).

The creation of a corps-size rapid-reaction force will give the SACEUR very much more than a representational instrument. In fact, it would constitute a serious potential for local war fighting wherever it might be deployed. The command headquarters for the organization should operate as a completely international body with a capacity for controlling national divisions and lesser size units attached to it on a rotating or as-required basis. General Galvin described normal US participation in the rapid-reaction force as a division, or possibly corps troops (non-divisional units directly subordinate to the corps headquarters), such as an aviation brigade or long-range artillery.[45] Of course, the international organization requires extensive communications, intelligence, logistics and strategic lift support in order to fulfil its prescribed role.[46]

Of particular note is the possibility that the force could be 'blocked out of the NATO structure for use in out-of-area emergencies', according to NATO Secretary-General Wörner. Under consideration is a dual-command structure that would have the organization responsive to both NATO and the WEU. According to this plan, the force would receive orders from the WEU when

[43] Miller, D., 'Multinationality: implications of NATO's evolving strategy', *International Defense Review*, Mar. 1991, p. 211.
[44] Gordon (note 18).
[45] Clauson, K., 'Galvin expects US to serve in Europe fast-response force', *European Stars and Stripes*, 12 Sep. 1991, p. 1.
[46] Hitchens (note 2), pp. 3, 28.

operating out of the NATO area. General Galvin's suggestion that the force ultimately encompass as many as five divisions (including armoured, mechanized, infantry, airborne and air mobile units) has heightened interest in the concept.[47]

As advantageous as the political aspects of multinational military organizations may be, there are many problems. Language is not the least of them. There are differences in training, equipment capability, organizational structure, operational procedures, communications patterns and supplies, not to mention such basic matters as troop diet and social standards and values. Continuing attention to the resolution of differences between the new US Army thinking and that being pursued at the political level will be needed in order for the Army to transition smoothly to its new responsibilities.

While some may argue that the US Army has had experience with multinational corps (e.g., the Australian Brigade attached to the US II Field Force in Viet Nam, and the 12th German Panzer Division subordinated to the US VII Corps in Bavaria), the matter is moot. The attachment of a unit of one nationality to a larger organization of another is not the same as the formation of an integrated, multinational force. The latter case generally requires many more internal adjustments and compromises for the various parts to be welded firmly into a cohesive body, particularly at the level of the controlling headquarters. It should be noted that while some allied units were attached to various US Army contingents in World War II, the major national forces in Europe were grouped at the operational level (i.e., army group) under General Omar Bradley and Field Marshal Bernard L. Montgomery. The multinational flavour of the enterprise occurred primarily at the theatre (strategic) level, under General Dwight D. Eisenhower.

A possible solution to the national identity problem may be a true multinationalization of the rapid-reaction corps, with a simpler mixture of divisions and some staff and support elements among the remaining formations. Current plans call for seven other corps: one, all-German, to be stationed in eastern Germany, the rest to be located west of the former inter-German border. Two of the corps would be commanded by German officers, one each by a US, a Belgian and a Dutch officer and one directed by a mixed German-Danish staff, possibly with rotating German and Danish commanders.[48] The arrangement is not greatly different from the current one, but the forces are certain to be smaller, with more cross-assignment of subordinate units for operational purposes. Some of the units, particularly those from Belgium and the Netherlands, may be stationed further to the west.

Still another development possibly impacting the shape of US theatre forces in Europe is the initiative by France and Germany to create a joint force that could operate outside the NATO structure. The concept would expand the 4200-member, French-German brigade to corps size. The force might number

[47] Politi, A., 'Alliance, WEU may command rapid reaction force', *Defense News*, 6 May 1991, p. 1.
[48] Montgomery, P., 'NATO is planning to cut US forces in Europe by 50 percent', *New York Times*, 29 May 1991, p. A-14.

between 35 000 and 100 000 troops, possibly with participation by other WEU member countries.

Recognizing that other national leaders were puzzled by the move, German Chancellor Helmut Kohl sought to reassure them. 'This is neither an expression of doubt of the stability of the Atlantic alliance nor an attempt to create a competing body', he told the Bonn Parliament on 6 November 1991.[49] Still, the proposal was initially upsetting to US military planners, and probably to others as well. Perceptions of need for NATO forces could diminish, as, indeed, they could for US forces in particular. No timetable has been set, so the details of subordination arrangements, for example, could remain unresolved for some time.

The most definitive statement regarding the future organizational structure of US ground forces in Europe was made by General Powell in testimony before the Senate Budget Committee on 3 February 1992. One division, he said, would be part of a multinational corps commanded by a US lieutenant general. The second division will be assigned to a German corps.[50] The arrangement comports with evolving NATO thinking, but it leaves unanswered the question of how the divisions will be supported. If they are to be as light and dextrous as the AirLand Battle-Future concept would indicate, they will require something more behind them than an international or different national control structure.

VII. The reinforcement problem: strategic lift

The US ability to reinforce NATO will depend to some extent upon its programmes for pre-positioned *matériel* and air- and sealift, but the issue is likely to be less critical for Europe than it has been in the past. While the CFE Treaty may impact negatively on the maintenance of POMCUS stocks (pre-positioned organizational *matériel* configured to unit sets) in Central Europe, the substantial increase in warning time, as discussed above, should afford NATO commanders adequate time for re-establishing a credible defence. Strategic lift will continue to be a major consideration for the world-wide contingency force, as it was for fulfilment of Operation Desert Shield. Early in the planning for that undertaking, the Commander-in-Chief, Central Command, General H. Norman Schwarzkopf, estimated that it would require 17 weeks to transport a force of some 200 000 to 250 000 troops to Saudi Arabia for defensive purposes.[51] As matters turned out, employing shipping from a broad spectrum of sources, a force of more than twice that size was in place, ready for offensive operations, in only slightly more time.

Strategic lift assets are items of highly volatile funding by the US Congress and the Department of Defense (DOD). While there appears to be substantial

---

[49] Fisher, M., 'NATO leaders seek new role', *New York Times*, 7 Nov. 1991, p. A45.

[50] US Army, Office of the Chief of Staff, *1992 US Congressional Hearing Summary* (summary of testimony of Defense Secretary Cheney and Chairman of the Joint Chiefs of Staff Powell), 3 Feb. 1992 (US Army, Office of the Chief of Staff: Washington, DC, 1992), p. 4.

[51] Comment by General Schwarzkopf in *Washington Post*, 3 May 1991, p. A-16.

support for new acquisitions in the wake of the Persian Gulf War, the enthusiasm could wane as other priorities arise. In 1981 the DOD undertook a congressionally mandated air mobility study which found that national airlift capabilities should be increased from 48 to 66 million ton-miles per day by the turn of the century. The study was based, of course, on an expectation of continued Soviet threat, and in April 1990, the DOD reduced the planned purchase of new C-17 transport aircraft by 43 per cent. Defense Secretary Cheney explained that the original number planned exceeded the requirements of 'the newly emerging strategic environment'.[52]

The record for sealift assets has been similar. Sealift requirements were estimated in 1989 to be one million short tons. The capacity at that time was approximately 797 000 tons, a shortfall of some 20 per cent. The DOD plans in 1990 envisaged an increase to 839 800 tons by the end of the century, but the plans were later dropped.[53]

Nevertheless, the success of Operation Desert Storm and the consensus regarding the stationing of most US forces in CONUS in the future have stirred renewed interest in strategic lift. Moreover, the proven value of pre-positioned ships in the Indian Ocean with stocks of war *matériel* for use in Saudi Arabia has increased enthusiasm for making additional investments in that approach to the reinforcement problem. Despite declining spending for defence over the next five years, the Bush Administration asked for an additional $1.2 billion for sealift over previously programmed funds for 1993 (for a total of $3 billion). A new classified strategic lift requirements study reportedly calls for construction of 20 new roll-on, roll-off vessels and additional pre-positioned depot ships around the globe.[54]

The Army, the principal potential beneficiary of strategic lift, has stated its future requirements in broad terms. It seeks support for the movement of a corps-size force of up to five divisions anywhere in the world, with a forcible initial entry if necessary. Its objective is to be able to place a lead brigade on the ground in the objective area four days after the unit is prepared to go. An entire division should be delivered in 12 days, and two divisions within a month. The full corps, together with supporting forces. should be delivered in no more than 75 days. Further, the Army seeks assurance that it will have sufficient supplies and ammunition for operations immediately upon arrival, and which would last until regular lines of communications and supply are established.[55] These requirements, of course, are intended primarily for potential theatres of operations other than Europe. However, the assets which may be acquired by the other ser-

[52] Schemmer, B. F., 'Lack of analysis behind C-17 cuts worries Army, Air Force, and Congress', *Armed Forces Journal International*, July 1990, p. 46.

[53] *Strategic Mobility: Getting There is the Big Problem*, Association of the US Army special report (Association of the US Army: Arlington, Va., Dec. 1989), p. 13.

[54] DiBenedetto, W., 'Budget pumps extra $1.2 billion into sealift fleet', *Journal of Commerce*, 30 Jan. 1992, p. 1.

[55] Granrud, Major General J. H., Assistant Deputy Chief of Staff for Operations and Plans, Force Development, HQ Department of the Army, in briefing to the Institute of Land Warfare, Association of the US Army, 6 May 1991.

vices to meet the Army's needs would be available to support a general reinforcement of Europe if a dangerous situation were to emerge there. After 1995
the Army plans to have one corps, composed of five active divisions, in a
highly ready configuration in CONUS. Behind this it will have a second corps
of three active divisions with reserve component brigades attached. Finally, it
will have a third corps, composed entirely of reserve component forces (eight
divisions), as a follow-on force if necessary. Two of the divisions of this corps
are expected to be maintained in cadre status and may require up to 15 months
to prepare for deployment.[56]

VIII. Reserve structure

All four services are dependent upon reserve forces for support and reinforcement in time of national emergency. For the Army and the Air Force, the
reserves include troops of the National Guard. For the most part, the dependence is valid and the support provided well worth the investment made in them.
In the Persian Gulf conflict 228 560 reservists were called to active duty to provide a wide variety of skills and services, including duty in the combat area.[57]

About 7 per cent of the reserves called up were in three National Guard brigades intended for attachment to Regular Army divisions ordered to deploy to
Saudi Arabia. Unfortunately, the brigades were found to be insufficiently
trained for combat duty and were held in the USA to complete their training in
case they were needed later. The problem was limited to combat manoeuvre
units, as many combat support (artillery, engineer, intelligence, etc.) units were
able to fulfil their required proficiency standards. The lesson for future Army
planning is quite clear. Combat support and combat service support (quarter-
master, transportation, ordnance, etc.) organizations with relatively narrow
technical functions may be expected to maintain their proficiency with standard
training as traditionally provided, but units designed for close combat, which
integrate with the full array of combat participants, require frequent and intensive training not normally afforded the reserves. The Army came to realize that
it was a mistake to rely upon these units to form part of force packages scheduled for early deployment in response to foreign crises. Accordingly, the Army
of the year 2000 is unlikely to depend upon reserve component manoeuvre
units for early reinforcement.

It may take time for the Army to define the linkage between its force planning and General Powell's conceptual force categories. Nevertheless, it is
apparent that the Atlantic Force, would encompass most of the slower arriving
units. Considering the length of warning time envisaged for a contingency in
Europe, it would seem reasonable to include reserves of all types. While man-

---

[56] Peay, Lieutenant General J. H. Binford, III, Deputy Chief of Staff for Operations and Plans,
Department of the Army, in a briefing to the Resolutions Committee of the Association of the US Army,
11 Oct. 1991.
[57] Sia, R. H. P., 'Army will restructure troops to avoid sending reserve units into early combat',
Baltimore Sun, 21 Apr. 1991, p. 12.

oeuvre units may take more time to prepare for combat, the time would probably be adequate if political leaders decided sufficiently early to call them to the colours to begin their training.

There are, of course, practical limits to such arrangements. Some intermediate size crises—like Desert Shield/Desert Storm—might require participation of units from both the Contingency and Atlantic forces. Clearly, the vast majority of units scheduled for early deployment would be part of the Regular Army, whatever force category they may be associated with. The principle exceptions would be those units of a specialized nature which have a high correlation between civilian and military skills, such as clerical, historical, decontamination and water purification detachments.

IX. A final word

This chapter would be incomplete if it did not include a statement of recognition that the quality of US theatre forces in the next century is dependent upon considerably more than the arms they might bear and the strategic and operational concepts under which they might operate. The orchestration of the full capabilities of the forces depends upon high-quality leadership, intelligent and rigorously trained personnel, and a spirit of dedication to mission accomplishment at all levels throughout the structure. These factors, in turn, are dependent upon a well-trained and educated officer corps, imaginative individual and organizational training, and a leavening of seasoned small unit leaders. However intangible these factors may appear, they are consumptive of resources and demanding of high-level attention and husbanding. The success of Operation Desert Storm was as much a product of these aspects of power as it was of the more prominent and measurable aspects discussed above. As kaleidoscopic as the other aspects may be, these are among the constants upon which all military efforts may turn.

10. High technology after the cold war

Benoit Morel

I. Introduction

In the post-war era, the Soviet Union developed a very impressive and powerful technology base, mostly in the areas of weaponry and space. This technological infrastructure is basically irrelevant for the civilian economic needs of the former Soviet republics. These new nations are undergoing economic, political and structural transitions of unprecedented scale. Little is understood about the forces driving the rapid changes in these nations and in their relations with the West. Technology is an important part of these forces, but its future impact is very uncertain. In addition, technology has both a civilian and a military or security component, which are intertwined in a complicated way. The impact of technological advance affects not only the country in which it takes place, but also other countries. This chapter attempts to shed some light on these not-so-hidden dimensions.

The chapter addresses this international aspect, beginning with a discussion of US technology and its relevance to relations between the USA and the post-Soviet republics. Although in its way the United States is also undergoing an economic conversion consisting of a reduction of its defence industry, the size and nature of this process is not comparable to the momentous changes taking place in the nations of the Commonwealth. Furthermore, the US effort at military exploitation of high technology is not weakening significantly. The discussion therefore tends to focus on this aspect of the US technological challenge.

The second part of the chapter deals with the post-Soviet Commonwealth nations. The situation in these countries is very confused. According to recent statements from the Russian Government, during the Soviet era up to 60 per cent or more of the Soviet manufacturing industry was reserved for the military. This is more than in the United States even during World War II. Of the 11 million or so people employed in the weapon industry in the area between the Atlantic Ocean and the Ural Mountains, about 8 million were in the Soviet Union. Even a very active policy designed to convert military into civilian production will at best consume a great deal of time before it leads to a military–industrial complex of comparable size to those of the Western democracies. It is clear from the start that even if the Commonwealth nations do not consider the military threat of the West as a relevant factor in the organization of their security today, they will be tempted to take advantage of their demonstrated skill in military technology for sheer economic reasons.

The third part of this chapter investigates some of the consequences of this fact on regional and global security. The final section of the chapter takes a general look at the role that the United States has chosen to play so far and may play in the future to affect the impact of technology on the historical processes taking place in the Commonwealth of Independent States.

II. Developments in US military high technology

Technology has always played a central role in US–Soviet relations, and it is safe to predict that this will continue to be the case in relations between the USA and the post-Soviet republics. Technology in this context has had an economic and a military component. This chapter focuses mostly on the latter.

High technology could become a major irritant in US–Russian relations. The USA will remain very concerned for some time about the security implications of letting its old rival acquire technologies from the West which have a potential military use. This is not an irrational attitude. The Soviet system was better organized for the military exploitation of new technologies than for introducing them in the civilian economy. This tradition may not disappear.

Furthermore, the military exploitation of high technology is an important component of the US military posture and may become relatively more important as equipment procurement budgets shrink. The USA will probably persevere in its dedicated attempt to exploit new technologies for military purposes. One important function of maintaining a superior military technology is to preserve or improve a power projection capability. The United States will need this if it wishes to enforce a 'new world order'. The efficiency of US military technology in the future will depend in part on the efficiency of counter-systems to US systems, and on their proliferation. It is in the remains of the Soviet military–industrial complex—scattered among the new republics, but with the highest concentration in Belarus, Russia and Ukraine—that the skills and will to develop and export that kind of system exist. The activities of the military–industrial complex of the republics and its access to US high technology will therefore be a major preoccupation.

US military high technology and its relentless development will unquestionably have some impact on US relations with the new nations arising from the wreckage of the Soviet Union. It should not be expected that military technology will be a preoccupation of each of the new nations, but it will most likely be of concern to Belarus, Kazakhstan, Russia or Ukraine because of their size, the size of their forces and because they have inherited most of the design bureaux and production capability of the Soviet military–industrial complex.

The Persian Gulf War

The Persian Gulf War was an opportunity for the USA to assess the performance of its new systems and see how they might be improved. For the USSR it was an opportunity to have a better—and bitter—assessment of the state of advancement of US military technology. The lessons that can be drawn from the war have to be put in the context of the specifics of the conflict.[1] What new lessons might the Iraqi rout teach, if any, regarding Soviet military technology and military doctrine? The Arab–Israeli wars in the Middle East and the impact of the Stinger missile, for example, on the Afghan conflict had already presented many opportunities for the USSR to reflect on the efficiency of its military technology and methods when confronted with US technology.

The Persian Gulf War showed what use US forces are now able to make of their newly acquired stealth and 'integrated strike and reconnaissance' capabilities. Very few 'traditional' aircraft, such as F-15s or F-16s, were shot down during the war, but not one F-117A stealth fighter was even scratched, despite the fact that the F-117As were used to bomb Baghdad, allegedly the best defended area in Iraq. The efficiency of laser-guided weapons is significantly increased when they are launched from survivable platforms that can stay above the target. The F-117A is only the first US aircraft to use stealth technology extensively.

The United States has also demonstrated that the Patriot air defence system has some limited anti-tactical ballistic missile (ATBM) capability. The Patriot–Scud episode in the Persian Gulf War may not have meant very much militarily, but it sent a message read by many as meaning that anti-missile defence is at hand. ATBM and anti-missile defence in general will most probably be an active area for US military modernization. A US ATBM capability (or the perception that the US forces will be difficult to target with tactical ballistic missiles) would enhance significantly the credibility of US forces engaged in power projection missions. It could even have a non-proliferation effect on ballistic missiles as it will deny them part of their efficiency.

Which technologies are of concern?

There is hardly any area of military high technology which is not relevant to the discussion here. The USSR had an approach to military technology which amounted to addressing systematically every aspect of technology with military application in mind. In fact Soviet research was more directly military-application oriented than is often the case with the US approach. Following are a few concrete examples to illustrate the nature of the asymmetry between the United States and the former Soviet Union.

As mentioned, the F-117A owes most of its accomplishments in the Gulf War to its stealth properties, and the USA is in the process of diversifying its

---

[1] The Iraqis were not able to offer very significant resistance. Except for an efficient use of decoys they did not give an impressive display of imaginative countermeasures or countertactics. In the air war, the task of the coalition was facilitated by the fact that the Iraqis failed to give more *élan* to their air force, despite its apparent ineptitude in the war against Iran. The fact that the USA had been given the secrets of the Iraqi high-tech systems by the providers, who happened to be in the coalition against Iraq, permitted the coalition to use efficient techniques against them. In other words, this was a lopsided war, and one should be prudent in drawing conclusions.

arsenal of stealthy aircraft by adding bombers, fighters and cruise missiles. There is even talk of making buildings 'stealthy' by spraying them with radar-absorbing materials. The United States has a very significant advantage in stealth technology over the rest of the world.

Another method of improving the performance of aircraft that was used with some success in the Persian Gulf is to provide fighters like the F-15 and the F-16 with the ability to fly at low altitude at night by the use of LANTIRN (Low-Altitude Navigation and Targeting with Infra-Red at Night). LANTIRN is at the technological heart of the US modernization effort. This system is based on advances in infra-red technology and uses high data-processing capabilities, two areas of spectacular technological success. An effect of LANTIRN is to complicate the comparison between US and Soviet fighters. Although the airframes of a Mig-29 or Su-27 are in no way inferior to those of an F-15 or F-16, LANTIRN and the rest of the avionics package provide the F-16 and F-15 with capabilities unmatched by the most advanced Soviet aircraft.

Automatic target recognition (ATR) is typically the kind of capability that could result from combining high data-processing power with high-quality infra-red imaging. Although LANTIRN did not achieve this technological feat, as was its original ambition, it contributed to spur interest in ATR, and made it an important area of research.

Although military technology evolved in many areas, one major engine of change—perhaps the main one—has been the staggering advance in Western civilian technology, in particular in the area of computers and data-processing capability which is also the area where there was the most significant gap between the USSR and the USA. These technologies find their military application in a variety of areas like reconnaissance, surveillance, target acquisition, battle management, long-range strike capabilities, communication and data distribution, penetration ability of aircraft and electronic warfare. The United States is only in an early phase of the process of military exploitation of those technologies. Some of the new weapon systems which have been developed are not yet mature, and the performance of those recently fielded is not necessarily representative of their future performance.

The United States is developing day–night all-weather surveillance and target acquisition capability through, for example, the development of airborne multimode radars like JSTARS.[2] When used in the moving-target indicator mode, JSTARS is a ground equivalent of AWACS (Airborne Warning and Control System), that is, it is supposed to detect moving targets, such as tanks, on the ground. In the synthetic aperture mode, it is supposed to give a map of the ground accurate enough to identify tanks or concentrations of military assets. This requires very high processing capability that so far only the USA has

---

[2] JSTARS (Joint Surveillance and Target Attack Radar System) is an airborne radar able to operate in a synthetic aperture radar (SAR) mode and as a moving-target indicator (MTI).

developed. France and the UK have no real competitors to JSTARS, which is expected to play a central role in the future.[3]

Although it has been credited with having performed well in the Persian Gulf War, the actual performance of JSTARS is still unclear. The Persian Gulf is a particularly favourable area for JSTARS, because the background on which the radar was supposed to detect its targets was a desert. JSTARS is supposed to identify tanks, or concentrations of tanks. Judging by the photographs from the Persian Gulf which were made public, JSTARS was able to recognize concentrations of armoured vehicles. It has its share of vulnerabilities which were not tested in the war, the main one being that it is a conspicuous and lucrative target, difficult to protect from guided missiles. If it is forced to fly further back from the combat zone because it might be attacked, its performance degrades rapidly. There are still strong reasons to question its wartime performance, especially if it turns out that the USSR had developed countermeasures against JSTARS, and its successors are now willing to share them with good buyers.

In peacetime, JSTARS could operate much closer to its theoretical performance. Used as an instrument of arms control verification, it could have a significant impact on the European theatre. By providing a higher quality of information on the military activities of the parties, JSTARS could contribute to avoiding miscalculation or misunderstanding in a crisis and thereby increase stability. Under the regime of the 1992 Open Skies Treaty, it could provide a platform for airborne monitoring or surveillance at night and in all weather. The USA will probably use JSTARS as a component of its national technical means of verification of the 1990 Conventional Armed Forces in Europe (CFE) Treaty. JSTARS will provide an ability to monitor military activities that no other nation can match.

JSTARS is only one among several US programmes in the general effort of modernization in the area of battle management, surveillance and target acquisition. Tactical command, control, communications and intelligence (C³I) is an area of modernization which has relatively small visibility despite its intensity. The communication field is another area in which Western civilian technology is evolving rapidly. Communications play such a central role for the military that it cannot afford to do otherwise than take full advantage of this progress. The US military is engaged in a somewhat frenetic process of exploiting the new possibilities offered by the progress in communication technology. Among the most visible new trends is the appearance of a wealth of intertwined networks of communication systems, making an increasing use of satellites or airborne platforms and changing the conditions of command and control substantially.

---

[3] France has the heliborne ORCHIDEE and the UK has ASTOR. Both are significantly less ambitious devices. Sweden is also developing side-looking airborne radar with some potential. The Open Skies Treaty could stimulate the development of more capable airborne SARs than these existing systems. According to Bill Sweetman, 'AWACS and JSTARS will dominate the surveillance and control scene for many years', see 'Planning for a new era', *Jane's Defence Weekly*, 14 Sep. 1991, p. 474.

JTIDS (Joint Tactical Information Distribution System) is an information or data-distribution system. It connects surveillance systems like AWACS or JSTARS (the eyes and ears) to tactical airborne or ground-based military units operating strike or weapon systems. Its primary purpose is to permit a fast and wide distribution of tactical data to the relevant units. For example, JTIDS would inform several aircraft involved in a mission above enemy territory of the movement and position of their target(s) and of enemy and friendly air-defence systems and aircraft.[4] This requires that all the relevant information which is gathered by several different devices be put together, processed, frequently updated and sent to the aircraft.[5] JTIDS is intended to provide that kind of support to a *whole front*. Needless to say JTIDS, still at the development stage, is an ambitious system, difficult to operate and requiring a very high level of intense training. The impact of JTIDS on the architecture of command and control, as well as in the design of operations, could be as profound as the adjustment required from the military forces which will have to learn to use and live with it. On the other hand, when completely digested (we are today only at the very tentative beginning of its introduction), JTIDS will create for US troops engaged in combat conditions of operation unmatched by those who do not enjoy equivalent logistical support.[6] JTIDS is only one among several major programmes in theatre and tactical C³ (together with TRITAC,[7] MSE,[8] PLRS,[9] SINCGARS,[10] TAOM/MCE,[11] etc.), some of which are of the same magnitude with the same far-reaching implications. The successful fielding of these

---

[4] Specifically, this information is displayed to the pilot on a television screen.

[5] JTIDS is a time-division multiple-access system requiring a high level of information processing. The information is then allocated into slots, from which the users have to extract what is relevant to them. Exact synchronization is essential for the collection of the right kind of information. The whole system occupies the bandwidth 962–1213 MHz (with a gap between 1030 and 1060 for IFF—identification, friend or foe—purposes). JTIDS is 'nodeless' in the sense that receivers are also emitters. The information is broadcast and encrypted in an error correcting code (the Reed Solomon code).

[6] It is also important to emphasize the reverse side of the picture represented by large-scale, revolutionary systems like JTIDS. First, they are so complicated that they might not need a malicious attack to break down, at least partially. When they are not fully operational, they act as force dividers as much as they are force multipliers when they perform well. If today such systems do not inspire a lot of confidence, one has to assume that their reliability will increase with time. In an age where the prospect of imminent war is dim, how those systems might perform in the future is perhaps what really matters most in assessing them. Second, JTIDS is best used as a link between computers. The suppression of human beings in the loop could be construed as contributing to overall efficiency or as in the logic of introducing such communication systems. The full exploitation of devices like JTIDS should be an incentive for greater reliance on computers. That way, it will be possible to see how JTIDS will contribute to a push for more automation of the battlefield.

[7] TRI-TAC is a system for tactical ground-to-ground communication. It uses sophisticated equipment (form transmission, switches, system control, etc.), and it involves several programmes.

[8] The Mobile Subscriber Equipment system is a radio communication system to provide corps and division users the equivalent of automatic and secure dial telephone service for both voice and data.

[9] The Precision Location Reporting System is an Army/Marine Corps system to provide commanders with real time identification and location of their forces on the battlefield.

[10] The Single-Channel Ground and Airborne Radio System (SINCGARS) is for acquiring a new family of manpack, vehicular and airborne, secure single-channel VHF radio. It is essentially an acquisition system of radios with a mean time between failures (MTBF) of 1550 hours.

[11] The Tactical Air Operation Module/Modular Control Equipment is a joint Air Force/Marine Corps effort. It is a transportable, automated air command and control system capable of controlling and co-ordinating the employment of a full range of air defence weapons, interceptors and surface-to-air missiles.

programmes is important for the efficiency of US military forces in the future. They are designed so that they are difficult to target. However, if they reveal some vulnerabilities in combat, the efficiency of the military forces would be seriously affected. If such vulnerabilities exist, the ex-Soviet military–industrial complex would probably be where they would be detected initially and where countermeasures to exploit them would first be developed.

Noteworthy is the fact that the United States is also developing and relying heavily on a world-wide communication network where many components are space-based. Only the USSR was, as its successors now are, in a position to develop a threat to its integrity through its anti-satellite (ASAT) capability.

The attitude towards military modernization

Nothing indicates that the drive for more exploitation of high technology by the US military will weaken. The rationale for intensifying efforts to modernize and rely even more in the future on military high technology has roots deep in the essence of US defence culture. The fascination with technology is a major component of the US military psyche. It is legitimized by the perception that (despite Augustine's Law)[12] technology can accomplish what the US defence needs most: savings without loss of security. Furthermore, technology seems to reduce the risk to US military personnel, while increasing military efficiency. The United States enjoys a visible superiority in military technology over the rest of the world from which it draws an obvious benefit. The policy of opposing the absorption of Kuwait by Iraq would not have been possible if the United States had not enjoyed this technological superiority. Maintaining that advantage has to be a top priority for the United States.

The US military is only at the beginning of the learning curve in its exploitation of new technological capabilities that the successors of the USSR do not master as well and are not in the position to develop. Some of the new nations arising from the collapse of Soviet power may be concerned to see the United States developing weapon systems which have the potential to revolutionize warfare and against which they cannot compete. The fact that other countries might feel threatened is irrelevant to US defence policy and might, because of the well-known security dilemma, put the Russian defence establishment under pressure. Could Russia let the United States be in the position of holding it hostage to a multiform military threat? The Russian Government has to assume that if political intimidation of Russia is an option for the United States, it is bound to be used when needed.

Given the expertise in military technology that Russia inherited from the Soviet system, it would only be prudent for the Russian Government to analyse carefully the evolution of the US military threat against its territory and develop protection against the most dangerous features. That means that despite the re-

---

[12] Augustine's Law refers to the observation by Norman Augustine, Head of Martin Marietta, that the price of individual weapon systems is increasing so fast that, sometime in the 21st century, the Air Force will be able to acquire only one aircraft.

design of the missions of the US forces to treat Russia at best as a secondary theatre, the US drive for military modernization is inherently a threat to Russia or other republics, and may provoke a reaction. The USA should not forget that it is in Russia and some of the other new republics that one finds the most advanced expertise in military high technology outside of the West. One effect of underestimating the importance for their security of US initiatives could be to inspire these governments to turn, of perceived necessity, to countermeasures.

The USSR made very detailed assessments of how advanced US systems worked, and explored all possible ways to degrade their performance. The new US systems tend to exploit new concepts at the limit of their applicability and to involve a high level of complexity of operation. Increased reliance on ATR capability could inspire efficient countermeasures. Very large-scale integration, important in maximizing the efficiency of high processing capabilities and one of the leitmotivs of US modernization, breeds new kinds of vulnerability. The failure of one component can have devastating effects on the whole system. The fact that, in the war against Iraq, no hidden vulnerability appeared in the new US approach to warfighting could be because the USSR did not tell Iraq all it knew. Such vulnerabilities may have been there, already known to some Soviet experts. The Persian Gulf War was an occasion to have a better idea of how well the new systems perform, but the lessons from that war have to be taken with a grain of salt. The war did not represent the most difficult combat conditions that these systems could have to meet.

US technical 'experts' tend often to voice scepticism about the cost-effectiveness of the modernization programmes. They point to the fact that not only are the new systems very expensive, but their reliability is sometimes questionable since they introduce new sources of military vulnerability. For example, one detailed study of cruise missiles suggests vulnerabilities and weaknesses, but these were not confirmed when they were used in the Persian Gulf War.[13] A closer examination of most new systems and of the technical complications they have to overcome to perform well, tends to prompt the same kind of scepticism. In some cases it turns out to be justified, in other cases to be wrong. In most cases, there is a learning curve and the systems of the second generation are far more capable and reliable than the ones first fielded. No 'expert' knows how to anticipate the shape of the learning curve.

III. The problem of technological development in Russia

Technology was perceived as vital to the economic development of what used to be the Soviet Union. Although the military dimension has lost part of its prominence in the life of Russia and the other republics, military technology has been and still is the most active area of technology in these countries. What used to be the Soviet military–industrial complex was so large, penetrated so

---

[13] Arnett, E., *Sea-Launched Cruise Missiles and US Security* (Praeger: New York, 1991).

deeply in the Soviet economy and geography, and employed such a large proportion of the élite, that it cannot and will not be dismantled easily.

However, military and civilian industry are profoundly different. Analysing the difficulties of converting one to the other is also an opportunity to see just how great this difference is. Although it might be de-emphasized somewhat, the military exploitation of technology in the republics will certainly not disappear. It is bound to be an important aspect of the security of the republics in the future, and probably a source of revenue through exports. Even if the confrontation between the USSR and the USA has passed into history, Russia, among other countries, will still be concerned about security and will watch carefully how the US military posture evolves. This to a large extent will be determined by the form and content of the US military modernization effort.

The economic dimension

Eventually security issues will surface one way or the other, but today they tend to be overshadowed by the economic and political chaos of the post-Soviet republics, which itself is loaded with potential security implications. One component of the economic life of the Soviet republics is 'economic conversion'. The idea is to reduce the size of the defence sector by transferring the labour force and production capability to the civilian economy. The Soviet policy of conversion is contemporaneous with the US conversion (i.e., the partial conversion of the US defence industry into a more vigorous civilian production), but they look very different.

The process of economic conversion of part of the military industry into civilian production was begun years ago during the Gorbachev era. It has not been a string of unmitigated successes. There are many reasons for this, some better understood than others. The interface with economic development is complex and depends on the specifics of the situation. In that regard, the Soviet economy itself was very poorly understood. Most discussions of it have dealt with organizational structure, as if that were the only factor relevant for discussion.

There is a cultural or ideological problem which prevailed at the onset of the now several-years-old Soviet policy of conversion. It was initiated in a planned economy. What in market economies would be an adjustment to a change in demand or the result of economic obsolescence, turns into a difficult adjustment in planned economies. In the words of Alexander: 'Because of the reluctance of accepting the very notion of economic obsolescence, planned economies and engineers in most economies search for technological solutions to shifting demands. These often take the form of detailed surveys intended to match technical capabilities with new uses, or searches for the optimal assignment of product to plant'.[14] Speed, responsiveness and adaptability (i.e., the organiza-

[14] Alexander, A., *The Conversion of Soviet Defense Industry*, P-7620, RAND Corporation, Santa Monica, Calif., Jan. 1990.

tional structure of the economy) determine the ease of the conversion. The Soviet approach proceeded along the lines of long-term planning: 'Long term planning is crucial . . . because the conversion process involves many sectors of production and must have constant political guidance as well as government supervision'. This guaranteed a certain element of rigidity limiting the adaptability of the system. The movement and availability of investment money is clearly a massive limitation.

The process of economic conversion cannot bring quick prosperity to the economy of a country like the Soviet Union or its republics: the historical precedents of the New Economic Policy of the 1920s, and even the Khrushchev experience of the late 1950s in economic conversion, are irrelevant or misleading approaches to understanding the difficulty of today's economic conversion. In terms of technology, times have changed. Low-quality civilian products have no economic value. The kind of high quality which is relevant to the civilian economy is very different from what defines high quality in the military. The two are end-points of a vastly different optimization procedure. The notion that a first-class engineer in a defence industry could in no time be as capable in the civilian economy is fundamentally flawed. What complicates the matter further is the fact that the civilian ex-Soviet economy has no use for the skills of the engineers of the defence industry. Conversion in the former Soviet Union tends to worsen the working conditions of the engineers and skilled personnel who used to be employed in the defence industry. For the privileged élite of the military–industrial complex accustomed to producing first-class military assets like aircraft missiles, nuclear weapons, space technology and the like, this will inevitably translate into painful intellectual and social demotion.[15]

A criticism of conversion policy is the waste of the research and development skill it implies in time and effort spent on mundane low-tech production. An attractive alternative is to maintain the activity of some key companies and, where appropriate, make their production more export oriented. The Soviet military–industrial complex has a lot to teach or sell in those developing countries where there is an interest in these matters. The Brazilian or Indian space programmes could benefit enormously from contracting, at high prices, with some well-chosen Russian enterprises. Space-vehicle launch services is another example of technology which could be exported.

Exporting military technology

The Soviet economy would benefit from any intake of hard currency: Regrettably, arms trade could be a source of export as good as any. One major legacy of the Soviet system is that it has developed a set of skills not directly useful to the civilian economy but which can be used otherwise as a source of income. It is not with token financial support that the West can hope to offset

[15] Belousov, N., 'The defence complex's attempted marriage with science and practical needs is turning sour', in Foreign Broadcast Information Service, *Daily Report–Soviet Union* (*FBIS-SOV*), FBIS-SOV-89-196, 12 Oct. 1989, p. 92.

the potential benefits that the Soviet Union could derive from weapon exports.[16] Furthermore, by being a weapon provider, Russia could recover part of the international influence it enjoyed in the past.

It is safe to assume that the republics will not launch ambitious military programmes targeted at containing the US threat against their territory. Protecting themselves against a US military threat is not the first priority of any of the republics. But within some republics, in particular Russia and Ukraine but also, at least, Belarus and Kazakhstan, there are people who used to work for the Soviet military–industrial complex and who can build on the research they conducted before the political change to develop privately, for example, some counterstealth capability for sale abroad.

The USSR has been developing stealth technology and might want to export it. Stealthiness is the result of a combination of factors. Shape is the most important. The USSR demonstrated in the past that the airframes of the aircraft it delivered were the products of a quite advanced design and manufacturing base. The ATBM is another area in which the USSR had made some headway years ago when testing its SA-12 air-defence systems against tactical ballistic missiles. What an operational ATBM would contribute to the security of the republics is less clear than the interest it could raise in some foreign countries.

The republics are at the moment of reckoning. They are in the process of identifying their real resources, natural and otherwise. As Gorbachev said in his farewell address, the USSR had talents in abundance, many of which were linked one way or the other to the military–industrial complex. The extent of advancement of that military technology is not precisely known, but this technology, together with the people who developed it, is one of the major assets of the republics. It could lead to the production of a high-performance system very suitable for export, which would be a matter of considerable relevance to the future world order.

The production and export by private companies of military high technology from the former Soviet Union has the potential to defeat the purpose of efforts like the Missile Technology Control Regime (MTCR). In the long-term, it may not be in the best interest of Russia to maintain this effort since it would deprive Russia of one of its main sources of revenue.

The West is not in a very strong position to prevent such an evolution. The Western countries seem to be entering into an era of fierce competition to sell their own military technology. From advanced aircraft to air defence systems and advanced vehicles, there does not seem to be any weapon system that at least one or more countries is not interested in exporting. Missile technology is the only area in which there seems to be a common political will in the West to hinder proliferation. It is noteworthy that some studies have concluded that the proliferation of strike aircraft is in many respects as dangerous if not more so than the proliferation of tactical ballistic missiles.[17] The only avenue that West-

---

[16] 'Arms factory can make bricks, but Russia asks is that smart?', *New York Times*, 24 Feb. 1992.

[17] Harvey, J. *et al.*, *Internal Report*, Center for International Security and Arms Control, Stanford, Calif., 1991.

ern governments have to try to affect the spread of Soviet military technology is negotiation with the new post-Soviet authorities, but this may not suffice. It may be difficult to prevent some Russian engineers from selling their services to developing countries, thereby defeating the purposes of the MTCR. An important component of a policy of conversion is to give increasingly more latitude to individual companies to take their future into their own hands, and find ways to integrate into the new economy. The net result is a diminution of the influence of government on those enterprises. Furthermore, one should not expect those governments to oppose strongly a policy which brings in hard currency.

The US response

Clearly, dark clouds on the horizon threaten the future of security relations between the USA and the new republics. The Russian Federation in particular (but also Ukraine and other republics) has the potential to be a major security preoccupation of the United States. This is not so much because of the size of its military forces, but because of the size and strength of its space and military–industrial complex. The protection of the economy of these countries will push them towards policies which will run counter to US interests. For example, they can compete in arms trade, sell their know-how or services in space technology and so on. In doing so, they would merely be defending their interests at a time when their economic weakness could be exploited by other nations.

The US Government's rhetoric is not much more impressive than its deeds. It behaves as if it were basically bankrupt—financially and intellectually. It does not display the mixture of imagination and vigour called for at this historic juncture. By developing ties preferentially with those republics which have the greatest natural resources (namely Kazakhstan, Kyrgyzstan and Ukraine), it is sending an intriguing message. The future of the democracies in most if not all the republics constituting the CIS is bleak at best. The changes which must be made are so radical and profound that they will take a long time, possibly longer than the political life of those politicians now in charge. The policy which is chosen to shape the future of the new nations must be one which has a long-term perspective.

IV. Impact on global and regional security

When the dust settles, Russia and the other republics will take their place in the international system and assert themselves wherever they can. For countries like Russia, recovering as much international influence as possible would not be a form of neo-imperialism, but rather a matter of survival as a sovereign and prosperous country. Russia is a country that is rich in intellectual talents, nuclear weapons and other military assets, but that is in economic disarray. It is a dangerous mixture. Furthermore, the Russian Federation shows every sign of internal instability under the centrifugal effect of ethnic pressure. Its democratic institutions are anything but solid. Its military establishment is very large and would provide a substantial power base for anyone wanting to use it that way.

Russia is in the process of securing much of the past influence of the Soviet Union: its seat on the UN Security Council, as much as possible of the Black Sea fleet, all Soviet nuclear weapons and more. Russia should be expected eventually to elbow its way into regional disputes relevant to its interests, and not necessarily with the aim of resolving tension. The Middle East, within the peace process or outside of it, could be an example of such a case, but other areas of future instability will provide new opportunities and markets for military systems. India, North Korea and perhaps Brazil, or other developing countries, could take advantage of the situation to boost their space and missile programmes or other forms of military buildup, such as nuclear submarines.

Tensions will predictably arise within and between republics owing to their different economic dynamics and the explosive character of their ethnic chemistry. US policy is not visibly attempting to attenuate the potential effect of the combination of these tensions with the presence of a very large (although partially dismantled) military establishment which is still quite powerful.

V. Managing technological competition

Technology introduces an element of change into the military balance by altering the relative efficiency of different weapon systems. High technology changes the way wars are waged. The programmes mentioned previously and most of the numerous other programmes of a similar nature each have their share of problems. However, together they constitute a multi-pronged effort to expand technological frontiers, which no doubt eventually will yield unprecedented new capabilities for US forces.

High technology has the potential perniciously to affect security arrangements, arms control regimes and other aspects of international relations. When technology enters into the realm of negotiations, as has been the case in nuclear arms control (e.g., the START or ABM Treaty), it tends to become a source of complication and friction, and to lead to unsatisfactory agreements. Still, removing technology from the arms control process is clearly not a satisfactory solution since it has become such a central factor in several aspects of security.

In theory, it would be possible to regulate by treaty the military exploitation of high technology. This is neither a realistic nor desirable option. The development and spread of technology is to a large extent inevitable. Limiting the key performances of weapon systems is another possible suggestion borrowed from nuclear arms control. High-tech systems are not like nuclear missiles; their military characteristics cannot be expressed by range, accuracy, payload or the like. Applied to a system like JSTARS, for example, it is difficult to see how this idea might be expressed. Furthermore, it would probably be unacceptable on grounds that it would limit the performance of a surveillance system.

Regulating military exploitation of high technology or the thrust of research, in short, is unattractive. It would raise all sorts of problems of enforcement and would have a very negative impact on technological innovation. In order to affect the impact of technology through constraints on the specifications of systems, more has to be understood about it than is currently the case. The military exploitation of data-processing capabilities cannot be predicted even with complete knowledge of what the performance and military impact of the resulting weapon systems will be. There are far too many uncontrolled factors.

To limit the negative impact of new systems, one could exploit the fact that the impact of high-tech systems depends on the specifics of the situation. If there are causes for legitimate concern, why should they not be discussed? This would be another kind of arms control, akin to transparency in defence planning. It would require a higher form of co-operation and communication (i.e., transparency) than has been the case so far. However, such exchanges could contribute very significantly by becoming a central component, and possibly an irritant, in international relations. Learning to communicate and discussing technological problems between states could help put an end to the current era of simplistic behaviour in that area.

The excessive prudence or reluctance of the USA to engage in ambitious joint space ventures with the USSR could backfire in encouraging joint space ventures between Russia and other countries (perhaps developing countries), and the net effect will be to accelerate the spread of missile technology. At this stage those are only hypothetical threats. It would be premature to attempt to prevent such developments before they even start, but it should be understood that someday the honeymoon will be over.

Engaging much more actively in joint space programmes with the new nations would also very significantly benefit the USA, European Space Agency (ESA) countries and others. Russia and Kazakhstan have the most powerful space infrastructure and their launching capabilities are superior to those of the United States. Their space station could provide a cheap way for the USA to learn what a space station can teach today, and the USA could as a result focus on long-term programmes more appropriate to its current level of space technology, such as returning to the moon to build a base and preparing for a Mars mission. President Yeltsin has suggested international co-operation for a world-wide strategic defence system where Russian expertise could be used. This idea has much merit technically and politically and deserves to be studied in great detail.[18]

Politically, it could put a graceful end to the obnoxious character of SDI (the Strategic Defense Initiative) by designing the GPALS (Global Protection Against Limited Strikes) system as protection for the entire planet against the ambitions of some to build ICBMs. This system could include more than just the USA and Russia. Some European countries and Japan could contribute. It could be a symbolic effort to deter the proliferation of ICBMs. Although such a

---

[18] Speech to UN Security Council, 31 Jan. 1992.

system would have a limited or zero capability against theatre ballistic missiles,[19] it would help demonstrate that the nuclear confrontation is over. It would in fact unify a co-operative abrogation of the ABM Treaty. A GPALS system would unavoidably involve many space-based components. Seeing the United States embarking unilaterally on a large space-based military buildup would create legitimate concerns. If instead this were part of an international programme, the impression created would be quite different.

Technically, a strategic defence system against a world-wide threat, even if limited in size, would involve many satellites and be very costly to build, deploy and maintain. Although the USA has a significant technological edge over the rest of the world in those technologies, the USSR had and the new republics still have a more efficient infrastructure and space-launch capability. They have space stations and could in such an endeavour find a useful role for their space infrastructure.

From the US point of view, the military–industrial complex of the Soviet republics will remain a major source of security concern. In today's era of unprecedented co-operation between the West and the new nations of Eurasia, it is somewhat frustrating to realize that so little seems possible as regards co-operative agreements which could be the foundation for a more secure future.

Arms control is supposed to be an exercise in co-operation in the domain of security. Arms control treaties are inherently rigid. When the problems become more subtle, as is the case with high technology, a more subtle approach than fixed agreements is of the essence. Moreover, it does not seem that confidence-building measures would help very much. Although the United States has a lot to lose in a policy of passively watching the new nations find their way out of their current mess, it would not be prudent policy for it to enter today into binding military agreements with countries whose military postures are degrading.

In this regard, some of the post-Soviet republics, it should be noted, could begin to be seriously concerned by the increased efficiency of the long-range US strike capability. 'Verification' technology, when it uses devices like JSTARS, can also provide pre-hostility target acquisition capabilities. This dual capability of JSTARS, coupled with the demonstrated US ability to deliver long-range weapons with pinpoint accuracy, could have an unsettling effect during a crisis. A prudent policy for the threatened party could be to conceal some key assets. This would be construed as a violation of the agreement since it would hinder verification. The net effect could be to poison the atmosphere.

The nuclear dimension

Although nuclear arms control is not a theme of this book, it is impossible to ignore the fact that the dismantlement of the Soviet Union provides a golden

---

[19] Garwin, R. L., 'Space-based defenses against ballistic missiles', *The Future of Smart Weapons*, Proceedings from a AAAS [American Association for the Advancement of Science] Symposium, Chicago, Ill., Feb. 1992 (Program on Science and International Security, American Association for the Advancement of Science: Washington, DC, 1992), pp. 45–52.

opportunity to change radically the nature of the nuclear threat. The most obvious effect of the decay of the centre has been to raise serious concerns as to who controls the strategic and tactical nuclear weapons and what is happening to the plutonium and weapon-grade uranium. The verbal assurances provided have failed to alleviate the legitimate concerns of the rest of the world. This is clearly a primary concern of the US Government, and it is actively attempting to help the Russian scientists and military maintain control of and destroy some of those vital weapons.

The unprecedented nuclear co-operation possible today could broaden to a redesign of the nuclear strategic environment. In the new world emerging from the catastrophic demise of the Soviet Union, the nuclear balance has lost its meaning. The status and purpose of nuclear weapons is undergoing a fundamental change.

A scenario of reduction where the USA in fact destroys large chunks of the Soviet nuclear forces has advantages, but also major disadvantages. It could institutionalize a superior US nuclear threat and disrupt an equilibrium that few like but which has been a stabilizing factor in some crisis situations. A reduction of the strategic arsenal based on Russian–US negotiations would probably be politically and psychologically more acceptable, but it would not be optimal either. It would force the two powers to look at each other as a potential enemy. Furthermore, it would miss a rendezvous with history which might be an option today—namely, to address the possibility of establishing a new world nuclear order less anarchic or threatening than has been and is the case. A larger framework involving all nuclear nations could achieve more towards defining this new world. Nuclear weapons are more visible than militarily useful, and when the dust settles again on them, the other dimensions of military technology—those which are relevant to US foreign policy—will regain prominence.

When arms control agreements are blind to technology, they run the risk of defining an evolving military equation which has only the appearance of a stable military balance. If 'stability' supposes among other things a shared confidence that no one is threatened by an incapacitating first strike of any kind, the combined effect of deep reductions, 'adequate verification' and technology, in the long run, can be to reduce the level of stability.

In today's turmoil in Europe these considerations seem irrelevant. However, when a new normality is established in that area, the redefinition of security balance will become important. The whole equation will be re-expressed in terms of new countries with different systems of alliance and with a need for new thinking about technological relations.

11. The metastable peace: a catastrophe theory model of US–Russian relations

*Irving Lachow**

I. Introduction

The last few years have witnessed dramatic changes in the USSR including its collapse in December 1991. Unprecedented events have occurred frequently and without warning. Future relations between the USA and Russia promise to be of a similar nature. Policy makers are faced with the formidable challenge of managing a highly unstable and dynamic relationship. This chapter was written with that challenge in mind; specifically, a framework is developed which may help policy makers analyse the complicated set of social and military variables which constitute US–Russian relations. The model presented here demonstrates a general method for describing military relations between the two nations. However, it might be more accurate to say that changes in force levels are used as a 'marker' to express the interaction of military, economic, political and psychological factors in the relationship. A case study is used to show that such a model can yield interesting insights. The example chosen concerns changes in the overall size of the conventional forces of the USA and the USSR between 1988 and 1991.

The backbone of the analysis is the observation that a dramatic change in the dynamics of US–Soviet relations occurred in 1988. In general, a discontinuity such as this is called a *bifurcation* or a *catastrophe*.[1] The types of bifurcations examined here are known as *local bifurcations* because they describe the dynamics of a small region around the point in question—they cannot describe what is happening to the system as a whole.[2] This chapter deals exclusively with local bifurcations.

The chapter begins by showing that linear models of arms race behaviour (e.g., Richardson's model) are no longer the most useful tools for examining the interaction of US and Russian conventional force levels. In order to comprehend the impact of this view, one must understand the difference between

---

[1] A bifurcation is 'the point at which the quantitative behavior of a system changes'. Sandefur, J. T., *Discrete Dynamical Systems: Theory and Applications* (Clarendon Press: Oxford, 1990), p. 185; see also Nicholson, M., *Formal Theories in International Relations* (Cambridge University Press: Cambridge, 1989), p. 167.

[2] It is difficult to have complete knowledge of a rapidly changing dynamic system because one never knows what is going to happen next.

* I would like to thank Dr Russell Moses and Ambassador James E. Goodby for their encouragement and support. Special thanks to Judyth Twigg and William Newmann for their helpful comments and insights. Finally, I would like to extend my deep appreciation to Dr Benoit Morel; this work could not have been completed without his guidance and oversight (especially the mathematical analysis). Of course, I alone accept responsibility for the contents of the chapter.

linear and non-linear views of the world. A *linear system* is a system where 'external effects on the system are purely additive'.[3] In other words, 'A linear model is one in which the concept of "superposition" holds. In a linear system the response to every disturbance runs its course independently of preceding or succeeding inputs to the system; the total result is no more nor less than the sum of the separate components of system response'.[4]

Thus the behaviour of a linear system can be expressed by one or more straight lines. By contrast, a system in which external effects are not purely additive is known as a *non-linear system*. Although the behaviour of such a system cannot generally be described with straight lines, it is sometimes possible to approximate a non-linear system with a linear one by looking at a small section of the non-linear one, a process known as *linearization*.[5] Unfortunately, this process can only be employed when the non-linear system is well-behaved (i.e., not too curved, no jumps in the curve, etc.). Bifurcations are by definition not well-behaved. Another tool is needed to examine what happens to a system which has undergone a bifurcation.

The tool utilized herein is *catastrophe theory* because it deals with local bifurcations: 'It [catastrophe theory] deals with sudden changes in the patterns of behaviour, whether benign, malign or neutral, in systems which for the most part exhibit continuous, smoothly moving (e.g., linear) forms of behaviour'.[6] In this chapter, catastrophe theory is used to describe the evolution of the bifurcation which took place in the USSR in 1988. The importance of several events which occurred in 1991—including the attempted coup and its aftermath—are also discussed in the context of the model.

How does catastrophe theory work? The first thing one tries to do is to identify which type of bifurcation has occurred by a process known as the *recognition problem*.[7] One of the methods used to recognize a bifurcation is to look at the system and see which type of bifurcation 'appears to make the most sense'. The idea is to find which type of local bifurcation best describes the physical (or social) situation one is attempting to model. In order to make this determination, one can refer to the fact that local bifurcations of fifth-order[8] or less are well understood and can be represented by simple diagrams.[9] The best-fitting bifurcation is identified by examining the dynamic properties of the various bifurcations which are known. An analysis can then be performed to

[3] Forrester, J. W., *Industrial Dynamics* (MIT Press and John Wiley & Sons, Inc.: New York, 1961), p. 50.

[4] Forrester (note 3), p. 50.

[5] Although linearizations can be helpful approximations of non-linear phenomena, the process results in a loss of information. An excellent discussion of the differences between linear and non-linear models is provided by Forrester (note 3), pp. 50–51.

[6] In other words, 'It [catastrophe theory] is a theory of jumps [i.e., bifurcations] in normally smooth systems'. Both quotes are from Nicholson (note 1), p. 167.

[7] For a detailed discussion, see Golubitsky M. and Schaeffer, D., *Singularities and Groups in Bifurcation Theory*, vol. 1 (Springer-Verlag: New York, 1985), pp. 51–116.

[8] The 'order' of a system is the number of solutions or equilibrium points the system has. A linear system is first-order, so it has one solution. A quadratic system is second-order, so it has two solutions, etc.

[9] A good presentation of these bifurcations is found in Golubitsky and Schaeffer (note 7), pp. 205–11.

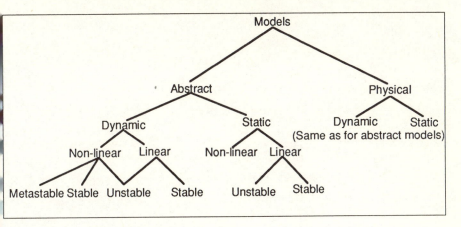

Figure 11.1. A taxonomy of mathematical models

determine if the dynamics of the bifurcation in question match the observed dynamics of the system. If the two do not match, the process is repeated until a match is found. In other words, an iterative process can be used to approach the best solution.

After determining what type of bifurcation the USSR underwent in 1988, a physical model is developed here to match the theoretical one since it is easier to understand the dynamics of a physical object than to speak in abstract terms about a system's behaviour. However, the dynamics of the two models are exactly the same. Figure 11.1 above may help one visualize this concept.[10]

In order to understand the findings of the analysis, one has to comprehend the notions of *stability, instability* and *metastability*. These terms are illustrated in figure 11.2 below.[11] The points marked A, B and C represent the three solutions of a third-order dynamic system. The two 'dips' in the curve—points A and C—correspond to the stable solutions of the problem, while the bump—point B—corresponds to the unstable solution. This is easily pictured by imagining a ball rolling down the slope of the curve. It can stop at any one of the three points. Point B is unstable because a tiny perturbation will cause the ball to roll off the bump into one of the two dips; points A and C are stable because the ball will tend to stay at those points.

However, the reader will notice that one dip is much deeper than the other. This is often the case in dynamic systems. If a dip is shallow enough the ball can be caused to roll out of that dip and into another one. In this example, it is possible for the ball to be pushed out of point A, over point B and into point C. A dip which is not very deep (relative to other dips) is called 'metastable' because the ball can be pushed to another solution fairly easily. On the other hand, a dip which is extremely deep would be considered 'stable' because it

---

[10] This illustration is based on a diagram in Forrester (note 3), p. 49.
[11] The diagram presents a 'potential-well' representation of a dynamic system.

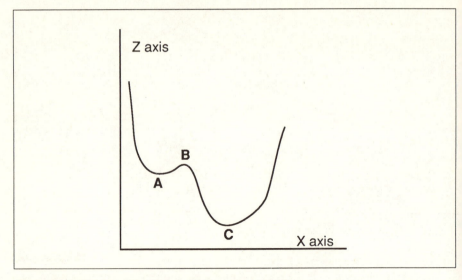

Figure 11.2. Diagram of stability, instability and metastability

would take a very large perturbation to move the ball. In this example, point A is a metastable solution; point B is an unstable solution and point C is a stable solution.

The analysis presented in this chapter shows that the USSR entered a region of metastability after the bifurcation of 1988. The events which have taken place since August 1991 (e.g., the coup attempt, the Ukrainian vote for independence, etc.) serve to reinforce this view. Being in a metastable state, the USSR was highly susceptible to perturbations from external sources, notably the USA. It is the view of this author that Russia remains in a metastable phase; the implications of this view are discussed in section IV of this chapter.

II. Why use a model?

Before continuing on to a description of the model, a simple but important question can be asked: why use a mathematical model to describe a complicated social situation? An answer to this valid query is that qualitative modelling is a useful tool precisely because of the uncertainty and complexity involved in the problem. Designing a mathematical framework around social phenomena forces one to be explicit about one's assumptions and beliefs. Furthermore, dynamic models allow one to determine the effect of various parameters on the overall behaviour of the system.[12] In other words, 'mathematical formulations

---

[12] Human beings tend to think in terms of two variables; for example: if the USA does X, then the USSR will do Y. A more realistic question—if the USA does A, B and C, what will the USSR do?—is very difficult to consider rationally due to the incredible complexity of such a question. Dynamic models are made to deal with exactly these types of questions. See Simon, H., *Models of Man* (Garland Publishing: New York, 1987).

of a complex problem point out possible outcomes and improve the selection of an optimum strategy of action'.[13]

Of course, there are dangers inherent in modelling: 'One is that the model does not tell us about the world, the other is that it is a faithful representation, and therefore we are overwhelmed'.[14] The model presented below is an extremely simplified and rough approximation of reality, but even a simple model can often capture the dominant dynamics of complicated system. To use the words of Puccia and Levins, 'Simplification is both legitimate and necessary as long as we are cautious, are willing to change the original underlying assumptions as necessary and build new models, and carefully interpret the model's predictions'.[15]

III. Which model to use?

There are a variety of approaches to modelling the behaviour of states in the international system. Two of the most common models are 'arms race' models, which describe the evolution of military forces over time, and 'attrition' models, which examine the evolution of conventional forces during an actual conflict.[16] This chapter does not use any type of attrition model, but instead employs an arms race model because it expresses the interaction between force levels, economics, threat perceptions and political grievances in a simple and easy-to-understand way.

First, this author's version of Richardson's linear arms race model is presented as applied to US–Soviet behaviour. Second, it is shown that the dynamic behaviour of the USSR passed through a bifurcation in 1988 which nullified the ability of a linear model to adequately describe the dynamics of the system. The model developed here as a response to this occurrence is a non-linear version of Richardson's model. By analysing this non-linear model using techniques from catastrophe theory it is possible to describe the evolution of the bifurcation which guided Soviet behaviour (and US–Soviet military relations) after 1988.

[13] Saaty, T. L., *Mathematical Models of Arms Control and Disarmament* (John Wiley & Sons: New York, 1968), p. 8.
[14] Levins, R. and Puccia, C. J., *Qualitative Modeling of Complex Systems* (Harvard University Press: Cambridge, Mass., 1985), p. 2.
[15] Levins and Puccia (note 14), p. 2.
[16] The best known attrition model is the Lanchester model, see for example Taylor, J. G., *Lanchester Models of Warfare*, vols 1 and 2 (Operations Research Society of America: Arlington, Va., 1983). An example of a newer, more flexible model is provided by Joshua Epstein in *Conventional Force Reductions: A Dynamic Assessment* (Brookings Institution: Washington, DC, 1990).

The bifurcation of 1988[17]

The year 1988 was no less than revolutionary for the USSR.[18] Four major events took place which had a dramatic impact on both internal matters and external relations: (*a*) the Soviet withdrawal from Afghanistan; (*b*) the 19th Communist Party Conference; (*c*) the Moscow summit meeting; and (*d*) Gorbachev's speech to the United Nations. Although a detailed description of these events is not provided here, it is useful to briefly discuss how truly profound these occurrences were.

The 15 May 1988 Soviet announcement that the USSR would begin to remove its troops from Afghanistan was of obvious importance: '1988, starting with Afghanistan, saw extraordinary developments in Soviet foreign policy'. However, few may realize the earth-shattering consequences of the 19th Party Conference held in July of 1988: 'it would become a watershed in the history of the Soviet state and of the Communist Party of the USSR'. The purpose of the conference was to change the roles of 'establishment, power, and privilege' in the Communist Party. Among the 10 'theses' approved by the Central Committee were the 'creation of the "rule-of-law socialist state"—an outright revolution', and several sections 'devoted to foreign policy formulations that radically revised past ideas'. Although the Moscow summit meeting between Presidents Gorbachev and Reagan produced no important agreements, it proved to be:

[A] true watershed in relations between the two superpowers . . . the outcome of the Moscow summit had an extraordinary psychological effect on public opinion in both countries, both of which were ready to abandon the heavy stereotypes of 'the enemy's image'. When Gorbachev and Reagan met for the fourth time [in Moscow], they knew they were acting out wide-spread desires in the world that had been stimulated by their own actions.[19]

The final event discussed in this chapter—the most important occurrence from the perspective of the model—is Gorbachev's speech to the United Nations. US Representative Les Aspin labelled the event a revolution: 'The first revolution began when President Mikhail Gorbachev announced to the United Nations on December 7, 1988, that he would withdraw some Soviet troops from Eastern Europe and unilaterally reduce Soviet forces'.[20] Specifically, Gorbachev declared that the Soviet army would eliminate 500 000 men, 10 000 tanks, 8500 pieces of artillery, and 800 aircraft. As part of this reduction, six divisions of 'assault troops' (the kind which most worried NATO planners)

---

[17] The following discussion is based on ideas and arguments presented in Chiesa, G. and Medvedev, R., *Time of Change: An Insider's View of Russia's Transformation* (Pantheon Books: New York, 1989), pp. 217–69. Any unidentified quotations in this section are from this work.

[18] It is also undeniable that the events of 1991 may make it the most important year in Soviet history since 1917. However, the dramatic nature of 1991 does not diminish the impact of the changes which took place in 1988.

[19] Chiesa and Medvedev (note 17), p. 259.

[20] Aspin, L., *National Security in the 1990s: Defining a New Basis for U.S. Military Forces* (House Armed Services Committee: Washington, DC, 1992), p. 1.

would be withdrawn from Eastern Europe. Although 'the immensity of the decision . . . cannot be underestimated', it was 'the philosophical context in which the new Soviet decision was announced' that had the greatest impact. Gorbachev shocked the world with his conclusion that 'today's problems could not be solved without "global coordination". . . . this applied to everyone—also, and above all, to Gorbachev's USSR'.

The events of 1991

The analysis presented in this chapter follows from the postulate that events in 1988 caused a fundamental change in US–Soviet military relations. However, it is obvious that the coup attempt of August 1991 and its aftermath had a tremendous impact on the USSR. If the events of 1988 caused a bifurcation in the behaviour of the USSR, does it not follow that the events of 1991 also point to a bifurcation? The answer is yes: 'The second revolution began in August 1991, when hard-liners in Moscow attempted to turn the clock back and resurrect the old totalitarian ways'.[21]

However, while it is true that some type of bifurcation took place in 1991, it is also true that this second catastrophe branched off from the original bifurcation. At this stage it is not clear whether the bifurcation of 1991 is a perturbation of the bifurcation of 1988 (which means that the fundamental dynamics associated with the latter are still valid) or whether it superseded the latter. If the second scenario holds true, the process presented in this chapter would have to be repeated to determine: (a) what type of bifurcation occurred in 1991; and (b) its implications for US–Russian relations. Unfortunately, it is still too early to determine with certainty which of the two cases described above is the most accurate; further discussion of this issue is presented in section IV of this chapter.

The Richardson arms race model[22]

The model described in this section was first developed by Lewis F. Richardson in 1960.

The model portrays the interdependent armaments behavior of two or more nations, and identifies three factors that determine armament levels: (1) the economic burden created by maintaining existing levels of military preparedness, (2) a nation's response to the threat presented by other nations and their armament levels, and (3) the grievances, ambitions, and prejudices that are unique to the internal politics of each nation.[23]

[21] Aspin (note 20), p. 2.
[22] For a basic description of Richardson's model, see Huckfeldt, R. R. et al., Dynamic Modeling: An Introduction, Sage University Papers no. 27 (Sage Publications: Newbury Park, Calif., 1982). The original model is presented in Richardson, L. F., Arms and Insecurity (Boxwood: Pittsburgh, Pa., 1960).
[23] Huckfeldt et al. (note 22), p. 46.

In order to obtain a simple expression for his model, Richardson linearizes about a stable point.[24] By doing so, he can ignore all of the non-linear terms in the expansion and create a linear model.[25] If X(t) and Y(t) denote the overall level of forces of the USSR and the USA at time t, respectively, (the terms 'armament levels' and 'force levels' are used interchangeably), then the continuous form of Richardson's equations can be written as follows:

$$\frac{dX}{dt} = rY(t) + cX(t) + d \qquad (1)$$

$$\frac{dY}{dt} = kX(t) + nY(t) + p \qquad (2)$$

where r = the threat felt by the USSR due to the size of US forces, c = the economic burden experienced by the USSR in attempting to maintain its armament level, and d = internal political and psychological considerations which affect the size of the USSR's forces.[26]

Similar definitions hold for parameters k, n and p in equation (2). The coefficients c and n are negative due to Richardson's assumptions that, 'Economics is a constraint on armament that tends to diminish the rate of armament by an amount proportional to the size of existing forces'.[27]

Because Richardson's equations are linear, a change in one variable, say X(t), will cause a proportional change in the other variable, Y(t). The proportion is determined by the coefficient relating the two variables in question (in the example just given, that coefficient would be k). In general, it is assumed that the coefficients (r, c, d, k, n and p above) in Richardson's model are constant during each iteration of the problem.[28] In other words, the assumption is made that the coupling between US and Soviet forces is fairly consistent during the time period being studied.[29] It is arguable that this assumption was valid for describing US–Soviet behaviour before 1988; however, after 1988 the situation changed dramatically.[30]

---

[24] In the case of an arms race model, a stable point would be a smoothly varying level of arms. In other words, Richardson assumes that there is no bifurcation in the system.

[25] Obviously, this can only be done when stable points exist. This assumption does not hold after 1988.

[26] The model being developing here deals only with conventional forces. If nuclear forces were included in the calculus, this would change the values of all of the coefficients, and might require changing the very form of the model. While it is probably true that nuclear forces have some impact on threat perceptions in the conventional arena, it is assumed that those considerations are secondary at the macro-level of analysis of this chapter.

[27] Saaty (note 13), p. 46. Many books present Richardson's equations with minus signs in front of the c and the n and define the coefficients as being positive. The two representations are equivalent.

[28] To be more precise, these parameters are allowed to vary in time, but since the time-scale of their variation is assumed to be much greater than the time-scales which drive the changes in force levels, the coefficients are essentially constant relative to the other parameters in the equations.

[29] Any time period can be chosen to update the value of the coefficients; this chapter deals with years.

[30] Some might argue that a bifurcation took place before 1988 (e.g., in 1986 when Gorbachev came to power). While this is an interesting point, the changes which took place in 1988 were so dramatic and profound that they clearly indicated a major break from previous patterns of behaviour.

A catastrophe theory model of US–Soviet military relations

US–Soviet relations experienced a profound and dramatic shift in 1988. The catastrophe which began to unfold in that year cannot be described with the linear equations of Richardson's model. For example, the coefficient describing the threat felt by the USSR due to US armament levels, r, can no longer be treated as a constant (i.e., slowly varying). Hence, the change in the armament level of the USSR,

$$\frac{dY(t)}{dt}$$

cannot be treated as a linear function.[31] In fact, armament levels are no longer the best unit to use in Richardson's equations. The reason for this change is as follows: Richardson expands his differential equations about $X(t)$ and $Y(t)$. The complete expression for these variables is:

$$X(t) = X(0) + \Delta X(t)$$

$$Y(t) = Y(0) + \Delta Y(t)$$

where the $\Delta X(t)$ and $\Delta Y(t)$ terms express variations about $X(0)$ and $Y(0)$. If the latter are stable points, then $\Delta X(t)$ and $\Delta Y(t)$ are negligible and linearization is possible. On the other hand, if $X(0)$ and $Y(0)$ are points of bifurcation, then the variations about those points cannot be ignored. In that case, equations (1) and (2) become:[32]

$$\frac{d(\Delta X)}{dt} = r[Y(0) + \Delta Y(t)] + c[X(0) + \Delta X(t)] + d \qquad (3)$$

$$\frac{d(\Delta Y)}{dt} = k[X(0) + \Delta X(t)] + n[Y(0) + \Delta Y(t)] + p \qquad (4)$$

These equations can be rewritten as:

$$\frac{d(\Delta X)}{dt} = r\Delta Y(t) + c\Delta X(t) + d' \qquad (5)$$

$$\frac{d(\Delta Y)}{dt} = k\Delta X(t) + n\Delta Y(t) + p' \qquad (6)$$

where

$$d' = rY(0) + cX(0) + d$$

$$p' = kX(0) + nY(0) + p$$

---

[31] While it cannot be denied that US forces are undergoing major changes as well, this discussion concentrates on the USSR because it was driving the dynamics of the system; the USA was playing a more reactive role. Major cuts in US conventional forces were discussed and planned, but no major changes took place during the period in question. See the discussion of the FY 1991 Congressional National Defense Authorization Act in chapter 9 in this volume

[32] It should be recalled that $X(0)$ and $Y(0)$ are constants, hence the derivative of these points equals zero.

Equations (5) and (6) have the same form as equations (1) and (2)—Richardson's equations—the only difference lies in the inhomogeneous terms (i.e., the grievance factors) and in the fact that the new equations express the dynamics of the changes in force levels, not simply the force levels themselves.[33] This is a subtle but important difference because, in essence, what is being studied here is a second-order effect. The implications of this finding are discussed later in the chapter.

Returning to the other change required in Richardson's equations, the correct functional form of r must be determined. During the cold war, parameters k and r were large (the coupling between US and Soviet force levels was tight). However, after 1988 the coupling between the superpowers diminished as economic and political considerations grew in importance.[34] Accordingly, the values of k and (especially) r decreased both absolutely and relative to the other coefficients. In other words, it appeared as though Soviet forces had 'decoupled' from US forces.

However, despite the apparent insensitivity of Soviet forces to outside influences, the Soviet military was highly sensitive to changes in US forces. This argument is based on the fact that President Gorbachev was counting on US co-operation in this area. If the USA had responded to Gorbachev's announcement of unilateral measures by increasing US force levels in Europe, the impact of this move on the USSR would have been tremendous—certainly greater after 1988 than it would have been several years earlier. The proposition can be restated as follows: after 1988, Soviet forces were no longer proportionally coupled to US forces.[35] This behaviour can be expressed by making the coefficient r a function of the size of US forces:[36]

$$\frac{d(\Delta X)}{dt} = r(\Delta Y)\Delta Y + c\Delta X + d' \qquad (7)$$

The Taylor expansion of ΔX shows that $r(\Delta Y)$ is a polynomial of degree $(n-1)$, so the term $r(\Delta Y)\Delta Y$ can be approximated with $(\Delta Y)^n$. Equation (7) then becomes:

$$\frac{d(\Delta X)}{dt} = e(\Delta Y)^n + c\Delta X + d' \qquad (8)$$

where e is the coefficient of the new term.

The next step is to determine the correct value for n. As stated earlier, this task is known as the recognition problem in catastrophe theory. In order to compare the equations here with those for known bifurcations, the form of

---

[33] In other words, the equations express the rate of change of variations in force levels; Richardson's equations express the rate of change of force levels.

[34] See Meyer, S., 'The sources and prospects of Gorbachev's new political thinking on security', *International Security*, vol. 13, no. 2 (fall 1988); and Snyder, J., 'The Gorbachev revolution: a waning of Soviet expansionism?', *International Security*, vol. 12, no. 3 (winter 1987/1988).

[35] In other words, the coefficient r can no longer be treated as a constant.

[36] To simplify the notation, $\Delta X(t)$ and $\Delta Y(t)$ will be written as ΔX and ΔY, respectively.

equation (8) must be changed so it depends only on one variable, not on both ΔX and ΔY.

This task can be begun by postulating that there is no bifurcation in the equation describing the dynamics of US forces (i.e., there was no dramatic jump in the size of US forces between 1988 and 1991).[37] Given this assumption, it follows that the function describing the coupling between changes in US and Soviet force levels from the US point of view is a smooth function.[38] Being a smooth function, the equation describing the variations in US force levels (not the rate of change of those variations) can be linearized without any loss of generality. If this is done, one arrives at the following result:

$$\Delta Y = k(\Delta X) + f \quad (9)$$

where k is the coupling coefficient between variations in US and Soviet forces, and f contains all the inhomogeneous terms of the equations (it is analogous to the variables d and p in Richardson's equations).

Equation (9) can be rewritten as:

$$\Delta Y = k[\Delta X + \frac{f}{k}] \quad (10)$$

$$\Delta Y = k(\Delta Z) \quad (11)$$

where

$$\Delta Z = \Delta X + \frac{f}{k} \quad (12)$$

The term f represents the various economic and political factors which affect US force levels. Parameter k represents the threat felt by the USA due to the size of Soviet forces. Thus, the ratio f/k is a measure of what actually drives the changes in US forces. If k is large, as before 1988, then ΔZ is approximately equal to ΔX. On the other hand, if one accepts the view that changes in US force levels are becoming more independent of changes in Soviet force levels, then the coefficient k is presumed to be small. If k is small, then the impact of f becomes significant.

Using equations (11) and (12), the desired form of equation (8) can be obtained. Making some simple substitutions, equation (8) can be rewritten as:

$$\frac{d(\Delta Z)}{dt} = ek^n(\Delta Z)^n + c(\Delta Z - \frac{f}{k}) + d' \quad (13)$$

or

$$\frac{d(\Delta Z)}{dt} = ek^n(\Delta Z)^n + c(\Delta Z) + (d' - \frac{cf}{k}) \quad (14)$$

---

[37] See note 31.

[38] The variable ΔY and its relation to ΔX is examined here; nothing is said about $\frac{d(\Delta Y)}{dt}$.

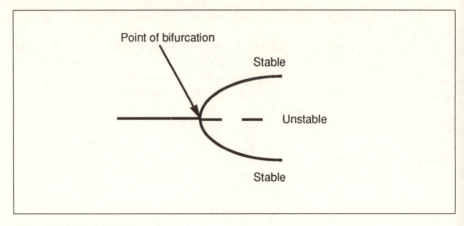

Figure 11.3. Pitchfork bifurcation

It is now possible to determine the correct value for 'n'. As mentioned earlier, this is done by comparing the dynamic behaviour of each family of bifurcations with the behaviour of the system in question. Although this process appears to allow great latitude in the selection of the correct type of bifurcation, in practice, the choices are quite limited.[39] Applying this method to the problem here, one finds that the simplest bifurcation which seems to capture the dynamics of Soviet behaviour is the pitchfork bifurcation. Because a pitchfork bifurcation is described by a cubic equation, it can be deduced that n = 3.[40] Figure 11.3 above provides a diagram of this bifurcation.

It is obvious how this bifurcation got its name; at the point of bifurcation the system splits into three possible paths: two of which are divergent curves while the third path continues linearly along the original direction. The two divergent solutions are stable. The solution which lies between the other two is unstable. This property may mirror what happened in the USSR.[41] However, before discussing these issues in detail, it is necessary to further develop the mathematical aspects of the analysis.

[39] See Golubitsky and Schaeffer (note 7), p. 203.

[40] The general form of the equation is $g(x, \lambda, \varepsilon) = x^3 - \lambda x + \varepsilon$. In an attempt to be as parsimonious as possible in deriving the model, the simplest bifurcation has been chosen which displays the 'correct' behaviour. It is possible, of course, that another more complicated bifurcation provides a better dynamic expression of US–Soviet force relations; however, the strategy used here is to start with the simplest possible explanation and test its usefulness. If it is found that the initial model is inadequate then appropriate changes will be made.

[41] The two stable solutions would represent reductions or increases in force levels, respectively. The middle solution would represent the status quo. The latter would be unstable because a slight 'perturbation' would lead to one of the extreme solutions; figure 11.2 shows how that representation reflects the dynamics just described.

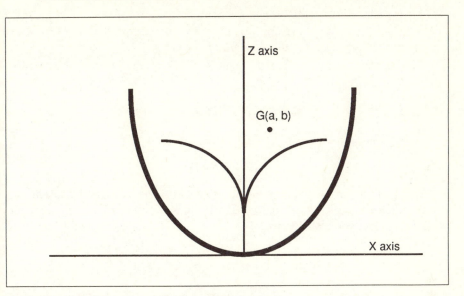

Figure 11.4. Model of the dynamics of the bifurcation

A physical model: the parabola

Although the mathematics which drive the model are now more comprehens-
ible, it is not yet clear how the various parameters in the model can be used to
gain an understanding of US–Soviet force relations. Because it will be difficult
to achieve such insights from a set of equations, an actual physical situation
will be used to 'model' the dynamics of the bifurcation. The physical model
used is a parabola sitting on a flat surface. Figure 11.4 above is a diagram of
this set-up.[42]

The behaviour of this system matches the dynamics of the pitchfork bifurcation: one stable solution exists until a specific point (the point of bifurcation) is
reached after which three possible solutions exist with the middle one being
unstable.

The point G(a, b) represents the centre of gravity of the parabola (the letters
'a' and 'b' describe the position of the centre of gravity in terms of the x–z
co-ordinates). The cusp inside the parabola represents the region where the
behaviour of the system bifurcates. If G is below the cusp, the system has one
stable solution (the parabola just sits there). On the other hand, if G is above the
cusp, then there are three possible solutions: (*a*) the parabola does not move;
(*b*) the parabola tilts to the right; and (*c*) the parabola tilts to the left. The first
solution is unstable because the slightest perturbation will cause the parabola to
move towards one of the other two solutions.[43]

---

[42] The equation of the parabola is $z = x^2$ (looking down the y axis).
[43] The higher the point G is relative to the x axis, the more unstable the parabola will be.

If it is assumed that G is somewhere in the region of the cusp, then the three possible solutions of the system (i.e., the three possible positions of G) can be characterized by measuring their distance from the ground.

If δ represents the distance from point G to the ground, then the expression for δ is, by definition:

$$\delta^2 = (x-a)^2 + (z-b)^2 \qquad (15)$$

However, since $z = x^2$, it is possible to write:

$$\delta^2 = (x-a)^2 + (x^2-b)^2 \qquad (16)$$

An equation for the possible positions of G can be obtained by taking the derivative of equation (16) and setting it equal to zero. If this is done, the following expression is obtained:

$$\frac{d\delta}{dx} = x^3 + \frac{1-2b}{2}x - \frac{a}{2} = 0 \qquad (17)$$

As expected, equation (17) has the same form as equation (14) with n = 3. Setting equation (14) equal to zero, produces the following:

$$\Delta Z^3 + \frac{c}{ek^3}(\Delta Z) + \frac{1}{ek^3}(d' - \frac{cf}{k}) = 0 \qquad (18)$$

The value of the point of entry (or bifurcation) into the cusp can be determined by examining the discriminant, Δ', of equation (17). The expression for Δ' is:

$$\Delta' = 2(1-2b)^3 + 27a^2 \qquad (19)$$

Thus, the cusp begins at the point b = 1/2 . Below this point, the discriminant is positive with one real root, hence there exists one stable solution (i.e., the situation before the bifurcation). Above b = 1/2, the discriminant is negative with three real roots: two of which are stable (the local minima for Δ'), and one which is unstable (a local maximum for Δ'). Obviously, equation (19) expresses the dynamics of a pitchfork bifurcation.

The question remains, what does all this mean in terms of the original dynamic model? First, the manner in which parameters 'a' and 'b' relate to the variables of the set of equations will be explored. Comparing equations (17) and (18) produces the following expressions:

$$b = \frac{1}{2} - \frac{c}{ek^3} \qquad (20)$$

$$a = \frac{2}{ek^3}(\frac{cf}{k} - d') \qquad (21)$$

IV. Model analysis

Position along the vertical axis (parameter 'b')

Examining equation (20) reveals that the USSR will cross into the cusp region if $c < 0$. It will be recalled that c was defined as 'the economic burden experienced by the USSR in attempting to maintain its armament level', and was assumed to be negative. If Richardson's assumption is correct, then the result appears to make no sense: if c is negative, then the centre of gravity is above the cusp and there is no point of bifurcation. However, before making any conclusions concerning the validity of the results, the role of parameter k in equation (20) needs to be discussed.

If k is small, then the term c/ek^3 is quite large. On the other hand, if k is large, then the same term approaches zero (regardless of whether c is positive or negative). If the assumption is accepted that US and Soviet forces were tightly coupled before 1988, then the value of b was approximately equal to 1/2. This means that the USSR was sitting very close to the point of bifurcation. At this point, the dynamics of the cusp region would have had only a minor impact on the USSR. In other words, it might not have been apparent to the USSR (or anybody else) that anything had changed.

However, as the coupling between the military forces of the USA and the USSR became less pronounced, the economic burden facing the USSR grew in importance (i.e., as k gets smaller, the term c/ek^3 gets larger). And as the economic burden of fielding its forces became more apparent, so did the realization that the USSR was falling deeper and deeper into a world driven by a new set of dynamics. After 1988, there was no denying the fact that the USSR had entered a region of profound tension between several distinct alternatives.

Position along the horizontal axis (parameter 'a')

Equation (20) described the vertical position of the centre of gravity in the parabola; similarly, equation (21) describes the horizontal position of G(a, b). Unfortunately, it is not possible to provide a definitive analysis of this equation. The uncertainty in the results is due to the nature of equation (21) itself. The value of 'a' is determined by the term: $(cf/k - d')$.[44] If 'a' is positive, the parabola will tilt to the right; this indicates an increase in the size of Soviet forces. If 'a' is negative, the parabola will tilt to the left which indicates a decrease in the size of Soviet forces.[45] If 'a' is zero, the parabola stands upright (but is unstable if $b > 1/2$) which indicates no change in the size of Soviet forces. In essence then an analysis of changes in Soviet forces requires examination of the term $(cf/k - d')$.

---

[44] The term $2/ek^3$ changes the magnitude but not the sign of 'a'. Since only the dominant characteristics of the system are of interest (i.e., which way the parabola falls), this term can be ignored here.

[45] To be more specific, the sign of 'a' indicates the sign of the variations in Soviet forces. A positive variation implies an increase in forces and vice versa.

The difficulty in analysing (cf/k – d') is due to the fact that the term contains four variables. Richardson's assumptions indicate that k is positive and c negative. If this hypothesis is accepted as fact, two variables (f and d') still remain which can be either positive or negative. If f and d' have the same sign, then the sign of 'a' follows trivially. If f and d' have different signs, then it becomes necessary to compare the magnitude of the terms cf/k and d' to see if 'a' is positive or negative. The following brief parametric analysis describes the behaviour of the system in broad terms.[46]

System behaviour

The magnitude of d' increased after 1988.[47] If the assumption is also made that internal political and psychological considerations pushed the Soviet Union to decrease its force levels, then d' must be negative. This leaves one free variable: f. Three different scenarios will be examined.

1. If f is negative, then 'a' is positive.
2. If f is positive and the magnitude of cf/k is greater than the magnitude of d', then 'a' is negative.
3. If f is positive and the magnitude of cf/k is less than the magnitude of d', then 'a' is positive.

If one believes that economic and political considerations pushed the United States towards lower force levels between 1988 and 1991, then f is negative and scenario 1 results.[48] However, if the Gulf War actually caused internal forces in the USA to push for increases in force levels during this period, then there are two possible cases: (*a*) if one agrees with Meyer's and Snyder's assertions (as this author does) that domestic factors were the dominant cause of change in Soviet force levels, then d' must be larger than cf/k, resulting in scenario 3; (*b*) if one disagrees with Meyer and Snyder, then d' must be smaller than cf/k, resulting in scenario 2. It is this author's contention that scenarios 1 and 3 are—depending on one's assumptions—the most likely explanations of what happened between 1988 and August 1991. Hence, this chapter will assume that 'a' is positive.

---

[46] Modelling is a mathematical expression of words and ideas. While it is helpful in many ways, modelling faces the same pitfalls and limitations which hinder anyone who attempts to study complicated social phenomena. One of those pitfalls is the difficulty of attempting to weigh the importance of various intangible factors in determining the behaviour of a group or organization.

[47] It should be recalled that the parameter d' represents internal political and psychological considerations which affect the size of the Soviet forces. For detailed discussion of this issue, see Meyer (note 34) and Snyder (note 34).

[48] Major cuts in US forces were discussed during this period, see note 31.

Results of analysis

The conclusion has been reached that 'a' is positive. In other words, the model shows that there would be a force pushing the USSR towards increasing its forces between 1988 and August 1991. This conclusion appears incorrect; in fact, the USSR decreased the size of its forces during the period in question. In order to explain this apparently erroneous result, the discussion of metastability at the beginning of the chapter must be recalled (see figure 11.2).

The three points of figure 11.2, marked A, B and C, represent the three solutions of the pitchfork bifurcation (or the parabola which has been discussed here). Points A and C correspond to the forks of the bifurcation, while point B represents the middle path. Point A is postulated to be a metastable solution. The notion of metastability has been introduced because it helps to explain two major findings of the analysis: a prediction that the Soviet Union would attempt to increase the size of its forces sometime after 1988, and the importance of 'coupling' between the two superpowers.

The coup attempt of 1991

The analysis presented here indicates that the USSR would attempt to increase the size of its forces after 1988; perhaps that is exactly what happened. As has been seen, the factors which determined whether Soviet forces would increase or decrease were primarily economic, political and psychological. Thus, the fact that 'a' is positive reflects the fact that economic, political and psychological forces were attempting to push the system away from Gorbachev's reforms. It is the view of this author that the coup attempt of August 1991 represents these dynamics described by the model.[49]

In the language of the model, the coup attempt was an effort to tilt the parabola to the right (i.e., 'a' was positive). What does the model have to say about the fact that the coup failed?

Referring to the previous discussion of stability, it is possible to deduce that the solution offered by the model was metastable. To put it another way, the ball fell into a shallow dip (the coup attempt) then rolled out of that dip and into another one (the aftermath of the coup). In terms of the parabola, this means that it began to tilt to the right but then tilted back towards the left. This idea is expanded on below.

---

[49] This assumes that Gennadi Yanaev and his fellow conservatives would slow down or reverse some of the changes Gorbachev had imposed on the Soviet military. Obviously, some conservative elements in the Soviet Union had resisted Gorbachev's military reforms from the very beginning. However, it was not obvious at the time that these forces would gather enough steam to actually attempt to overthrow the government. An interesting question to raise here concerns the impact of the Persian Gulf War on the internal dynamics of the Soviet Government. It is possible that the apparent ease with which the USA defeated Soviet weapons catalysed the hard-liners in the USSR. A more detailed discussion of Soviet attitudes *vis-à-vis* the war is found in chapter 10 in this volume.

Metastability and Soviet behaviour

Metastability has been used to explain the connection between the 1991 coup attempt and the model's indirect prediction of that event. The discussion will now be expanded to include Soviet behaviour after the coup; specifically, between August and December 1991: four months which witnessed great change in the Soviet political, economic and military climate. Two events, in particular, were turning points for the future of the nation: the Ukrainian vote for independence and the declaration of the Commonwealth of Independent States by Belarus, Russia and Ukraine. These two occurrences will be addressed briefly from the point of view of the model.

It has been postulated that the model's observation that the USSR would attempt to increase the size of its forces was a metastable solution. It appears, however, that the solution which the system *actually* fell into was also metastable. This is possible because the system being studied is evolving very quickly over time. In fact, it is not completely clear whether the bifurcation used for describing events between 1988 and August 1991 is appropriate for describing events after the coup attempt. There are two possibilities:

1. The events after the coup represent a fundamental change in the dynamics of the system.
2. The events after the coup represent a minor perturbation of the pitchfork bifurcation, in which case the underlying dynamics of the system remain unchanged.

Of these two cases, the latter scenario is probably more appropriate. The reason for this choice is that it is the most parsimonious theory which can adequately explain the events which took place. Suppose that an accurate representation of the period in question looks like figure 11.5 below.

The region in question contains several metastable solutions (points A, C and E) and unstable points (B, D, and F) as well as a stable attractor (point G). Thus, a variety of fairly small perturbations could cause the system to jump from one solution to another. Although such a system would appear to be highly unstable to an outside observer, the system might simply be converging towards some 'globally' stable solution. In other words, some force (or a variety of forces) could be pushing a ball from dip to dip in order to reach the deepest one.[50]

For example, it is possible that the stable attractor (point G) represents the birth of a new nation (i.e., the CIS) in place of the former USSR. If this postulate is accepted, then events between August and December 1991 would correspond to the metastable solutions of the diagram. On the other hand, the birth of the Commonwealth could also be a metastable event and the system as a whole could continue to evolve towards some unknown solution.

---

[50] A physical interpretation would be that the system is attempting to minimize the potential energy of the ball.

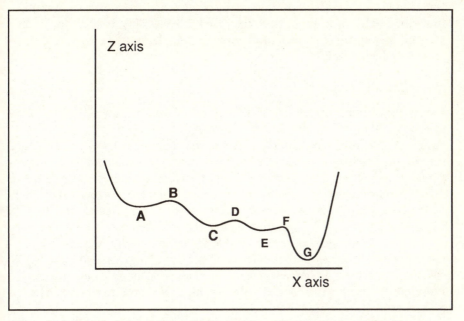

Figure 11.5. Hypothetical potential-well representation of Soviet behaviour, 1988–91

Coupling between US and Soviet forces

Few would argue with the assertion that the coupling between US and Soviet conventional forces decreased after 1988. Domestic issues clearly became the primary concern of the Soviet Government, and the United States no longer saw the Soviet Union as a major threat.[51] One would naturally have expected the military coupling between the two nations to have had less of an impact on the dynamics of their interactions than before 1988. We have seen that such a conclusion is not necessarily correct. This counter-intuitive result follows from the relationships among the parameters in the model.

Equations (20) and (21) have shown that despite the pre-eminence of economic and political factors in the model, the coupling parameter k has some influence in determining the possible solutions of the system (see the discussion of 'system behaviour' above). If it is assumed that one of the potential solutions is metastable, it is possible that a change in the coupling term alone could push the system from one solution to another. In other words, a parameter which is relatively small in magnitude (the coupling term) can have significant impact on the system as a whole.

In addition, parameter k is sensitive to action–reaction cycles that may be started by either nation. For example, the overwhelming success of the USA in the Gulf War worried some officials in the USSR (the value of r increased).

---

[51] For example, 'Mr. Bush's remarks tonight [27 Sep.] represented a recognition that there is no longer an imminent threat of war with the Soviet Union in Europe', see Rosenthal, A., 'U.S. to give up short-range nuclear arms; Bush seeks Soviet cuts and further talks', *New York Times*, 28 Sep. 1991, p. 5.

Had the USSR reacted to this pressure by redeploying some of its conventional forces, the value of k would have increased as well. This, in turn, could have affected the overall dynamics of the system (i.e., the position of the centre of gravity in the parabola).

Non-military coupling

It was shown in the discussion of 'system behaviour' that the dynamics of the system are highly dependent on the ratio cf/k. Up to this point, the discussion has concentrated on the military aspects of the coupling between the USA and the USSR (variable k); however, it is apparent that economic, political and psychological considerations (variables c and f) can play a significant role in the model. An example of this phenomenon is demonstrated in declarations made by Presidents Bush and Gorbachev concerning short-range nuclear forces.[52] On 27 September 1991, President Bush announced that the USA 'would eliminate all tactical nuclear weapons on land and at sea in Europe and Asia, called long-range bombers off their 24-hour alerts and offered to negotiate with the USSR for sharp reductions in the most dangerous kinds of globe-spanning missiles'.[53] President Gorbachev responded with a similar but more extensive offer on 5 October.[54]

President Bush's initiative had a tremendous impact on the USSR. First, 'The President's speech reflected a fundamental change in the way Americans think about the Soviet threat'.[55] Second, the US position pressured the Soviet Government to take control of nuclear forces which were located in 'independent-minded' republics. In addition, the fact that Bush chose to deal with Gorbachev instead of the republics themselves legitimized Gorbachev's role in the face of a disintegrating Union. The fact that Bush undermined this position two months later by (a) agreeing to recognize an independent Ukraine 'expeditiously'; and (b) by then announcing that Secretary of State James Baker would visit Kiev to 'discuss American concerns about the control of nuclear weapons on Ukrainian territory' two days after Ukraine voted for independence, provides further evidence of the significant impact the USA had on the dynamics of the USSR.[56]

Although they will not be discussed here, two other issues which could be examined in connection with the model are: US policy during the coup attempt, and the economic ties between the USA and the USSR during the period studied here. Decision makers should play close attention to the *apparent* decoupling between US and Russian forces in Europe. It is possible for 'small' effects to lead to major events. If one can determine the role various factors play in the system, it may be possible to prevent destabilizing situations from

[52] The model does not include nuclear forces in any way; this example has been chosen only for illustrative purposes.

[53] See Rosenthal (note 51), p. 1.

[54] Schemann, S., 'Gorbachev matches U.S. on nuclear cuts and goes further on strategic warheads', *New York Times*, 6 Oct. 1991, p. 1.

[55] Aspin (note 20), p. 3.

[56] Wines, M., 'Baker will visit Ukraine to discuss nuclear question', *New York Times*, 3 Dec. 1991, p. 1.

occurring.[57] This may become more important now that the disintegration of the USSR is a *fait accompli*; relations between the USA and Russia will be vitally important to the stability of the region and Europe in general.[58]

V. Final observations

Caveats

Two caveats must be entered into the discussion. The first concerns the importance of being explicit when making assumptions about the impact of various parameters on US–Soviet force structure relationships. The term c/k can be examined as an illustration of such an assumption. A decrease in the value of the coupling coefficient (k) implies an increase in the relative magnitude of economic considerations (c) *if* one assumes (as was done in this chapter) that the value of c does not decrease proportionally to k. If one believes that the magnitude of c decreased *more* than the magnitude of k, then the conclusion one would reach is that economic considerations actually decreased in relative importance.

The second caveat concerns the use of catastrophe theory: it is a descriptive device. Since it deals only with local bifurcations, catastrophe theory cannot predict the global behaviour of the system. A good example of this property is the finding that dynamic forces were pushing the USSR to increase its armament levels. Although this solution reflected a dynamic process which was taking place in the USSR, the model could not predict whether it was metastable or globally stable; only in retrospect was it possible to identify the nature of the solution. Furthermore, the model does not describe all of the forces which are at work in the system described.[59] Rather what has been provided is a layout of the environment in which the forces play out their game. Using an analogy from golf, the model (and catastrophe theory in general) describes the characteristics of the course—where the holes are, what the greens are like, etc.—but it cannot say with certainty which hole the ball will go into.[60]

Units of analysis

Early in the chapter the units of analysis were changed from overall force levels to variations in force levels. This was done because overall force levels did not provide a stable point about which it was possible to linearize. The implications of this are quite interesting: rather than using the size of forces as an indicator

---

[57] An excellent example of the need for such analyses is found in the issue of technological coupling between the two superpowers. This is a significant problem affecting US–Russian relations, but one which has received little attention so far. See chapter 10 in this volume.

[58] Two examples which come readily to mind concern the US role in settling the disagreement between Presidents Yeltsin and Nazarbayev regarding control of nuclear weapons in Kazakhstan, and US policy *vis-à-vis* a military conflict between Russia and Ukraine.

[59] Nor could any other model; models are by definition incomplete descriptions of reality. See Morgan, M. G. and Henrion, M., *Uncertainty: A Guide to Dealing with Uncertainty in Quantitative Risk and Policy Analysis* (Cambridge University Press: New York, 1990), p. 68.

[60] This metaphor comes from Dr Benoit Morel.

of stability, one needs to look at changes in force levels. To be more precise, the dynamics of the system are not driven by the rate at which forces change size over time but by the rate at which changes in forces take place.

For example, rather than observing the rate of change of Soviet force levels from 1988 to 1991, one could examine the frequency of the changes in Soviet force levels during the period. Did the changes occur gradually or quickly? Did they involve increases, decreases or restructuring of forces? Although the issue raised here is subtle, it should certainly be examined further.

Conclusion

This chapter has employed catastrophe theory to study the relationship between US and Soviet conventional forces between 1988 and 1991. It has shown that a non-linear dynamic model (and the techniques of catastrophe theory) can be a useful tool for helping policy makers analyse some aspects of US–Russian relations. The analysis highlighted the role various factors—threat perception, economic burden, domestic politics and psychology—played in affecting the dynamics of the system. It was found that the decline of the perceived threat between US and Soviet forces in Europe allowed other factors to have a greater impact than they had previously.

The USSR underwent two dramatic shifts in behaviour in 1988 and 1991. The result of the first shift—which was definitely a bifurcation—was that the USSR entered a region of metastable behaviour which led to the coup attempt of August 1991 and its aftermath. Although it could not be determined whether the coup attempt was an actual bifurcation, it appeared that the USSR remained in a region of metastability after the coup, and that Russia is probably in a metastable state today.

It was also found that, despite a decrease in magnitude, the military coupling between the USA and the USSR remained an important factor in determining the dynamic behaviour of the relationship. In fact, it was the interaction between the military coupling and the other 'non-military' factors which determined the fundamental direction of the system—see equations (20) and (21). Thus, it is possible that an instability which one nation is experiencing can have a tremendous impact on the relationship between the two countries (not a surprising conclusion).

Although it is not clear where either nation is headed, it is apparent from the analysis presented here that the fates of Russia and the USA are significantly intertwined. Although economic and domestic political considerations may dominate the agenda of the Russian Government, it is evident that military considerations are vital to the stability of the region. The analysis has shown that relatively small forces can have a tremendous impact on a dynamic system. It is incumbent upon both Russia and the USA to identify such forces and prevent them from destroying a promising future. It is hoped that the framework presented in this chapter can assist decision makers to do just that.

Part IV
Building a new security relationship

12. Co-operation or competition: the battle of ideas in Russia and the USA

Steven Kull

I. Introduction

Discussions of Russian–US security co-operation most often focus on the problems and advantages of specific concrete proposals. However, underlying these discussions, and playing a potent role in shaping outcomes, are the attitudes of Russian and US policy makers about the very concept of security co-operation.

Taking into account Soviet as well as recent Russian experience, these attitudes have gone through a long and circuitous process of evolution. To some extent this has been an interactive process as each side has responded to the attitudes perceived to be held by the other side but there has also been a dimension of internal conflict or ambivalence about the prospect of security co-operation. As this chapter demonstrates, on both sides there have been at least two streams of thought, one enthusiastic about the potential fruits of co-operation, and another more concerned about the constraints such co-operation may impose on the nation's freedom of unilateral action to pursue its immediate interests or its long-term ideological goals.

II. The roots of the interest in security co-operation

The primary factor prompting interest in Soviet–US security co-operation was concern about the growing destructiveness of warfare engendered by the power of modern technology. On the US side this concern preceded the Soviet–US competitive relationship. After World War I there was a widespread revulsion in the United States against the destruction of the war and the prospect for future destruction in light of the devastating power of aerial bombing. A strong stream of thinking emerged which held that it was no longer viable for nations to resolve disputes through war, which stressed the value of disarmament and which undertook to find new means to resolve international disputes through co-operation, for example, through international law. President Woodrow Wilson was a champion of this point of view, proposing the League of Nations as a collective security system.

This line of thought was not universally accepted at the time in the United States. Before World War I, there had been a tradition that glorified military conquest and happily embraced the notion of, and even the term, imperialism. Support for the notion of a collective security system was so lukewarm that even though the formation of the League of Nations had been spearheaded by President Wilson, the United States Senate refused to ratify US membership.

The Soviet Union also resisted this new emphasis on a co-operative approach to security. The Soviet Marxist ideology established by V. I. Lenin embraced military violence as a legitimate instrument of policy and an essential feature of socio-economic evolution. Efforts to suppress military violence through such forms of co-operation as international law or disarmament were rejected as intrinsically biased in favour of the status quo and therefore inconsistent with the revolutionary Soviet ideology. In a tract derisively titled *The 'Disarmament' Slogan*, Lenin wrote:

Socialists cannot be opposed to all war in general and still be socialists. . . . To put 'disarmament' in the programme is tantamount to making the general declaration: We are opposed to the use of arms. There is as little Marxism in this as there would be if we were to say: We are opposed to violence! . . . we are living in a class society from which there is no way out. . . . [Disarmament] is tantamount to complete abandonment of the class struggle point of view, to renunciation of all thought of revolution.[1]

Accordingly, the Soviet Union was initially very suspicious of international institutions, and it was not a member of the League of Nations for many years after the League's founding in 1920. Typical of the Soviet attitude to the League is the following communiqué, issued by the Soviet Narkomindel, the Commissariat for Foreign Relations: 'The Soviet Government is still convinced that this allegedly international body really serves as a mere mask, designed to deceive the broad masses, for the aggressive aims of the imperialist policy of certain Great Powers or their vassals'.[2]

By the 1930s, however, the Soviet Union began to accommodate to the international trend towards collective security. Stalin apparently came to view the League of Nations as a potential brake on the aggressive actions of other states.[3] In 1934 the Soviet Union became a member of the League, but in 1939 it invaded Finland thus leading to its expulsion from the League.

Though the League turned out to be ineffective in preventing the outbreak of World War II, the horrors of that war and the spectre of the potential for atomic war revitalized the interest in establishing a co-operative international order. The USA took the lead in founding the United Nations. The universalist thinking that undergirded the idea of the United Nations was particularly prominent in the United States. The prospect of world government was viewed seriously and numerous US Senators identified themselves as world federalists. Even then President Harry Truman said that he carried in his pocket a copy of the portion of Tennyson's poem 'Locksley Hall' that predicted a 'Parliament of Man, the Federation of the world', Truman explaining 'that's what I have been

[1] Lenin, V. I., *Collected Works*, vol. 23 (Foreign Language Publishing House: London, 1960), p. 95.

[2] 'Narkomindel reply to the invitation to attend the League of Nations Conference on Naval Disarmament', 15 Mar. 1923, ed. J. Degras, *Soviet Documents on Foreign Policy*, vol. 1 (Oxford University Press: London, 1953), p. 381.

[3] See Degras (note 2), vol. 3, p. 45.

working for'.[4] There was a remarkable willingness to consider subordinating national sovereignty to international institutions, most notably in the unsuccessful effort to establish an international body that would control atomic weapons—a notion that would not be seriously considered today.

This does not mean that the USA was entirely willing to subordinate itself to international institutions. Apparently, for many US policy makers, US willingness to promote such international institutions was predicated on the assumption that the USA could effectively dominate them. Nevertheless the *Zeitgeist* at that time was one of great enthusiasm for international institutions.

On the surface, the Soviet Government joined in the formation of the United Nations and embraced Western notions of international co-operation, but apparently, these moves were primarily cynical efforts to soften the West. The Soviet Union was still deeply steeped in a highly competitive ideology aimed at ultimately overcoming the capitalist West. The ideal of ideological expansion was still seen as a higher priority than that of maintaining peace.

The USA, correctly assessing Soviet attitudes (though perhaps overestimating the willingness of the USSR to take military risks in the pursuit of its goals), pulled back from the heady universalism of the early post-war period. Having rapidly disarmed after the war, the USA began an intensive period of military expansion, increased the size of its defence budget several fold and maintained it at high levels for the ensuing decades. Interest in such co-operative international structures as the UN or ideas such as the international control of nuclear weapons, dropped off precipitously. Instead, the dominant paradigm for the international order became the military and political containment of the Soviet Union.

The stream of US thinking that had previously resisted efforts at international co-operation now consolidated around the 'realist' school, whose key spokesmen were Hans Morgenthau and George Kennan. The distribution of military power, it was stressed, not a co-operative international order, is necessarily the key factor that shapes international relations. Specifically for the USA, this thinking pointed to the policy of seeking to contain the Soviet Union through a forward-based military presence around its periphery.

The US policy of containment and the military buildup that flowed from it, confirmed the Soviet concept of an inevitable conflict between socialism and capitalism. As the Soviet Union accelerated its own military buildup, developing atomic and then thermonuclear weapons much sooner than the USA anticipated, the cold war and its attendant arms race were soon in full bloom.

Not long after Joseph Stalin's death in 1953, though, the dangers of military competition with the West became apparent. This arose from an awareness of the destructive potential of nuclear weapons. Georgiy Malenkov, then Chairman of the Council of Ministers, asserted that a general nuclear war would mean 'the destruction of world civilization'.[5] This idea was not well received,

---

[4] Gaddis, J. L., *Strategies of Containment* (Oxford University Press: Oxford, 1982), p. 56.
[5] Quoted in Holloway, D., *The Soviet Union and the Arms Race* (Yale University Press: New Haven, Conn., 1983), p. 31.

and it apparently played a role in Malenkov's fall from power. Nevertheless, in 1956 Party General Secretary Nikita Khrushchev recognized that nuclear weapons made war so destructive that a revision of Marxist-Leninist dogma was needed. A general war with the West, previously viewed as a necessary outcome of the tension between capitalism and socialism, was no longer seen as 'fatalistically inevitable'.

Khrushchev also began to articulate some of the key features of the condition of mutual vulnerability between powers with large nuclear arsenals. He explained that in a war between nuclear-armed states even 'the state which suffers [an all-out surprise attack] . . . will always have the possibility to give the proper rebuff to the aggressor'. With more emphasis, he asserted, 'Nuclear war is stupid, stupid, stupid! If you reach for the button you reach for suicide'.

III. The effort at *détente*

As the reality of nuclear vulnerability began to make a more fundamental impression on Soviet thinking it led to a greater interest in the prospect of co-operation with the United States on security matters. In the late 1950s efforts were initiated, some of them ultimately successful, to control the levels of the superpowers' armaments and to regulate nuclear testing. In the late 1960s, under Leonid Brezhnev, the Soviet Union also embraced the principle that the superpowers should pursue a policy of co-operation with the USA on security matters, a policy jointly dubbed *détente*. Warmed by this new Soviet posture, the USA experienced a renewal of hope in the potential for such co-operation.

This new approach reached its zenith in 1972 with the signing of the first Strategic Arms Limitation Treaty (SALT I) which included an Interim Agreement limiting strategic offensive weapons and a treaty of unlimited duration banning anti-ballistic missiles (ABMs). This latter agreement was significant because it, in effect, made explicit the condition of mutual vulnerability and committed both sides to refraining from attempts to upset it through defensive systems. Concurrently, the superpowers also signed a joint statement on the Basic Principles of Relations between the Soviet Union and the United States. This agreement said that the two countries:

will proceed from the common determination that in the nuclear age there is no alternative to conducting their mutual relations on the basis of peaceful coexistence. . . . The US and the USSR attach major importance to preventing the development of situations capable of causing a dangerous exacerbation of their relations. Therefore, they will do their utmost to avoid military confrontations and to prevent the outbreak of nuclear war. They will always exercise restraint in their mutual relations, and will be prepared to negotiate and settle differences by peaceful means. . . . The prerequisites for maintaining and strengthening peaceful relations between the US and the USSR are the recognition of the security interests of the Parties based on the principle of equality and the renunciation of the use or threat of force. . . . The USA and the USSR regard as the ultimate objective of their efforts the achievement of general and complete disarmament and the establishment of an effective system of international security.

Such thinking established a framework for a regime of security co-operation. This regime gained such strength that negotiations on arms control and confidence-building measures (CBMs) persisted even during periods when US–Soviet relations were at a low ebb. Nevertheless the fruits of these efforts were minimal and very hard won because the co-operative framework had still not displaced a fundamentally competitive relationship.

This competitive attitude was apparent on both sides.[6] In a variety of ways the USA tried to pursue unilateral advantages contrary to the spirit of *détente*. Some US policy makers tended to view *détente* as a means of getting the Soviet Union to accept a secondary position in international affairs. Nevertheless, the co-operative notion of *détente* was consistent with US values and many US policy makers saw themselves as genuinely trying to promote co-operation.

For the Soviet Union, though, this newly co-operative attitude was simply grafted onto the body of Soviet thinking in a piecemeal fashion; it did not really alter the underlying competitive foundation. In response to concerns about whether *détente* signified a departure from the Leninist path, Brezhnev reassured the faithful that he was simply pursuing Lenin's method of peaceful coexistence, which would mollify the West while giving socialist forces a chance to build their strength. He explained that *détente* 'creates favorable conditions for the struggle between the two systems and for altering the correlation of forces in favor of socialism'.[7] The Soviet Union continued to pursue a competitive foreign policy, supported socialist factions in the Third World, dramatically expanded the size and capabilities of its conventional and nuclear forces, and ultimately invaded Afghanistan.

These developments dashed hopes about the potential for *détente* and left many in the USA with the impression that the entire effort had been little more than a charade to put the West off its proper guard while, underneath, the USSR had not really changed. The factors that led the Soviet Union to seek out *détente*, however, were very genuine. The problem was that many of these factors contradicted key principles of Leninism. Since the Soviet leadership was not ready to directly challenge Lenin, these new insights existed side-by-side with traditional Leninist thought.

IV. New thinking

All this changed when Mikhail Gorbachev took the helm of the Soviet state in 1985 and, in the following years articulated what he called 'new thinking', an

---

[6] For an excellent account of how *détente* was undermined by the efforts of both superpowers to seek unilateral advantages see Breslauer, G., 'Why détente failed: an interpretation', ed. A. George, *Managing U.S.–Soviet Rivalry* (Westview: Boulder, Colo., 1983), pp. 319–40.

[7] Quoted in Weeks, A. L. and Bodie, W. C., *War and Peace: Soviet Russia Speaks* (National Strategy Information Center: New York, 1983), p. 6.

orientation to international relations that unequivocally stressed the need for co-operative international structures to displace military power as the means for maintaining security. Gorbachev underscored that the cornerstone of new think-ing was recognition of the reality and implications of the condition of mutual vulnerability. He explained that this condition effectively undermined the idea of war as a means for promoting socialist revolution:

In developing our philosophy of peace, we have taken a new look at the interdepend-ence of war and revolution. In the past, war often served to detonate revolu-tion. . . . But when the conditions radically changed so that the only result of nuclear war could be universal destruction, we drew a conclusion about the disappearance of the cause-and-effect relationship between war and revolution. . . . At the 27th CPSU Congress we clearly 'divorced' the revolution and war themes . . .[8]

More broadly, he stated that the condition of mutual vulnerability effectively undermined the concept of class struggle as the central theme of international relations: 'with the emergence of weapons of mass, that is universal destruction, there appeared an objective limit for class confrontation in the international arena: the threat of universal destruction'.

Now, he explained, the 'primary thing that defines' international relations is 'the immutable fact that whether we like one another or not we can survive or perish only together'.[9] As a result, he explained on many occasions, class values or interest have to be subordinated to universal human values: 'The backbone of the new way of thinking is the recognition of the priority of human values, or, to be more precise, of humankind's survival'.[10]

Perhaps most telling, in Gorbachev's speeches there was a complete absence of any reference to the ultimate victory of socialism. Instead, Gorbachev asserted that 'the world is moving' not towards socialism but 'to a pluralism which is natural for the new times'.[11] Thus, he said 'The increasing varieties of social development in different countries' call for: 'respect for other people's views and stands, tolerance, a preparedness to see phenomena that are different as not necessarily bad or hostile, and an ability to learn to live side by side. . . . Thus, the question is of unity in diversity'.[12]

At times Gorbachev was even quite direct in acknowledging that his ideas signified an important break with Marxism-Leninism. Clarifying the distinction between his new perspective and Lenin's strategy of 'peaceful coexistence', Gorbachev explained: 'there have been changes in Lenin's concept of peaceful coexistence. . . . At first it was needed above all to create a modicum of external conditions for the construction of a new society in the country of the socialist

[8] Gorbachev, M., *Perestroika: New Thinking For Our Country and the World* (Harper & Row: New York, 1987), pp. 147–48.

[9] 'An interview with Gorbachev', *Time*, 9 Sep. 1985.

[10] Gorbachev (note 8), p. 146.

[11] 'In a friendly atmosphere', *Pravda*, 19 Oct. 1988, p. 2, in Foreign Broadcast Information Service, *Daily Report–Soviet Union (FBIS-SOV)*, FBIS-SOV-88-202, 19 Oct. 1988, p. 41.

[12] 'M. S. Gorbachev's speech at the UN organization', *Pravda*, 8 Dec. 1988, pp. 1, 2, in FBIS-SOV-88-236, 8 Dec. 1988, p. 13.

CO-OPERATION OR COMPETITION 215

revolution [but it] subsequently became a condition for the survival of the entire human race, especially in the nuclear age'.[13] On another occasion he stated baldly that many of the ideas of Marxism-Leninism 'have "exhausted" their usefulness and receded into history'.[14]

V. The new emphasis on co-operation

One of the key principles flowing from new thinking was a strong emphasis on the value of co-operation and reciprocity in international relations. Gorbachev wrote: 'Life itself . . . require[s] a transition from confrontation to co-operation among peoples and states irrespective of their social system'.[15] This perspective did not rule out competition, especially between nations of differing social systems. However, it stressed that this competition both can and should be contained within a co-operative context. Gorbachev wrote: 'Economic, political and ideological competition between capitalist and socialist countries is inevitable. However it can and must be kept within a framework . . . which necessarily envisages co-operation'.[16]

The pursuit of a co-operative world order was not only seen as a necessary adaptation to a more dangerous world, it was also attributed with an intrinsic normative value, in some cases on the same plane as the traditional competitive effort to achieve world revolution. Shevardnadze said that: 'co-operation for the salvation of civilization . . . this is the sacrosanct struggle. This is our world revolution . . . not the world revolution that our predecessors spoke of . . . we must [be] co-operative with everyone'.[17]

To achieve this co-operative order, new thinkers outlined a number of key principles. A critical one was to abandon the maximalism of traditional Bolshevism and to embrace compromise. Closely related was the idea that one must take the other party's interests into account and then try to find some sense of fairness or a 'balance of interests'. Gorbachev said, 'big politics . . . cannot be built entirely on one's own interests, which are inevitably one-sided',[18] and Shevardnadze spoke of the need, in negotiations, to 'take as a basis an old principle of . . . reciprocality'.[19]

New thinking called for an expanded regime of security co-operation directly between the superpowers. Gorbachev emphasized the need for arms control and

[13] Quoted in Sanakoyev, S., 'Peaceful coexistence in the context of military–strategic parity', *International Affairs*, Feb. 1988, p. 75.
[14] Quoted in Mikhalyov, A., 'USSR–Poland: toward new frontiers', *Za Rubezhom*, 8–24 Nov. 1988, in FBIS-SOV-88-230, 30 Nov. 1988, p. 23.
[15] Gorbachev, M., 'The socialist idea and revolutionary *perestroika*', *Pravda*, 26 Nov. 1989, pp. 1–3, in FBIS-SOV-89-226, 27 Nov. 1989, p. 75.
[16] Gorbachev (note 8), p. 148.
[17] D'Alema, M. and Sergi, S., 'Interview with Eduard Shevardnadze', *L'Unita*, 28 Nov. 1989, pp. 11–13, in FBIS-SOV-89-231, 4 Dec. 1989, p. 4.
[18] Maslennikov, A., 'Another stage completed: thoughts following the visit', *Pravda*, 3 June 1988, p. 5, in FBIS-SOV-88-108, 6 June 1988, p. 19.
[19] Speech by Eduard Shevardnadze at the International Open Skies Conference, Ottawa, 12 Feb. 1990, *TASS*, 12 Feb. 1990, in FBIS-SOV-90-030, 13 Feb. 1990, p. 3.

disarmament, calling for the superpowers to lower their respective military forces to the minimal level of sufficiency. Ultimately, nuclear weapons should be completely eliminated and nations should only have forces necessary for their territorial defence. In arms control negotiations the Soviet Union became much more conciliatory in its effort to achieve agreements and much more willing to submit to intrusive verification.

In regions of the Third World where the United States and the Soviet Union had been supporting opposing factions, new thinking called for a policy of national reconciliation. Accordingly, the superpowers would refrain from trying to seek an advantageous outcome and instead would encourage the feuding factions to seek a resolution of the conflict, ultimately through democratic elections. New thinking also called for the superpowers to mutually reduce their transfers of conventional arms.

Another key idea in new thinking was that the superpowers should reduce their military presence throughout the world. The Soviet Union proposed that the superpowers should withdraw all their troops within their national boundaries by the year 2000. Gorbachev particularly emphasized the idea of reducing the superpowers' naval presence through naval arms control. The Soviet Government made numerous proposals for reducing superpower presence and other CBMs in specific regions. It also reiterated its support for the various proposals for establishing a 'zone of peace, friendship and neutrality' in specific regions around the world (the Indian Ocean, South-East Asia, the south Atlantic), which stipulate that both superpowers should reduce or eliminate their military presence.

VI. The US response to new thinking

In 1988 I did a series of interviews with officials in the State Department, the Defense Department and the National Security Council to understand the US response to the new Soviet proposals for an expanded co-operative security regime.[20] Officials expressed continued interest in negotiations to reduce conventional weapons in Europe and strategic nuclear weapons and a lukewarm interest in the limited CBMs already under consideration. They seemed, however, to give little attention to or expressed doubts about the prospect of expanding Soviet–US security co-operation into non-traditional areas.

For example, I asked respondents for their opinions about explicit or tacit rules of the game in the Soviet–US relationship under which both would exercise restraint in seeking unilateral advantages. Many respondents resisted the idea, recalling that the Basic Principles of Relations of 1972 had not produced the hoped-for results. Three recurrent arguments were given for why it was not a good idea to try to develop such a regime of mutual restraint. Some argued

---

[20] This technique was one I also used in a study of the psychological processes involved in making defence policies. That study resulted in a book entitled *Minds At War: Nuclear Reality and the Inner Conflicts of Defense Policy Policymakers* (Basic Books: New York, 1988). In this book readers can find an expanded description of the methodology I use in my interviews.

that because of the unique ideology of the Soviet Union it was inherently untrustworthy. Those of a more hawkish persuasion argued against the notion of rules that might constrain the USA from promoting its ideology. As one Administration figure explained: 'What's the name of the game? To move the balance against your opposition. To expand democracy. That's my rule. I am not here to build an international order which is condominium, and where I live at the expense of millions of essentially political prisoners of the rest of the world. I just don't think that's compatible with American basic values'.

However, the most common argument against the notion of having rules of the game was the realist argument that such a system was not feasible because there was no means of enforcement. Ideas of having such rules were rejected as 'illusions' or 'wishful' in contrast to the necessary 'realism'. Some respondents even said that, given the inherently deceitful nature of states, the Soviet Union should not trust the United States to abide by a regime of mutual restraint.

Yet, despite the sceptical attitudes about the potential for Soviet–US security co-operation, there was still a distinct undercurrent of interest in the prospect. Even when criticizing certain possibilities for co-operation, respondents would refer to them as 'desirable', 'nice' or 'like heaven'. Some respondents were quite definite that if the Soviet Union could be trusted to abide by rules of restraint, the USA would be willing to be restrained as well, even if that meant accepting some undesirable outcomes. One high-level official who served in the Bush Administration said: 'If we were convinced the Soviets would keep their hands off we would let the chips fall where they may. This is a new position though, as we have become more confident that the Soviets don't have a siren song'.

He elaborated how, deep down, Americans still have the kind of co-operative, universalist attitudes that prompted the United Nations. 'We do have this sort of universalistic notion, so that the UN Charter, which is what we wrote, really, however cynical we are about it now, represents the way we really think about the world'. Such responsiveness to international norms, he explained, is really seen as essential to success in the world: 'I think we feel, deep down inside, that we're only going to succeed if we in fact act in what we perceive to be the world interest, if you will, and that if we are simply acting selfishly and cloak it with a rationale of legality, that we'll lose'.

VII. The Bush Administration

When the Bush Administration came into office there was no immediate change in attitude about the potential for Soviet–US security co-operation. In light of the 'new thinking' in the Soviet Union, the Administration in its first year conducted a review of US policy. However, the conclusion of the study was that the United States should basically follow a business-as-usual policy dubbed 'status quo plus'. Eventually though, in response to the Iraqi invasion of Kuwait, the Bush Administration did begin to embrace the idea that the principles and institutions of collective security, especially the United Nations, would play a more central role in the post-cold war world.

When the Gulf crisis broke out the Bush Administration first tried to rationalize US involvement in narrow economic terms pointing to concerns about access to oil and maintaining US 'jobs'. These rationales fell flat with the US public, but when the Bush Administration invoked the principles of international law and collective security a political consensus emerged in support of US action in the Persian Gulf. With Soviet support in the UN Security Council, the USA was able successfully to lead a coalition of countries against Iraq and to have it almost universally viewed as legitimate.

In the ensuing months Bush seized on this new consensus and elaborated the idea of a 'new world order'. He spoke of 'a vision of a new partnership of nations . . . a partnership based on consultation, co-operation, and collective action'.[21] He emphasized that this partnership will not only be a vague commitment, but will be governed by 'the rule of [international] law, not the law of the jungle'.[22]

He made it clear he was talking about a revival of the universalist undercurrent in US thought, saying that the new world order will be based primarily in the United Nations, which is now 'poised to fulfill the historic vision of its founders'[23] and 'its promise as the world's parliament of peace'.[24] As a State Department official I interviewed at the time explained: 'There is almost a rebirth of idealism in the sense of Wilsonian idealism about what you can accomplish and what you can do. In a world where there isn't this terrible Russian bear out there which is scaring the wits out of you, it seems to me that the American people want us to be on the side of law and justice much more so than before'.

Bush implied that this new world order would also impose constraints on the powerful. Quoting Winston Churchill, he defined the new world order as one in which 'the principles of justice and fair play protect the weak against the strong'.[25] Perhaps most dramatically he implied that nations are constrained from using military force without international authority, saying that 'a just war must also be declared by legitimate authority' which he specified as the United Nations.[26]

Later, however, Bush seemed to back-pedal from this universalist vision and to echo the more unilateralist strand of US thought. Addressing a military audi-

---

[21] 'Transcript of President's address to the UN General Assembly', *New York Times*, 2 Oct. 1990, p. A12.

[22] President Bush, 'Operation Desert Storm launched', address to the nation broadcast from the White House at 9.00 p.m. (EST), 16 Jan. 1991, US Department of State, *Dispatch*, vol. 2, no. 3 (21 Jan. 1991), p. 38.

[23] President Bush, 'The world after the Persian Gulf War', address to Joint Session of Congress, 6 Mar. 1991, US Department of State, *Dispatch*, vol. 2, no. 10 (11 Mar. 1991), p. 162.

[24] 'Transcript of President's address to the UN General Assembly', *New York Times*, 2 Oct. 1990, p. A12.

[25] See note 23.

[26] President Bush, 'Persian Gulf War: supporting a noble cause', excerpts from an address before the National Religious Broadcasters Convention, 28 Jan. 1991, US Department of State, *Dispatch*, vol. 2, no. 5 (4 Feb. 1991), p. 67.

ence in February 1991, Bush asserted that after the Persian Gulf War the world will understand 'that what we say goes'.[27] On 13 April 1991 he revised his earlier definition of the new world order as constituting 'rules of conduct' saying that it is not 'a blueprint that will govern the conduct of nations, or some supranational structure or institution'. Rather he injected a much more unilateral character saying, instead, that the new world order 'really describes a responsibility imposed by our successes'. He downplayed potential constraints on the USA, implied by the need to look for international consensus, by arguing that there is already an emerging consensus based on a set of 'shared ideals' which 'have received their boldest and clearest expression in our great country, the United States'.[28]

Despite these ambiguities the Bush Administration made a series of important and unprecedented steps towards greater security co-operation with the Soviet Union and later Russia, beginning in the dying days of the Soviet Union and persisting through the transition to an independent Russian Federation. The two nations worked together, in some cases under UN auspices, to resolve conflicts in Angola, Cambodia and El Salvador. The USA showed a willingness to co-operate with the Soviet Union in areas in which it had previously shown reluctance: agreeing to a UN-sponsored mutual cessation of aid to the Afghan factions and co-sponsoring with the Soviet Union a Middle East peace conference. The United States also took the unprecedented step in September 1991 of initiating significant unilateral cuts in its nuclear arsenal, successfully prompting a corresponding cut on the Soviet side. Security co-operation entered a new phase when the USA and Russia acted in concert to prevent the proliferation of new nuclear weapons states as the Soviet Union disintegrated.

VIII. Security co-operation as seen by Russian foreign policy experts

Although Russia will clearly play a lesser role in world affairs than the Soviet Union did after World War II, it will still be a major player and one with which the USA will need to deal. It is possible, though not probable, that the Commonwealth of Independent States (CIS) will come to be a prominent and coherent actor on the world stage. It is more likely that the Commonwealth will become so loose as to be irrelevant, in which case the USA will still be dealing with the Russian Federation as a major power. Throughout the history of the Soviet Union, Russia was the dominant political force, constituted the majority of its population and possessed the overwhelming majority of its land mass and manufacturing base. Even without the republics it has hitherto dominated, Russia is still the largest single land mass in the world, has tremendous natural

---

[27] Balz, B. and Derrdy, A., 'Bush keeps earlier vows to set terms', *Washington Post*, 23 Feb. 1991, p. 10.
[28] Yang, J. E., 'Bush defends nonintervention in Iraq', *Washington Post*, 14 Apr. 1991, p. A27.

resources, has a huge array of military forms and is strategically positioned to help or hinder the achievement of a wide array of Western objectives.

What can be anticipated about the future willingness of Russia to co-operate in a security regime with the United States? Can it be assumed that new Russian leaders will closely adhere to the co-operative principles of new thinking?

On questions of international relations the Russian leadership will probably show substantial continuity with the Gorbachev era. The members of the Russian foreign policy-making élite have emerged from the same cultural milieu as the Soviet foreign policy élite and, indeed, many of the individuals that were part of the Soviet foreign policy establishment have simply shifted over to working for Russia. For example, the Russian Foreign Minister, Andrey Kozyrev, was originally a high-level official in the Soviet Foreign Ministry.

This does not mean that it can be assumed that Russian foreign policy will be entirely devoid of competitive elements. In recent years the Soviet/Russian leaders made so many dramatic steps in the direction of greater co-operation that it is easy to forget that they also persisted in behaviour with a competitive edge and at odds with their own principles of new thinking, such as maintaining an enormous military, an extensive programme of arms transfers and a global military presence.

Between 1988 and 1991, I carried out an extensive series of interviews with members of the Soviet foreign policy-making élite in which I asked them for the rationale for Moscow's arguably competitive behaviour. Naturally, I initially looked for signs of persisting Leninism. Indeed, some respondents did express some traditional Leninist thought. However, such thinking was not very widespread, was usually mixed—often in an illogical fashion—with elements of new thinking, and over the years of the study became increasingly less prevalent. There was another stream of thought that supported some of the more competitive features of Soviet policy but was clearly not rooted in Leninism. This stream of thought, remarkably similar to Western realist thinking (a number of Soviet respondents even noted the similarities), emphasized that the Soviet Union is a 'great power' and that great powers will inevitably compete. As one political analyst explained:

Look we are rivals, historical rivals. . . . You cannot negate the political realities, this is the objective result of history that the Soviet Union and the United States have become two major powers of the world after the Second World War and even if we have some agreements which would regulate somehow our rivalry, that would not exclude the rivalry from the relationship completely. . . . Even if Russia was non-Communist, say Czarist Russia or something like that, we still would have this type of relationship with the United States.

Such rivalry, several Soviet experts explained, is rooted in the inevitable tendency of great powers to try to expand their sphere of influence. When I asked why great powers do this, the answer was often tautological. A political analyst explained, while making a rhythmic expanding movement with his hands, 'That is simply what great powers do. They try to expand'. Likewise a Soviet Foreign Ministry official explained Soviet military presence and its military support for allies: 'Like you, we also have global interests and we have allies and friends in all parts of the world. . . . You will agree that it is an inevitable function for a superpower. Well, it is an open question whether we are still a superpower, but still we see ourselves as such'.

This was not meant to imply, though, that mutual restraint and co-operation between great powers is impossible. Exponents of this great power thinking also embraced the new thinking principle that, given the risks of nuclear confrontation, it is incumbent on the great powers to be constrained by a framework or regime based on a 'balance of interests'. To achieve this balance of interests, it was argued, the first step is for the great powers to maintain a military balance between them. A Soviet Foreign Ministry official who now works in the Russian Foreign Ministry explained: 'We cannot achieve the balance of interests other than through a balance of power. . . . Given the conflicting interests of the sides, the balance of them can be achieved only through the hope that we can return to the concept of deterrence'.

More recently with the collapse of the Soviet Union and the severe economic problems throughout the former Soviet Union, the Russian leadership has taken numerous steps to reduce its great power posture—diminishing the size of its military, eliminating support to allies and cutting back its naval activities. Nevertheless, there are strong indications that great power concerns are still very much alive in the Russian leadership and will probably continue to shape their future behaviour. For example, Russian President Boris Yeltsin has made it clear that he is still keeping a close eye on the geopolitical balance of power. In a 12 December 1991 speech to the Russian Parliament, he explained that the initiative for establishing the Commonwealth was prompted by a concern that an independent nuclear-armed Ukraine would be a 'serious violation of the geopolitical balance'.[29]

The Russian Foreign Minister Andrey Kozyrev, shortly before the final demise of the Soviet Union in December 1991, affirmed that: 'Russia will remain a great power. It may not be a superpower, but it will be a great military power and part of the global strategic balance. . . . Russia will be the continuation of the Soviet Union in the field of nuclear weapons'.[30]

At times Russian policy makers have recognized that owing to their internal problems they must step down a bit in the international arena, but they also stress that they see this as only temporary. Oleg Derkovsky, deputy head of the Russian Foreign Ministry's Middle East Department has said, 'Russia was, is and will be a great power, regardless of the problems we are passing

[29] Excerpts from Yeltsin speech, 'Union pact ruthlessly trampled sovereignty', *New York Times*, 13 Dec. 1991, p. A22.
[30] Remnick, D., 'In new commonwealth of "equals", Russia remains the dominant force', *Washington Post*, 22 Dec. 1991, p. A39.

222 THE LIMITED PARTNERSHIP

through. . . . Sooner or later, with economic reform, we will be able to play the role of a great power again'.[31]

At the same time though in the interviews I conducted, there was no hint that Russia might try to use its military forces to resurge as an imperialist power. In every case in which an interviewee defended competitive Soviet behaviour based on great power principles, that individual would also emphasize that he favoured even more the objective of creating a co-operative world order together with the United States. Great power behaviour was portrayed as a necessary interim *modus operandi*.

It appears that the political culture of the new Russian Government is heavily imbued with the principles of new thinking even though Gorbachev is gone and unlamented. Russian Government officials with whom I have spoken emphasize that the only difference they have from their Soviet predecessors is that they intend to more completely fulfil the principles of new thinking. Members of the Russian Government élite use great power terminology to stress that they still view themselves as being a great power and that they do not intend to simply bow out of the world arena. However, the thrust of their position seems to be that they are willing to match the USA in subordinating their great power aspirations to a co-operative international order.

IX. Conclusion

Currently, for the first time, a remarkable symmetry exists in the normative orientations of US and Russian leaders on the question of international security co-operation. In the past, as well as the present, US leaders have embraced such co-operation as the preferred ideal, though they have often pursued competitive policies in the name of pragmatism. For the Russians, in the past, it was just the opposite: their highest normative framework called for a competitive approach to foreign policy in the name of promoting certain ideals, while co-operation was seen as a short-term pragmatic tactic. The Russians have gone through an ideological revolution and, for now, co-operation is their pre-eminent ideal, while competition may be a necessary short-term tactic.

None the less, it can be expected that there will continue to be some degree of competitive great power behaviour between Russia and the USA. Some of this behaviour may be purely ritualistic in nature in the sense that its main purpose will be to claim its great power status. However, while both sides embrace the co-operative ideal, it will be politically difficult to act in a starkly unco-operative fashion.

On the Russian side there are also a number of structural factors encouraging co-operation. The massive problems Russia now faces will prompt it towards co-operation. To the extent that Russians wish to prevent the United States from

---

[31] Quoted in Ford, P., 'Russia relegates Mideast ties in wooing West', *Christian Science Monitor*, 5 Feb. 1991, p. 1.

becoming the singular world hegemon, their best hope may be to accept a co-operative security order as a means of imposing constraint on the USA.

For the United States though, as has been demonstrated here, these vectors are more mixed. While the USA has been ideologically committed to security co-operation in the past, it now has the option of pursuing its interests in a uni-lateral fashion relatively unfettered by the constraints of a co-operative security system. For some in the USA pursuing US interests unilaterally is more com-pelling, even morally, than promoting co-operative security. Because the USA has these options, the decisions it makes will be one of the most important variables determining the level of security co-operation in the coming decades.

13. Building a Eurasian–Atlantic security community: co-operative management of the military transition

William W. Newmann and Judyth L. Twigg

I. Introduction[1]

At the end of World War II, one of the major tasks of the Allied powers was to reintegrate West Germany into the community of democratic nations. The creation of NATO as a security framework that would forge co-operation to ensure Western solidarity against the Soviet threat was one of the cornerstones of this process. A similar challenge exists today, although the nature of the threat is more complex. The end of the cold war requires the integration of the nations of the Commonwealth of Independent States (CIS) into a Eurasian–Atlantic community that can co-operate and co-ordinate its actions to defend against the political instabilities unleashed by the collapse of the Soviet empire.[2]

Many observers herald the coming of a 'new world order', but it is unclear whether this new order will be more or less peaceful than the cold war era.[3] While it may be true that the world no longer lives under the spectre of a US–Soviet nuclear war, and that ideological struggle between the superpowers is over, the instabilities and basic ethnic, border and resource conflicts that could lead to violence still govern the realities of international behaviour. These instabilities are primarily caused by the two simultaneous transitions which are taking place today: the breakup of the Soviet Union into 15 separate nations

---

[1] Secondary journalistic sources were used in the collection of some data on recent events. Individual articles are cited only as necessary. These sources are: *New York Times, Washington Post* and *Los Angeles Times*.

[2] An early assessment of the needs of a comprehensive security regime is contained in Carter, A. B., Perry, W. J. and Steinbruner, J. D., *A New Concept of Cooperative Security* (Brookings Institution: Washington, DC, 1992).

[3] Scholars are beginning to address the issue of global stability now that the USA and the CIS are moving towards co-operation. Did client relationships with nuclear powers in a deterrent but competitive relationship act as a brake on the ambitions of many Third World regimes? Or did such relationships merely prolong conflicts as the superpower supply line prevented either side from denying its opponent the resources necessary to continue fighting? The conflicts in the Persian Gulf and Yugoslavia support the former hypothesis, while events in Afghanistan, Africa, East Asia and the Arab–Israeli conflict suggest the latter. Early contributions to this debate are: Mueller, J., *Retreat From Doomsday* (Basic Books: New York, 1989); an insightful review of Mueller's work in Kaysen, C., 'Is war obsolete? A review essay', *International Security*, vol. 14, no. 4 (spring 1990), pp. 42–64; Fukuyama, F., 'The end of history', *The National Interest*, summer 1989, pp. 3–18; Snyder, J., 'Averting anarchy in the new Europe', *International Security*, vol. 14, no. 4 (spring 1990), pp. 5–41; Mearsheimer, J., 'Back to the future: instability in Europe after the cold war', *International Security*, vol. 15, no. 1 (summer 1990), pp. 5–56; and Cohen, E., 'The future of force and American strategy', *The National Interest*, fall 1990, pp. 3–15.

attempting to move towards democracy and market-oriented economies, and the evolution of these new nations' relations with the USA and the West. The CIS may turn out to be a temporary phenomenon; even if it survives politically and economically, it is not clear that the military structures of its members will be integrated under a single umbrella. Russia, by virtue of sheer size and possession of nuclear weapons, will remain the dominant military power within the Commonwealth. The attempts of the other former republics to escape possible Russian domination, and efforts by all of the Commonwealth members to arrive at a mutually acceptable distribution of former Soviet military assets, are the political fodder that might feed likely threats to security in the region during the transition period. In addition, problems involving ethnic minorities and border disputes, if unchecked, could lead the CIS towards the same fate as Yugoslavia.

The integration of the CIS nations into a Eurasian–Atlantic security community can ease the fears and dangers of this transition. There is a need for an overarching security system to monitor and manage the extensive political-military transition taking place on former Soviet soil. A positive side-effect of this process will be to help stabilize the former Soviet military itself. The currently disillusioned and desperate state of all ranks of the military forces of the Commonwealth nations holds tremendous potential for instability. Ironically, one of the primary goals during the formation of this Eurasian–Atlantic security community must be to help rebuild the former Soviet forces into a professionally satisfied, politically neutral entity.

The Conference on Security and Co-operation in Europe (CSCE) can most effectively play this role (though its performance in the Yugoslav crisis suggests that the CSCE has yet to develop its potential). Its membership has already grown to include the CIS nations and the Baltic states; its security arrangements must also be expanded to account for the special dilemmas posed by the unique situation of the Commonwealth nations.

Other institutions, such as NATO and the United Nations Security Council, may also play a role, but the USA and the CSCE should take the lead in this process. The UN Security Council does not include all the CIS nations. As a permanent member, Russia's veto power in the Security Council presents special problems; since future instabilities may pit Russia against other members of the Commonwealth, it is hardly a proper forum for institutionalizing the entire Eurasian–Atlantic security community. It might, however, prove to be a useful vehicle for potential joint US–Russian military operations beyond CIS borders. NATO as an institution is historically hostile to the Commonwealth nations; until it is ready to include them in its membership, its role in the new community will remain minimal. Although the North Atlantic Cooperation Council (NACC) is reaching out to the Commonwealth nations, it does not have the institutional structure to perform the missions suggested here.

The CSCE is the only organization that both includes all of the relevant nations and possesses an institutional framework for dealing with security problems from Vancouver to Vladivostok. The potential for the USA to play a special role within the CSCE is born of the legacy of superpower competition and the vast nuclear arsenals that created a unique relationship between Moscow and Washington; this relationship seems already to have outlived the cold war. Whether the USA approaches these problems bilaterally or multilaterally will depend on the nature of the specific issue at hand, and on the extent to which the USA decides to involve itself in Commonwealth affairs.

This chapter focuses on means by which the USA can take advantage of its special historical bilateral relationship with the Soviet Union in order to help Russia and the other members of the Commonwealth become members of this Eurasian–Atlantic security community. It begins with a discussion of the political–military crisis currently facing the CIS nations. Second, it proposes near-term measures intended to ensure that the withdrawal of Soviet forces from Eastern Europe and the redeployment and redesignation of forces within former Soviet borders takes place smoothly. Third, it examines possible military-to-military co-operative mechanisms between the USA and the Commonwealth nations designed to draw the former Soviet republics into the broader Eurasian–Atlantic security community. Finally, it anticipates the possibility of eventual joint East–West military operations.

Before discussing these measures, however, the potential political obstacles to such a scheme within the USA must be addressed briefly. Attempts to deliver even moderate amounts of food and medical aid to the former Soviet republics have met potent political opposition from some corners. House Armed Service Committee Chairman Les Aspin's one billion dollar aid proposal, for example, was at first ridiculed, then supported, by the Bush Administration; finally Congress balked on the plan. The fundamental questions are these: How much of the 'peace dividend' is the USA willing to give to the Commonwealth nations? Most of the mechanisms discussed in this chapter do not involve direct financial assistance, but deepening the US involvement in the affairs of the former Soviet Union at any level will consume governmental energy and taxpayers' dollars. In addition, how ready is the USA to make a perceptual and psychological transition towards viewing the CIS nations fully as allies? These questions must be addressed within the US political system before any progress can be made towards genuinely transforming the old US–Soviet security relationship into one suitable for the 21st century.

II. Conflict and chaos in the Soviet military

The aborted August 1991 right-wing coup in the Soviet Union paradoxically brought about the very phenomenon it was primarily designed to prevent: the disintegration of the country. Within days after Boris Yeltsin's triumphant victory celebration in front of the Russian White House, most of the international community had recognized the independence of the Baltic nations; within months, the Union had been replaced by a Commonwealth of independent nations composed of the former republics.

The collapse of the Soviet Union has created considerable confusion and consternation in the West as to the future disposition of the Soviet armed forces, and about identifying an appropriate response. Indeed, Sovietologist Pilar Bonet has likened the Soviet Union-turned-Commonwealth to a person having an epileptic fit: anyone wishing to intervene can either place a spoon in the epileptic's mouth (hardly possible in the Soviet case), or cushion his environment to protect him from his own kicks.[4] This section outlines some of the sources of potential military-related instability within the Commonwealth in preparation for a discussion of the means by which the USA might provide some 'cushions'.

Political instability

Major political tensions will continue to arise from the fact that republic borders are not set in stone. There have been numerous border changes within the Soviet Union since the 1917 Bolshevik revolution. Ninety transfers of territory took place between 1921 and 1980, and 60 requests for territorial transfers were communicated to General-Secretary Mikhail Gorbachev between 1985 and 1990.[5] Immediately after the attempted coup in August, for example, representatives of Russian President Yeltsin responded to non-Russian republican independence declarations by hinting that Russian borders were not necessarily permanent, and that Russia might at some point wish to repatriate adjoining territories with ethnic Russian majority populations. The Crimean peninsula in particular is likely to arouse tension, since it was transferred to Ukrainian jurisdiction only four decades ago, and since only half its population voted in favour of Ukrainian independence in December 1991.

Military threat assessments in the entire region are being explicitly rethought as a result. Baltic and Ukrainian military leaders are currently in the process of formulating military doctrines based far more on wariness of Russia than of NATO.[6] Similarly, Lithuanian Defence Minister Audruus Butkevicious has stated that he perceives a potential security threat from Belarus and Ukraine, and that he views collective defence as implemented through the CSCE as his only alternative.[7]

Ethnic problems within individual republics are also likely to pose a threat to the security of the former Soviet Union in the near future. Immediately after the aborted coup, President Yeltsin declared that all territory which was currently Russian would remain Russian. Even within Ukraine, ethnic borderlines are not

---

[4] Remarks by Pilar Bonet, Kennan Institute for Advanced Russian Studies, 6 Dec, 1991, quoted by Dr Alex Pravda at The Implications for Soviet Defence and Arms Control Policies of the Devolution of Power from the Centre to the Republics, a conference sponsored by the Ford Foundation and the British Academy at Wolfson College and Oxford University, 10–11 Dec. 1991,

[5] Goble, P., 'Can Republican borders be changed?', *Report on the USSR*, 28 Sep. 1990, pp. 20–21.

[6] Foye, S., 'CIS: Kiev and Moscow clash over armed forces', *RFE/RL Research Report*, 17 Jan. 1992, pp. 1–3.

[7] Kinzer, S., 'Lithuania's new defense minister: young man with a non-violent strategy', *New York Times*, 4 Sep. 1991, p. A6.

cleanly drawn. Western Ukraine remains a nationalist stronghold; the Eastern part of the republic contains many ethnic Russians with close ties to Russia; the Crimea and Odessa in the South are not historically part of Ukraine at all. This division is reflected in the Ukrainian Parliament, where there has never been a complete consensus on Ukrainian independence.

This kind of ethnic distribution raises the distinct possibility of a Yugoslavia-type situation: a war that is specifically about areas of republics with non-native ethnic majorities in some border regions. In the weeks before the Ukrainian independence referendum, for example, demonstrations were held in various parts of Ukraine to protest Soviet Ministry of Defence plans to stage military exercises along the Russian–Ukrainian border. These manœuvres were ostensibly for the purpose of monitoring the combat readiness of local troops, but Ukrainians interpreted them as a means to intimidate voters.[8] The problem extends to Eastern Europe as well; Poland has expressed concern about an independent Ukrainian military, and has indicated that it might seek reallocation of weapons limited under the Conventional Armed Forces in Europe Treaty (CFE) among the former members of the Warsaw Pact in order to counter the Ukrainian threat.[9]

Centre vs. republic armed forces

One of the major sources of tension within the former Soviet military is the formation of independent armed forces in most of the newly independent republics. As of January 1992, only Armenia, Kazakhstan, Kyrgyzstan, Russia and Tajikistan were committed to unified command over general purpose forces on their territory.[10]

The central CIS military and political authorities, based primarily in Moscow, continued to insist throughout early 1992 that the Commonwealth retain integrated military structures, although Russia indicated that it would develop its own armed forces if the actions of other republics left it no choice. The centralist arguments focus on the need to maintain a coherent 'military–strategic space' on the territory of the old Union; the prohibitive costs of establishing independent republic armed forces, including weapons research and procurement, salaries and housing of officers and servicemen, and job retraining for discharged servicemen; and the need to protect Soviet armed forces pensioners currently living in the now-sovereign republics.[11] Former Chief of the General Staff Vladimir Lobov has exhorted each republic to

[8] Canadian Friends of Rukh news release, 13 Nov. 1991, from electronic mail communication to one of the authors, 27 Nov. 1991.
[9] Hitchens, T. and Leopold, G., 'Pressure grows for republics to adhere to CFE', *Defense News*, 13 Jan. 1992, pp. 1, 29.
[10] Sheehy, A., 'Commonwealth of Independent States: an uneasy compromise', *RFE/RL Research Report*, 10 Jan. 1992, p. 3.
[11] See Ryabikin, S, 'Pozitsiya Ministerstva Oborony SSSR' ['Positions of the USSR Ministry of Defence'], *Krasnaya Zvezda*, 29 Oct. 1991, p. 1 (in Russian); and Shaposhnikov, Y., 'Povinuyus' sovesti i zakonu' ['I will obey my conscience and the law'], *Pravda*, 25 Sep. 1991, pp. 1, 3 (in Russian).

'weigh a thousand times' the question of independent armed formations, given the probability that their very existence will prompt their use to settle inter-ethnic, interstate and inter-republic political conflict.[12] Some CIS military leaders see the cost factor as so overwhelming that they dismiss as a 'childhood illness of sovereignty and state independence' the whole notion of republic armed forces separate from the centre; Black Sea Fleet Deputy Commander Ivan Kapitanets boldly predicts, for example, that the Black Sea Fleet will 'sink at its moorings' within two or three years under Ukrainian jurisdiction without Russian military and industrial backing.[13]

These caveats have done little to stem the drive for military independence among most newly independent republics and even among some semi-autonomous regions within these new nations. For example:

1. The Belorussian Supreme Soviet voted on 23 September 1991 to create an independent defence and state security system. Troops conscripted there now serve only on Belorussian soil. On 25 October a national guard, 5000–8000 men strong, was formed on the basis of existing combat-ready and mobile units of the Soviet armed forces. In January 1992, Belorussian Minister of Defence Petr Chaus declared that all Belorussian officers serving outside the country could return home and take up comparable positions in the Belorussian Army; as of 15 January, 170 officers had done so.

2. In October 1991 the Moldovan Ministry of Internal Affairs called on Moldovan officers and non-commissioned officers (NCOs) serving with border troops outside the country to return home. In December, the Moldovan Government announced that its armed forces would consist of one motorized rifle division, plus border and internal troops.

3. The Supreme Soviet of the self-proclaimed 'Dnestr republic,' having unilaterally seceded from Moldova, on 9 January 1992 resolved to place all 20 000 former Soviet troops stationed on its soil under Dnestr authority. It tripled the salaries of officers, instituted its own military oath of allegiance and introduced conscription on the territory it claims. The Fourteenth Army based there supports secession and has placed itself under Dnestr government authority.

4. The Central Asian countries bordering on the Caspian Sea (Azerbaijan, Kazakhstan and Turkmenistan) indicated in January 1992 that they want control over part of the 85-vessel Caspian Sea Flotilla.

By far, however, the most substantial potential for centre–periphery tension arising from national desires for military independence lies with Ukraine. As early as 15 July 1990, Ukraine declared its right to have its own military.[14] On

[12] Lobov, V., 'Politika, doktrina i strategiya v menyayushchemsya mire' ['Politics, doctrine and strategy in a changing world'], *Krasnaya Zvezda*, 23 Oct. 1991, pp. 1–2 (in Russian). Although Lobov has been dismissed from his position as Chief of the General Staff, he apparently remains a prominent political figure and continues to freely voice his opinion on military affairs.

[13] Kapitanets comments to Reuters, 'Russia and Ukraine try to settle military dispute', *New York Times*, 12 Jan. 1992, p. 3.

[14] Mihalisko, K., 'Laying the foundation for the armed forces of Ukraine', *Report on the USSR*, vol. 3, no. 45 (8 Nov. 1991), p. 19.

22 October 1991, the Ukrainian Parliament authorized the formation of a 420 000-man independent Ukrainian Army, appointing Colonel General Konstantin Morozov the Ukrainian Minister of Defence. Even this large a number would involve considerable downsizing from the current 1.5 million troops on Ukrainian soil. The figure of 420 000 was not the product of an elaborate military doctrine, but rather one arrived at through ratios and comparisons with other relatively non-militarized countries. According to Ukrainian calculations, 420 000 is 0.8 per cent of its total population of 52 million, which corresponds to an acceptable European level of 0.8–0.9 per cent of a given population in military service. Ukrainian military leaders cited in particular France, which currently has 453 100 of its 57 million people in uniform, as their model.[15]

Stepan Khmara, a member of the Ukrainian parliamentary committee on defence, has explicitly rejected the notion that Ukraine will join a military bloc composed of the other members of the Commonwealth. Again, France is used as the base case: Khmara said that Ukraine wants a status in the Commonwealth similar to that of France in NATO, as a member of the political council but not of military structures.[16] He further added that the Commonwealth does not have the right to speak or act on behalf of Ukraine in foreign affairs.

So far, two of Ukraine's concrete steps towards military independence have particularly threatened to tarnish Ukrainian–Russian relations: cutting off communication between the CIS military command and the units on Ukrainian soil,[17] and declaring the Black Sea Fleet to fall under Ukrainian jurisdiction. The latter has by far caused more tension.

The initial declaration of the CIS in December 1991[18] declared that all of the former republics have the right to their own national armed forces, with the exception of 'strategic forces' which are to remain under Commonwealth control. The determination of what constitutes a 'strategic' force lay at the heart of the debate over the Black Sea Fleet.[19] In early January 1992 Ukraine ordered all

---

[15] The unofficial three-stage blueprint for the Ukrainian change-over to national armed forces looks something like this: (a) by the end of 1992, the formation of a Ukrainian General Staff and its assumption of command; (b) in 1992–93, the placement of all troops stationed in Ukraine under the jurisdiction of the Ukrainian Ministry of Defence, the redrawing of military district lines (currently Ukraine embodies three former Soviet military districts), the commissioning of the first Ukrainian air force units, and the reorganization of the Black Sea Fleet and the Ukrainian higher military schools; and (c) in 1994–95, the final departure of non-Ukrainian troops not willing to serve in Ukraine and the emergence of a fully Ukrainian command structure. Mihalisko, K., 'Defense and security planning in Ukraine', Report on the USSR, 6 Dec. 1991, pp. 15–19. See also chapter 8, p. 121.

[16] Moscow Radio Rossii network, 28 Dec. 1991, in Foreign Broadcast Information Service, Daily Report–Soviet Union (FBIS-SOV), FBIS-SOV-91-250, 31 Dec. 1991, p. 48.

[17] In January 1992, Kiev military officials seized primary communication control over 300 000 troops of the former Soviet Army in Ukraine. Moscow is now deprived of its instantaneous communication network with these various land and non-strategic air forces, and now has to rely on much slower conventional telephones.

[18] The 8 Dec. 1991 Text of the Minsk Agreement Establishing a Commonwealth of Independent States, an agreement made by Belarus, Russia and Ukraine, is reprinted in Washington Post, 10 Dec. 1991, p. A32 and in SIPRI, SIPRI Yearbook 1992: World Armaments and Disarmament (Oxford University Press: Oxford, 1992), appendix 14A, pp. 558–59.

[19] The Black Sea Fleet is larger than the British or French navies, with over 100 000 servicemen and roughly 400 vessels, including 30 diesel-powered submarines. 400 ground-based aircraft are also attached to the fleet, of which 140 are capable of carrying nuclear weapons, along with a naval infantry brigade

ground forces on its territory and the sailors and officers of the Black Sea Fleet either to take an oath of loyalty to Ukraine, to retire from the armed services or to transfer out of the republic. It claims that the fleet is not 'strategic' because it is not currently armed with strategic nuclear weapons, and that it is therefore subject to Ukrainian control since its home port is the Ukrainian city of Sevastopol. The central naval command counters that the fleet is indeed strategic, since it carries out the strategic mission of opposing the US Sixth Fleet in the Mediterranean, and because half of its ships are capable of carrying nuclear arms.

Russia has offered to transfer several of its ships to Ukraine for coastal defence, but insists that the full fleet remain under the command of Russia because of Russia's historical claim to the fleet, and its position as the legal successor to the Soviet state.[20] In addition, the fleet constitutes the only warm-water port in the western part of the former Soviet Union. Ukrainian President Leonid Kravchuk counters that Ukraine should be a maritime state, and that it 'has a genuine desire for a maritime military force'.[21] An uneasy January 1992 settlement between the two powers declared that a commission of military experts would determine how the ships would be divided between them; both sides have pledged 'not to take any unilateral actions'.[22]

Ukraine will probably encounter considerable difficulty carrying out its ambitious military plans even without direct interference from Moscow. The central authorities are probably correct in observing that the costs of building an independent Ukrainian army may be prohibitive. The Commonwealth Ground Forces Main Staff claims that no one has ever seriously calculated how much it costs to operate the three military districts (Carpathian, Kiev and Odessa) now under Ukrainian jurisdiction.[23]

based at Sevastopol and a 'coastal defence' motorized rifle division based at Simferopol, both on Crimea. The bulk of the ships and aircraft are also based on Crimea. 45 nationalities are represented in the fleet; 19% of its officers and 30% of its petty officers and seamen are Ukrainian.

[20] The Black Sea Fleet was the core of the Russian Imperial Navy beginning in the 18th century. Its home port, Sevastopol, a historically Russian city located on the Crimean peninsula, was besieged by the Turks and their allies in the Crimean War. Crimea was made part of Ukraine as a 'gift' from Russia less than 40 years ago. Ukraine reacted furiously to Russia's January reassignment of its largest aircraft-carrying cruiser, the *Kuznetsov*, from the Black Sea to the Northern Fleet; it had little right to do so, however, since that redeployment had been scheduled for the previous August and was delayed due to lack of fuel and lubricants. See Bohlen, C., 'Yeltsin, in rebuff to Ukraine, lays claim to Black Sea Fleet', *New York Times*, 10 Jan. 1992, pp. A1, A6.

[21] Clarity, J. F., 'Ukraine woos Soviet troops' loyalty', *New York Times*, 10 Jan. 1992, p. A6.

[22] Foye, S., 'CIS: Kiev and Moscow clash over armed forces', *RFE/RL Research Report*, 17 Jan. 1992, pp. 1–3. Before this agreement, Russia made or planned several moves clearly designed to thwart Ukraine's efforts to build an independent military. A rumour circulated in early November 1991 that Russia plans to build a new Black Sea naval base in the Russian region of Krasnodar, since the fleet's current headquarters is located on Ukrainian territory. One month before, after Kravchuk's redesignation of all troops and equipment on Ukrainian soil to Ukrainian jurisdiction, Moscow reportedly sent secret orders for 420 of the top Soviet military construction experts and hundreds of items of sophisticated construction equipment to be quietly returned to Russia. The Supreme Soviet of Ukraine responded with orders to Ukrainian cities to ban the dispatch of men or hardware to Moscow. See Radio Kiev, 24 Oct. 1991, in FBIS-SOV-91-207, 25 Oct. 1991, p. 49.

[23] The Kiev military district currently has 2025 tanks and 2500 infantry fighting vehicles (IFVs); the Odessa 400 tanks and 1900 IFVs; and the Carpathian 2600 tanks and 3000 IFVs. In current state rouble prices, a T-72 or T-80 tank costs 1.5 million roubles, and a BMP-2 IFV costs 257 000 roubles. These

Disillusionment of the military leadership

The leadership of the former Soviet military is currently divided and increasingly dissatisfied with the political course being taken by Russian President Yeltsin and his associates. In October 1991, Defence Minister Yevgeniy Shaposhnikov threatened to resign his post due to determined resistance from conservative military forces attempting to block his reform efforts.[24] Numerous informed observers of the Commonwealth political scene have warned about the potential consequences of the ongoing struggle for power within the military leadership, particularly due to the continued presence in the high command of a number of generals supposedly involved in the August coup attempt.[25] In December 1991, General Lobov was fired as Chief of the Soviet General Staff, accused by Shaposhnikov of 'splitting the higher echelon of the military administration' and of attempting to make the General Staff independent of the Ministry of Defence. On 10 December the *Washington Post* linked Lobov's firing to rumours that a disgruntled faction of the General Staff was planning to seize power.[26] One month later, a stormy assembly of thousands of army officers in the Kremlin expressed its dissatisfaction with the current situation, demanding the retention of a unified army and improved social guarantees for servicemen.[27]

A growing sense that the current Russian political leadership is simply incompetent underlies much of the discontent within the armed forces leadership. Russian Vice President Alexander Rutskoi has spearheaded these charges. Colonel Rutskoi, a graduate of the Voroshilov General Staff Academy and a hero of the Afghan conflict, has dubbed the Russian Government 'urchins', claiming that it contains no 'practical workers'.[28] Ruslan Khasbulatov, Chairman of the Russian Parliament, has also accused the present Government of incompetence in economics, defence and foreign affairs. Apparently a growing number of military officers and defence industrialists share this sentiment, fondly reminis-

prices do not reflect probable increases due to the attempted transition to a market economy, and do not include fuel, ammunition or maintenance. Training costs are also enormous. In autumn 1991 rouble prices, a single company tactical exercise cost 36 000 roubles; a battalion exercise, 134 000 roubles; a regiment, 1.2 million roubles; and a division, 6 million roubles. In one year therefore a division would cost 10 million roubles in exercises alone, and an army 30 million roubles. Given that there is generally more than one army in a military district, and that there are three military districts in Ukraine, training costs alone become astronomical. See Krayniy, A., 'The politicians can only divide it up, it is for the taxpayers to increase it', *Komsomol'skaya Pravda*, 15 Nov. 1991, p. 2, in FBIS-SOV-91-223, 19 Nov. 1991, pp. 77–78.

[24] *Svenska Dagbladet*, 17 Oct. 1991, in FBIS-SOV-91-203, 21 Oct. 1991, pp. 41–42.

[25] See, in particular, noted military reformer Colonel Vladimir Lopatin and former Soviet Foreign Minister Eduard Shevardnadze, quoted in 'Weekly record of events', *Report on the USSR*, 22 Nov. 1991 and 26 Nov. 1991, respectively.

[26] Foye, S., 'From Union to Commonwealth: will the armed forces go along?', *Report on the USSR*, 20 Dec. 1991, pp. 4–7.

[27] See Adams, P., 'Russian military poses threat to Yeltsin government', *Defense News*, 10 Feb. 1992, pp. 1, 28.

[28] TASS–Russian Information Agency report, 'Vice President in doubt', *Rossiyskaya Gazeta*, 29 Nov. 1991, p. 1, in FBIS-SOV-91-233, 4 Dec. 1991, p. 48. Rutskoi has dismissed rumours of another coup but adds the caveat that 'you cannot play endlessly with people who bear arms', because it 'may end in disaster'.

cing about the old Union which at least knew how to manage industry and write a budget.[29]

Yeltsin's political appointments have evidently been based less on expertise than on demonstrations of loyalty and personal ties. In addition, his political reach does not extend far beyond Moscow; the Russian Government's horizontal network has remained undeveloped due to under-representation of outlying regions in the centre, and to the fact that central 'emissaries' to outlying regions spend too much time in Moscow. Local defence and defence industry authorities increasingly view both Yeltsin and Rutskoi as inaccessible and impenetrable, and are beginning to view self-governance as their only alternative.

Discontent in the military ranks

The Commonwealth's problems of feeding, housing and maintaining its military and military industry personnel have created considerable disenchantment among the lower strata of the former Soviet military. One Soviet Parliament official warned in October 1991 that 'the army has become the sixteenth republic, hungry and unsettled, but well armed and trained'. He foresees a possible social explosion that 'could sweep away democracy and the market'.[30]

The problem of feeding CIS military units has grown with the dissolution of the central supply organs. Before the recent reform-driven price increases, because state food prices were so low and because suppliers pay only a minor fine for not fulfilling state orders for the military, those suppliers chose to ignore military orders and instead sell their wares to other buyers at much higher contract prices. The price increases, which have brought state prices more into line with contract prices, have not significantly improved the military's situation; on a fixed budget, it cannot afford to accommodate the dramatic inflation.

Furthermore, with the dissolution of the Soviet economic structure, regional enterprises and producers are giving legal priority to orders from their own republics, exercising their right to turn down military consumers at will. Rouble-financed trade is being replaced by barter in a growing number of transactions between economic entities, with products as diverse as building materials, metals, foodstuffs, consumer goods and motor cars all serving as media of exchange. Because they have few hard products to barter, military bases often therefore have no choice but to develop their own agricultural and food processing facilities, a time-consuming endeavour that certainly distracts them from what should be their main tasks.[31]

---

[29] Recent private comments to one of the authors by a former high-ranking Soviet General Staff officer. This officer strongly fears that disenchanted defence industry directors may be forming an alliance with equally displeased local military commanders, setting off a potentially explosive chain of events.

[30] Interview with Chairman of the USSR Supreme Soviet Commission on National Security Viktor Minin, *Krasnaya Zvezda*, 25 Oct. 1991, pp. 1–2 (in Russian). An October joint report issued by the Military–Political Department of the USA and Canada Institute, the Institute of Europe, and the Analytical and Economic Administration of the KGB reached similar conclusions.

[31] Currently the St Petersburg Naval Base is developing an animal husbandry complex to supply 90% of base personnel needs in meat, milk and other products. For more detail, see McMichael, S. R., 'Market

The housing problem of the CIS military, as severe as the food shortages, is well known. The construction of military housing and other social service facilities is on the brink of failure due to incomplete and uneven delivery of reinforced concrete products and bricks.[32] More than 185 000 men, including 43 000 officers and warrant officers, have been withdrawn from Czechoslovakia, Hungary and Mongolia; 370 000 men total are to be withdrawn from Germany, including 100 000 officers and 185 000 of their family members. Even before these withdrawals, over 175 000 Soviet officers and their families were homeless. CIS military officials therefore calculate that at least 300 000 apartments or other living spaces are desperately needed. The USSR Supreme Soviet committee chairman responsible for social protection for the military comments that for the military to be without housing 'is not only immoral, but politically dangerous'.[33] Indeed, one helicopter pilot from a regiment withdrawn from Czechoslovakia, having lived with his compatriots and their families for 18 months in so-called 'Afghan-style' module barracks, declared that 'we have opened our holsters, but have not decided where to fire'.[34] Germany has earmarked DM 7.8 billion for military housing construction, but apparently this money has been inefficiently allocated. In 1991 the Western Group of Soviet Forces received none of its planned allocation of 36 000 apartment units.[35] German officials have replied that the collapse of the Soviet Union has greatly complicated their construction plans. The most pessimistic scenario involves ultra-conservative, communist or nationalist political leaders hiring these well-trained, disenchanted soldiers as the building blocks of mercenary armies to help them further their cause. These mercenary armies could usher in an era of chaos, in which feuding warlords carve out pieces of former Soviet territory.[36]

Workers in military industry are similarly troubled. Major defence enterprises and entire cities built around the defence industry are currently at a standstill; recent dramatic reductions in arms procurement orders,[37] combined with botched attempts at defence industry conversion to civilian production, have resulted in huge pockets of unemployment.[38] The defence industry has already

relations threaten combat-readiness of Soviet armed forces', *Report on the USSR*, 18 Oct. 1991, pp. 11–15.

[32] Salmin, V., 'Pechal'naya stabil'nost' ['Sorrowful stability'], *Krasnaya Zvezda*, 18 Sep. 1991, p. 2 (in Russian).

[33] Interview with Deputy Chairman of the USSR Supreme Soviet Committee for Defence and Security Affairs V. Ochirov, *Krasnaya Zvezda*, 18 Oct. 1991, p. 1 (in Russian). To make matters worse, apparently servicemen and officers do not always receive their salaries; sailors in the Northern Fleet reportedly were not paid for two months in autumn 1991.

[34] TASS, 'Military "social explosion" poses problems', 30 Dec. 1991, in FBIS-SOV-91-251, 31 Dec. 1991, p. 28.

[35] Burlakov, M., 'Firm belief in peace and good neighbourly relations', *Die Welt*, 28 Dec. 1991, p. 8, in FBIS-SOV-91-251, 31 Dec. 1991, pp. 26–28. Col. Gen. Burlakov is Commander-in-Chief of the Western Group of Soviet Forces.

[36] This possibility was repeatedly cited as quite realistic in recent private remarks to one of the authors by prominent Russian military and political officials.

[37] Procurement spending declined by 23% in 1991, according to the Soviet Ministry of Defence. This rate of decline was planned to continue through 1992. Production of long-range missiles is down by 40%, tanks by 66% and aircraft by 50% from 1989 levels.

[38] See Capelik, V., 'Yeltsin's economic reform: a pessimistic appraisal', *RFE/RL Research Report*, 24 Jan. 1992, pp. 26–32.

struck back in subtle ways; for example, the defence plants that built and traditionally operated the heating system for the city of Saratov shut the entire system down in November 1991 due to 'financial difficulties'.

The potential for arms sales

With military units and enterprises unable to feed and maintain themselves, and with barter becoming a primary form of economic exchange, armaments are increasingly becoming a unit of currency in both domestic and foreign transactions. Weapons are now frequently being exported at dumping prices, often through non-governmental channels. Many defence-oriented factories feel that if they can demonstrate their viability through arms exports, they might escape demands for conversion. The Far Eastern Military District, for example, plans to sell 4000 of its tanks to South-East Asian countries and South Korea.[39] Some Commonwealth political leaders have speculated that Ukraine plans to keep only the smaller ships of the Black Sea Fleet for border security and to combat terrorism, and will sell the larger ships for billions of dollars in hard currency on the world market. Russian military authorities consider the problem of stolen weapons serious enough to have held a special assembly of Moscow military district commanders on questions of safekeeping of weapons and ammunition.[40]

Decline in training standards

It is generally acknowledged that, because of the political and economic turmoil in which the military has had to operate, its combat training regimen has come virtually to a standstill. Local military commanders are completely preoccupied with the task of figuring out how to feed, clothe and pay their personnel, often accomplished by selling off their assets to the communities in which they are stationed; their attention is most certainly not focused on a rigorous training schedule. In 1991, for example, the ground forces did not carry out any division-level tactical training.[41] One reason for this phenomenon is that, with ministries of defence and national guards being established in the former republics, and the equipment of the Soviet armed forces being proclaimed republican property, military leaders judge that any movement of military equipment or troops may excite public opinion.[42] Other reasons include prohibitive costs, manpower shortages and limits imposed by international agreements.

[39] Moscow Central Television, 23 Oct. 1991, in Joint Publications Research Service–USSR Military Affairs (JPRS–UMA), JPRS-UMA-91-027, 5 Nov. 1991, p. 22.
[40] Semyanovskiy, F., 'Chto protivopostavit' raskhititelyam oruzhiya' ['Who opposes the plundering of weapons'], *Krasnaya Zvezda*, 13 Nov. 1991, p. 2 (in Russian).
[41] This according to Col. Gen. Eduard Vorobyov, deputy commander in chief of ground forces in charge of combat training. See Moscow Postfactum, 2 Dec. 1991, in FBIS-SOV-91-232, 3 Dec. 1991, p. 52.
[42] TASS, 'Tactical exercises cut', 12 Dec. 1991, in FBIS-SOV-91-240, 13 Dec. 1991, p. 28.

III. Near-term measures

The potential for conflict in the near term between former Soviet republics and within elements of the evolving structures of the CIS military forces is evident. The military or non-military instruments traditionally used to de-escalate or resolve conflicts of this type are nearly always applied too late, after the battle has already erupted. Two things are needed: (*a*) an early-warning system, with mechanisms that would enable political and military specialists to ward off conflict and engage potential opponents in constructive dialogue before conflict occurs, and (*b*) a system of mechanisms to identify and remove potential sources of conflict.[43]

These measures must be more comprehensive and intrusive than the 'preventive diplomacy' suggested by UN Secretary-General Boutros Boutros Ghali and the CSCE's peaceful settlement of disputes (PSD) mechanism as it has developed thus far.[44] While both the UN and the CSCE are in the process of improving approaches to crisis prevention and crisis management, the nature of the Commonwealth and its problems demands specially designed arrangements. These mechanisms can, however, be implemented and institutionalized through the CSCE, its emergency meeting procedures for the Committee of Senior Officials (CSO) and its Conflict Prevention Center (CPC). As an organization that includes the USA, and now all of the nations of the Commonwealth, it is an appropriate institution for addressing issues of Eurasian and North American concern.

In all these measures there is a great need for off-the-shelf, multilaterally funded and operated verification capabilities, since some of the new nations—perhaps those who might need the service the most—cannot afford their own aircraft (for Open Skies Treaty-based verification measures), verification technology or well-trained inspection teams for these purposes.

This capability could be institutionalized within the CPC and budgeted within a CIS Transition Assistance Fund. Indeed, this fund could be established by CSCE nations to finance all the measures discussed here, including dismantling and restructuring the military systems of Commonwealth nations and the implementation of various verification procedures. This type of financial assistance is already underway for the removal and destruction of Commonwealth nuclear systems. The bulk of this aid would, of course, come from the West.

---

[43] See Royen, C., 'After the USSR: questions for the West', *Report on the USSR*, 22 Nov. 1991, pp. 9–14.

[44] In January 1992, the UN Security Council asked UN Secretary-General Boutros Boutros Ghali, to study, among other things, the UN's capacity for preventive diplomacy. The Secretary-General reported the results of the study in June 1992 in a document entitled *Agenda for Peace*. The Helsinki CSCE summit meeting of July 1992 agreed on several early warning and peaceful settlement procedures.

Easing inter-republic political tension

The two major problems which could cause political tension between the former Soviet republics are the intermingling of populations and the possibility of massive refugee problems if ethnic persecution leads to major population movements. CSCE and UN arbitration mechanisms should anticipate these types of problems before they become violent, and look into solutions such as devolution of government authority to the lowest possible level and dual republic and national citizenship. A CSCE forum might usefully oversee refugee issues as the UN High Commissioner for Refugees already does. This might be a role for the CSCE High Commissioner for Minorities, who now is mainly concerned with providing early warning of problems.

With the breakup of the Soviet Union into its constituent republics, the potential for political intimidation through military means such as exercises and troop movements has multiplied. The solution to this problem involves a simple extension of the Stockholm and Vienna measures[45] to all of the former Soviet Union, probably allowing for third party inspections since the Baltics and other small, economically strapped nations may not be able to afford frequent inspections. Border keep-out zones between some of the former Soviet republics, where major troop presence is prohibited, would also contribute to stability; military exercises and troop transport could be limited to specific concentration areas. Open Skies arrangements can ease verification of this type of agreement.[46]

Monitoring troop movements

Belarus and Ukraine are well endowed with tanks that were part of the equipment of the Soviet Army. A large number of Soviet forces remain in the Baltic countries: 3 tank divisions, 7 motorized rifle divisions, 2 1/3 air assault or airborne divisions, and 1 artillery division.[47] In addition, about two-thirds of the forces currently in Ukraine will have to move or be destroyed if the Ukrainian army is to be downsized as planned.

One of the major elements of the CIS military transition is therefore likely to be the movement and destruction of conventional armaments within Commonwealth borders. Incorporation of the non-Russian republics under the CFE umbrella will include provision for Western inspection and observation of the movement and destruction of conventional forces. In order to monitor these

---

[45] In brief, the Stockholm and Vienna agreements signed by all CSCE members allow for transparency and inspections of specific types of national and multinational military exercises within the Atlantic-to-the-Urals region. For the text ot the 1986 Stockholm Document see SIPRI, *SIPRI Yearbook 1987: World Armaments and Disarmament* (Oxford University Press: Oxford, 1987), appendix 10A, pp. 355–69. The 1990 Vienna Document is reprinted in SIPRI, *SIPRI Yearbook 1991: World Armaments and Disarmament* (Oxford University Press: Oxford, 1991), appendix 13B, pp. 475–88.

[46] Open Skies-type arrangements, that allow for aerial reconnaissance inspections of the territory of signatories, can facilitate verification of agreements.

[47] International Institute for Strategic Studies, *The Military Balance 1990-1991* (Brassey's: Oxford, 1990), p. 39.

movements, primarily so that no republic can use these movements to threaten another, they should come under more intense scrutiny.

The ongoing withdrawal of Soviet forces from Germany and Poland provides an excellent example of the tension that movement of military forces within and among the former Soviet republics might create. The Soviet–German agreement on the withdrawal of the Western Group of Forces called for the transport of these forces from Germany to the USSR through Poland. The Polish Government was neither consulted, nor its permission asked, to allow implementation of this agreement, a slight which caused serious tension between Warsaw and Moscow.[48] On several occasions Polish border troops stopped Soviet troop and equipment transport trains at the border and sent word to Moscow that passage would not be allowed.[49] The Soviet Union was forced to counter the problem by using alternate routes by sea and through the Baltics.

The core of a monitoring and inspection regime for these forces would be schedules and timetables for transport and restructuring of the forces involved, and designated routes for movement of large units and heavy equipment between former republics. These schedules could either be agreed to bilaterally between the countries involved and then submitted to the CSCE for purposes of monitoring and inspection, or the schedules themselves could be negotiated if necessary through the CSCE or the CPC.[50]

Ample precedent exists for this sort of agreement. Between 1956 and 1958, 'Status of Forces' agreements between the Soviet Union and its Warsaw Pact allies (the German Democratic Republic, Hungary, Poland and Romania) were signed as consolation for the 1956 Soviet invasion of Hungary and crushing of rebellion in Poland.[51] These agreements theoretically made the movement of Soviet forces within the territory of its Warsaw Pact allies transparent and subject to notification. The 1957 Soviet–Polish agreement was used as the basis for negotiations that settled the problems of Soviet troop withdrawal from Poland after the collapse of the Warsaw Pact.[52] Its provisions included:

[48] 'Parys on "difficult" Soviet troop pullout talks', *Warsaw Rzeczpospolita*, in Foreign Broadcast Information Service, *Daily Report–Eastern Europe (FBIS-EEU)*, (FBIS-EEU-91-049, 13 Mar. 1991, p. 36.

[49] Popov, S. and Khabarov, V., 'Vyvod voysk . . . s prepyatstviyami' ['Troop withdrawal . . . with obstacles'], *Krasnaya Zvezda*, 5 Feb. 1991, p. 1 (in Russian); and 'Government refuses Soviet troops crossing rights', Warsaw PAP, in FBIS-EEU-91-059, 27 Mar. 1991, p. 24.

[50] The schedules might also involve notification of Commonwealth use of military facilities on non-Russian republic soil. Russia risked creating considerable tension by firing an unarmed long-range nuclear missile over the Kamchatka peninsula from a base in Kazakhstan on 20 December 1991; the USA was informed before the test launch, but Kazakhstan was not. See 'Russia first tells U.S., then launches missile', *New York Times*, 22 Jan. 1992, p. A4. Kazakh officials say that they do not have the technical means to control flights from their own launch facilities at Tyuratam.

[51] Wolfe, T., *Soviet Power and Europe* (Johns Hopkins University Press: Baltimore, 1970), pp. 82, 149.

[52] 'General Siwicki on Soviet troop withdrawal', *Zulnierz Rzeczypospolitei*, in FBIS-EEU-90-087, 7 May 1990, p. 46. For more details on this withdrawal, including a map of the transport routes taken by the Western Group of Forces, see Clarke, D. L., 'Poland and the Soviet troops in Germany', *Report on Eastern Europe*, vol. 2, no. 4 (25 Jan. 1991), pp. 40–44.

1. The Soviet Northern Group of Forces Commander must inform the Polish Defence Minister of any changes in troop manning, equipment, and the like, every six months.

2. All military movements must follow designated pre-arranged transit routes.

3. Five to seven days prior permission must be granted from the host country before any troops or equipment can be moved. The request must include information on the timing of the move, planned transit route, destination and type of equipment involved.

This model could more than adequately deal with troop movements out of the Baltic countries and Ukraine, and with any other former republic which is undergoing military restructuring and/or requesting withdrawal of Soviet forces stationed on its territory. Several additional provisions might be necessary: inspection and observation of movements of large concentrations of forces; adequate, distributed timetables for complete troop withdrawals and force restructuring; and notification and provisions for observation or inspection of base closures and equipment destruction. Again, the best forum for distribution of this information is the CSCE.

Indeed, *ad hoc* measures of this type have already taken place. The Soviet Union, and later Russia, promised Lithuania that it would be informed of any troop movements. On 8 September 1991, such a notification took place, and Lithuanian police escorted Soviet troops from Vilnius to Kaliningrad.[53] It would be useful to formalize this type of arrangement both because of the potential political problems involved, and the sheer number of troops to be moved. Soviet forces will be withdrawing from Germany until 1994, and in order to get back to Russia, they will have to pass not only through Poland, but also through the newly independent nations of Belarus, Estonia, Latvia, Lithuania, Moldova or Ukraine.[54] The restructuring of troop deployments in the CIS nations will likely take far longer. Given the degree to which these new countries have already encountered political friction with Russia over military matters, it probably makes sense for troop movements not only to be bilaterally monitored, but also backed by the CSCE and inspected by third parties.

The complicated movement of troops out of Eastern Europe also required the identification of roads and railways which could handle Soviet equipment, and the rebuilding of some routes to accommodate that equipment.[55] This was not a trivial task; a similar process must now take place within the Commonwealth nations. The USA and the CSCE nations can expedite this process by providing engineering resources for the necessary structural integrity tests and potential

---

[53] Girnius, S., 'Dismantling Soviet armed detachments in Lithuania', *Report on the USSR*, vol. 3, no. 41 (11 Oct. 1991), p. 31.

[54] Ukraine has stated that it is no longer willing to serve as a transit zone for returning Soviet troops, and the Baltic nations are not happy with current arrangements either.

[55] On some of the difficulties of moving Soviet forces out of Eastern Europe, see 'Agreement reached on Soviet troop withdrawal', Budapest Domestic Service, in FBIS-EEU-90-024, 5 Feb. 1990, p. 44; and 'Preparations underway for Soviet troop transit', Warsaw PAP, in FBIS-EEU-90-010, 15 Jan. 1991, p. 39.

road and railway modifications. The West may also wish to provide financial resources for these tasks analogous to the assistance given for dismantling of the Soviet nuclear arsenal.[56]

Easing the return home for withdrawn troops

The former Soviet troops withdrawing from Eastern Europe often cannot look forward to a bright immediate future. Indeed, many Soviet military officers in this position are now refusing to obey withdrawal orders without first receiving guarantees that their social welfare will be looked after.[57] Some officers in the Baltic countries have formed an independent organization and demanded that the central military authorities consult with them before making plans to transfer them out of the region. Their fears of poor social conditions when they return home are most certainly justified, but their situation where they are currently based may soon not be much better; the Baltic countries stopped supplying food to Soviet troops stationed on their soil as of 1 January 1992. According to one high-ranking commander stationed there, 'the present situation with the Soviet troops in the Baltics is like a powder keg that could explode at any moment'.[58]

Given the economic situation in the Soviet Union and German anxiety about the continued presence of Soviet troops on its soil, the Soviet Union had little difficulty convincing Germany to foot the bill for the movement of Soviet troops eastward and for their housing once they returned home. Russia is now asking the Baltic nations to do the same. The West could easily further facilitate these types of arrangements by creating, through the CSCE or the UN, a Commonwealth Transition Assistance Fund. In this context the fund would stabilize political relations between and among the Eastern European nations and the former Soviet republics by underwriting the management and monitoring of force movements.

To mitigate the dangers evident in a situation where current and former military personnel are selling their armaments in order to support themselves, the USA might also provide assistance in organizing job retraining for former servicemen. Inter-republic retraining centres could be financed with part of the DM 200 million that Germany has earmarked for the personnel of the Western Group of Forces. This task would be particularly beneficial for specialized troops; chemical troops, for example, possess a unique material base and experience which could be transformed into ecological troops. These ecological troops could perform monitoring functions in unmasking and preventing environmental crimes, and in performing services such as assisting in the environ-

---

[56] Policy makers who question the irreversibility of Moscow's democratic reforms might have reservations about this particular form of assistance.

[57] Kionka, R., 'Officers in the Baltic take the initiative', *Report on the USSR*, 15 Nov. 1991, pp. 27–29.

[58] Mironov, V., 'Yesli smotret' cherez prizmu medlitel'nosti i neopredelennosti' ['Looking through the prism of sluggishness and uncertainty'], *Krasnaya Zvezda*, 1 Jan. 1992, p. 3 (in Russian). Col. Gen. Mironov is the commander of the Northwestern Group of Forces.

mental clean-up after the Persian Gulf War.[59] The closing of military bases in the USA and Europe has left local municipalities with the task of cleaning up pockets of environmental damage. The same is certainly the case in the CIS. Ecological troops could be charged with cleaning up these areas as well.[60]

Monitoring military activity within the Commonwealth

The military forces of the newly independent republics are likely to establish standard training and exercise routines and schedules. In times of political turmoil, these normal military activities could become a destabilizing factor in unusual, unrelated political situations. Predictability, stability and normalcy are the watchwords; given the already tenuous political situation, the CIS nations want to prevent unpleasant surprises.

Preventing the normal military activities of the European nations from causing unintended or unexpected tension was always an underlying goal of the negotiations that developed the Stockholm and Vienna agreements. These agreements, however, cover only the area within the designated Atlantic-to-the-Urals (ATTU) region. For the sake of stabilizing the military relationship between the nations of the Commonwealth, a regime of notification and observation of certain military activities must be expanded to all Commonwealth territory. This is, of course, more than a near-term measure; presumably it would remain as a permanent part of the integration of the CIS nations into the Eurasian–Atlantic security community. The USA, third party, or multilateral off-the-shelf inspection teams may at some point be requested to carry out inspections for any CIS member, since inspections within the Commonwealth may themselves cause political tension.

IV. Military-to-military co-operation

This section addresses two goals for military-to-military co-operation between the USA and the CIS nations: in the medium term (following the redesignation of Soviet forces under whatever military structure evolves within the Commonwealth), stabilizing the military services of the CIS nations by assisting them in their transition to a professional military on a Western model; and in the long term, building an alliance relationship between Commonwealth and US forces.

First, stabilizing the military forces of the Commonwealth nations calls for rebuilding their professionalism, *esprit de corps* and purpose. As discussed above, much of the Soviet military is being decommissioned. The remaining forces, whether joint forces or the forces of new nations, require a new rationale and new methods of conscription, training and peacetime operation.

[59] Minin (note 30), pp. 1–2.
[60] Suggestions for similar use of NATO troops can be found in Lowe, K., 'US armed forces in the new Europe', ed. J. Simon, *European Security After the Revolutions of 1989* (National Defense University Press: Washington, DC, 1991), pp. 130–32.

Second, the military structures within the Commonwealth must become open, operating as allied rather than adversarial forces in Western eyes. For 45 years the US and Soviet military establishments had one major goal—to prepare for combat with each other. It will take some time and effort to turn adversaries into partners. The former Soviet military, or at least some elements of it, clearly continues to view the USA and its sophisticated military technologies as a security threat.[61] The goal here is not to foster trust—that may take a generation—but instead simply to create military relationships that befit allies. The first step on the path to a more co-operative relationship will be for the military forces of East and West to gain a more intimate knowledge of each others' standard military operating procedures, doctrines and training practices.[62] Precedents for this type of military-to-military co-operation and understanding already exist. During the *détente* of the 1970s, for example, the USA and the USSR signed the May 1972 Agreement on the Prevention of Incidents On and Over the High Seas.[63] This agreement was negotiated by a civilian-military delegation from the USA and by an entirely military delegation from the Soviet Union that consisted of some of its Navy's highest officials. The agreement established an official channel of communication through the naval attachés in each nation's capital for discussing incidents at sea, an annual review conference and continuing negotiation of unresolved issues. More recently, US and Soviet military leaders negotiated and signed the Agreement on the Prevention of Dangerous Military Activities.[64] This document established the Joint Military Commission, which meets at least annually to discuss implementation, compliance and expansion of the agreement.

Among numerous military-to-military contacts, including exchange programmes, tours of military facilities and bilateral talks, the USA and the USSR have participated in two CSCE-sponsored seminars on military doctrine.[65] The first, held in Vienna in February 1990, allowed military leaders from the CSCE nations to discuss their individual national military doctrines.[66] The second, convened from 8–18 October 1991, built on the foundation laid by the first.

The new era in US–Commonwealth relations demands an expansion of these ties. In order to address actual military activities within US and CIS territory,

---

[61] See, for example, Rebrov, M., 'Ne skudeyet ruka dayushchego' ['Don't discard the hand of the future'], *Krasnaya Zvezda*, 17 Sep. 1991, p. 3 (in Russian). The performance of US weaponry in the Persian Gulf War was particularly astonishing to the Soviet Union.

[62] These measures are analogous to those proposed by Judyth Twigg on transparency and co-operation in US and Commonwealth nation defence planning (see chapter 15 in this volume).

[63] Lynn-Jones, S. M., 'A quiet success for arms control: preventing incidents at sea', *International Security*, vol. 9, no. 4 (spring 1985), p. 171.

[64] For an analysis of the agreement's provisions and its text see Carnahan, B. M., 'Decreasing the danger in military activities: the meaning of the new US–Soviet agreement', *Arms Control Today*, Aug. 1989, pp. 13–17. The agreement entered into force on 1 Jan. 1990.

[65] On the extent and benefit of bilateral military-to-military contacts see Williams, W. J., 'Expanding the US–USSR military dialogue', ed. B. Blechman, *Preventing Nuclear War* (Indiana University Press and Center for Strategic and International Affairs, Georgetown University: Bloomington, Ind., 1985), pp. 144–67; and Sagan, S., 'Reducing the risks: a new agenda for military-to-military talks', *Arms Control Today*, July/Aug. 1991, pp. 16–21.

[66] Almquist, P., 'The Vienna military doctrine seminar: flexible response vs. reasonable sufficiency', *Arms Control Today*, Apr. 1990, pp. 21–25.

we propose routinizing a programme of observation visits for US and Commonwealth officers to the military bases of their counterparts. This programme would include all services, but only those bases where units are stationed in peacetime. Visits would be for the purpose of observing scheduled exercises, and hence would not constitute inspections like those mandated by the Stockholm and Vienna agreements or the INF, CFE and START treaties. The goal of this visitation programme would be to familiarize each nation with the standard training practices of the others, and possibly more important, to allow the military officers and troops of the Commonwealth nations to redesign their own training programmes based on the US model.

V. Joint missions and allied operations

The construction of a Eurasian–Atlantic security community not only calls for multilateral security co-operation, but also implies the possibility of joint military operations in defence of community interests. These operations could call on the military forces of the CIS nations to serve side by side with Western forces in many capacities: enforcing UN provisions against aggressors, as in the Persian Gulf War, participating in multilateral peacekeeping and preventive diplomacy operations throughout the world and assisting in anti-terrorist or anti-narcotic operations. This new security relationship necessitates a joint training programme for the military forces of the USA and the CIS nations.

Apparently CIS military officers are anxious to adopt new forms of tactical thinking and training. According to British officials involved with then Defence Minister Dmitri Yazov's visit to Great Britain in the summer of 1989, the Soviet delegation used their trips abroad as sources of inspiration for their own institutions. Indeed, Admiral Chernavin, when accompanying Yazov aboard the HMS *Invincible*, completely ignored the ship's hardware and instead asked countless questions about training and conditions of service.[67] The Soviet military analysis of the Persian Gulf War stressed the need to think three-dimensionally when training, and to close the gap between outmoded tactics and modern means of waging battle;[68] US and NATO training techniques and facilities, particularly their skilful use of technical simulations, were clearly objects of admiration.[69] The Russian KGB has explicitly expressed a desire to co-operate with Western secret service agencies in combating terrorism, drug trafficking and the proliferation of biological and chemical weapons, not merely in the form of information exchange, but with the creation of joint units.

During the 1980s the US military began to operate combat training centres specially designed to simulate actual combat operations. The US Army operates

[67] Thompson, G. N., 'Soviet military collaboration: the thirties revisited?', *Jane's Soviet Intelligence Review*, Jan. 1991, pp. 12–15.

[68] See, for example, Vorobyev, I., 'Umeyem li myslit' po-novomu?' ['Do we know how to think in new ways?'], *Krasnaya Zvezda*, 5 Sep. 1991, p. 2 (in Russian).

[69] See Markushin, V., 'Shtil' posle shtormovykh preduprezhdeniy' ['Calm after storm warnings'], *Krasnaya Zvezda*, 18 Sep. 1991, p. 5 (in Russian).

several centres of this kind: the Combat Maneuver Training Center (CMTC) in Hohenfels, Germany; the National Training Center (NTC) at Fort Irwin, California, which trains mechanized infantry and armoured forces; and the Joint Readiness Training Center (JRTC) at Fort Chafee, Arkansas, which was developed for training light infantry.[70] These centres train US Air Force units from Military Airlift Command (MAC) and Tactical Air Command (TAC), in addition to US Army forces. The war-games at the centres are made more realistic by a specially trained Opposing Force (OPFOR) that challenges the training unit by simulating enemy tactics.[71] The goal of the training centres is to create situations as close as possible to those that would confront units in actual combat, through the use of force-on-force war-games. Although the OPFOR at the NTC was initially trained to simulate Soviet battle tactics, following Iraq's invasion of Kuwait, the NTC and the OPFOR were remodelled to resemble Iraqi forces and defences in the Kuwaiti Theatre of Operations.[72] Units at the NTC then tested various tactical operations to get a sense of what they might confront during ground operations in the Gulf.

The US Marine Corps operates two centres in California based on the same combat simulation principles: the Marine Corps Air–Ground Combat Center at Twenty-Nine Palms and the Marine Corps Mountain Warfare Center in Bridgeport.[73] The Air Force operates its own training centre at Nellis Air Force Base, Nevada. Its 'Red Flag' exercises include not only Air Force tactical air units, but also units from the armies, navies and air forces of allied nations as well.[74] The Army and Air Force plan to build two joint combat training centres: the Joint Warfare Center at Hurlburt Field, Florida, and the Warrior Preparation Center at Ramstein Air Base in Germany.[75] One convenient mechanism to assist the Commonwealth in these matters would be for its representatives to be present at, or even participate in, the design and construction of these two new centres in the USA. The war-games played at these centres can be modified to reflect new realities, replacing scenarios for defence against Soviet forces with

[70] Steele, D., 'Eleven days in Arkansas test light infantry mettle', *Army*, Feb. 1989, p. 39. The JRTC had been located at Ft Chafee, Arkansas; however, this was not designed to be its permanent base of operation. Ft Chafee was included on Secretary of Defense Dick Cheney's list of bases to be closed.

[71] For more details on the operation of the NTC and the JRTC see the following: Steele (note 70), pp. 39–46; Goldsmith, M., *Applying the National Training Center Experience: Incidence of Ground-to-Ground Fratricide* (RAND Corporation: Santa Monica, Calif., Feb. 1986); Levine, R., Hodges, J. and Goldsmith, M., *Utilizing the Data from the Army's National Training Center: Analytical Plan* (RAND Corporation: Santa Monica, Calif., June 1986); Ganley, M. and Schemmer, B., 'Getting the US Army ready for war', *Armed Forces Journal International*, May 1987, p. 62; and Steele, D., 'Lessons learned: "what happened out there?"', *Army*, Jan. 1989, pp. 33–35.

[72] Baker, C., 'California desert rehearsals provide key to Gulf', *Defense News*, 15 Apr. 1991, p. 12.

[73] For further details on the US Marine combat training centres see *Department of Defense Appropriations for FY 1989*, Hearings before the Committee on Appropriations, US Senate, 100th Congress, 2nd Session (US Government Printing Office: Washington, DC, 1988), part 1, pp. 260–61.

[74] Like the NTC, the Nellis Air Force Base exercises were remodelled into 'Desert Flag' exercises during the Gulf War. See Scott, W. B., 'Air Force modifies red flag exercises to reflect Gulf combat environment', *Aviation Week and Space Technology*, 25 Feb. 1991, p. 46.

[75] *Department of Defense Appropriations for FY 1991*, Hearings before the Senate Appropriations Committee, 101st Congress, 2nd Session (US Government Printing Office: Washington, DC, 1990), part 3, p. 146.

those designed to simulate peacekeeping, interpositional (preventive diplomacy) and counter-terrorist operations.

Developing a similar system in the Commonwealth would entail seminars for the CIS military on the operation of such centres and visits by its officers to actual US combat training centres. Any visits to training centres would not be inspections as in the CFE or Stockholm and Vienna provisions, but instructional tours. US teams would help the Commonwealth military design its own combat training centres and might even assist in the initial stages of their operation. Ultimately, US and CIS forces could participate in joint operations at each others' training centres.[76]

VI. Conclusion: institutionalizing the Eurasian–Atlantic security community

Precedent exists for joint US–CIS measures on managing the transition from Soviet to Commonwealth military structures in the areas of both nuclear and conventional weaponry, The USA and Europe have made extensive efforts to see that the Soviet nuclear arsenal is transformed into a Russian arsenal without the creation of new nuclear states or the proliferation of nuclear systems, technology or expertise. Early on, during US congressional debates on aid to the Soviet Union, Congress appropriated $400 million for warhead dismantlement.[77] In October 1991, the USA and the USSR began to discuss the possibility of formal negotiations on joint management of the movement and dismantling of Soviet nuclear systems outside Russia; these talks began officially between the USA and Russia in January 1992.[78] These talks, dubbed the Safety, Security, and Dismantlement (SSD) Talks, resulted in agreements at the Bush–Yeltsin summit meeting of June 1992. The USA will provide Russia with containers for the transportation of nuclear systems, armoured blankets for the protection of these containers during transportation and accident-response 'clothing and equipment'.[79] In addition, Germany, Russia and the USA, with assistance from Canada, Japan and the European Community, have established an International Science and Technology Center. The Center is designed to create jobs for ex-Soviet nuclear scientists, thereby preventing the possibility that they might seek employment in developing countries that are hoping to gain access to nuclear weapon technology and expertise.[80]

---

[76] For an excellent analysis of the challenges posed by joint operations, see Grau, L. W., *Confrontation to Cooperation: An American/Soviet Military Coalition?* (Soviet Army Studies Office: Ft Leavenworth, Kans., Mar. 1991).

[77] For discussion of congressional debates on aid, see Newmann, W. W., 'History accelerates: the diplomacy of co-operation and fragmentation', chapter 3 in this volume.

[78] Lockwood, D., 'US, Russia, see limited progress in warhead dismantlement talks', *Arms Control Today*, vol. 22, no. 3 (Apr. 1992), p. 16.

[79] Bunn, M., 'Bush–Yeltsin summit brings deep new strategic arms cuts', *Arms Control Today*, vol. 22, no. 5 (June 1992), p. 27.

[80] Lockwood, D., 'International center designed to limit brain drain', *Arms Control Today*, vol. 22, no. 2 (Mar. 1992), p. 24.

The West and the Commonwealth nations have also co-operated to remodel the NATO–Warsaw Pact CFE Treaty to fit post-Soviet Eurasia. Soviet military assets as divided among Commonwealth nations must be adapted within modified CFE sublimits. The 10 CIS nations that lie within the ATTU region signed an agreement with NATO and ex-Warsaw Pact states on this updated conventional forces treaty, CFE 1A, on 9 July 1992.[81]

The European and North American leaders who attended the Paris CSCE Summit meeting of November 1990 hoped to usher in a new order for Europe—an age of peace, stability and finally, a lasting end to the conflicts that had ravaged the continent for over a century. It seemed that with the end of the cold war, the nations of Europe needed only move towards collective security arrangements that could identify and oppose aggressor states. The multilateral effort against Iraq appeared to be a shining example of the type of measure that would maintain the peace in the 'new world order'. It seems apparent, however, that there is much left over from the old world in this new world order. The civil war in Yugoslavia and the breakup of the Soviet Union were a cold splash of water in the face of those who saw the collapse of communism as 'the end of history'.[82] For states such as Estonia, Latvia, Lithuania, all the Commonwealth nations, and Croatia and Slovenia, history is only beginning. The dangers in Europe do not lie in the possibility of new aggressor states seeking conquest and territory.[83] For a number of reasons, the age of this sort of aggression in Europe seems over.[84] The end of the cold war, however, may have reopened the Pandora's box of territorial and ethnic violence that had been the cause of conflict before ideological struggles overshadowed other national ambitions.[85] It is the spread of regional conflict that will be the cause of future instability in Europe.

Many analysts have written on the new instabilities in Europe and offered sweeping plans for bringing order to situations which seem to grow increasingly chaotic. The above discussion of integrating the CIS nations into a

---

[81] Feinstein, L., '25 nations sign CFE follow-on', *Arms Control Today*, vol. 22, no, 6 (July/Aug. 1992), p. 29. A comprehensive discussion of adapting the CFE process of conventional arms reductions to the new European security environment is in Dean, J. and Forsberg, R., 'CFE and beyond: the future of conventional arms control', *International Security*, vol. 17, no. 1 (summer 1992), pp. 76–121.

[82] Fukuyama (note 3), pp. 3–18.

[83] Former US National Security Advisor and Secretary of State Henry Kissinger has argued that a co-operative security regime such as that proposed here may be dangerous and counterproductive. He fears that assisting Russia in remodelling its military may lay the groundwork for a resurgent Russian Army that could once again threaten to dominate Europe. See Kissinger, H., 'Charter of confusion', *Washington Post*, 5 July 1992, p. C7. This view directly contradicts the basic assumptions of this chapter, which sees instability, rather than traditional geopolitical rivalry, as the larger threat to European security over the next several decades.

[84] Some analysts claim that nuclear weapons have irreversibly changed the nature of the military instrument as a political tool, while others see a more peaceful era as a result of evolving historical, economic and political forces. On the former point, see Gaddis, J. L., *The Long Peace* (Oxford University Press: Oxford, 1987); and Bundy, M., *Danger and Survival* (Vintage Books: New York, 1988). For the latter argument, see Mueller (note 3); and Kaysen (note 3), pp. 42–64.

[85] Brzezinski, Z., 'Post-communist nationalism', *Foreign Affairs*, vol. 68, no. 5 (winter 1989–90), pp. 1–25; Van Evera, S., 'Primed for peace: Europe after the cold war', *International Security*, vol. 15, no. 3 (winter 1990–91), pp. 7–57; and Larrabee, F. S., 'Long memories and short fuses: change and instability in the Balkans', *International Security*, vol. 15, no. 3 (winter 1990–91), pp. 58–91.

Eurasian–Atlantic security community offers a less comprehensive set of institutionalized security arrangements than some would suggest. This lower level of institutionalized security, however, may be most appropriate for the near- and medium-term future; it allows the future of Eurasian–Atlantic security to remain a high-level political issue rather than the domain of a rigid, easily by-passed multilateral bureaucracy.

Some observers have called for a new Concert of Europe that relies on the major powers to guarantee European security.[86] Presumably, the powers that would reorder Europe and then police that new order would include nations with either nuclear weapons or large conventional armed forces. The former group would include Britain, France, Russia and the USA The latter group would add Germany and Ukraine, if Kiev follows through on its plans to maintain a sizeable military.

The problem with a concert system is most easily illustrated by the inclusion of Germany and Russia as members of the group of major powers charged with maintaining order. The revolutions of 1989, the disintegration of the USSR and the trepidation felt by some nations as Germany reunites are all manifestations of the same simple, yet profound notion—the desire of the peoples of Europe to chart their own destiny as free men and women. Both world wars and the cold war were struggles about the rights of nations to self-determination and the ability of smaller nations to be free of intimidation and domination by the major powers. It seems intuitively wrong to suggest that smaller nations would now willingly give up sovereignty over their security to the major powers so soon after gaining real independence. The nations of Eastern Europe and those that have emerged from the USSR have had enough of 'Big Brother'. It is important to remember that, although the trend in Western Europe is towards unification, the Eastern Europeans and peoples of the Commonwealth nations are more likely to concentrate on rebuilding their societies and developing independent futures now that the era of communism is over.[87]

This is not to suggest that co-operative security arrangements are unlikely. It simply means that there are upper limits to what is feasible at this time. Proposals that call for supranational authority over security issues are sure to be greeted with little enthusiasm and will quickly be ignored if somehow established.[88] For these reasons, this chapter suggests the use of the CSCE to create mechanisms specifically designed to address present security problems. These

[86] Kupchan, C. and Kupchan, C., 'Concerts, collective security, and the future of Europe', *International Security*, vol. 16, no. 1 (summer 1991), pp. 114–61.

[87] Historians may look back on this era as one tinged with irony. While Western Europe unified the communist bloc divided. The EC and the successor to the Soviet Union may come to resemble each other in the next few decades—the EC moving from independent, quarrelling, even warring states to a union of equals, while a Soviet Union dominated by the communists in Moscow moves to a looser confederation of economically linked states with co-ordinated foreign policies. The compelling irony of the developments in Europe was captured in early December of 1991. As the leaders of Belarus, Russia and Ukraine met to negotiate the Brest Declaration and declare the USSR dead, in Maastricht, the Netherlands, West European leaders came together to fine tune their coming union.

[88] An example of one such proposal calling for a supranational body with independent powers can be found in Mueller, H., 'A United Nations of Europe and North America', *Arms Control Today*, vol. 21, no. 1 (Jan./Feb. 1991), pp. 3–8.

measures are intended to become elements of a security regime between equal partners in the maintenance of peace in the new Europe. This security regime would be based upon political bargaining to solve problems, not the use of sovereignty-inhibiting pan-European institutions or international bureaucracies.[89]

The CSCE is the proper forum for negotiating and implementing such measures. Article X of the Vienna Document charges the CPC with holding annual meetings to discuss present and future confidence-building measures similar to the ones discussed here. It is within the CPC that these measures can best come to fruition. The political nature of the CSCE—its limited institutional arrangements and the high national bureaucratic level at which the Council of Ministers and Committee of Senior Officials meet—helps to assure that the actions of the CSCE will reflect the real political dynamic of any given security concern and not wishful thinking. Above all else, if the CSCE is to play a role in maintaining the security of Europe, it must remain attuned to the shifting balance of power in Europe and Eurasia.

At present, the CSCE's potential may be overshadowed by its ineffective performance during the current situation in Yugoslavia. The principles of non-intervention in internal disputes and consensus in decision making that prevent the major powers from dominating the minor powers also prevent the CSCE from becoming involved in issues that are still defined as domestic problems.[90] The August coup attempt and the rapid dissolution of the Soviet Union have made things easier for those hoping to avert a Yugoslavia-type conflict among the successor states of the USSR. As these nations become fully independent, issues that had been domestic become international concerns. All of the Commonwealth nations have joined the CSCE and are therefore subject to the agreements and principles it has established. The USA, normally reluctant to view the CSCE as an expanding set of institutions, should take this opportunity to use the CSCE as a method of stabilizing the transition of its former Soviet enemy into a present and future ally.

[89] On the necessity for a European security based on political realities and not multinational, semi-autonomous institutions see Goodby, J. E., 'A new European concert: settling disputes within the CSCE', *Arms Control Today*, vol. 21, no. 1 (Jan./Feb. 1991), pp. 3–6.

[90] At the Paris conference of November 1990, the CSCE began to chip away at these principles by declaring that, in the case of one state seeking clarification from another concerning unusual military activities, the consensus rule need not apply. The Berlin conference of June 1991 added provisions for emergency meetings of the CSO without the consensus of all members. In essence, no CSCE member state can veto another's request for information or discussion. See Weitz, R., 'The CSCE's new look', *RFE/RL Research Report*, vol. 1, no. 6 (7 Feb. 1992), p. 30.

14. Russian–US security co-operation on the high seas

Steven E. Miller

I. Introduction

During the cold war, naval forces never figured prominently on the Soviet–US arms control agenda. Indeed, by the end of the 1980s, it seemed an anomaly that naval forces, alone of all the major weapon systems, remained largely outside the extensive web of arms control measures that had been developed between East and West. While a few limitations on navies have been achieved, mostly (though not entirely) as by-products of negotiations on non-naval issues, it is still basically true that, as Johan Jørgen Holst put it, 'Naval forces remain beyond regulation'.[1]

With the end of the cold war and the collapse of the Soviet Union, the prospects for security co-operation with the Soviet successor states have greatly increased. There now exists an opportunity to replace the highly adversarial cold war security relationship with one marked by high levels of co-operation, and perhaps even including collaboration on some issues. In the naval realm, moving in this direction falls overwhelmingly in the province of US–Russian relations, since Russia inherited the vast bulk of the Soviet Navy.[2]

The ultimate character of US–Russian relations depends, of course, on the outcome of the internal processes presently under way in Russia, but the state of current relations with a Russia evolving into a democracy and market economy suggests a tremendous potential for co-operation. Indeed, the Charter for American–Russian Partnership and Friendship signed during the summit meeting between Presidents George Bush and Boris Yeltsin in June 1992 not only declares that the two states are not adversaries but also that they are 'developing relations of partnership and friendship'.[3] Further, the Charter explicitly emphasizes increased security co-operation: 'In view of the potential for building a strategic partnership between the United States of America and the Russian

---

[1] Holst, J. J., 'European security: a view from the North', eds A. Cless and L. Ruhl, *Beyond East–West Confrontation: Searching for a New Security Structure in Europe* (Nomos Verlagsgesellschaft: Baden-Baden, 1990), p. 328.

[2] Russia inherited in their entirety the two main Soviet fleets, the Northern and Pacific Fleets, as well as the less capable Baltic Fleet. The Black Sea Fleet is subject to dispute between Russia and Ukraine, and Kiev will gain custody of some portion of this force. In the context of the concerns of this chapter, this development is inconsequential. On the Black Sea Fleet controversy, see Eberle, J., 'Russia and Ukraine: what to do with the Black Sea Fleet?', *The World Today*, Aug./Sep. 1992, pp. 158–60.

[3] 'US–Russian summit documents: a charter for American–Russian partnership and friendship', *US Department of State Dispatch*, vol. 3, no. 25 (22 June 1992), p. 490.

Federation, the parties intend to accelerate defense cooperation between their military establishments'.[4] This statement of intent has been accompanied by agreements on reductions in strategic nuclear weapons and on co-operation on nuclear weapon safety and security issues, and by joint statements envisioning collaboration on ballistic missile defence, space co-operation, chemical weapons, defence conversion and nuclear proliferation. As this incipient security co-operation between Russia and the United States takes root, it is plausible that there will be reason and desire to extend the co-operation to sea.

This chapter explores the ways in which naval forces might be drawn into a co-operative security relationship between Russia and the United States. It first discusses the reasons why it would be desirable to expand security co-operation at sea. It then describes the existing framework of agreements and limitations that apply to Russian and US naval forces and serve as the starting point in building a more extensive regime of co-operation at sea. Finally, it explores ways in which security co-operation at sea might profitably be expanded.

II. Why expand the arms control regime at sea?

During the cold war, the opposition to naval arms control of the United States and some of its NATO allies was so strong and unwavering that many concluded it would be impossible to achieve meaningful limitation.[5] Ironically, now that the cold war has passed and the prospects for co-operation are greatly increased, movement towards an expanded arms control regime at sea may be inhibited by the argument that naval arms control is now unnecessary. After all, the Russian and US fleets are shrinking in any case, the likelihood of confrontation or crisis at sea seems low and the aggressive cold war interactions of these two navies have abated. There is little to be gained, in this argument, by spending the effort to enlarge security co-operation at sea.

While this argument is not without merit, there are nevertheless a number of reasons for thinking that it would be beneficial to do so. First is a negative consideration: the political instability in Moscow could bring to power a leader or government that is unattractive and hostile. It is worth contemplating what sorts of naval arms control measures would be desirable to have in place in the event that relations with Moscow once again became adversarial. Failing to capitalize on the present phase of extremely good relations may well come to be a cause of regret if tension resurfaces and co-operation and agreement again become difficult or impossible.

Second, while the extraordinary political transformation in East–West relations has placed the entire military relationship in a different, more benign, context, perceptions and realities have changed more slowly at sea than else-

---

[4] 'US–Russian summit documents' (note 3), p. 492.

[5] For a description of the US opposition to naval arms control, see Miller, S. E., 'Naval arms control and northern Europe: constraints and prospects', ed. S. Lodgaard, *Naval Arms Control* (Sage: London, 1990), pp. 85–87.

where.[6] The US Navy's continued embrace of a forward maritime strategy, including an anti-SSBN (nuclear-powered, ballistic missile submarine) mission, still leads, for example, to occasional accidents and mishaps.[7] In addition, those of the USA's allies poised on the maritime borders of Russia retain residual concerns about the preponderant potential threat they face; the retrenchment of the Russian Navy has only exacerbated this concern by increasing force concentrations in their neighbourhood.[8] Persisting concerns of this sort could be mollified via naval arms control.

Third, it may be possible to minimize the likelihood of mishaps, accidents and dangerous encounters, whether in normal circumstances or in crises, via improved communications and greater mutual understanding of operational preferences and requirements. Militaries are large, complex, socio-technical organizations whose normal operations afford ample opportunity for things to go wrong, and the chances of trouble are increased when they operate under stress: technologies may fail, data may be misinterpreted, commanders may get confused and flustered—which is how allies get attacked by allies, units get attacked by friendly fire and civilian airliners get shot down.[9] Moreover, even when military command systems work 'well' they may produce the 'reasonable choice of disaster', given the bias towards self-defence in the face of uncertainty.[10] Even the fact of good relations is not protection against all such possibilities; and of course the possibility of future confrontational crises cannot be dismissed altogether. Some constructive measures are already in place, but there is undoubtedly room for improvement. Co-operation to mute these problems would be most valuable in adversarial relationships, but the opportunity afforded by improving political relations to put more extensive measures in place should not be squandered—especially in view of the potential for unhappy outcomes in Moscow.[11]

---

[6] For a full explication of this point, see Miller, S. E., 'Maritime threat perceptions after the cold war', ed. L. Valki, *Changing Threat Perceptions and Military Doctrines* (Macmillan: London, 1992), pp. 112–30.

[7] As indicated by a 1992 submarine bumping incident in the Barents Sea. See also Sagan, S. D., 'Reducing the risks: a new agenda for military-to-military talks', *Arms Control Today*, July/Aug. 1991, pp. 16–21, which also makes the point that risks of accident and misunderstanding have persisted beyond the end of the cold war.

[8] See, for example, Tamnes, R. (ed.), *Soviet Reasonable Sufficiency and Norwegian Security*, Forsvarsstudier 5/1990 (Norwegian Institute for Defence Studies: Oslo, 1990); and Huitfeldt, T., Ries, T. and Øyna, G., *Strategic Interests in the Arctic*, Forsvarsstudier 4/1992 (Norwegian Institute for Defence Studies: Oslo, 1992), especially pp. 182–224.

[9] For a stimulating discussion of this issue, see Rochlin, G. I., 'Iran air flight 655 and the USS *Vincennes*: complex, large-scale military systems and the failure of control', Paper prepared for the Conference on Large-Scale Technological Systems, Berkeley, Calif., 14 June 1990. For a recent example, see 'Two US missiles mistakenly hit Turkish ship during exercise', *Boston Globe*, 2 Oct. 1992.

[10] The phrase is taken from Lanir, Z., 'The reasonable choice of disaster: the shooting down of the Libyan airliner on 21 February 1973', *The Journal of Strategic Studies*, Dec. 1989, pp. 479–93.

[11] Ball, D., 'Improving communications links between Moscow and Washington', *Journal of Peace Research*, vol. 28, no. 2 (May 1991), p. 155, makes this point very well: 'The fact that current political developments in the Soviet Union and in the US–Soviet strategic relationship are dramatically reducing the likelihood of strategic confrontation is not a reason for inaction. Rather, these developments provide an unprecedented opportunity for cooperative efforts to dramatically improve communications links between the superpowers. Posterity will not be forgiving if the opportunity is forsaken'.

Fourth, the current good relations between Russia and the United States, coupled with the ongoing transformation of the 'Soviet' military, may provide a remarkable and unprecedented opportunity to influence the internal debate over and the evolution of the Russian Navy. Establishing a continuing dialogue, including navy-to-navy contacts and possibly negotiations, could provide US input on everything from doctrine, budget, and force size to practical issues such as personnel policies and housing.

Finally, and most promisingly, expanding naval co-operation may provide the basis for fuller collaboration between the Russian and US Navies. This could encompass very specific functional measures such as mutual assistance in the event of accidents or co-operation to ensure environmentally sound disposal of nuclear-powered vessels. More ambitiously, it could entail joint peace-keeping operations—which would further imply joint training and exercises. This would truly reflect the extension of a co-operative 'new world order' to the high seas.

In short, there are grounds for seeking to incorporate the sea into the co-operative security framework that presently appears to be emerging in Russian–US relations: to have desirable measures in place in the event of negative outcomes in Moscow; and to fully capitalize on the opportunities that would arise if positive trends continue. The following discussion outlines the modest arms control regime which currently exists at sea and the ways in which it might be enlarged.

III. Existing measures

There already exist a number of arms control measures that apply at sea. Most of these impose restrictions on a particular weapon, activity or region without affecting in any fundamental way the forces or operations of the Russian and US Navies. Thus, for example, the Limited Test Ban Treaty prohibits nuclear tests at sea. The Antarctic Treaty demilitarizes the area south of latitude 60°S, including territory, ice shelves and ocean. The Seabed Treaty proscribes the placement of weapons of mass destruction on the sea floor. The Ballistic Missile Launch Agreement requires advance notification of missile launches, including submarine-launched ballistic missiles (SLBMs). In addition, strategic arms control agreements, past and prospective, place limits on the number of SSBNs. Thus, it is apparent that military activities at sea are not entirely unconstrained,[12] but none of these agreements addresses the main forces and activities of the US and Russian Navies. Accordingly, they cannot really serve as the foundation of a more co-operative superpower regime at sea.

---

[12] The texts of all the relevant treaties are conveniently reprinted in Fieldhouse, R. (ed.), SIPRI, *Security at Sea: Naval Forces and Arms Control* (Oxford University Press: Oxford, 1990), as Annexe B, 'Current international agreements relevant to naval forces and arms control', pp. 256–85. Fieldhouse also includes the Tlatelolco and Rarotonga Treaties, which aim at the denuclearization of Latin America and the South Pacific, respectively, but they are omitted from the recitation above because they are not presently overburdened with signatories.

However, there also exist a few agreements that do impinge or might impinge directly on the behaviour of the general purpose naval forces of the USA and Russia. These agreements can more reasonably be regarded as the framework on which one must build in order to enlarge the role of co-operative approaches in Russian–US relations at sea. They are few in number and relatively modest in scope, but they address legitimate sources of concern in pragmatic and useful ways.

The Incidents at Sea Agreement

The centre-piece of all discussion of existing Soviet–US arms control at sea is the 1972 Incidents at Sea Agreement.[13] Though it long languished in obscurity and was only a few years ago described as 'a virtually forgotten remnant'[14] of the arms control heyday of the early 1970s, by the end of the 1980s it had emerged as everybody's favourite naval arms control measure. Even the US Government, which has long been notorious for its lack of enthusiasm about arms control at sea, lauds the Incidents at Sea Agreement as naval arms control that 'works' and regards it as a 'model of cooperation'.[15]

The problem addressed by the agreement is very straightforward. Soviet and US naval forces often operated in proximity to one another; their ships occasionally became intermingled; they participated as uninvited 'guests' in one another's exercises; they routinely tailed the major vessels of the other side, and so on. This gave rise both to accidents (bumps, collisions and near-misses) and to harassment (intentional close approaches, shouldering and blocking, aggressive surveillance, simulated attacks and other purposeful interference with the operations of the other side).[16] There have been hundreds of such incidents over the past several decades, including well over 100 since the signing of the Incidents at Sea Agreement in 1972.[17] The ratio of accidental to intentional incident is probably impossible to know with any precision, but the larger

[13] The literature on this agreement is not extensive. The first and best serious treatment is Lynn-Jones, S., 'A quiet success for arms control: preventing incidents at sea', eds S. E. Miller and S. Van Evera., *Naval Strategy and National Security* (Princeton University Press: Princeton, 1988), pp. 359–89. See also Lynn-Jones, S., 'Applying and extending the USA–USSR Incidents at Sea Agreement', in Fieldhouse (note 12), pp. 203–19; Hilton, R. P., 'A CBM at work: the 1972 United States–USSR Incidents at Sea Agreement', in United Nations, *Naval Confidence-Building Measures*, Disarmament Topical Papers no. 4 (United Nations: New York, 1990), pp. 151–66; and Allen, T. B., 'Incidents at sea', *US Naval Institute Proceedings*, Sep. 1990, pp. 40–45. The text of the agreement may be found in Fieldhouse (note 12), pp. 256–58.

[14] Lynn-Jones, S., 'A quiet success for arms control' (note 13), p. 359.

[15] US Department of Defense, *Report on Naval Arms Control*, Apr. 1991, p. 33.

[16] For detailed treatments of this issue, see Fisher, C. S., 'Controlling high-risk US and Soviet naval operations', and Durch, W., 'Things that go bump in the bight: assessing maritime incidents, 1972–1989', both in Blechman, B. *et al.*, *The US Stake in Naval Arms Control* (Stimson Center: Washington, DC, 1990), pp. 193–244, 245–300. Also instructive is Arkin, W. M., 'Controlling superpower naval operations', in Fieldhouse (note 12), pp. 147–57.

[17] Durch (note 16), p. 249, identifies 114 incidents involving Soviet and US naval forces between 1972 and 1989.

number are thought to have been intentional, the by-products of aggressive naval behaviour.[18]

However, whether accidental or intentional, such incidents are, from an arms control perspective, undesirable.[19] They put at risk men and equipment. They can (and during the cold war did) serve as irritants in relations between Moscow and Washington, increasing tension and perceptions of hostility. They can increase the difficulty of managing crises and, in the worst case, may increase the likelihood of escalation. These would be the reasons for trying to minimize the number of incidents and the effects of those that do occur.

This is the broad purpose that the Incidents at Sea Agreement is meant to serve. It attempts to do so in several ways. First, it establishes some rules of behaviour for naval manœuvres and operations (including aircraft but excluding submarines). It mandates, in Article II, that Soviet and US naval forces 'observe strictly the letter and spirit' of the International Rules of the Road (known formally as the International Regulations for Preventing Collisions at Sea). It further requires (in Article III) that ships operate 'in all cases' so as to avoid risk of collision, and specifies that ships shall not operate in a manner that impedes formations, that surveillance take place at a safe distance and that ships not act in ways that hinder the other side's operations, particularly when launching or landing aircraft or engaging in under-way replenishment. Aircraft are enjoined to 'use the greatest caution and prudence' in approaching aircraft and ships of the other side, to forgo 'various acrobatics over ships' and to refrain from dropping objects in a manner that might be hazardous to ships. Second, certain categories of harassment are specifically prohibited. Notably, simulated attacks, whether ship against ship, aircraft against ship, or ship against aircraft, are banned. Similarly, the blinding of ships by brightly illuminating their navigation bridges is forbidden.

Third, the agreement imposes a requirement of communication between ships in a number of circumstances. Thus, ships must employ the International Code of Signals for mariners (or other agreed signals) to convey intended operations when manœuvring in sight of one another. In addition, the presence of submerged submarines should be signalled during exercises. When operating near to one another, the intention to launch aircraft should also be signalled. In 1976, special signals were worked out under the auspices of the Incidents at Sea Agreement that allow clear communication of distance, direction and intention and clear issuance of warnings; these have been published as a supplement to the International Code of Signals. In 1987, the Soviet and US Navies intro-

---

[18] Barry Blechman has concluded, for example, that 'only a small number of incidents are accidental'. As quoted in Fisher, C., 'Arms control and confidence-building in northern waters', in eds B. Blechman and G. Gunnarson, *Arms Control and Confidence-Building in Northern Waters: A Conference Report* (University of Iceland Press: Reykjavik, 1990), p. 25. See also Fisher (note 16), pp. 194, 199.

[19] As Lynn-Jones points out, there may be utility in certain forms of harassment, in terms of training, intelligence and deterrence, which means that incidents are not undesirable from every perspective. This would explain why so many intentional incidents are thought to have occurred. Introducing the arms control element sets potential costs against alleged benefits. See 'A quiet success for arms control' (note 13), p. 367.

duced bridge-to-bridge radio communications. These communications measures are important because, as Thomas Allen has commented, prior to the agreement 'US and Soviet warships and warplanes had no dependable way to warn each other about hazardous maneuvers'.[20]

Finally, the Incidents at Sea Agreement imposes obligations to exchange information and to engage in consultation. There is, first, a stipulation that three to five days warning should be provided of actions (such as exercises or test launches) that pose a danger to navigation or aircraft in flight. Additionally, there is a commitment to exchange information, through the respective naval attachés, regarding any incidents which do occur. Article IX of the agreement also mandates regular consultations on the implementation of its provisions, to be held on an annual basis (or more frequently if both sides so desire).

The Incidents at Sea Agreement seems to have been, by all available accounts, a great success. The number of incidents has declined. Such incidents as do occur are addressed in a professional environment in the annual consultations, which have taken place regularly since the agreement was signed, through the high points of Soviet–US relations and the low. Robert Hilton, a retired rear admiral and himself a participant in the Incidents at Sea consultations, reports, for example, that a diplomat on the US delegation professed himself 'utterly amazed at the frankness, professionalism, and objectivity of the exchanges during our sessions'.[21] Moreover, the agreement provides a venue for navy-to-navy contacts, and can thereby contribute to mutual professional understanding as well as adding a human dimension to the interaction of these two navies.[22]

Not insignificantly, the agreement seems to have attracted the strong support of both navies, which, after all, determine whether and how this collection of rules and consultations work. Then Chief of Naval Operations, Admiral Trost, said in 1989, for example, in the context of making the argument that most naval arms control does not make sense, 'What *does* make sense is careful and prudent conduct of operations at sea. Since 1972, when our nations signed the Incidents at Sea Agreement, we have seen a reduction in the kinds of incidents that formerly occurred at sea. Recently . . . we had the annual meeting of our respective delegations to review the past year's events. It was very cordial'.[23] Admiral Chernavin, former Commander in Chief of the Soviet Navy, likewise has given the agreement a very positive appraisal:

The Soviet Union attaches great significance to the 1972 Treaty between the Soviet government and the US government on the prevention of incidents on the open sea and in the air above it. . . . The treaty is an effective instrument for smoothing mutual rela-

---

[20] Allen (note 13) p. 42.

[21] Hilton (note 13), pp. 162–63.

[22] See, for example, Allen (note 13), p. 45, for anecdotes supporting this point. Hilton also remarks on the value of the navy–navy contact, see note 13, pp. 160–63.

[23] 'Trost responds', *US Naval Institute Proceedings*, Dec. 1989, p. 47 (emphasis in original). See also the very positive opinion expressed by former Secretary of the Navy, John Lehman, as reported in US Arms Control and Disarmament Agency (ACDA), *Arms Control and Disarmament Agreements: Texts and Histories of the Negotiations* (ACDA: Washington, DC, 1990), p. 143.

tions between the fleets of our countries. Thanks to this document, we have a constant communication channel through naval attachés for the settlement of many operational issues. The provisions for regular consultations between representatives of the Soviet and US navies also have great significance. These meetings permit the discussion of emerging problems in a businesslike manner and on a high professional level. They also . . . promote more accurate thinking by each side about the other, and overcome stereotypes that have formed over the years'.[24]

The Incidents at Sea Agreement was, in short, the most substantial and effective agreement that was reached regarding Soviet and US naval forces.[25] It is from this starting point that one might attempt to build a larger co-operative framework for Russian and US forces at sea.

The Prevention of Dangerous Military Activities Agreement

In June 1989, as a product of burgeoning military-to-military diplomacy between senior officers of the USA and the USSR, the heads of the Soviet and US militaries signed the Prevention of Dangerous Military Activities (PDMA) Agreement.[26] It is an agreement that resembles the Incidents at Sea Agreement, but applied to all armed forces—including naval forces.[27] It specifically addresses four categories of military activity that could cause dangerous incidents: (a) military operations near the territory (including the territorial waters) of the other state; (b) use of lasers, which are potentially harmful to personnel; (c) operations in areas of high threat, risk or tension (which the parties to the agreement can designate as Special Caution Areas); and (d) interference with command and control networks. The agreement creates a responsibility in each of these cases to behave with caution, to communicate so as to avoid incidents and problems, and to terminate injurious activities if notification of a problem is received from the other side. There is an obligation to exchange appropriate information when and if incidents do occur. The agreement provides detailed arrangements for communications and agreed signals among ships, aircraft and ground vehicles, including the arrangement of radio frequencies to be used and

[24] 'Chernavin responds', *US Naval Institute Proceedings*, Feb. 1989, pp. 77–78. This article, a companion to the one cited in note 23, represented part of an effort to achieve a dialogue between the Soviet and US naval communities. Admiral Trost's comments were published also in the Soviet naval journal, *Morskoi Sbornik*, Sep. 1989.

[25] A 1973 protocol to the agreement incorporates the obligation to notify non-military ships of the other side in accordance with the terms of the agreement regarding mutual safety.

[26] The best account of the genesis and content of the PDMA agreement is Campbell, K. M., 'The US–Soviet Agreement on the Prevention of Dangerous Military Activities', *Security Studies*, vol. 1, no. 1 (autumn 1991), pp. 109–31. See also Almond, H. H., 'Dangerous military activities', *US Naval Institute Proceedings*, Dec. 1989, pp. 97–99; and the essays by General Butler and Major General Bolyatko, in Butler, G., Bolyatko, A. and Sagan, S., *Reducing the Risk of Dangerous Military Activities* (Center for International Security and Arms Control: Stanford, Calif., July 1991). For a brief discussion of the naval implications, see Fisher, (note 16), p. 198. The text of the agreement may be found in Fieldhouse (note 12), pp. 278–85.

[27] See, for example, Borawski, J., 'Superpower cooperation for risk reduction at sea', *Naval Forces*, vol. 11, no. 1 (1990), p. 10, which describes the PDMA as 'building upon' and 'extending' the Incidents at Sea Agreement.

the provision to test the reliability of these communications connections. Finally, the agreement establishes a Joint Military Commission, which will meet at least once a year, and more frequently when thought necessary, to assess compliance and to consider enhancement of the agreement.

While not a naval agreement *per se*, this agreement can be regarded, in the naval context, as an augmentation of the Incidents at Sea Agreement, in the sense that it establishes rules of behaviour to another set of military activities at sea and provides, in the Joint Military Commission, another forum in which to discuss problems that might arise at sea. The PDMA entered into force on 1 January 1990, so it has not been in place long enough to judge whether it will come to be as highly regarded as the Incidents at Sea Agreement. However, it obviously contains the same elements which made the Incidents at Sea Agreement so successful: concrete and specific measures to address pragmatic operational problems, with provision for direct military consultations to deal with any difficulties that might arise.

The Stockholm CSBMs Document

In 1986, after nearly three years of negotiations, the 35 participants in the Conference on Security and Co-operation in Europe (CSCE) agreed upon a document outlining a set of politically binding confidence- and security-building measures (CSBMs).[28] These included in particular provisions for notification and observation of exercises, constraints on exercises and measures (including on-site inspection) to allow verification that constraints were being followed. For the most part, these provisions are irrelevant to the maritime environment, for independent naval activities were specifically excluded from the negotiation.[29]

However, the situation at sea is not completely untouched by the Stockholm Document, despite the failure to address independent naval activities. Thus, Annex I of the Stockholm Document defines the zone of application for CSBMs to be 'the whole of Europe as well as the adjoining sea area and air space', and notes that in the latter two 'the measures will be applicable to the military activities of all the participating States taking place there whenever these activities affect security in Europe as well as constitute a part of activities

---

[28] The best account is Goodby, J. E., 'The Stockholm Conference: negotiating a cooperative security system for Europe', eds A. George, P. Farley and A. Dallin, *US–Soviet Security Cooperation: Achievements, Failures, Lessons* (Oxford University Press: Oxford, 1988), pp. 144–72. Also useful is Darilek, R. E., 'The future of conventional arms control in Europe: a tale of two cities: Stockholm, Vienna', SIPRI, *SIPRI Yearbook 1987: World Armaments and Disarmament* (Oxford University Press: Oxford, 1987), pp. 339–54. A detailed analysis of the agreement may be found in Ben-Horin, Y., Darilek, R. E., Jas, M., Lawrence, M. and Platt, A., *Building Confidence and Security in Europe: The Potential Role of Confidence and Security Building Measures*, RAND R-3431-USDP (RAND Corporation: Santa Monica, Calif., Dec. 1986). The text of the Stockholm Document may be found in *SIPRI Yearbook 1987* (note 28), pp. 355–69.

[29] For discussion of this point, see Peters, I., 'CSBM policy after the cold war', *Aussenpolitik*, vol. 42, no. 2 (1991), pp. 132–34.

taking place within the whole of Europe . . . which they will agree to notify'.[30] In practice, this means that naval activities are notifiable whenever (but only when) they are part of combined sea-land exercises whose size and scope are notifiable under the terms of the agreement.

In addition, certain specific provisions of the Stockholm Document bear on a narrow range of naval activities. For example, the agreement requires notification of and information exchange about exercises involving amphibious landings of 3000 troops or more in the zone of application. It also obliges signatories to provide advance notification about naval ship-to-shore gunfire and other ship-to-shore support and to make available information about the level of command organizing naval force participation. Thus, while the Stockholm Document does not apply to most naval activities, it does apply conditionally to all naval forces (when involved in notifiable combined arms exercises in Europe), and it does include provisions that address a narrow slice of naval activity (amphibious exercises and ship-to-shore support). Consequently, the Stockholm Document must be regarded as part of the existing framework of arms control at sea, even if it is the case that, literally and figuratively, it only nibbles at the edges of the problem.

The Bush–Gorbachev reciprocal unilateral initiatives

On 27 September 1991, President Bush announced a dramatic set of unilateral initiatives affecting US nuclear forces and deployments. These included several measures which had the effect of denuclearizing the general purpose naval forces of the United States. The President proclaimed that:

the United States will withdraw all tactical nuclear weapons from its surface ships, attack submarines as well as those nuclear weapons associated with our land-based naval aircraft. This means removing all nuclear Tomahawk cruise missiles from US ships and submarines, as well as nuclear bombs aboard aircraft carriers. The bottom line is that under normal circumstances, our ships will not carry tactical nuclear weapons.[31]

Some of the nuclear weapons removed from US naval forces were to be destroyed; the remainder were to be removed to central storage.

On 5 October 1991, Soviet President Mikhail Gorbachev responded to Bush's speech by announcing a similarly sweeping set of initiatives to be applied to Soviet nuclear forces.[32] These included the identical measures for the denuclearization of the general purpose forces of the Soviet Navy. In combination, the Bush–Gorbachev initiatives entailed a major change in the security environment at sea; this was the most substantial act of naval arms control in the

---

[30] 'Appendix 10A. Stockholm Document', SIPRI, *SIPRI Yearbook 1987* (note 28), pp. 367–68.

[31] 'President George Bush, September 27', *Arms Control Today*, Oct. 1991, p. 4.

[32] 'President Mikhail Gorbachev, October 5', *Arms Control Today*, Oct. 1991, p. 6. A concise summary of the Bush and Gorbachev initiatives is 'Nuclear weapons: going, going', *The Economist*, 12 Oct. 1991, p. 54.

entire post-World War II era—even if it did result, not from formal negotiations, but from reciprocal unilateral initiatives.[33]

In sum, these three agreements—Incidents at Sea, Prevention of Dangerous Military Activities and the Stockholm Document—plus the Bush–Gorbachev initiatives constitute the co-operative infrastructure that presently applies to Russian and US general purpose naval forces. There is much that these measures do not do: the size and character of naval force postures are not limited by agreement, and naval operations and independent naval exercises are unconstrained. Nevertheless, it is evident that the military environment at sea is not completely unregulated and that a number of pragmatic steps have been taken to reduce potential problems associated with naval interaction and to cope with those problems that do arise. It is from this modest but sound foundation that a more ambitious arms control regime at sea would be built.

IV. Expanding security co-operation at sea

There are a number of steps, ranging from the quite modest to the extremely ambitious, that might be taken to increase the role of security co-operation at sea. The following discussion examines a number of measures that seem worthy of serious consideration. The focus, as in the rest of this volume, is not on formal arms agreements *per se* but on other useful forms of security co-operation.

Expanding the coverage of existing institutions to maritime incidents and crises

One way of enhancing security co-operation at sea would be to modify existing institutions to cover the maritime environment. Two such institutions seem appropriate for such treatment. First, there are the Nuclear Risk Reduction Centres, (NRRCs) created by a Soviet–US agreement in 1987 and in operation since 1 April 1988. As the US Arms Control and Disarmament Agency (ACDA) has explained it, 'The Centres are intended to supplement existing means of communication and provide direct, reliable, high-speed systems for the transmission of notifications and communications at the Government-to-Government level. . . . The principal function of the Centres is to exchange information and notifications as required under certain existing and possible future arms control and confidence building agreements'.[34]

These centres have heretofore been used primarily for notification of ballistic missile launches. However, Article 3 of Protocol 1 of the Nuclear Risk Reduction Centres Agreement allows the parties to use the centres for whatever pur-

---

[33] For an evaluation, see Pugh, M. C., 'Unilateral nuclear disarmament at sea', *Arms Control*, vol. 13, no. 1 (Apr. 1992), pp. 108–20 (which expresses the concern that unilateralism is a means of circumventing the need for inspection and verification measures).

[34] Arms Control and Disarmament Agency (note 23), pp. 336–37. For the text of the agreement, see pp. 338–44.

poses they deem constructive. These centres are therefore flexible instruments that could be adapted for use in the context of a more co-operative regime at sea.

Similarly, the Conflict Prevention Centre (CPC) of the CSCE, established primarily to support the implementation of the Stockholm CSBMs regime, could also be given maritime responsibilities. Indeed, the existing functions of the CPC could be construed as having naval application, since the CPC is meant to provide a mechanism for consultation in the event of unusual military activity or hazardous military incidents. However, paragraph 3 of the CPC founding document allows it to assume other functions as assigned by the Council of Foreign Ministers of the CSCE.[35] The CPC is both Eurocentric and multilateral, and hence might be regarded as a supplement rather than an alternative to the bilateral NRRCs as a mechanism for maritime communication.

What would be the point of applying these institutions to the naval situation? There are several rationales for doing so. First, these are standing institutions, unlike the Incidents at Sea gatherings or the Joint Military Committee of the PDMA, which normally meet only once annually. Hence, they would provide more regular means of interaction. Second, they would provide a level of interaction that fell between the tactical/operational, on the one hand (as provided by the PDMA) and the head of state, on the other (as provided by the Hot Line Agreement). Presumably there will be occasions when something more than ship-to-ship communications is necessary or desirable but activating the Hot Line is not warranted. Third, one or both of these institutions could be exploited for the purpose of information exchange and notification should a more extensive regime of naval CSBMs emerge.

This would be a modest but pragmatic step, one whose utility might grow as co-operation at sea expanded. For those accustomed to resisting all thoughts of naval arms control, this might be an acceptable first step.

CSBMs at sea?

As noted above, the Stockholm Agreement of 1986 established a fairly extensive set of CSBMs to be applied in Europe—a regime that has been enlarged in subsequent negotiations. The stipulated measures fall into two basic categories: those intended to increase military transparency in Europe via information exchange and notification and observation of exercises; and those that impose constraints on the size, location and frequency of exercises and major military activities, conjoined with appropriate verification procedures. The overarching purpose of this regime is to provide reassurance about military activities—such as large-scale exercises in border areas—that could cause justifiable alarm on the part of neighbouring states.

---

[35] See 'Supplementary document to give effect to certain provisions contained in the Charter of Paris for a new Europe', eds A. D. Rotfeld and W. Stützle, SIPRI, *Germany and Europe in Transition* (Oxford University Press: Oxford, 1991), p. 227.

A common refrain in recent years has been that the Stockholm CSBM regime, or portions thereof, could be extended to the maritime environment. Indeed, because structural naval arms control—negotiated limitations on the size and character of naval forces—seemed so unpromising,[36] much of the considerable attention devoted to naval arms control in the late 1980s was focused on the question of CSBMs at sea.[37] If there was to be additional arms control at sea, it seemed, the feasible measures were to be found in the category of CSBMs.

However, the subject was far from uncontroversial. Indeed, opponents of naval arms control constructed an extensive case against the application of CSBMs at sea, calling into question both the necessity and the desirability of doing so. They argued that naval forces cannot take and hold territory and that, in the Soviet–US context, they did not represent a surprise attack threat. Therefore, there was no reason why naval activities should produce 'justifiable alarm'. Further, it was argued that naval forces are already transparent, even without CSBMs, for several reasons: major naval forces are visible to national technical means of reconnaissance; the mutual, if uninvited, observation of naval deployments and exercises has long been routine; and major exercises occur on a regular schedule and are known well in advance. Hence, there is no need for CSBMs at sea.

Further, an additional three considerations were offered to suggest the undesirability of CSBMs at sea. First, there was concern that CSBMs might impede the operational flexibility of naval forces, thereby undermining their utility as instruments of national policy. Western navies are wholly committed to the principle of freedom of the seas and resist fiercely any measure that might inhibit their ability to operate when, where and how they want. Second, some CSBMs would require inspection regarded as excessively intrusive by navies and their supporters. As the US Department of Defense (DOD) put it, intrusive verification procedures 'could compromise the technologically advanced state of Western naval communications, armaments, and sensors, as well as the more intricate fleet tactics of the US and its allies'.[38] Third, it was argued that CSBMs would undermine deterrence by reducing the uncertainties posed by Western navies to Soviet war planners; in this logic, the openness and

[36] A characteristic judgement on this point is Hill, J. R., *Arms Control at Sea* (Naval Institute Press: Annapolis, 1989), which concludes on p. 154: 'The possibilities of limiting general-purpose or conventional maritime forces . . . look to be uniformly bleak'.

[37] Three substantial studies illustrate this point: Haesken, O., Kjølberg, A., Lütken, C., Omang, F. and Solstrand, R., *Confidence-Building Measures at Sea*, FFI/Rapport-88/5002 (Norwegian Defence Research Institute: Oslo, 1988); Lacy, J. L., *Within and Beyond Naval Confidence-Building: The Legacy and the Options*, RAND Note N-3122-USDP (RAND Corporation: Santa Monica, Calif., 1991); and UN, *Naval Confidence-Building Measures* (note 13). An excellent study of CSBMs in a regional setting is Ball. D., *Building Blocks for Regional Security: An Australian Perspective on Confidence- and Security-Building Measures in the Asia/Pacific Region*, Canberra Papers on Strategy and Defence, no. 83 (Strategic and Defence Studies Centre, Australian National University: Canberra, 1991).

[38] US Department of Defense, *Report on Naval Arms Control*, Submitted to the House and Senate Armed Services Committees, Apr. 1991, p. 29. (This document illustrates most of the arguments described here, and concludes on p. 32 that 'Under the guise of openness and transparency . . ., CSBMs would actually decrease the efficacy and readiness of Western maritime forces'.

transparency usually sought in CSBM regimes are more destabilizing than reassuring.[39]

While some of these arguments were overstated and others are anachronistic in the new political environment, even-handed assessments of the promise of CSBMs at sea would concede that their benefit is less than on land. Because naval forces routinely operate in proximity to one another, the maritime environment is inherently more transparent. Because, in the East-West context, war at sea would be an appendix to war on land, the risks associated with naval forces were more limited.

Nevertheless, there do appear to be some components of the Stockholm CSBM regime that ought to be acceptable in the maritime environment now, even if they were not politically viable before the end of the cold war. There would seem to be little reason, for example, why substantial information exchange (provision of annual exercise calendars, for example) cannot routinely and regularly take place. The reasons for opposing exchange of observers at exercises should be much less compelling in the new political context. Similarly, it ought to be possible to design constraints on naval exercises that provide reassurance about routine and innocuous activities without interfering unduly with the flexibility and utility of naval power in routine deployments or crisis responses.[40] Another possibility would be to discuss the idea of declaring temporary safety and exercise zones when large-scale naval activities are under way, for the purpose of reducing the risk of accident. Even if the benefits of putting such measures in place are limited, the reasons for not doing so have disappeared with the end of the cold war.

By the same token, it can be asked what the purpose of CSBMs is in the new environment. Why are CSBMs at sea needed when relations between Russia and the USA are good? One answer is that it may be sensible to develop a maritime CSBMs regime against the possibility that US–Russian relations could sour—an eventuality that would seem likely if politics in Moscow should take an unfortunate turn. It is probably sensible to arrange now, in the current hospitable environment, measures whose value would be greatest if hostile relations should revive. Another reason would be to strengthen the promising but still tenuous security relations between Moscow and Washington and to promote the habit of security co-operation. A further consideration is that, while the USA and its Western allies presently have little need for reassurance, the same may not be true in Russia. There are clearly political forces in Moscow which doubt the West's intentions are entirely benign in its eagerness to contribute to the shrinking and reshaping of Russia's military forces; CSBMs at sea might be one way of helping to neutralize Russia's doubters. In short, while naval

---

[39] This argument is clearly articulated in O'Rourke, R., *Naval Arms Control*, CRS Issue Brief IB89132, Congressional Research Service, 25 Oct. 1989, p. 10.

[40] See, for example, the thoughtful discussion of the application of the Stockholm model to sea in Hill, J. R., 'Bilateral and regional approaches to confidence-building measures', Paper presented at the Conference on Arms Control and Confidence-Building in Northern Waters, Akureyri, Iceland, 14–16 Aug. 1990. See also Hill's *Arms Control at Sea* (note 36), pp. 190–95.

CSBMs are not a panacea and their value should not be overstated, there are constructive purposes that they can serve.

Military-to-military relations I: doctrine and force posture

During the latter years of the Gorbachev era, military-to-military diplomacy emerged as an increasingly prominent component of US–Soviet security relations.[41] This has entailed everything from port visits to meetings of senior military officers. The PDMA was one tangible product of this new diplomacy, but the less tangible results of this process seem to have been equally impressive. General Butler, for example, reflecting on his experience as head of the US negotiating team for the PDMA talks, emphasized 'the confidence that we gained and the insights that we shared about operational patterns and procedures, which have unlocked our understanding of each other. It so widened the regime of contacts as to have lifted us to an entirely new level of interaction'.[42] Similarly, the US DOD, even in the context of mounting a comprehensive critique of naval arms control, observed that navy-to-navy contacts, if developed, would 'lay a foundation for mutual understanding that will facilitate resolution of concerns about the two navies'.[43]

These interactions can be (and are being) continued and could be expanded to serve as a vehicle for discussion of a whole range of issues. One obvious topic for discussion is naval doctrine. During the cold war, Western concerns about Soviet naval doctrine and Soviet alarm about US naval doctrine were a chronic source of friction; and there were recurrent worries that the interaction of these two doctrines produced undesirable risks and dangers, especially in crisis situations.[44] There is already multilateral precedent for doctrine discussions in the military-to-military context: the CSCE has held two Seminars on Military Doctrine in Vienna in 1990 and 1991.[45] These seminars provided an occasion for military officers from participating CSCE states to describe their national military doctrines and the force posture implications thereof; and they were meant to provide an opportunity for discussion of the defensive restructuring of forces.

US–Russian navy-to-navy discussions on doctrine could build on this precedent, but could well be even more fruitful because bilateral talks would avoid the complications associated with several dozen participants, because the talks would be more narrowly focused on naval doctrine and because the discussions could be made part of a continuing, regular dialogue between the two navies

[41] See, for example, Campbell, K., 'The soldier's summit', *Foreign Policy*, no. 75 (summer 1989), pp. 76–91.
[42] Butler, G., 'Negotiating the Dangerous Military Activities Agreement', in Butler, Bolyatko and Sagan (note 26), p. 6.
[43] US Department of Defense (note 38), p. 36.
[44] See, for example, Posen, B. R., 'Inadvertent nuclear war? escalation and NATO's northern flank', in eds Miller and Van Evera (note 13), pp. 332–58.
[45] See Lachowski, Z., 'The Second Vienna Seminar on Military Doctrine', SIPRI, *SIPRI Yearbook 1992: World Armaments and Disarmament* (Oxford University Press: Oxford, 1992), pp. 496–97.

rather than once every year or two military 'summits'. These discussions could enhance understanding of past doctrinal orientations and could clarify the recent evolution of their naval doctrines. This could be especially important to the Russian Navy, whose current doctrine—if one exists—is far from clear; it will likely be struggling in the coming months and years to redefine its role and mission in the post-Soviet period. Hence, an ongoing joint study of alternative naval strategies could be especially opportune and potentially influential in informing the internal naval debate in Russia. One sensible topic of discussion would be the design of Russian and US naval doctrines that allowed each to fulfil its essential maritime missions without bringing the two navies into collision; in the new era this would seem to be a feasible objective—at least, certainly one worth exploring together.[46]

Similarly, both the US and Russian Navies are in the midst of adjusting, both to the end of the cold war and to shrinking military budgets. It is clear that they are going to reduce their forces substantially in the coming years. This will happen whether or not there is navy-to-navy dialogue on the issue. However, since each navy's calculation of its requirements will be determined in part by perceptions of the other, explicit discussion of the evolution of the two fleets could well facilitate force planning on both sides.

Military-to-military relations II: politics, organization and management

The Russian Navy is in the middle of a wrenching transformation. This has only partly to do with a shrinking budget and a shrinking fleet. If all goes well in Russia, it will also have to reorient itself in a democratic polity. This raises fundamental questions of civil–military relations, and there is no reason to expect that this organization will have any expertise or experience in how to comport itself in a democratic setting. The Russian Navy may well also have to transform itself from a conscript-based to a volunteer-based personnel system. This raises fundamental issues of management. It seems likely that every aspect of the Russian Navy, including personnel recruitment, payment schedules, training, provision of housing and medical care, and so on, will need to be reconsidered and probably restructured. Anyone who has had the opportunity to visit a Russian base will attest that an enormous task lies ahead in creating an attractive career path in the Navy that will be competitive with the civilian sector in obtaining and retaining personnel.

While care should be taken to avoid the presumption that the US Navy is the end of wisdom on all these questions, it does possess a tremendous amount of experience, and has dealt with considerable effectiveness, with just these sorts of issues. In the context of a vigorous and growing naval dialogue, it might be

---

[46] The one remaining area in which the Russian and US Navies have unavoidably colliding interests is strategic anti-submarine warfare (ASW). The United States will regard Russian strategic submarines as a potential nuclear threat to the USA and will therefore continue to pursue strategic ASW capabilities against them; and Russia will undoubtedly continue to regard the strategic submarines as a critical part of its nuclear deterrent, and therefore seek to protect them.

possible to impart this experience to the Russian Navy so as to influence or assist its inevitable effort to remake itself.

The suggestions for navy-to-navy dialogue in this and the previous section are not novel. Indeed, much of what is suggested here has already been undertaken, to one extent or another, in a variety of official and unofficial, formal and informal settings.[47] So what is required is not a sharp departure from current practice, but continued efforts to find constructive uses of the continuing dialogue.

Military-to-military relations III: discussing rules of engagement

Military forces in operational deployments are provided a set of guidelines—known as rules of engagement—which determine the circumstances under which they can use force, the amount and character of the force that can be used and the targets against which they can use force.[48] The rules of engagement can be adjusted, made more restrictive or more permissive, depending on the perceived risks and dangers of the situation in which the forces are operating. In dangerous settings, in which the risk of conflict is high, rules of engagement can be critically important instruments of crisis management because they determine thresholds which would trigger the use of force.[49] They therefore bring into play what Alexander George has described as 'the tension experienced in many crises between relevant military considerations and the equally, if not more urgent requirements for managing and terminating such confrontations before they escalate to war or to higher levels of violence'.[50]

The dilemma in setting rules of engagement is that restrictive guidelines may handicap the ability of forces to defend themselves, while permissive guidelines may result in unwanted and potentially escalatory use of force. Thus, in 1987, the USS *Stark* was deployed in the Persian Gulf under rules of engagement that emphasized the avoidance of provocative incidents and encouraged commanding officers to be fully confident in their identification of targets before firing; this contributed to the *Stark*'s tragic failure to defend itself against an Exocet missile attack, resulting in the death of 37 US sailors.[51] On the other hand, a year later the USS *Vincennes*, operating in the Persian Gulf under more permissive rules of engagement promulgated after the *Stark* disaster, shot down

[47] For example, the US Naval War College, in co-operation with the Center for Foreign Policy Development at Brown University, has hosted discussions with the Russian Navy on doctrine. Similarly, Professor Robert Blackwill of Harvard's Kennedy School of Government has run a series of seminars for senior Russian military officers on subjects such as civil–military relations in a democracy.

[48] For an excellent discussion, see Sagan, S., 'Rules of engagement', *Security Studies*, vol. 1, no. 1 (autumn 1991), pp. 78–108. See also Roach, J, A., 'Rules of engagement', *Naval War College Review*, Jan.–Feb. 1983, pp. 46–55; and Parks, W. H., 'Righting the rules of engagement', *US Naval Institute Proceedings*, May 1989, pp. 83–93.

[49] This theme is explored in Hayes, B. C., *Naval Rules of Engagement: Management Tools for Crisis*, RAND Note N-2963-CC (RAND Corporation: Santa Monica, Calif., July 1989).

[50] George, A. L., 'Crisis management: the interaction of political and military considerations', *Survival*, Sep./Oct. 1984, p. 224. George's discussion of the rules of engagement issue is found on pp. 227–28.

[51] Sagan (note 48), pp. 94–97; Vlahos, M., 'The *Stark* report', *US Naval Institute Proceedings*, May 1988, pp. 64–67.

an Iranian Air commercial flight, in the mistaken belief that it was a hostile military aircraft; in this case, the commander, prompted by new rules of engagement and with the *Stark* incident undoubtedly in mind, chose tragically to err on the side of safety.[52]

Balancing restrictiveness and permissiveness in naval rules of engagement is rendered especially difficult by the fact that there is, in many tactical settings, a pronounced first-strike advantage in naval warfare.[53] Consequently, restraint can be had only by accepting the risk of military disadvantage.[54] This means that naval forces deployed in threatening situations—a fairly common occurrence—will always be walking a fine and risky line.

Mutual appreciation of this sensitive issue is undoubtedly desirable. This would probably be most valuable in confrontational situations: understanding the operational perceptions and thresholds of the other side could help contain risks and prevent inadvertent triggering of the use of force. However, even if the Russian and US Navies are operating together (about which, more later) it is desirable that there be some harmonization of views about rules of engagement—if only to prevent those of one power from dragging the other into unwanted escalation. Accordingly, another component of military-to-military relations between these two navies could be an ongoing joint study group on rules of engagement.

Accident assistance

Occasional accidents are facts of life in operating naval vessels.[55] Indeed, during the cold war, there were more than 1200 known naval accidents and undoubtedly hundreds more of which there is no public record.[56] Because naval forces often operate near or intermingled with formations of the other side or near to the territory of other states, it will sometimes be the case that the most immediate or best source of help in the event of accident will be provided by the other party.

During the cold war, however, there was reluctance to call for help from other parties, for fear of revealing technical or operational secrets. In one recent

[52] Sagan (note 48), pp. 97–101; Friedman, N., 'The *Vincennes* incident', *US Naval Institute Proceedings*, May 1989, pp. 72–79. For the commander's perspective on the incident, see Rogers, W., Rogers, S. and Gregston, G., *Storm Center: The USS Vincennes and Iran Air Flight 655* (Naval Institute Press: Annapolis, Md., 1992).

[53] See Hughes, W. P., *Fleet Tactics: Theory and Practice* (Naval Institute Press: Annapolis, Md., 1986), which describes 'attack effectively first' as the 'fundamental maxim' of naval tactics (see pp. *xv*, 25).

[54] A protest against the handicap of restrictive rules of engagement is Crews, E. 'ROEs that kill', *US Naval Institute Proceedings*, Sep. 1988, p. 121. See also Bunn, G., 'International law and the use of force in peacetime: do US ships have to take the first hit?', *Naval War College Review*, May/June 1986, pp. 69–80, which analyses the conditions under which the general rule of self-defence permits firing first.

[55] For recent examples, see Sanger, D., 'Two explosions and fire hit a US carrier off Japan', *International Herald Tribune*, 22 June 1990; and 'Blast said to kill officer on Russian atomic sub', *Boston Globe*, 4 June 1992.

[56] The best source on this subject is Arkin, W. and Handler, J., *Naval Accidents, 1945–1988*, Neptune Papers no. 3, (Greenpeace: Washington, DC, June 1989), which identifies 1276 known accidents (p. 78) and speculates (p. 1) that many hundreds more are undocumented, largely due to the secrecy of and the lack of data from the Soviet Union.

case in April 1989, for example, a nuclear-powered Soviet submarine, the *Komsomolets*, caught fire in waters north of Norway.[57] The crew struggled unsuccessfully for six hours to bring the fire under control, all the while desperately appealing to the Soviet naval complex in Murmansk, 806 kilometres away, for help. When *Komsomolets* finally sank, most of the crew escaped, but half the 'survivors' perished in the frigid waters of the Barents Sea before help arrived—some seven hours after the emergency began. Had Soviet authorities sought assistance from Norway, which had assets closest to the scene of the accident, it is likely that most of these lives would have been saved. While this particular example does not involve the United States, it does illustrate especially well the advantage of having in place some sort of framework for providing assistance when accidents occur.

Whatever inhibitions previously existed about providing or accepting assistance in response to accidents, they are surely not appropriate in the current era of US–Russian relations. Hence, this is a topic ripe for explicit discussion, probably in the military-to-military setting. At a minimum, assurances ought to be exchanged that help will be provided and accepted when needed. Perhaps this could be codified in an agreement. This could be done, for example, as an expansion of, or in a protocol to, the PDMA, whose extensive provisions for communications among Russian and US forces could be exploited for this purpose. In some regions, as the example above indicates, these bilateral arrangements would be sensibly augmented by multilateral co-operation—with Norway in northern European waters, with Japan in the north Pacific. An arrangement of this sort would build on the pragmatic, operationally oriented tradition of the Incidents at Sea and the Prevention of Dangerous Military Activities agreements.

Military–environmental co-operation at sea

There is growing understanding that military activities can produce adverse environmental consequences, and that the reduction and restructuring of the cold war military establishments will leave behind some enormous problems in need of cleaning up.[58] This will be true for both Russia and the United States, and can apply at sea as well as on land. This leads to at least two potential avenues for maritime co-operation.

First, it is already evident that there are major environmental problems associated with the past behaviour of the Soviet Navy. Much of the concern derives from the revelation that for several decades the Soviet Navy disposed of its

---

[57] Several harrowing accounts of this incident exist in English. See in particular Carley, W. M., 'Inferno at sea: how secret Soviet sub and its nuclear arms sank north of Norway', *Wall Street Journal*, 14 Mar. 1990; and Cherkasin, N., 'Fire down below', *Soviet Weekly*, 28 June 1990, pp. 8–10. See also 'Forty-two lost as Soviet submarine sinks', *The Guardian*, 16 Apr. 1989; and Handler, J., Wickenheiser, A. and Arkin, W., *Naval Safety 1989: The Year of the Accident*, Neptune Papers no. 4 (Greenpeace: Washington, DC, 1990).

[58] A vivid illustration of the point is Shulman, S., *The Threat at Home: Confronting the Toxic Legacy of the US Military* (Beacon Press: Boston, Mass., 1992).

radioactive wastes by dumping them into the waters of the Barents and Kara Seas—a practice that apparently ended only in 1991.[59] The deposited material is reported to include weapon-grade plutonium, spent reactor fuel and even reactors and parts from retired nuclear-powered submarines. If properly undertaken, this practice would not necessarily lead to severe environmental problems, but there are worrying indications that lax safety standards were followed. Other environmental risks may result from nuclear weapons or nuclear power plants that have been left on the ocean floor as a result of accidents.[60]

It will clearly be a large and expensive task to assess the extent of the problem, to determine the best response and to take corrective action.[61] Given the economic crisis in Russia, the money necessary for this undertaking is likely to be lacking. Moreover, it is far from clear that Russia possesses an abundance of expertise on the issue of environmental clean-up.[62] Accordingly, this would appear to be an issue ripe for international co-operation. Russia's northern neighbours, particularly Norway and Finland, are deeply concerned about these issues (including, but not limited to, the military environmental question) and have already begun to involve themselves, via joint studies and financial support, in helping to address them.[63] The USA could sensibly do likewise.

[59] A lengthy and informative expose on this issue is Tyler, P., 'Soviets secret nuclear dumping raises fears for Arctic waters', *New York Times*, 4 May 1992. See also Trevelyan, M., 'USSR is said to have sent atomic waste into the sea', *Boston Globe*, 24 Sep. 1991; and 'Russia Sea called a nuclear dump', *Boston Globe*, 26 Feb. 1992. For an overview of this issue, see Heininen, L., 'Environmental threats of military presence in northern waters and the Arctic', ed. L. Heininen, *Arctic Environmental Problems*, Tampere Peace Research Institute, Occasional Papers no. 41 (Tampere Peace Research Institute: Tampere, Finland, 1990), pp. 42–69. See also Schoenfeld, G., 'Underwatergate: a submarine Chernobyl', *The New Republic*, 27 Apr. 1992, pp. 20–21, which describes an instance of accidental nuclear contamination.

[60] Note, for example, the concern that the *Komsomolets* submarine lost in the 1989 accident might be leaking radiation. For expressions of concern, see 'Sunken Soviet sub is found to be leaking radiation', *Boston Globe*, 24 Nov. 1992; and Gordon, M., 'Russians asked US aid to raise lost atom sub', *New York Times*, 25 Nov. 1992. Disputing this allegation are 'Norway: Soviet sub no threat', *Boston Globe*, 25 Nov. 1992; and Chandler, D., 'Scientists study risks of Soviet radioactive waste dumped in sea', *Boston Globe*, 27 Nov. 1992. A related but distinct set of concerns is associated with the Soviet nuclear test site on Novya Zemlya, a large island that marks the eastern boundary of the Barents Sea. There has been worried speculation that Soviet safety standards were not as rigorous as they should have been, and that radioactive emissions from Soviet underground nuclear tests may have caused contamination in northern waters. See, for example, 'Soviet nuclear testing in the Arctic', *The Canadian Arms Control Centre Barometer*, summer 1991, p. 1.

[61] A sense of the potential scale of the task can be gathered by way of comparison with the problems the USA faces in cleaning up its own military-related nuclear messes. See, for example, Office of Technology Assessment, *Complex Cleanup: The Environmental Legacy of Nuclear Weapons Production* (US Government Printing Office: Washington, DC, 1991).

[62] Dr Willy Ostreng, Director of Norway's Nansen Institute, which has interacted with Russia on these issues, has commented, for example: 'They do not have the resources and they are facing a major environmental challenge and they do not know how to handle it'. Quoted in Tyler (note 59).

[63] See, for example, 'Norway to fund Soviet cleanup', *The Guardian*, 12 Sep. 1990; and Tyler, P., 'On Norway's border, Russian Arctic in crisis', *New York Times*, 10 May 1992. On Norway's involvement in the naval dumping problem, see Tyler (note 59). The Finns have also been very active in arranging environmental co-operation with Russia. See, for example, *Agreement between the Government of the Republic of Finland and the Government of the Russian Federation on Cooperation in Murmansk, the Republic of Karelia, in St. Petersburg and the Leningrad Area*, Press Release no. 26/7 (Ministry for Foreign Affairs: Helsinki, Finland, 3 Feb. 1992), which specifies the 'solving of environmental problems' as one of the areas for co-operation. Illustrative of the type of project being undertaken is *Conceptual Design of Safety Improvements of Kola Nuclear Power Station* (Ministry of Trade and Industry, Energy Department: Helsinki, Finland, 9 Apr. 1992). Also noteworthy is *Environmental Priority Action Pro-*

Second, in the coming years, as the post-cold war Russian and US Navies shrink, a substantial number of nuclear-powered vessels will be retired. Russia, for example, may retire as many as 50 nuclear-powered submarines in the next few years. The disposition of retired nuclear-powered vessels has been a subject of international controversy, in particular because disposal at sea has been a preferred solution.[64] Some argue that properly prepared decommissioned nuclear-powered vessels are safely sunk in the ocean, while others believe that nuclear dumping at sea should be reduced to zero to preclude any further risk of contamination.[65] Embracing the latter view necessitates, of course, finding some alternative environmentally sound way of decommissioning nuclear-powered vessels. Since this is a difficult and expensive problem that both the US and Russian Navies will inevitably face, this issue could profit from explicit discussion, joint studies and co-operation in eliminating retired vessels. Working together to prevent future environmental messes is just as sensible as collaborating in the clean-up of past messes. This could be a large and long-term undertaking.

Joint exercises and operations

The notion of 'strategic partnership' contained in the Charter for American–Russian Partnership and Friendship implies more than just remedial co-operation to belatedly apply CSBMS at sea or to address specific problems—useful though such steps be. It suggests that there may emerge areas in which US and Russian interests are harmonized and in which joint naval action is useful or desirable. This leads directly to consideration of joint exercises, which are probably necessary if collaborative naval operations are to be undertaken in any serious way.

Joint exercises would serve at least two purposes. First, they should increase mutual understanding and dampen mutual fears.[66] The protracted isolation of these navies from one another contributed to 'worst case' mentalities in both directions, and probably allowed exaggerated worries to fester. Joint exercises should hasten the process of breaking down such images and inoculate against a further outbreak of fear-based, worst-casing.

Second, and more tangibly, naval collaboration—for example, in peace-keeping or collective security operations—is not easily done on an impromptu basis. To an extent that is often underappreciated, naval forces that have not practised together cannot operate smoothly together. In the Persian Gulf War,

---

gramme for Leningrad, Leningrad Region, Karelia and Estonia (Ministry of the Environment: Helsinki, Finland, Sep. 1991).

[64] See, for example, Hunt, J. 'Dispute on submarine dumping', *Financial Times*, 30 Oct. 1989, which reports on the deliberations of the London Dumping Convention on whether disposal of submarines at sea violates the international moratorium on disposal of nuclear waste at sea.

[65] An extensive analysis of the issue is Eriksen, V. O., *Sunken Nuclear Submarines: A Threat to the Environment?* (Oxford University Press: Oxford, 1990).

[66] It should be noted that the US Navy's evolving strategy has already de-emphasized global war with Moscow and is focusing instead on regional security challenges. See 'US Navy adopts new sea strategy', *Boston Globe*, 2 Oct. 1992.

for example, the US Navy experienced difficulty communicating among its own battle groups, because it does not exercise formations as large as that assembled in the Gulf and accordingly command and control procedures were not in place; co-ordination with the other US services proved problematic as well.[67] Similarly, co-ordination with the USA's NATO allies was not always smooth, although these navies do periodically exercise together.[68]

Yet multinational naval operations of one form or another—including the possibility of both Russian and US participation—have attracted growing interest, not least because of the experience in the Persian Gulf War and because of the hope that the United Nations can come to play a more effective role in the post-cold war environment. Several proposals illustrate the point. British scholar Gwyn Prins, among others, has suggested the creation of a UN Standing Naval Force (UNSNF)[69] A recent study of NATO's maritime future emphasizes the need for multinational naval response;[70] the NATO and Western European Union naval deployments in the Adriatic in response to the crisis in Bosnia suggest the practical relevance of the idea. UN disarmament specialist Derek Boothby sees promise in the idea of regional and subregional multinational naval co-operation.[71] Nothing in the idea of multinational naval co-operation inherently requires both US and Russian participation, but joint US–Russian naval involvement in maritime peace-keeping or collective security operations would certainly be compatible with the new character of their relations and could be politically, and perhaps even militarily, attractive.

In short, Russia and the United States could undertake occasional, perhaps even regular exercises, with an eye to preserving good relations and preparing for joint peace-keeping operations. In time, if good relations deepen, even joint planning for multinational naval action could take place. These ideas, which would have been dismissed as preposterous only a short time ago, are not very far-sighted even today. The first joint exercise between the Russian and US Navies has already taken place.[72] Further, the US and Russian Navies have already participated together, albeit on a modest scale, in the same operation, since the USSR contributed several vessels to the Gulf War coalition.[73] Looking

[67] See Moore, M., 'In Gulf War, US services also fought rivalry', *International Herald Tribune*, 11 June 1991.

[68] See, for example, Marlowe, L., 'Ships near-collision raises coordination fears', *Financial Times*, 3 Sep. 1990; and White, D., 'A multinational force in name alone', *Financial Times*, 9 Aug. 1990.

[69] Prins, G., 'The United Nations and peacekeeping in the post-cold war world: the case of naval power', *Bulletin of Peace Proposals*, vol. 22, no. 2 (June 1991), p. 144. See also Staley, II, R. S., *The Wave of the Future: The United Nations and Naval Peacekeeping* (Lynne Rienner: Boulder, Colo., 1992); and Sands, J. I., 'Blue hulls: multinational naval cooperation and the United States', unpublished MS, Center for Naval Analyses, 10 Nov. 1992.

[70] Prina, L. E., 'CSIS report seeks new course for NATO', *Sea Power*, Oct. 1992, p. 23.

[71] Boothby, D., 'Sailing under new colors', *US Naval Institute Proceedings*, July 1992, p. 50.

[72] See 'US, Russian Navies to break the ice in joint Arctic exercise', *Boston Globe*, 2 July 1992. The brief exercise with Russian vessels based at Severomorsk, on the Barents Sea, was named 'Operation Northern Handshake'.

[73] See Posen, B. R., 'Military mobilization in the Persian Gulf conflict', SIPRI, *SIPRI Yearbook 1991: World Armaments and Disarmament* (Oxford University Press: Oxford, 1991), pp. 646, 650.

to the possibility of joint operations in the future would thus not be unprecedented, but rather would build on these modest beginnings.

V. Conclusion

To a large extent, naval arms control was left out of the Soviet–US arms control framework. There is no reason why this need remain true in the context of US–Russian relations. While the passing of the intense rivalry between Washington and Moscow may have made security co-operation at sea less urgent, it also has created an unprecedented opportunity to put co-operative measures in place. The purpose is not to pursue arms control for the sake of arms control. Rather, the discussion above has tried to suggest that there are still constructive steps that can be taken, despite the end of the cold war. Some of the steps would be of greatest value if adversarial relations were to return; but now is the time to initiate such steps. Other of the measures examined here build on the premise of co-operative US–Russian security relations, and would contribute to that end by increasing mutual understanding and facilitating the transition of both navies to the post-cold war era. The most ambitious possibilities envision at least some limited degree of US–Russian collaboration at sea, including the prospect of joint naval peace-keeping operations. Thus, if a strategic partnership between Russia and the United States should emerge, naval forces could be incorporated into the fabric of their security co-operation.

15. Defence planning: the potential for transparency and co-operation

Judyth L. Twigg

I. Introduction

An earlier chapter in this volume[1] proposed that the United States and the members of the Commonwealth of Independent States (CIS) join with the nations of Europe to form a Eurasian–Atlantic security community that would institutionalize joint management of the military aspects of the transition from the cold war to a new world order. This type of co-operative security arrangement is important for two reasons. First, it is not at all clear that the collapse of the Soviet Union will necessarily erase the potential for political or military factions in both the USA and former Soviet republics to perceive real military threats from the other side.[2] A well-established regime of co-operative security can dramatically reduce the possibility of this type of mutual misperception, and can also diminish the political legitimacy of any individual or group attempting to create or invoke a foreign devil for any purpose.

Second, and probably more important, is the need to create a stable process of change now that events in the realm of CIS politics are proceeding at such a dizzying pace. The former commander of US Army forces in Europe may have put it best: the chief enemy for the West at this point is no longer the USSR or the Warsaw Treaty Organization (WTO), but instability and uncertainty.[3] Currently it is impossible to ascertain whether the breaking up of the Soviet Union will entail greater or fewer security risks to Europe and the rest of the world, since the CIS itself has yet to sort out the solutions to its staggering array of problems. A system of co-operative security encompassing the USA and the Commonwealth nations can help ensure that the transition to whatever the future holds is a stable one. Indeed, US contributions to the process of military reform in the former USSR could help cement a lasting security alliance between the two former superpower adversaries.

Chapter 13 deals with the new US–CIS military relationship in terms of actual forces deployed in the field. Elements of the defence planning process—decision making for military doctrine and strategy, force planning, military

[1] See Newmann, W. W. and Twigg, J. L., 'Building a Eurasian–Atlantic security community: co-operative management of the military transition', chapter 13 in this volume.

[2] Russian military officers remain particularly concerned about US attempts to exploit its advantage in military high technology. See Rebrov, M., 'Ne skudeyet ruka dayushchego' ['Don't discard the hand of the future'], *Krasnaya Zvezda*, 17 Sep. 1991, p. 3 (in Russian).

[3] Saint, C., 'For NATO, concerns stay', *New York Times*, 4 Sep. 1991, p. A7.

education, defence budget formulation, the weapon procurement process and related issue areas—are equally critical to the creation of a common security community. This chapter discusses the means by which aspects of the defence planning process might be incorporated into the US–CIS co-operative security agenda.

Two categories of issue area are addressed here: the tangibles and intangibles of defence planning. The former concerns decisions with concrete, verifiable manifestations—force structure and weapon procurement. The latter includes such considerations as military budgets, doctrine, strategy and education which, although involving primarily declaratory policies without physical resultant, still contribute significantly to threat perception.[4]

Within each of these categories two types of security co-operation are discussed: transparency and assistance. Making defence planning more transparent brings openness to processes which were shrouded with a veil of secrecy during the cold war that exacerbated mutual misperception and mistrust. Increased transparency would benefit not only the US–CIS security relationship, but also relations between the members of the CIS as they carve up the assets of the former Soviet military. US military assistance to the defence planning processes of the Commonwealth nations is necessary if the former Soviet military structures are to be reoriented towards co-operation with their former enemies and placed under democratic civilian control.

In order to lay the groundwork for this discussion, it is necessary first to examine the parameters of the US and Soviet/CIS defence budgeting and procurement processes.

II. Budget and procurement processes

The US defence budget and procurement process

The US decision process for military budgets and procurement is well known.[5] The military budget sequence operates in conjunction with the overall federal budgetary cycle. The formation of the national budget begins almost a year before it is submitted to Congress. During that year the Office of Management and Budget (OMB) engages in evaluation and negotiation with other federal agencies. In December the President makes a final decision on economic policy based on the OMB's recommendations, and final changes are made in agency budgets, including defence, in accordance with that policy.

The basis for the annual budget negotiated between the Department of Defense (DOD) and the OMB—and ultimately the budget submission to Congress—is established within the framework of five-year defence plans

---

[4] On this point, see Naumann, K., 'Doctrines and force structures', eds I. M. Cuthberson and O. Volten, *The Guns Fall Silent: The End of the Cold War and the Future of Conventional Disarmament*, Occasional Paper Series no. 17 (Westview Press: Boulder, Colo., 1990), pp. 51–66.

[5] For details on the budget and procurement process, see Weida, W. J. and Gertcher, F. L., *The Political Economy of National Defense* (Westview Press: Boulder, Colo., 1987).

(FYDP). The annual planning and programming debate formulating these plans within the DOD centres around how military programme elements relate to current defence objectives and how defence funds should be allocated to these programme elements.

Having taken the submissions of the DOD and other federal agencies into account, the President sends a final budget proposal to Congress on the 15th day after Congress convenes in January.[6] Throughout the spring and summer, congressional budget, authorization and appropriations committees hold hearings and conduct analyses resulting in a final budget submission in time for the beginning of the fiscal year (FY) on 1 October. Once funds are allocated, the weapon procurement process—consisting of the standard phases of basic research, applied research, concept formulation, exploratory development, advanced development, prototype testing, serial production and deployment—can proceed.[7]

The Soviet/CIS defence budget and procurement process

It now appears as though there will be no single CIS military budget and weapon procurement process, since several of the newly independent republics have explicitly rejected the option of remaining within a central CIS military structure. Although the types of co-operative security arrangements discussed here are potentially applicable at either the overall CIS or republic level, for reasons of simplicity the discussion here focuses on the Russian republic as a prototype.

Before the attempted coup in August 1991 and the subsequent disintegration of central Soviet economic structures, the Soviet military budget formulation and procurement process involved inter-agency negotiations over the allocation of scarce resources similar to those in the USA, the major differences being the still relatively closed nature of the process and the dramatically reduced role of the legislature.[8] The Soviet process was best characterized as occurring at three distinct decision levels: (*a*) the top political leadership, including the Politburo and Defence Council; (*b*) intermediate institutions such as the Ministry of Defence, the General Staff and its chief, and the state economic planning agencies; and (*c*) lower level actors, including the military services and industrial ministries. It was assumed by Western analysts that the budget process in

---

[6] The FYDP is updated three times annually: in January to reflect the January Presidential submission to Congress, in May to reflect programme proposals by the individual military services, and in September to reflect service budget estimates from decisions made by the Secretary of Defense on service programme proposals.

[7] The stages of this complex process, of course, have been characterized and labelled in a variety of different ways. See Long, F. A. and Reppy, J., *The Genesis of New Weapons* (Pergamon Press: New York, 1980); and Long, F. A. and Rathjens, G. W., *Arms, Defense Policy, and Arms Control* (W. W. Norton: New York, 1975).

[8] For a description and analysis of the Soviet process, see Meyer, S. M., 'Economic constraints in Soviet military decision making', eds H. S. Rowen and C. Wolf, *The Impoverished Superpower: Perestroika and the Soviet Military Burden* (Institute for Contemporary Studies Press: San Francisco, Calif., 1990), pp. 201–19.

the Soviet executive branch took place within a time-frame similar to that in the USA, with the top level setting a cap on overall resource allocations for defence as opposed to other budget priorities; the intermediate-level actors determining the shape of distribution of those resources among military missions; and the lower levels, within those constraints, subdividing the apportionments among individual weapon programmes.[9]

The role of the legislative branch in the USSR evolved into something more than a rubber stamp of decisions already made by the executive only at the very end of the 1980s. At the very least, Supreme Soviet committees seem to have played an important role in determining the overall size of the 1991 Soviet defence budget. Apparently the initial 1991 Ministry of Defence proposal for defence spending amounted to 98.6 billion roubles. During Supreme Soviet debates on national expenditure, the Committee on Defence and State Security (CDSS), heavily populated with representatives from the military and military–industrial sector, objected that this sum was not sufficient to maintain a reliable defence, and proposed an increase of 1.1 billion to 99.7 billion roubles. The Deputy Chairman of the CDSS argued that levels of spending lower than that target figure would result in 70 000 lost jobs and force industrial profits down by 240 million roubles, costing the state 110 million roubles in tax revenues. However, citing pressing budget deficits and the general economic crisis, the Planning, Budget and Finance Committee decided to ignore the protestations of what its chairman labelled the defence industry's 'clients' and reduced allocations for defence by two billion roubles. The resulting figure of 96.6 billion roubles was indeed eventually approved by the Supreme Soviet as a whole.[10] After the failure of the attempted coup, the relationship between the reformist executive and conservative legislative branches in the Russian Government has been dynamic and chaotic. The exact shape of the Russian budget formation process is therefore unresolved.

Since the collapse of Soviet power and the concomitant removal of central economic structures, the military economy of the former Soviet republics has been reduced to a shambles. The vertical links between central administrators and military producers, which had governed military production completely, are now gone; the sluggish pace of market-oriented economic reform has prevented horizontal networks of customers and suppliers (for military or civilian products) from filling the resulting void in the defence industry.[11] Military budgets are now written quarter by quarter and are frequently finalized long after the relevant fiscal period has begun, leaving defence enterprises with little or no

---

[9] See Meyer (note 8).

[10] See accounts of this process in Lukashevich, V., 'Pochemu my okazali' bez byudzheta' ['Why we ended up without a budget'], *Krasnaya Zvezda*, 9 Jan. 1991, p. 1 (in Russian); Urban, V., interview with V. N. Ochirov, 'Pochemu "ushli" dva milliarda' ['Why two billion "departed"'], *Krasnaya Zvezda*, 12 Jan. 1991, p. 1 (in Russian); 'Differences block defense budget debate', TASS News Agency, 10 Jan. 1991, in Foreign Broadcast Information Service, *Daily Report–Soviet Union (FBIS-SOV)*, FBIS-SOV-91-008, 11 Jan. 1991, p. 16.

[11] See Dolgikh, A., interview with V. Dementyev, 'Ne pogubit' nauku' ['Don't destroy science'], *Krasnaya Zvezda*, 16 Oct. 1991, p. 4 (in Russian).

guidance as to what percentage of their military production will remain intact in the face of massive procurement cutbacks, and to what extent they must look elsewhere for customers.

Even after defence enterprises receive budget allocations for military production, these rouble figures are often meaningless to them owing to both the astonishing rate of currency inflation now plaguing the Russian economy and the manner in which resources have traditionally been allocated for military procurement. Because the rouble is not internally convertible, resources for defence procurement and construction have traditionally been allocated in terms of material balances—tonnes of steel, kilograms of plutonium—because that is the way the production of those inputs was specified in the national annual and five-year central economic plans. Only accounts which were manpower-intensive, such as salaries, pensions, and research and development (R&D), were allocated in rouble figures. For procurement, rouble values were simply assigned later in the process for accounting purposes, but because of the political priority traditionally afforded the defence sector those figures were artificially low and meant next to nothing in terms of the real opportunity costs of the goods involved.[12] The defence sector could not effectively exploit its political priority if all that priority entailed was sheer infusion of money, since roubles were no guarantee of access to resources. Material supplies in a command economy, where the laws of supply and demand do not apply, have to be rationed by government fiat, not by price.[13]

In other words, the rouble figures for weapon procurement in the Soviet defence budget were not true indicators of the defence burden. This situation began to change when regulations on self-financing went into effect for defence industries on 1 January 1989. These laws dictated that all Soviet industrial enterprises had to at least nominally balance their books in rouble terms. In conjunction with defence budget cuts and demands for defence industry conversion, the defence industrial sector found itself in the difficult position of not being able to afford (or in most cases even find) necessary material inputs for its traditional military and new civilian product lines. It therefore increased the prices of many weapon systems: the price of a tank has doubled since 1989, for example, and that of an aircraft has increased by 150 per cent.[14] These price increases explain the apparent discrepancies in the published annual Soviet defence budget figures over the past three years—the claim of deep cuts in defence spending versus increases in several categories of the defence budget.

[12] Isayev, A., 'Reforma i oboronnyye otrasli' ['Reform and the defence industries'], Kommunist, no. 5 (Mar. 1989), pp. 89–99 (in Russian).

[13] With the Commonwealth economy in chaos, the questionable value of the rouble has led to a vast increase in barter arrangements throughout society. The St Petersburg city council, for example, has sent representatives throughout the country to make ad hoc arrangements to exchange finished industrial goods for the foodstuffs and raw materials necessary to keep the city afloat. See Barringer, F., 'Wide bartering keeps Leningrad going', New York Times, 4 Sep. 1991, pp. A1, A10.

[14] Other price increases: strategic missiles by 2.4 times, ammunition, 2.8 times, self-propelled and towed artillery, 2.9 times, and various armoured vehicles, 4.2 times. Shcherbakov, V., statement to TASS News Agency, 6 Aug. 1991, FBIS-SOV-91-152, 7 Aug. 1991, pp. 33–34. See also Akhromeyev, S., 'Skol'ko stoit oborona' ['How much does defence cost'], Izvestia, 12 Jan. 1991, p. 3 (in Russian).

For example, while 1991 rouble figures for procurement went up by 8.6 billion roubles, Soviet defence sector representatives claimed that, when the average 67 per cent increases in industrial wholesale processes are taken into account, the 1991 budget actually represented a real procurement cut of 25–27 per cent.

Now that each new Commonwealth nation is trying to protect its own political sovereignty and economic interests, difficulties with trade between the former republics are also hampering defence industry attempts to continue to function in the new environment. Enterprises now often find that independent contracts which they have signed with suppliers in other Commonwealth nations are thwarted by republican customs officials.[15] British Prime Minister John Major has remarked that while it is clear that the people of the CIS have chosen the path to democracy and freedom, it is not certain whether they will proceed towards a market economy together or as 15 separate nations.[16] As early as 1990, Ukraine and Belarus issued instructions to enterprises to fill republic orders first and send only any excess to the centre or to other republics. Unless these tendencies are mitigated by some sort of inter-republic economic order, continued economic decay seems inevitable. For example, while Ukraine produces more than 90 per cent of the nation's locomotives, it gets the parts for them from more than 800 different factories across the Union.[17] A disintegration of trade across republic borders will bring much of the CIS's economy to a standstill.

The reductions in procurement and general chaos in the defence economy have resulted in massive layoffs and unemployment among military industry employees. The situation is serious enough to have prompted the formation of an All-Union Trade Union of Workers of the Defence Industry, a body independent of any government structure uniting 80 per cent of the workers in the former Soviet military plants and scientific research centres. The union's task is to offer 'social protection' to its workers during the transition to a demilitarized market economy.[18] Indeed, entire cities once devoted to military production are now becoming ghost towns.

The governments of the Commonwealth nations have proposed solving the defence industry unemployment problem (as well as a myriad of other ills, including overall national economic reform and demilitarization of the society) through conversion of the defence industries to civilian production. Thus far, however, conversion efforts have succeeded sporadically at best. From the beginning the Soviet Government had failed to recognize that substantial investment was necessary to retool plants and retrain workers;[19] only in 1991 did

---

[15] Gladkevich, Y., 'Submariny na slkade, ili komu nuzhna takaya konversiya' ['Submarines for the warehouse, or who needs this kind of conversion'], *Krasnaya Zvezda*, 24 Oct. 1991, p. 2 (in Russian).

[16] Whitney, C. R., 'Gorbachev asks British leader for economic aid', *New York Times*, 2 Sep. 1991, p. 5. For general information on trade problems, see Slay, B., 'On the economics of interrepublican trade', *Report on the USSR*, 29 Nov. 1991, pp. 1–8.

[17] Clines, F. X., 'Survive, then mend', *New York Times*, 1 Sep. 1991, p. 6.

[18] TASS, 20 Nov. 1991, in FBIS-SOV-91-228, 26 Nov 1991, pp. 56–57.

[19] See Gladkevich (note 15).

278 THE LIMITED PARTNERSHIP

it begin to allocate substantial sums for these purposes.[20] However, even with these start-up funds it seems unlikely that conversion can succeed without a proper macro-economic environment. The rouble is still not convertible (and therefore no information on consumer supply and demand is available); horizontal links among economic actors are still woefully underdeveloped; and little attention is being given to the potential applicability of advanced military technologies to civilian purposes. In the absence of effective market-oriented economic reform, conversion's near- and medium-term prospects seem slim.[21]

The defence industrialists in the former USSR have tried to counter their new uncertain environment, including demands for conversion, with two strategies: the formation of joint-stock companies and arms sales. The joint-stock companies (supposedly operating as investment houses and commodity exchanges under the guise of market principles) are generally simply umbrella organizations formed by former governmental industrial ministries in an attempt to retain central economic administrative structures.[22] Their intent is most likely to attempt to escape the impact of market reform by retaining central supply allocation structures, and to exercise political influence over the government to maintain higher levels of military procurement spending. Arms sales are being proposed by individual defence enterprises, in the hope that continued defence production for foreign customers will enable them to maintain full employment and production capacity and thereby escape conversion, and also by governmental organs anxious for any possible source of hard currency.[23] Both of these strategies are likely to hinder the market economic reform and demilitarization processes, and a surge in arms sales would certainly damage political relations of the Commonwealth nations with their new Western friends.

[20] Ten billion roubles are in the Russian 1992 budget for conversion; Ukraine, however, could afford only 450 000 roubles for 1992. See Tedstrom, J. (ed.), 'Economic and business notes', *RFE/RL Research Report*, 7 Feb. 1992, pp. 44–45.

[21] Even obvious candidates for conversion, such as military aircraft, may not be as promising as a first glance would indicate. Take, for example, the issue of operating environment: military systems are designed to endure extremely strenuous environments for a short period; commercial applications should function under relatively benign environments for long periods. Cost considerations are similar: military producers are accustomed to achieving technical sophistication with relatively little attention to cost; producers for civilian industry must keep market competition in mind and therefore must make constant quality/cost trade-offs. These observations imply that the more sophisticated military technologies and plants may have limited, if any, application to the civilian sector.

[22] For more on the joint-stock companies, see Pimenov, A., interview with Morozov, V. A., 'Nuzhen konsortsium voyennykh birzh' ['A consortium of military exchanges is needed'], *Krasnaya Zvezda*, 21 Nov. 1991, p. 2 (in Russian); and Moscow All-Union Radio First Program, 2 Nov. 1991, in FBIS-SOV-91-215, 6 Nov. 1991, pp. 38–40.

[23] See Ayupov, A. I., 'Air battles in high-ranking officials' offices', *Rabochaya Tribuna*, 15 Oct. 1991, p. 3, in Joint Publications Research Service–USSR Military Affairs (JPRS-UMA), JPRS-UMA-91-028, 14 Nov. 1991, pp. 30–31. Russian President Yeltsin has hinted that he might support an arms export strategy. See Bohlen, C., 'Arms factory can make bricks, but, Russia asks, is that smart?', *New York Times*, 24 Feb. 1992, pp. A1, A6.

III. The tangibles: weapon procurement

Transparency

There are two basic categories of potential types of transparency: (*a*) simple categories and line items, and (*b*) stages of the procurement process. The first is self-explanatory. Transparency measures can be applied to overall procurement totals, specific procurement categories or individual line items, depending on the appropriate level of detail. The second is more complex because of the differences which existed between the US and Soviet weapon procurement processes, and because of the chaos currently governing the defence economies of the Commonwealth nations. The process of overall budget formation in the executive branch, the course of legislative debate and oversight, and the formal stages of the weapon procurement process are likely current candidates for increased transparency.

The desirability of transparency measures applied to the tangibles of defence planning seems to vary with their degree of intrusiveness. Certainly it is difficult to argue with the benefits of data exchanges and regular dialogues on some budget and procurement figures. However, a co-operative security regime for defence planning that is too extensive, perhaps involving actual limitation of defence budgets or procurement, is likely to meet with strong objection, particularly from some political sectors in the USA. First, constitutional issues must be considered. The US Congress is uniquely legally empowered to authorize and appropriate the distribution of federal funds; any bilateral executive agreements impinging on that authority would have to be negotiated carefully to side-step this issue.[24] The use of joint executive/congressional negotiating teams would circumvent this potential difficulty.

Perhaps more important are potential objections relating to the purpose of US military power and the threats against which that power is arrayed in the post-cold war era. As the USA brings its grand strategy in line with the shape of the new world order, particularly in the aftermath of recent events in the former USSR, it becomes clear that contingencies such as the war in the Persian Gulf are the likely threat scenario to which it will be required to respond in the future.[25] The CIS becomes a potential ally or more likely an interested by-stander in eventualities of this type. Projected CIS weapon procurement requirements are therefore quite different from those of the USA, and it is reasonable to argue that bilateral limitations in those categories give the CIS an unwarranted degree of decision influence in areas which are no longer legitimately its concern.

This line of argument becomes even more pressing if transparency measures are extended to the R&D phase of weapon procurement. The USSR tradition-

---

[24] The author thanks William Newmann for discussions on this point.

[25] The Pentagon recently suggested seven likely future scenarios for military action. See Tyler, P. E., 'Pentagon imagines new enemies to fight in post-cold war era', *New York Times*, 17 Feb. 1992, pp. A1, A5.

ally perceived sophisticated US military technologies as most threatening to its national interest, primarily because it was unable to duplicate them. High technology has always constituted the realm of greatest US comparative advantage; the USA is therefore unlikely to be willing to discuss limitations or even transparency with regard to advanced military technology, particularly in light of its staggering utility in the victory in the Persian Gulf. Intrusive transparency measures or limitations on military technology have a difficult time passing the test of feasibility as well. A myriad of barriers render successful restraints on technological innovation unlikely; they include:[26]

(a) the impossibility of placing the entire innovation process under a centralized authority;

(b) the futility of attempting to predict future applications and consequences of scientific advance;

(c) the vested interests which inevitably form around the development of technology;

(d) the international character of technology, implying that bilateral constraints are ill-advised, and that limits must therefore be negotiated with all advanced or potentially advanced industrial societies;

(e) the inherent secrecy surrounding an endeavour where significant developments can spring from one person in a closet-sized laboratory;

(f) the fact that modern weapons derive from an extensive technological base increasingly common to civilian applications as well; and

(g) the related point that similar technologies can have stabilizing or destabilizing military applications, for example, satellites as force multipliers or as early-warning and surveillance devices.

The irony of these observations is that, in terms of controlling potentially destabilizing inaccurate threat perceptions, transparency and control measures are most effectively applied at the early stages of the research–procurement cycle when they are least feasible. Recent proposals in both the USA and Russia to adopt an economizing weapon procurement philosophy involving development only to the prototype stage may influence this dynamic in either direction. If the USA emphasizes research and early development over production, it may become more secretive and protective than ever with regard to sophisticated military technologies; on the other hand, the new political environment has prompted recent proposals for joint Russian–US R&D on such technically sophisticated systems as ballistic missile defence. If such plans are

---

[26] For extended discussion of the difficulty of restraining military technology, see Karkoszka, A., 'The impact and control of technology', eds Cuthberson and Volten (note 4), pp. 141–53; Greenwood, T., 'Why military technology is difficult to restrain', *Science, Technology, and Human Values*, fall 1990, pp. 412–29; Berkowitz, B. D., *Calculated Risks* (Simon & Schuster: New York, 1987), pp. 91–134. Soviet analysts echo these points. See Solnyshkov, Y. S., 'O voyenno-tekhnicheskikh zakonomernostyakh razvitiya vooruzhennykh sil' ['On military-technical regularities of the development of the armed forces'], *Voyennaya Mysl'*, Nov. 1990, pp. 40–45 (in Russian).

dopted, then transparency in military R&D will give way to collaboration in a
ashion unimaginable during the cold war era.

Assistance

It is clear that the difficulties the Commonwealth nations face in rationalizing
and reforming their defence economic system present not just a severe constraint on the feasibility of meaningful transparency for procurement in the near
term, but also an opportunity for co-operation. The USSR, and now the CIS,
has been coming to the West seeking aid for many months. While direct financial assistance remains a sticky political and financial issue, a more creative
and, in the long run, perhaps a more effective solution is US assistance in the
process of developing and implementing military-economic reform. Various
measures have been envisaged and some implemented, including: seminars and
discussions on market economics; long-term exchanges of defence industrialists
and businessmen both in classrooms and factories; and extensive assistance in
both creating commodity and material exchanges, and in making those
decisions about the applicability of military technologies to civilian products,
which are so necessary for successful defence industry conversion. One of the
most useful services the West can immediately provide is its technological
expertise, and perhaps telecommunication hardware, to create efficient and
accessible data bases so that potential customers, suppliers and investors in the
defence and civilian sectors can identify one another. The continued lack of
horizontal communication between economic actors in the Commonwealth
nations is appalling.

While many activities of this type have been taking place on an *ad hoc* basis,
they will be more effective if institutionalized and provided with governmental
financial assistance. Russian President Boris Yeltsin, for example, has created
the All-Russian Reserve Officers' Training Centre for business education of
discharged military officers; the West could usefully assist in both helping to
finance this and other similar centres, and in providing faculty and curriculum
advice.[27] The USA can play an invaluable role in teaching managers of CIS
defence enterprises facing market conditions for the first time how to choose a
product, formulate a business plan, attract capital investment, market a product
to potential customers and make the thousands of other day-to-day decisions
that Western businessmen take for granted.

Proposals involving more direct financial assistance must be treated cautious-
ly. Current conversion efforts in the Commonwealth nations, as outlined above,
are unlikely to succeed in the absence of a proper macro-economic environ-

---

[27] See Popov, R. N., interview with Korchagin, V., 'Iz ofitserof–v biznesmeny' ['From officers to
businessmen'], *Krasnaya Zvezda*, 1 Nov. 1991, p. 1 (in Russian). Indeed, even such simple and
inexpensive activities as providing textbooks would prove invaluable. One recent US visitor to a Russian
economic think-tank found its head using a US economics text as the basis for his proposals and advice to
the Russian Government; when asked why he chose that particular text, he replied that it was the only one
he had. See also chapter 13, p. 245.

ment. Direct investments therefore, either at the government-to-government or business-to-business level, will probably end up as money down the drain. Until the rouble is convertible, so that capital markets can function normally and foreign investors can extract profits on terms other than barter, and until the large Soviet defence industry conglomerates are broken down into manageably sized firms and privatized, the best service the West can perform for conversion and defence economic reform in general is to provide information and advice on creating the proper overall economic conditions. Perhaps the only necessary long-term financial aid is a rouble stabilization fund of the type currently under consideration.

IV. The intangibles: military budgets, doctrine, strategy and organization

Transparency

At the most basic level, data exchanges on defence budgets would build on the submissions using the United Nations format which have taken place since the Vienna Agreement of November 1990. This agreement guaranteed each state the opportunity to submit questions for clarification about any other state's submitted military budget within two months of receipt, with all parties agreeing to make every effort to answer such queries fully and promptly. The UN format divides expenditures into individual military services and commands along one axis, and categories of personnel, operations, procurement, construction and R&D (including a total of 20 subcategories) along the other.

This format certainly constitutes a good start, but it might be hoped that more formalized routine discussion of budget matters would lead to revelation of Russian data at a level of detail equivalent to that revealed by its government to the US public. Such procedures would enable both sides to gather information on those elements of military spending which have traditionally been buried in civilian budget categories.[28] Senior Russian military officials have rebutted complaints that their published defence budget conceals a great deal by observing that the USA does the same to a certain extent. These officials have advocated going beyond the UN budget format to include data on indirect expenditures such as expenses for the US space programme, coast guard, strategic material reserves and payment of pensions to DOD civilian employees.[29] Direct bilateral exchanges and detailed discussion of these issues might lead to objective, agreed-upon standards for what constitutes military spending, so that the question of what data to exchange can become unambiguous and allow still-unanswered questions about CIS defence spending to be resolved.

---

[28] Some steps have been taken in this direction recently, including the adoption of a single format for calculating defence budgets to ensure comparability between NATO and the former East Bloc countries. See Hitchens, T., 'NATO, ex-Warsaw Pact nations agree on budget format', *Defense News*, 12–18 Oct. 1992, p. 62.

[29] See Akhromeyev (note 14).

Table 15.1. The structure of US and Soviet defence expenditures, 1990

Figures are percentage shares of 1990 military budgets.

Category	USA	USSR
Procurement	27.14	43.70
Research and development	12.83	18.60
Military construction	1.99	3.76
Housing	1.14	1.47
Operation and maintenance	29.19	17.65
Personnel	26.77	9.57
Pensions	7.07	3.44

Sources: Cheney, D., *Annual Report to the President and the Congress* (US Government Printing Office: Washington, DC, 1990), p. 69.

One potential roadblock in making defence budgets more transparent is the history of tremendous asymmetries in US and Soviet defence spending. Efforts to negotiate absolute or relative limits on particular budget and procurement categories will have to take into account the radically different military philosophies of the two sides.[30]

First, the US and CIS armed forces are structured differently. The USA has three armed services; the CIS has four—strategic deterrent forces, ground defence forces, air forces and navy.[31] Pure geopolitics dictated that the USSR, a huge land mass with lengthy and traditionally unfriendly borders, emphasize its ground forces. In contrast, the air force and navy have historically enjoyed larger budget shares in the USA, a nation isolated from potential threats by thousands of miles of ocean.

Second, the dramatically different economic priorities of the two superpowers resulted in important differences in the allocation of resources for defence. As table 15.1 demonstrates, the USA spends a much greater proportion of its defence budget on daily operating costs (personnel, operation and maintenance) than did the former USSR which invested more heavily in hardware. Manpower policies primarily account for this difference; the USA must offer attractive salaries and benefits to entice qualified recruits into a professional army, while the USSR was able to pay its conscripts only a nominal salary and force them to endure horrendous living conditions.[32] Presumably these relative proportions will come more into line as the CIS moves to some degree towards a volunteer military based on contract service.

[30] Much of the following discussion is drawn from Rogov, S., *From the Cold War to Military Cooperation: Controlling Military Technology and Defense Spending*, unpublished manuscript, May 1990.

[31] On the recent reorganization of the Soviet military into four services from the previous five, see Clarke, D. L. 'Soviet military reform: a moving target', *Report on the USSR*, 22 Nov. 1991, pp. 15–16.

[32] For details of the living standards of Soviet military personnel, including accounts of officers withdrawn from Eastern Europe forced to live in tent cities for want of adequate housing, see Herspring, D., The Soviet military today: reshaping in response to a moving target', *Orbis*, vol. 35, no. 2 (spring 1991), pp. 179–94.

However, these figures also reflect the relatively little attention the Soviet Government paid to maintaining its defence infrastructure as compared to th USA. The low priority accorded operations and maintenance has been mani fested in recent complaints from CIS military officers about poor training stand ards, and even more strikingly in numerous accounts of costly accidents involv ing shoddy and poorly maintained equipment.[33] The day-to-day operations o the military services have clearly suffered from overall budget reduction: Funds allocated for the purchase of capital equipment already in the procure ment pipeline must be spent in order to carry through prior investments, and s the cuts chip away primarily at repairs and purchases of spare parts and fuel. Indeed, Russian Air Force technicians are now routinely cannibalizing relative ly new aircraft for spares.

Assistance

Implied in the concept of additional transparency in the sphere of th intangibles—the analysis and formation of military budgets, doctrine, strateg and tactics, and debates and decisions on future military organizational arrange ments, such as manpower and force structure—is the fact that the Common wealth nations, as they undertake their military restructuring process, will lear a great deal from their US military counterparts. Assistance is therefore organi to the transparency process. These types of measure might range from the obvi ous routine joint discussions through extensive arrangements for US advice a assistance to the former Soviet republics as they travel through the militar reform process. They might take the form of military-to-military communica tion, including military academy and other academic exchanges, joint militar war-gaming and modelling exercises, and military-to-civilian contacts.

The obvious precedent for joint discussion is the annual military doctrin seminar, first held over a period of three weeks in Vienna's Hofburg Palace i January 1990.[35] Representatives from all of the then WTO, NATO, and Euro pean neutral and non-aligned countries attended. Each country's general staf was allotted 25 minutes to outline its own military doctrine, and then othe specialists were given time to discuss the seminar's other three topics: forc structure, training and exercises, and budgets. Provisions were also made fc general discussion of issues which may have aroused particular attention durin the initial presentations. The participants hailed the event not only as a learnin

---

[33] For just a few naval accident horror stories, see Puteyev, K., '"Nekonditsionnyye" atomokhod: ['"Nonstandard" nuclear submarines'], *Krasnaya Zvezda*, 7 May 1991, p. 2 (in Russian); Gladkevich, Y 'Pochemu pogibla podlodka "*Komsomolets*"' ['Why the submarine "*Komsomolets*" was destroyed'] *Krasnaya Zvezda*, 8 Aug. 1989, p. 2 (in Russian). For a fuller account, see also Tsypkin, M., 'Quanti versus quality in today's Soviet navy', *Journal of Soviet Military Studies*, Mar. 1991, pp. 124–40.

[34] Maryukha, V., 'Konversiya, rynok, sudoremont' ['Conversion, the market, and ship repair' *Krasnaya Zvezda*, 22 Jan. 1991, p. 2 (in Russian).

[35] This and other details of the Vienna discussions are taken from Almquist, P., 'The Vienna milita doctrine seminar: flexible response vs. defensive sufficiency', *Arms Control Today*, Apr. 1990, pp. 21–2: and Einvardsson, J., *Draft Interim Report*, North Atlantic Assembly, Sub-Committee on Confidence- an Security-Building Measures, part 1, Geneva and Vienna, Nov. 1990.

experience but also as an opportunity to explain and clarify concerns. The second military doctrine seminar, in October 1991, built on the groundwork laid by the first.[36]

Given the precedent of the Vienna discussions, military-to-military communications at all levels have begun to sprout up on an *ad hoc* basis. In October 1990, for example, then Chief of the Soviet General Staff Mikhail Moiseyev visited NATO headquarters in Brussels to take part in a conference of chiefs of staff of the NATO countries' armed forces. At that time it was agreed that regular, planned contacts between military representatives would be arranged. These contacts might, for example, take the form of the May 1990 visit to the Taman Guards Motorized Infantry Division by military attachés and assistants from 51 countries, including the USA, organized by the Soviet Ministry of Defence External Relations Directorate.[37] This interaction provided an opportunity for observation not only of company tactical training, but of the equipment, lifestyle and everyday routines of the regiment's personnel. Were these exchanges to take place on a regular, reciprocal basis, some confidence might be established that they were more than mere Potemkin villages, and that the visitor was receiving a meaningful glimpse into the other side's habits and practices.

In terms of US assistance to the CIS military reform process, military-to-military discussions might be particularly useful if they centre around the CIS move away from universal conscription towards some form of volunteer, contract service. Many of the issues at the heart of the debate on this topic in Russia and the other newly independent states would sound familiar to students of this subject in the US context: the relative cost of a volunteer army which must attract recruits with higher salaries than those paid to conscripts; the difficulties of attracting high-quality volunteers into military service; and the risk of accusations of ethnic or racial inequities, as economic concerns leave many people from less advantaged educational and socio-economic backgrounds with military service as one of their only employment alternatives. The US military has vast experience in dealing with these issues, particularly with calculating the cost of a conscript versus volunteer army, which its CIS counterpart might find invaluable. Of course, the caveats outlined above concerning US assistance to the CIS reform process apply here as well.

On another level, the USA and the CIS have already taken preliminary steps towards formalized exchanges of students in military education facilities. In 1990, for example, three Soviet students attended the US Coast Guard Academy, and several East Europeans attended the US Army War College; legal provisions, currently under review, are the only barriers in the way of similar arrangements for the other US service academies. NATO began in late 1991

[36] Other CSCE-sponsored East–West military seminars in early 1992 focused on democratic civilian control of the military and defence industry conversion. See *Focus on Vienna*, no. 26 (Dec. 1991), p. 4.
[37] Pogorelyy, A., 'Visiting Taman', *Krasnaya Zvezda*, 27 May 1990, p. 3.

to invite officers from all CSCE nations to attend courses in its higher education establishments; Soviet officials were anxious to attend.[38]

The Soviet Union has historically boasted an extensive system of military education, including at the highest rung the Voroshilov General Staff Academy, and ranging down through 16 advanced service-specific officers' academies and over 100 military colleges and high schools.[39] With the dramatic reduction in the number of CIS military officers resulting from the 500 000-man unilateral force cuts of 1988, the further cuts certain to ensue from the failed coup and the decline in competition for academy admissions resulting from the diminished prestige of the military, this system is currently undergoing major reform.[40] Many of these schools have been closed completely; others have been revamped to improve technical training; still others are being transformed into more well-rounded universities to include a broad liberal arts education. There is even talk of beginning to admit women. Exchanging students at these educational facilities, at all levels, would not only begin to build co-operative bonds between military counterparts, but the presence of US students in the CIS system at this particular time would provide a clear window into these processes of reform in this critical sector of CIS military activity.

Another avenue of military-to-military contact might be joint military modelling and war-gaming. CIS military officers in particular have expressed increased interest in modelling techniques recently, probably because of financial constraints. As one retired Russian general recently observed, modelling can to some degree replace expensive real-time and scale exercises and manœuvres; he estimated that every divisional-scale exercise in the USSR cost on the order of one million roubles.[41] Subject matter for joint modelling consideration might at first centre around military response to civilian disasters, such as hurricane or earthquake relief or a nuclear power plant accident. As the two sides become more comfortable with co-operative gaming, they might proceed towards joint modelling of real military scenarios, perhaps acting both as allies and adversaries in various contingencies.[42]

Finally, considerable benefit might accrue from enhanced or even routine civilian-to-military contacts. In mid-1990, for example, 58 journalists repres-

---

[38] Markushin, V., 'Shtil' posle shtormovykh preduprezhdeniy' ['Calm after storm warnings'], *Krasnaya Zvezda*, 18 Sep. 1991, p. 5 (in Russian).

[39] For details of the Soviet military education system, see Seaton, A. and Seaton, J., *The Soviet Army: 1918 to the Present* (Meridian Press: New York, 1986), pp. 212–14; Scott, H. F. and Scott, W. F., *The Armed Forces of the USSR* (Westview Press: Boulder, Colo., 1984), pp. 189, 348–87.

[40] See Lobov, V., 'Vysokoye kachestvo: glavnyy kriteriy boyevoy bezopastnosti' ['High quality: the main criterion of military security'], *Kommunist Vooruzhennykh Sil*, no. 1, Jan 1989 (in Russian); Urbanovsky, C., 'The Soviet officer corps : time for reform?', *Jane's Soviet Intelligence Review*, Apr. 1991, pp. 157–60; and Green, W. C. and Karasik, T., *Gorbachev and His Generals: The Reform of Soviet Military Doctrine* (Westview Press: Boulder, Colo., 1990), pp. 134–36.

[41] Larionov, V., 'Modeli voyny, modeli bezopasnosti' ['Models of war, models of security'], *Mirovaya Ekonomika i Mezhdunarodnoye Otnosheniye*, Oct. 1990, pp. 26–36 (in Russian).

[42] Joint modelling might also give the West a window on the current reconceptualization of Russian force structure; for details on the reported move from a division military structure to one based on corps and brigades, see Clarke, D. L., 'Soviet military reform: a moving target', *Report on the USSR*, 4 Nov. 1991, pp. 14–19.

enting the USA and several other countries were given a tour of units stationed in what were then the Belorussia, Kiev and Leningrad military districts. The tour organizers, the Soviet General Staff and Novosti News Agency, offered visits to firing ranges and training facilities, and even a taste of the soldiers' meals.[43] Along another dimension of civilian interaction, earlier in the same year, members of the Armed Services Committee of the US House of Representatives received members of the Supreme Soviet Committee on Defence and State Security (CDSS), as a reciprocal for a visit the former had paid the latter in 1989.[44] The CDSS members not only testified at length before Congress, but also toured the Pentagon, the Los Alamos National Laboratory, the North American Air Defense Command (NORAD), the Strategic Air Command (SAC) Headquarters, the Kennedy Space Center and several air bases, weapon production facilities, naval bases and training centres. The participants agreed that their interaction was productive not only in terms of confidence-building, but also as a precedent for helping the Soviet Union to learn from the US experience with the legislative and budgetary processes. Even more striking, in late 1991, 28 senior Soviet military officers attended a two-week crash course at Harvard University's John F. Kennedy School of Government on how to help build a democracy.[45] Their classes, planned months before the aborted coup, focused on the proper role of the military in a popularly elected government; the curriculum ranged from the US legal system, to theories of arms control, to the role of the superpowers in Europe. Expanding these types of arrangement into regular patterns of interaction should serve as a cornerstone of a US–CIS co-operative security regime.

One potentially sensitive area of political acceptability of the measures described here is the degree to which these elements of a co-operative security regime are structured to include participation from European countries, both East and West.[46] First, the USA must remain aware of the continued possibility of tension between Russia on the one hand, and the non-Russian republics and newly emerging democracies of Central Europe on the other. Care must be exercised not to create exclusive ties between the superpowers that unwittingly threaten smaller European neighbours. Second, expanding on the former point, the USA and Russia must avoid action that smacks of superpower condominium. Either the NATO and former WTO states must be included in these agreements, or bilateral activity must be supplemented with similar arrangements to assuage the sensitivities of European allies.

[43] 'Foreign journalists given tours of army units', TASS, 8 Aug. 1990, in FBIS-SOV-90-154, 9 Aug. 1990.

[44] US Congress, House Armed Services Committee, *The New Soviet Legislature: Committee on Defense and State Security*, 101st Congress, 2nd session (US Government Printing Office: Washington, DC, 11 Apr. 1990).

[45] Schmitt, E., 'Soviet forces begin a drill in democracy', *New York Times*, 10 Sep. 1991, p. A5.

[46] The author is grateful to Jeffrey Simon for discussions on this point.

V. Conclusion: moving towards an uncertain future

Caution must be exercised along several dimensions when discussing any type of assistance measures. While the USA unquestionably possesses experience and expertise that will be invaluable to the Commonwealth republics as they undertake military reform, two pitfalls must be carefully guarded against: cultural insensitivity and arrogance. The former simply involves the recognition that, while the CIS certainly seems to be moving towards political and economic structures which more closely resemble their Western counterparts than in the past, it is doing so within a unique economic, cultural and situational context that is bound to render US analogies occasionally less relevant than might be apparent on the surface.[47] US military representatives 'teaching' the former Soviet republics about market-oriented economic reform and the pursuit of military affairs in a democracy must keep this in mind. The latter danger, arrogance, concerns the possibility that Western assistance will be offered when and where it is not wanted. The US military, and US democracy, have not always found all the 'right' answers to the problems they have encountered; the West should remain aware that in some areas the CIS may decide to reject, or not even consider, the Western experience and travel its own path unassisted.

It is even more important now than before that the USA and the former Soviet Union be more than disinterested mutual observers as each makes its way into the future. A process of co-operative security engagement such as that outlined above and in the other chapters of this volume, including measures of both transparency and co-operation in defence planning, can ensure that at the very least there are no unpleasant surprises on the path that lies ahead, and at best that the superpowers emerge from that path as allies having worked together through a difficult transitional period.

---

[47] On this point, see Cohen, S. F., 'The election's missing issue', *The Nation*, 23 Nov. 1992, pp. 622–24.

16. Some limits on co-operation and transparency: operational security and the use of force

William W. Newmann

I. Introduction[1]

With the end of the cold war comes not simply a new *détente*, but a growing friendship between the USA and Russia.[2] The greatest testament to the changed relationship between the USA and the USSR is the actions taken by the United Nations Security Council since 1986. Co-operation between Moscow and Washington to settle regional conflicts from Cambodia to Nicaragua, and the startling alliance during the Persian Gulf War clearly signalled the coming of a 'new world order'. Although new leaders have taken residence in Moscow, its foreign policy at present seems to be consistent with the trends that ended the cold war during President Mikhail Gorbachev's tenure in the Kremlin.

In spite of this trend towards multilateralism, the USA showed during its intervention in Panama in 1989 that it is still willing and able to use force unilaterally in pursuit of its national interests. Washington also demonstrated during the Persian Gulf War its willingness to play the role of the 'arsenal of democracy'. This chapter examines the relationship between the continued use of force and the new level of co-operation in world affairs. Specifically, this chapter focuses upon the limits on co-operation and transparency during multilateral and unilateral employment of military forces.

It is possible to divide the use of military force after the cold war into four categories: (*a*) traditional peace-keeping operations such as the United Nations Emergency Force (I and II) in the Middle East; (*b*) proposals for off-the-shelf military capability at the disposal of the UN Security Council to be used primarily in a preventive diplomacy context; (*c*) multilateral enforcement actions such as the UN-sponsored forces during the Korean War and the recent Persian Gulf conflict; and (*d*) unilateral military action.[3]

---

[1] Secondary journalistic sources were used in the collection of some data on recent events. Individual articles are cited only as necessary. These sources are: *New York Times, Washington Post, Los Angeles Times* and *Wall Street Journal*. The dates and times used in this paper refer to Eastern Standard Time.

[2] In this chapter, Russia is considered the post-cold war partner of the USA. Moscow will continue to control the majority of the former Soviet nuclear systems, if not all, and the Bush Administration has set the precedent of treating the new Moscow Government as the successor state to the USSR.

[3] The author would like to thank Jim Goodby for suggesting this framework. It excludes anti-terrorist and anti-narcotic operations, as well as the use of naval forces for coercive diplomacy.

Proposals for expanding the UN's traditional peace-keeping role and its capability for rapid 'preventive diplomacy'—including the use of UN forces as interpositional forces that can act as a deterrent to conflict before the shooting starts instead of as peace-keepers after the shooting has stopped—are being studied within the UN, in academia and in government.[4] Categories (*a*) and (*b*) are not discussed in this chapter. Although some proposals call for the use of US and Russian troops in these operations to give UN peace-keeping or deterrent forces more credibility, these two categories are not relevant to the discussion here.[5] There is a great difference between the 'use of military forces' and the actual 'use of force' by a nation's military. The 'use of military forces' is a broader term that includes the employment of military units in operations that extend from non-combat missions such as emergency airlifts to the use of nuclear weapons. The term 'use of force' implies a coercive, hostile military context, such as in the case of armed interventions or their defence, overthrow of governments or the seizure of territory by military forces, and involvement in regional conflict as a belligerent. Neither peace-keeping operations nor emergency airlifts, though requiring the use of military forces, would constitute the 'use of force' by this definition.

Categories (*a*) and (*b*) deal with the use of military resources to prevent combat. These operations are visible, even publicized, to ensure the high profile necessary for recognition as a peace-keeping or interpositional force. Categories (*c*) and (*d*) deal with the use of military resources in pursuit of international or national goals to initiate combat operations or to defend against invading forces. These operations often require stealth and deception to achieve their missions. Essentially, the first two categories include operations that intend to keep the peace while negotiations settle differences; the latter two categories deal with operations that intend to enforce a 'peace' as defined by those who undertake the use of force.

The premise of this chapter is that even after the cold war there will be limits to co-operation and transparency in the case of the use of force in the latter two categories: multilateral enforcement operations and unilateral military interventions. To explore this point analysis is made of US attempts to maintain operational security (the military euphemism for secrecy) during the Grenada intervention of 1983, the Panama intervention of 1989 and the Persian Gulf War of 1990–91. The Multinational Force operation in Lebanon is deliberately excluded from this analysis, since it was an attempt at peace-keeping. The focus is on co-operation and openness during the decision-making process for intervention. It leads to the central question of this section: how much information

---

[4] The Secretary-General reported on the UN's capability for these expanding roles in a document entitled *Agenda for Peace* in June 1992. Comprehensive treatments of the UN's new role now that consensus can be reached within the Security Council can be found in *Survival*, May/June 1990, in particular, Urquhart, B., 'Beyond the "sheriff's posse"', pp. 196–205; and Blodgett, J. Q., 'The future of UN peacekeeping', *Washington Quarterly*, winter 1991, pp. 207–20.

[5] A suggestion for the use of US and what were then Soviet forces in support of the United Nations is contained in Russet, B. and Sutterlin, J., 'The UN in a new world order', *Foreign Affairs*, vol. 70, no. 2 (spring 1991), pp. 69–83.

on the decision-making process for future military actions can any nation share with any ally? The assumption is made that even large multilateral operations will be dominated by the forces of one nation, as was the case during the Persian Gulf conflict. The US decision-making process for intervention, as open a decision-making process as any, is used for the test cases.

Operational security includes all measures taken by decision makers to ensure that knowledge of an impending military operation remains limited to the primary decision group and military forces directly involved. Simply put, the success of the military operation and the lives of the forces involved depend upon achieving either strategic or tactical surprise.[6] For the purposes of this chapter, simplified notions of strategic and tactical surprise suffice. Strategic surprise is attained if the victim of the attack does not know that an attack is, in fact, on the way. Tactical surprise, in contrast, is achieved if—once aware that an attack is imminent—the victim still remains unaware of the exact timing and shape of that attack. The extent of operational security that must be preserved depends upon whether strategic and/or tactical surprise is necessary for the success of the operation. The extent of surprise needed for a successful operation depends upon the nature of the military operation; the amount of information that can be shared therefore also depends on the nature of the military mission.

The importance of surprise (and therefore operational security as a method to achieve surprise) to ensure the success of an operation in the minds of US decision makers cannot be overstated. The success of a military operation is not judged only on the battlefield, but in the US political arena as well. Many analyses of the Viet Nam War suggest that wars must be won first on the home front before they have a chance to be won on the battlefield.[7] Before the military can be expected to achieve its operational goals, it must have the support of the American people. This belief acknowledges that national will is as much a key to military power as weaponry.[8] US decision makers, however, recognize the peculiar reality that support for military action within a democracy seems to be dependent upon the success of that military action rather than the importance or morality of the political objective.[9] Public support for military operations

[6] Betts, R., *Surprise Attack* (Brookings: Washington DC, 1982), pp. 4–5.

[7] This notion that the failure to gain public support for the Viet Nam War was critical in the failure of the war effort is outlined in detail by Summers, H., *On Strategy* (Presidio Press: Novato, Calif., 1982), pp. 33–70. Summers' book can be viewed as the official US Army post-mortem on Viet Nam. It was commissioned by the US Army War College and is used as a text throughout the Pentagon university and college system.

[8] The concept is hardly new, dating back at least to Clausewitz's classic work of 1832. See Clausewitz, K., *On War* (Viking Penguin: New York, 1982), pp. 251–54. See also Howard, M. E., 'The forgotten dimension of strategy', *The Causes of War* (Harvard University Press: Cambridge, Mass., 1983), pp. 101–15.

[9] This notion is illustrated by a series of Columbia Broadcasting System (CBS)/*New York Times* polls taken during the US conflict with Iraq. In polls taken 11–15 January, the days immediately preceding initiation of the air campaign against Iraq, 47% of those polled supported military action, while 46% supported continuing a policy of sanctions. A second poll conducted immediately after the air strikes began (17–20 January) and were hailed as a great success by military and political leaders illustrated that 75% of those polled favoured military action, while only 20% would have rather continued sanctions. A third poll taken 28 February–1 March, after the rapid success of the ground campaign, showed 82% support for

before the operation is underway is less important to policy makers than public support after the operation has begun.[10]

In quick-strike operations such as Grenada and Panama there is not time to gain public support for intervention beforehand. Any type of national debate on the merits of intervention would give the proposed victim of the strike strategic warning and make military action more difficult, if not impossible. In these types of operations the key to support at home is quick success on the battle-field. Bluntly stated, but none the less true, nothing stifles debate like success—if the mission is successful, the majority of US citizens will support it. In this sense, to decision makers, operational security is a key factor in ensuring a successful mission and therefore a key factor in ensuring public support and political survival.

In a larger operation like Iraq where strategic surprise is not possible, and therefore a national debate on the merits of intervention is possible, public support before an operation is important, but public support once the operation is underway remains the measure of success. The political and military leadership can be blamed for losing the war. Such was the case in Viet Nam. Chairman of the Joint Chiefs of Staff General Colin Powell explains this notion: 'The American people want their interests protected and they want their values protected . . . but at the same time, being very reasonable, practical people, they hope we will do it quickly, efficiently and successfully. The quicker you can do it, the better off you are'.[11] Again, operational security becomes a critical aspect of success, even if it is only assuring tactical surprise.

The analysis above suggests that the USA will be reluctant to share information concerning its decision processes for intervention. As the following analysis illustrates, it seems unlikely that any greater openness in the case of armed intervention is possible. Each case illustrates that in the minds of the decision makers the need for operational security to ensure the success of the military operation and the safety of the troops going into battle seems to outweigh any need to foster openness in the new security environment.

In each case the focus will fall upon US openness and transparency towards the USSR. During the cold war, the USSR was the primary US antagonist. In the early years following the cold war, it was still the nation whose military forces posed the greatest threat to the USA, although that capability did not necessarily translate into intention.

It is interesting to note how the Reagan Administration communicated with British Prime Minister Margaret Thatcher during the Grenada crisis. The highest hopes for a post-cold war US–Russian relationship would imagine a relationship similar to the US–British relationship. While this is unlikely, at least in the short run, the US–British relationship during the Grenada crisis can be in-

---

military operations and only 14% who still thought sanctions the better course. Applebome, P., 'At home, war healed several wounds', *New York Times*, 4 Mar. 1991, p. 1.

[10] The Presidency of Lyndon Johnson will ever be a reminder to presidents and their advisers of the validity of this point.

[11] Rosenthal, A., 'Military chief: man of action and of politics', *New York Times*, 17 Aug. 1990, p. 1.

structive. If seen as an analogy for the future of US–Russian relations, US notification to Britain of the Grenada intervention (a situation where unilateral US action troubles an ally's leadership, but does not damage relations) can be compared to US notification of both Britain and the USSR during the Panama intervention and the Persian Gulf conflict with Iraq. The comparison illustrates that during the Panama operation, the USA treated Great Britain and the USSR equally, notifying each shortly before operations began. In the case of the Persian Gulf War, British military forces were a major part of the operational force involved, while Soviet forces did not participate. For this reason, British and Soviet notifications are not analogous; however, the USSR was provided with swift notification.

As is discussed below, it seems that the USA has already been providing Moscow, or any ally, with as much information about the use of its armed forces as it feels it can without sacrificing operational security. This aspect of co-operation seems to have reached the limits of its potential.

II. Grenada

The invasion of Grenada serves as a case study of cold war decision making and an illustration of the measures taken to preserve operational security when the USA and USSR were bitter rivals. As discussed below, it is a case in which strategic surprise was necessary to achieve the desired outcome. In addition, the crisis over Grenada not only placed the USA and the USSR on opposite sides of the conflict, but it placed the USA and Great Britain at odds. Grenada, as a member of the British Commonwealth, shared a special relationship with Great Britain. As a result, US intervention in Grenada caused great consternation at 10 Downing Street.[12]

In 1979, the leftist New Jewel Movement (NJM) came to power on the Caribbean island of Grenada.[13] Its leader Maurice Bishop led a successful coup that gave him the title of Prime Minister. Bishop's leadership of the NJM came under increasing fire from more hard-line elements within the NJM and from the Reagan Administration, which singled out Grenada as one of the targets in its anti-communist crusade. In October of 1983, the hard-line faction under the leadership of General Hudson Austin of the NJM made its move, arresting Bishop and executing him on 19 October. Dealing with General Austin's overthrow of Bishop and subsequent declaration of martial law was made more urgent by the presence of US students at St Georges Medical School. The Reagan Administration feared that these students might become hostages of Austin's military junta.

---

[12] Adkin, M., *Urgent Fury: The Battle for Grenada* (Lexington Books: Lexington, Mass., 1989), p. 123; and 'Britain's Grenada shut-out', *The Economist*, 10 Mar. 1984, p. 34.

[13] In this chapter only the briefest outline of the events leading to the US intervention in Grenada are necessary. A more detailed history can be found in Dunn, P. and Watson, B. (eds), *American Intervention in Grenada* (Westview Press: Boulder, Colo., 1985); Schoenhals, K. and Melanson, R., *Revolution and Intervention in Grenada* (Westview Press: Boulder, Colo., 1985); and Adkin (note 12).

Following the assassination, National Security Council (NSC) crisis-management mechanisms were activated and a meeting of the Crisis Pre-Planning Group (CPG) was scheduled for the early morning of 20 October.[14] During the CPG meeting, chaired by Deputy National Security Advisor Admiral John Poindexter, it was decided that the crisis demanded secrecy even during these early planning stages. First, if an invasion was a real possibility, it would need surprise in order to succeed. Second, there was a distinct fear that the US medical students at St Georges Medical School could be taken hostage if word of possible US intervention leaked.

The NSC-level Special Situation Group (SSG) chaired by Vice President George Bush met on the afternoon of 20 October. At that meeting, several decisions were made. Two naval task forces headed for Lebanon were diverted to Grenada. In addition, all decision makers scheduled to attend a second SSG meeting on 22 October were instructed to use different entrances to the White House and to go about their business as if no crisis existed.[15] President Ronald Reagan and Secretary of State George Shultz had a previous commitment to travel to Augusta, Georgia for a weekend of golf. The weekend of golfing was not cancelled, since this might have aroused suspicion that the USA was planning a major response to the events in Grenada. One slight alteration to the President's plans was the inclusion of National Security Advisor Robert McFarlane on the trip.[16]

Attempting to cover the planning for Grenada with a shroud of secrecy was easier decided upon than achieved. Reports that something was in the works began trickling out even before a decision had been made to intervene.[17] The diversion of the *Independence* Carrier Battle Group and the Marine Task Force

[14] For details of this meeting, see Menges, C., *Inside the National Security Council* (Simon & Schuster: New York, 1988), p. 56. Approximately 1000 US medical students attended St Georges; *Full Committee Hearing on the Lessons Learned as a Result of US Military Operations In Grenada*, Hearing before the Committee on Armed Services, House of Representatives, 98th Congress (US Government Printing Office: Washington, DC, 24 Jan. 1984), p. 1.

[15] This meeting of the SSG crisis management group is detailed in Adkin (note 12), pp. 118–19; and Menges (note 14), pp. 59–60. The SSG included Bush, Weinberger, Shultz, Chairman of the Joint Chiefs of Staff General John Vessey, Attorney General Edwin Meese, acting CIA Director John McMahon, Under Secretary of Defense Fred Iklé, US Ambassador to the Organization of American States William Middendorf, Under Secretary of State for Political Affairs Lawrence Eagleberger, Assistant Secretary of State for Inter-American Affairs Langhorne Motley and NSC staffers Oliver North and Constantine Menges. The forces instructed to go to Grenada were the *Independence* Carrier Battle Group; a Marine Amphibious Task Force that included the 22nd Marine Amphibious Unit had left the USA several days earlier on its way to replace forces of the Multinational Force peace-keeping operation in Lebanon. These forces eventually took part in the invasion.

[16] Shelton, G. and Johnston, O., 'Invasion mapped at Georgia golf course', *Los Angeles Times*, 26 Oct. 1983, p. 1.

[17] The diversion of the *Independence* Carrier Battle Group and the Marine Amphibious Task Force was reported first on 22 October. See Shelton, G. and Wood, D., 'US to post task force off Grenada', *Los Angeles Times*, 22 Oct. 1983, p. 1; Ayers, B. D., 'US Marines diverted to Grenada in event Americans face danger', *New York Times*, 22 Oct. 1983, p. 1; Hiatt, F., 'US says situation still unclear as naval force nears Grenada', *Washington Post*, 23 Oct. 1983, p. A24. A deployment of Marines to Barbados on 24 October was reported in the morning papers as the invasion was underway. See Kaufman, M., '59 Marines land at Barbados field', *New York Times*, 25 Oct. 1983, p. 1; Turner, K., 'Marines land in Barbados as "option" for evacuation', *Washington Post*, 25 Oct. 1983, p. A14. On Caribbean news reports see Gwertzman, B., 'Steps to the invasion: no more paper tiger', *New York Times*, 30 Oct. 1983, p. 1; and Speakes, L., *Speaking Out* (Charles Scribner's Sons: New York, 1988), p. 152.

was reported in the US press on 21 October. The following day the Caribbean news media reported that an invasion of Grenada was imminent.

Although the Cuban Government and the military junta in Grenada responded to these reports by sending diplomatic messages to the USA that its citizens in Grenada would be safe, the USA had yet to inform any other nation that it was mulling over the possibility of intervention; the final decision was made at a meeting of the National Security Planning Group (NSPG) on 23 October originally scheduled to discuss the bombing of the Marine barracks in Beirut.[18]

Secrecy remained the top priority.[19] Military preparations by troops stationed in the USA began soon after the decision was made.[20] Chairman of the Joint Chiefs of Staff General John Vessey and Secretary of Defense Caspar Weinberger had decided that only the President, Shultz and McFarlane should know details of the military operation. The Chief of Logistics Operations of the Atlantic Command (LANTCOM) was not informed of invasion plans until 24 October, a day after the operation had been decided upon, a full seven days after planning had begun within LANTCOM and only 22 hours before the operation would begin. The head of logistics for the Joint Staff was not told at all.

The operation actually began on the night of 23 October when Navy sea, air, land teams (SEALS) attempted a reconnaissance mission on Grenada. The mission failed as rough seas swamped the SEALS' boat, and a second insertion was scheduled for the next night.[21] What is interesting about this mission, however, is that it took place before the USA formally agreed to intervene on behalf of the Organization of Eastern Caribbean States (OECS).[22] Earlier on the night of 23 October, as US Special Forces operations had already begun, a US diplomatic representative met with Prime Ministers Tom Adams of Barbados, Edward Seaga of Jamaica, and Eugenia Charles of Dominica to finalize plans for the diplomatic end of the intervention.[23] The three leaders were told of the Special Forces mission the next morning.

To ensure that the press and therefore the American people would remain unaware of US intentions towards Grenada, decisions were made at the highest

---

[18] Gwertzman (note 17), p. 1; and Adkin (note 12), pp. 116, 127–28. The NSPG differed from the NSC in that within the NSC the Chairman of the Joint Chiefs of Staff Vessey, and the CIA Director William Casey were officially only advisers. Within the NSPG, these two positions were elevated to principal membership.

[19] The Administration's attempts to maintain secrecy are detailed in Menges (note 14), p. 69; and Adkin (note 12), p. 132.

[20] On the night of 23 October, the Ranger battalion stationed at Ft Lewis, Washington was airlifted to Ft Stewart, Georgia to link up with another Ranger battalion. Gabriel, R., *Military Incompetence* (Hill & Wang: New York, 1985), p. 153. Marine forces were already in the Caribbean; preparations by the 82nd Airborne Division did not begin until the night of 24 October. Adkin (note 12), p. 219.

[21] The second mission failed as well. Adkin (note 12), pp. 167–69. Four SEALS were killed during these operations; Fialka, J. and Perry, J., 'As Panama outcome is praised, details emerge of bungling during the 1983 Grenada operation', *Wall Street Journal*, 15 Jan. 1990, p. A12.

[22] The OECS asked the USA to intervene on the behalf of states in the Caribbean that feared the spread of Cuban influence and the character of the new government in Grenada. See Schoenhals and Melanson (note 13), pp. 140–43. The OECS consists of Antigua and Barbuda, Dominica, Grenada, Montserrat, Saint Christopher (Kitts) and Nevis, Saint Lucia, and Saint Vincent and the Grenadines.

[23] Adkin (note 12), pp. 99–100.

level to shut Press Secretary Larry Speakes and White House Communications Director David Gergen out of the communication loop.[24] On the eve of the invasion, Speakes responded to a question about the possibility of US military intervention by repeating what the NSC had told him—that reports of a military response in Grenada were 'preposterous'. This exchange would create considerable tension between both Speakes and the press, and Speakes and several members of the Administration.

While the nature of the military's relationship with the press is not discussed here, the Pentagon went to surprising lengths to keep the US press off the island of Grenada.[25] Reporters from the *Washington Post*, *Miami Herald* and *Newsday* who had reached Grenada were taken off the island and held by the US military to prevent them from relaying word of the invasion to their newspapers in the USA. Vice Admiral Joseph Metcalf, commander of US forces in the operation, even instructed US ships to fire warning shots at any boats attempting to bring reporters to Grenada. US-based ham radio operators in contact with Grenada were shut down by the Federal Communications Commission (FCC) as well.

The need for operational security was explained by Under Secretary of Defense Fred Iklé in answer to a question on the consequences of the invasion becoming public knowledge: 'then everybody runs down there—the Cubans and Russians and everybody else, and gets on the beach ready to oppose us when we are coming in. Do you really expect us to tell them ahead of time in open press conference what we are going to do and jeopardize more American lives in the doing?'[26]

However, for the purposes of this chapter, the question is when other nations were informed. In the case of Grenada, informing the USSR would seem out of the question.[27] One of the primary missions of the intervention was to rid the island of Soviet and Cuban influence. US allies were not notified until shortly before the operation began.[28] Prime Minister Thatcher, who would surely have been critical of US meddling in Commonwealth matters, was notified of the operation by President Reagan at 7.00 p.m. on 24 October, less than 12 hours before the invasion began. At the same time, US Ambassador to Barbados

---

[24] Details of how Speakes was left uninformed, then deliberately misled by the NSC staff are described in Speakes (note 17), pp. 150–59. In defending the decision at a congressional hearing, Under Secretary of Defense Fred Iklé explained that Speakes was not told because the Administration knew that he would be asked. See Hearing before the Committee on Armed Services (note 14), p. 44.

[25] Gailey, P., 'Administration bars coverage of Grenada action: news groups protest', *New York Times*, 27 Oct. 1983, p. 1; and Speakes (note 17), p. 158. On the debate over press restrictions during the intervention in Grenada, see *1984: Civil Liberties and the National Security State*, Hearings Before the Subcommittee on Courts, Civil Liberties and the Administration of Justice, Committee on the Judiciary, House of Representatives, 98th Congress (US Government Printing Office: Washington, DC, 1984), pp. 425–515.

[26] Hearing before the Committee on Armed Services (note 14), p. 44.

[27] General Manuel Noriega claimed that then Vice President Bush called him and asked Noriega to relay a message to Fidel Castro that a US invasion of Grenada was underway and that Castro should keep Cuban forces out of the conflict. Bush denied the account. Weymouth, L., 'Why is Elliott Abrams picking on Panama's Noriega', *Washington Post*, 11 Oct. 1987, p. H1.

[28] Notification of and communication between the USA and its allies are detailed in Adkin (note 12), pp. 100 and 122. Thatcher sent a cable back to the USA protesting the invasion one hour after the British Government was notified.

Milan Bish was allowed to tell Prime Minister Adams of Barbados that the operation was scheduled for the next morning. This is particularly interesting since troops from Barbados were involved in the operation, and Barbados' Seawall International Airport was a major staging base for the operation.

In the case of Grenada, the Reagan Administration was willing to withhold information from elements of its own bureaucracy, the US public and even its allies involved in the operation for the sake of operational security. Only when the operation was already underway did the Administration feel secure in passing that knowledge to others.

III. Panama

Although the cold war had ended, the intervention in Panama in 1989 reveals a similar tale of secrecy. As in the case of Grenada, the need for operational security was paramount in the minds of US decision makers. Again, strategic surprise was necessary to ensure a successful operation.

US dissatisfaction with the regime of General Manuel Noriega built up gradually over several years during the Reagan and Bush administrations.[29] Noriega had been an important ally of the USA in Latin America, working with the Central Intelligence Agency (CIA) since the early 1970s. However, his involvement in drug trafficking, repeated incidents between Noriega's Panamanian Defence Forces (PDF) and US soldiers stationed in Panama (the home base of US Southern Command—SOUTHCOM), and fraudulent elections in May of 1989 convinced US leaders that Noriega would have to go. In the summer of 1989, US forces in Panama and units stationed in the USA began several series of training exercises to intimidate Noriega and prepare for the possibility of invasion.[30] The forces in Panama had the added task of attempting to desensitize Noriega and the PDF to possible warning signals that real action was underway. In spite of these preparations, the invasion still necessitated strategic surprise; the USA had yet to decide whether it would indeed be necessary for US forces to intervene to remove Noriega from power.

A failed coup attempt against Noriega in October convinced the Bush Administration that US forces were needed to oust him. In December of 1989,

---

[29] Again, this chapter requires only a cursory look at US–Panamanian relations during the Noriega years. For complete accounts see Koster, R. M. and Sanchez, G., *In the Time of the Tyrants* (W.W. Norton and Co.: New York, 1990); Dinges, J., *Our Man in Panama* (Random House: New York, 1990); Buckley, K., *Panama: The Whole Story* (Simon & Schuster: New York, 1991); and Watson, B. and Tsouras, P., *Operation Just Cause* (Westview Press: Boulder, Colo., 1991).

[30] For details of US preparation for the possibility of intervention see Ropelewski, R., 'Planning, precision and surprise led to Panama successes', *Armed Forces Journal International*, Feb. 1990, p. 28; *Department of Defense Appropriations for FY 1991*, Hearings before a Subcommittee of the Committee on Appropriations, House of Representatives, 101st Congress (US Government Printing Office: Washington, DC, 1990), Part 2, p. 161; Hughes, D., 'Night airdrop in Panama surprises Noriega's forces', *Aviation Week and Space Technology*, 1 Jan. 1990, p. 30; Fulgham, D., 'Army tells Congress that aviators rehearsed US invasion of Panama', *Aviation Week and Space Technology*, 11 June 1990, p. 23; Healy, M., 'Panama lessons: soldiers need police and urban war training', *Los Angeles Times*, 14 Feb. 1990. p. A6; and *Department of Defense Appropriations for FY 1991*, Senate Committee on Appropriations, 101st Congress (US Government Printing Office: Washington, DC, 1990), Part 2, p. 216.

Noriega gave the Bush Administration a justification for intervening. Noriega's self-appointed National Assembly appointed him 'maximum leader of national liberation' and declared that the USA and Panama were in a state of war. Several incidents between US forces and the PDF that resulted in the death of one US Marine led the Bush Administration to choose to intervene to overthrow Noriega as soon as possible.

Once the final decision was made on 17 December 1989, the attention of the decision makers turned to keeping the operation secret until it began three days later. Secretary of Defense Dick Cheney's role in this was to see to it that only a few senior Pentagon officials knew of the invasion.[31] Apparently he was successful. The spokesman for the Joint Chiefs of Staff explained after the invasion that 'there were a handful, really a small number of people in this entire building [the Pentagon] who knew this operation was going to happen'.[32] The CIA was reportedly kept in the dark about the operation for fear that some members of the CIA might leak the information to Noriega, who had been on the CIA payroll for a number of years.[33]

It seems that keeping a secret in Washington is nearly impossible. There were only 53 hours between the decision to intervene on 17 December and the initiation of operations on 20 December. Preparations for intervention began almost immediately, and continued meetings of the principal decision makers gave clues that something was underway.[34] Bush himself fuelled speculation by announcing on Monday, 18 December, that the USA was contemplating the use of military force in Panama.[35]

On Tuesday, 19 December, the airwaves in the USA were filled with reports of military activity.[36] The National Broadcasting Company (NBC) reported that transport planes were flying into Panama every 10 minutes and included foot-

[31] 'Inside the invasion', *Newsweek*, 25 June 1990, p. 29.

[32] Church, G., 'Showing muscle', *Time*, 1 Jan. 1990, p. 23.

[33] *Newsweek* (note 31), p. 30. On Noriega's relationship with the CIA see Dinges (note 29).

[34] C-141 aircraft began to move to bases from which they would ferry troops to Panama early on the morning of 18 December. These airlift operations in the USA culminated with the movement of troops to Panama included one-quarter of all US strategic airlift assets, 11 active Military Airlift Command (MAC) units, 17 reserve MAC units and the use of 21 bases. For details of these operations see *1989 Events in Panama*, Joint Hearings before the Senate Armed Services Committee and the Senate Select Committee on Intelligence, US Senate, 101st Congress (US Government Printing Office: Washington, DC, 1990), p. 122; *Department of Defense Appropriations for FY 1991*, Hearings before a Subcommittee of the House Committee on Appropriations, 101st Congress (US Government Printing Office: Washington, DC, 1990), Part 1, p. 271; and Crowell, L., 'The anatomy of Just Cause', eds Watson and Tsouras (note 29), pp. 76–77.

[35] Rosenthal, A., 'President calls Panama slaying a great outrage', *New York Times*, 19 Dec. 1989, p. 1. This is an interesting point. Why would a President who had decided to begin an invasion of another nation an hour after midnight on Wednesday announce on Monday to all the world that he was contemplating military action? This was probably Bush's way of deflecting congressional critics who felt he was already letting his opportunity for action disappear as he had done in October when the USA did not intervene to assist the PDF officers attempting to overthrow Noriega. Bush could reassure them by announcing that he was thinking about using force, without having to let anyone in Congress know any details. For details on the October coup and US decision making, see Joint Hearings before the Senate Armed Services Committee and the Senate Select Committee on Intelligence (note 34).

[36] See Horowitz, S., 'Indication and warning factors', eds Watson and Tsouras (note 29), p. 57; Senate Committee on Appropriations (note 30), p. 245; Crowell (note 34), p. 83; and Gordon, M., 'US increases Panama forces, hinting action', *New York Times*, 20 Dec. 1989, p. 1.

age of C-141s landing at Howard Air Force Base. The Cable News Network (CNN) and the Columbia Broadcasting System (CBS) broadcast reports of aircraft leaving Fort Bragg, home of the 82nd Airborne Division. The Pentagon attributed all the activity to readiness exercises.

In addition to these public reports that could have warned Noriega of the invasion, the National Security Agency (NSA) detected a phone call to Noriega in which the caller claimed to have been told by US Government officials that an invasion was on the way.[37] News reports indicated that a US Government official did call a friend on the Panama Canal Commission to tell him to be careful on the night of the invasion. Several Panamanians reportedly overheard US soldiers speaking about the 1.00 a.m. start of operations. The result of these leaks and possible others was a Panamanian radio announcement broadcast from the Commandancia (headquarters of the PDF) that US forces would arrive at 1.00 a.m. and a television announcement at 11:45 p.m. that all Dignity Battalions (Noriega's élite forces) should prepare for US attacks.[38] Although Noriega and the PDF had word of the invasion, it seems that the flurry of US military activity since the October coup had served its purpose of desensitizing Panamanian forces to warning indicators. Actual preparations for the invasion and reports of these activities were shrugged off by most of the Panamanian leadership as more exercises.[39]

The *furor* over the Pentagon's treatment of the press during the Grenada operation had led the Pentagon to devise a pool system in which a group of reporters would be allowed access to a military operation as representatives for the entire US press. However, the Pentagon's stress on secrecy once again caused controversy over the military's handling of the press. Assistant Secretary of Defense for Public Affairs Pete Williams was not allowed to inform the media or those at SOUTHCOM responsible for media accommodations and transportation that a press pool would be sent to Panama until the night of the operation. With such short notice media representatives and SOUTHCOM public affairs officers were so unprepared that the press pool arrived in Panama at 5.00 a.m. after much of the fighting had ended.[40]

The notification of foreign leaders had become nearly formalized within the Bush Administration. President Bush had held to a pattern of personal diplomacy since coming into office. During the Panama intervention, Bush called many foreign leaders himself. Latin American leaders began to be notified at 9.00 p.m., four hours before H-Hour (initiation of the operation).[41] The rest of the world, including Soviet President Gorbachev and Prime Minister Thatcher,

[37] On reports of the compromising of operational security see Crowell (note 34), p. 83.
[38] 'Security leaks compromised invasion', *Jane's Defence Weekly*, 10 Mar. 1990, p. 421; and Senate Committee on Appropriations (note 30), p. 245.
[39] *Newsweek* (note 31), p. 30.
[40] Watson, B., 'Assessing press access to information', eds Watson and Tsouras (note 29), pp. 136–38. The results of these efforts to maintain secrecy were so problematic that Williams called for an investigation. A report, released 20 March 1990, criticized the Pentagon for its 'excessive concern for secrecy'.
[41] Dowd, M., 'Doing the inevitable', *New York Times*, 24 Dec. 1989, p. 5.

was informed after 11.00 p.m., two hours before H-Hour.[42] These notifications continued until 4.00 a.m.

This notification of the USSR is more relevant to the future of US–Russian relations than the lack of notification during the Grenada operation. Grenada was a small battle in the cold war. The island had become a client of the USSR and Cuba, and US objectives of the intervention included ending that relationship. In the case of Panama, the USSR was treated as any other nation. It received prior notification of the intervention only hours before it began. This is likely most advanced warning of impending military activities that the US concern for operational security can allow during small, quick-strike operations. As the case of the Persian Gulf War illustrates, even in a multinational operation, the USA can provide only a few hours advance notice of the initiation of combat operations.

IV. The Persian Gulf War[43]

Any analysis of operational security during the Persian Gulf War must recognize the differences between the Gulf crisis and the Panama and Grenada crises. To be successful the interventions into Grenada and Panama required both tactical and strategic surprise—the leaders of Austin's junta in Grenada and Noriega's PDF in Panama had to be unaware not only of the timing of any US military operations, but also of whether military intervention was even a possibility. US military operations were predicated upon achieving complete tactical and strategic surprise with a swift and devastating strike. Only 34 hours passed between decision and H-Hour during the Grenada operation and a mere 53 hours went by between decision and H-Hour during the Panama operation.[44]

In contrast, in the case of Iraq, President Bush gave final approval for a troop deployment at 4.00 p.m. on 6 August 1990, and H-Hour for air operations began slightly over five months later at 7.00 p.m. on 16 January 1991. Success in the case of the Persian Gulf War was predicated upon achieving only tactical surprise—keeping the Iraqi leadership unaware of the timing and shape of the attack. Strategic surprise was unattainable. UN Security Council Resolution 678 of 29 November 1990, established a deadline of 15 January 1991. The USA made it clear that it considered this deadline to be Iraq's Rubicon—the presence of Iraqi forces in Kuwait on 16 January was considered grounds for the use of force to liberate Kuwait. This was a clear message that an attack was on its way sometime after the passage of the deadline. The Bush Administration set a similar deadline for an Iraqi pullout even after air operations were underway. Failure of Soviet negotiations with Iraq by this deadline on 23 February gave the

---

[42] Nelson, J., '"Enough is enough" President declared', *Los Angeles Times*, 22 Dec. 1989, p. A1.

[43] The best sources for decision making within the Bush Administration during the Persian Gulf War can be found in Woodward, B. and Atkinson, R., 'Mideast decision: uncertainty over a daunting mood', *Washington Post*, 26 Aug. 1990, p. 1; and Friedman, T. L. and Tyler, P., 'From the first: US resolve to fight', *New York Times*, 3 Mar. 1991, p. 1.

[44] Schoenhals and Melanson (note 13), p. 143; Adkin (note 12), pp. 127–28; and Church, (note 32), p. 23.

USA warrant for proceeding with ground operations. Therefore, only the exact day, time and shape of the attack were held secret from those outside the top level of US decision makers in Washington and US military commanders in the field. As is illustrated below, not even the other members of the international coalition were notified when military operations would begin until immediately before the fact.[45]

Two other aspects of US policy in the Gulf conflict allowed for less secrecy surrounding US operations: (*a*) a strategy of coercive diplomacy, and (*b*) the size of the operation. First, the Bush Administration hoped to gain Iraqi withdrawal from Kuwait through a strategy of coercive diplomacy.[46] The USA hoped that a high profile deployment of troops would illustrate US resolve. The USA announced every deployment, and the Pentagon supplied a great deal of information to the media detailing the extensive logistical operations undertaken to move forces to the Persian Gulf. The first US deployments, announced on 7 August, were intended to show US commitment to the defence of Saudi Arabia, while the UN embargo was to force Iraq out of Kuwait. The additional deployments, announced on 8 November, were intended to show Iraq that the USA was willing to use force to push Iraqi troops out of Kuwait. In both cases, it was hoped that US deployments would convince Iraq that it must abandon any plans it may have had for expanding its borders southward.[47]

In addition, the mere size of the US operation prevented it from being undertaken in secrecy.[48] As illustrated above, both the Grenada and Panama interventions were compromised by media reports of the movement of US forces. During the Grenada operation the USA deployed 7 1/2 battalions, about 6500 men; including air support, airlift and naval operations a total of approximately

[45] Although this is true, and the Bush Administration did attempt to keep the timing and details of the shape of the attack secret, it seems that just about every aspect of the operation leaked out at some point. Both the UN deadline for military action of 15 January and the Bush-imposed deadline for ground operations of 23 February were clear indications of when the attacks might take place. Air Force Chief of Staff General Michael Dugan's detailed outline of the type of air attack the USA might use also telegraphed a great deal of US military plans. A number of military officials including Central Command (CENTCOM) Commander General H. Norman Schwarzkopf and CENTCOM Deputy Commander Lt General Calvin Waller stated publicly that they did not believe that US ground forces would be ready to fight by the 15 January deadline. These revelations detailed the air attack and also implied that such an attack would proceed weeks before any ground operations would begin. However, it seems that the Iraqi leadership was in fact surprised by the timing and form of the international coalition's operations. See, for example, Schmitt, E., 'Air Force chief dismissed for remarks on Gulf plan: Cheney cites bad judgement', *New York Times*, 18 Sep. 1990, p. 1; and Pazstor, A., 'Ground troops won't be set for assault on Iraq till February, commander says', *Wall Street Journal*, 26 Dec. 1990, p. A32.

[46] The classic theoretical and analytical work on coercive diplomacy can be found in Schelling, T., *Strategy of Conflict* (Harvard University Press: Cambridge, Mass., 1960); Schelling, T., *Arms and Influence* (Yale University Press: New Haven, Conn., 1966); and George, A., Hall, D. and Simons, W., *The Limits of Coercive Diplomacy* (Little, Brown and Co.: Boston, Mass., 1971).

[47] In both instances the strategy failed. Instead of withdrawal from Kuwait the Iraqi response to the initial US deployments was to increase the number of forces in Kuwait to 430 000 and to fortify its defensive position. The additional deployments were also met by continued Iraqi intransigence. In the end bargaining failed, and the USA was required to destroy Iraqi forces to remove them from Kuwait.

[48] On the size of the Grenada operation, see Bolger, D., 'Operation Urgent Fury and its critics', *Military Review*, July 1986, p. 62; House Committee on Armed Services (note 14), p. 30; Fialka and Perry (note 21), p. A12; and Adkin (note 12), p. 128. On the scope of the Panama operation, see House Committee on Appropriations (note 34), p. 271; Senate Committee on Appropriations (note 30), p. 229; and 'Excerpts from briefings on US military action in Panama', *New York Times*, 21 Dec. 1989, p. 10.

20 000 troops was involved. The Panama operation included the deployment from the USA of 1 1/3 division of light forces, around 11 500 troops; including forces already stationed in Panama, air support, airlift and Naval forces, the operation employed 27 081 troops.

In contrast, the Persian Gulf operation included the deployment of 7 2/3 divisions, of which 5 2/3 could be considered heavy forces. The operation necessitated the movement of over 500 000 troops to the Gulf region.[49] It also required the call up of 228 000 National Guard or Reserve troops whose departure from their ordinary jobs affected communities throughout the nation.[50] Such a deployment could not have been kept secret even if the Administration had tried. In the early days of August after the initial announcement that forces would be sent to Saudi Arabia, the Administration was reluctant to announce which Marine units would be deployed to the Gulf. However, after repeated media reports that the Marines stationed at Camp Pendleton were phoning relatives to 'say good-bye', and sightings of large troop convoys on the California expressways, the Marine Corps announced that it would be sending elements of its California-based forces.

In spite of the publicity accompanying the deployments, the Bush Administration did try to maintain operational security concerning them. It reached an agreement on deployment with the Government of Saudi Arabia over the weekend of 4–5 August, and President Bush signed the order to send troops at 4.00 p.m. on 6 August. The USSR was informed that same day, although the public was not informed of the US decision to deploy troops until 7 August.[51]

A larger amount of secrecy was maintained concerning the decision to reinforce the initial deployments and give US commanders in the Gulf the capability to push the Iraqi forces out of Kuwait. If US forces were only to be used to defend Saudi Arabia, they would be deployed for an indefinite period and would need to be replaced by fresher forces at some point in the future. Secretary of Defense Cheney was to decide on such a rotation plan by the end of October. Within the President's decision circle, however, many were already realizing that the USA would have to free Kuwait militarily—Iraq was not going to withdraw without a fight.[52] After repeated briefings by General H. Norman Schwarzkopf and much debate between Cheney and Chairman of the Joint Chiefs Powell, the Administration decided upon the flanking manœuvre actually used to defeat Iraqi forces on the ground.[53] This manœuvre

---

[49] Bond, D., 'Troop and material deployment missions central elements in Desert Storm success', *Aviation Week and Space Technology*, 22 Apr. 1991, p. 94.

[50] Baker, C. and Finnegan, P., 'US questions war role of reserve combat units', *Defense News*, 15 Apr. 1991, p. 34.

[51] Warner, M. G., 'The Moscow connection', *Newsweek*, 17 Sep. 1990, p. 25. The first wing of F-15s left for Iraq at 5.00 p.m. on 6 August.

[52] President Bush's decision circle included Secretary of State James Baker, Secretary of Defense Dick Cheney, Chairman of the Joint Chiefs of Staff General Colin Powell, National Security Advisor Brent Scowcroft, Vice President Dan Quayle, and Deputy National Security Advisor Robert Gates. Chief of Staff John Sununu, Secretary of the Treasury Nicholas Brady and Secretary of Energy James Watkins also participated on occasion.

[53] On these debates within the Administration see Atkinson, R. and Woodward, B., 'Prolonged buildup reflects doctrine of invincible force', *Washington Post*, 2 Dec. 1990, p. 1.

would necessitate the deployment of additional troops. These new deployments and the abandonment of a rotation policy were approved by the Administration on 31 October.

Although the USA announced that it might deploy as many as 100 000 additional troops earlier on 25 October, the Administration attempted to keep the full extent of the 31 October decision secret until after the November elections. Except at the senior level within the Joint Staff, most officers in the Pentagon continued to prepare for a rotation plan; the announcement of new deployments on 8 November came as a great surprise.

The plan approved on 31 October called for a second period of transporting forces to the Persian Gulf, followed by an air attack starting in mid-January and ground operations beginning in mid-February.[54] This operational plan was followed during the transition from Desert Shield to Desert Storm. It is unclear if the USA informed other nations in the coalition of this timetable for operations. One can assume, however, that nations whose forces would be involved in these operations were at least told to be ready for operations by the days scheduled by the Bush Administration. For the purposes of this chapter the focus will be placed on the sharing of information with the USSR—a nation not directly involved in the military effort against Iraq.

With the failure of Secretary of State James Baker's 9 January meeting with Iraqi Foreign Minister Tariq Aziz, the congressional approval of the use of force on 12 January and Saudi consent for the USA to use Saudi territory for conducting offensive operations against Iraq, the Bush Administration simply waited for the 15 January deadline to pass. General Schwarzkopf recommended commencement of the air phase of the operation for the evening of 16 January, and the date and time were set by the Administration on the evening of 13 January. Only the President, Cheney, Baker, Powell, National Security Advisor Brent Scowcroft, his deputy Robert Gates, about 20 officers in the Joint Staff and, of course, the Central Command (CENTCOM) commanders in the Persian Gulf knew of the decision to launch the attack.

Only on 16 January, the day of the attack, did the Administration begin to notify its allies. At 8.00 a.m., the Saudi Ambassador to the US, Prince Bandar bin Sultan, was informed that the attack would begin later that night at 7.00 p.m. In the afternoon, both the USSR and Israel were notified by Secretary Baker.[55]

The USA maintained a similar policy of notification as the October-scheduled date for ground operations began. Following a meeting in Saudi Arabia with General Schwarzkopf, Secretary Cheney and Chairman Powell informed the President on 11 February that the General would like a 'window' for ground operations beginning on 21 February. Several days later, General Schwarzkopf gave the President a more precise date, asking the President for an

---

[54] Friedman and Tyler (note 43), p. 1.
[55] It is interesting to note that congressional leaders were informed after the notification of major allies in the coalition.

H-Hour of 8.00 p.m. on 23 February.[56] Last minute efforts by the USSR to negotiate an Iraqi withdrawal began on 18 February, but were cut short by a US-imposed deadline for withdrawal of Iraqi forces for noon on 23 February. President Gorbachev was informed of the deadline before it was announced publicly. On 23 February, President Bush left Washington for Camp David knowing that he would return that evening to announce the start of ground operations. Shortly after the deadline passed, Gorbachev was informed by Bush that the ground war would begin that evening at 8.00 p.m.

As in the case of the pre-H-Hour missions by US Navy SEALS during the Grenada mission, two US Marine Air–Ground Task Forces (MAGTFs)—a total of 3000 men—had moved 16 kilometres into Kuwaiti territory two days before the operation officially began. While President Gorbachev was still negotiating with Iraq to prevent a ground war, US forces had already begun their operations. Such information, if publicly known, could have jeopardized the lives of the members of these units whose mission required stealth for success.

V. Implications

It is unlikely that in the future US decision makers participating in multinational enforcement operations or unilateral interventions will agree to provide Russia (or any nation) with more advanced notification of impending military operations than that provided during the Panama and Persian Gulf crises. The need to maintain operational security as a path to ensuring a successful operation is simply too critical for decision makers to overrule.

It is also important to remember that all governments, including the Moscow Government, are subject to the same bureaucratic and organizational politics as any other. In all the cases described above, the USA withheld information not only from foreign powers but from segments of its own bureaucracy. In sharing information with other nations, the USA must consider whether that information might pass down through its bureaucratic layers to officials who might have reasons to leak the information. The H-Hour for the Panama operation did leak to Panama through the US bureaucracy. The CIA was even cut out of the decision-making loop to prevent just such a possibility. In the early days of the Persian Gulf crisis, segments of the Soviet Foreign Ministry were reluctant to condemn the Iraqi invasion of Kuwait.[57] Iraq had been an ally of the USSR, and presumably some Soviet officials had friends and colleagues within the Iraqi Government. One can only wonder whether these sympathetic officials might have tipped off any Iraqi friends (as US officials did during Panama) if they had known the date and time when operations would begin.

It seems that US decision makers operate by a general rule that if the leaking of certain information could jeopardize the mission, it simply cannot be shared

---

[56] Details on the decision making related to the timing of the ground war can be found in Apple, R. W., 'Cheney and Powell meet 9 hours with US commanders in the Gulf', *New York Times*, 10 Feb. 1991, p. 1; and Friedman and Tyler (note 43), p. 1.

[57] Warner (note 51), pp. 24–25.

with many individuals outside the President's inner circle—whether within the US Government or foreign governments. Essentially, top decision makers seem to take the attitude that if it leaves the room where the decision was made, it becomes public knowledge.

As the results of the Persian Gulf crisis illustrate, this does not obscure the potential for US–Russian alliances, multilateral enforcement operations and co-operative crisis management. Notification of foreign governments can begin once the operation is safely underway, although details of the nature of the operation will most likely remain a secret, again, to ensure the success of the operation. In the future, if US and Russian forces participate in joint operations (with the exception of peace-keeping and interpositional deterrent operations which require not surprise, but high visibility in the presumably non-hostile atmosphere of a negotiated cease-fire), command arrangements and the sharing of military operational details will have to be worked out between the military and political leadership of the two nations.

About the authors

Edward B. Atkeson (USA) is a retired Major General of the US Army and a former member of the National Intelligence Council. He is now a senior fellow at the Institute of Land Warfare, Association of the US Army.

Mikhail E. Bezrukov (Russian Federation) is a Research Fellow at the Institute of USA and Canada (Moscow) and, since 1991, Director of the Russian Science Foundation (Moscow). He is a contributor to *Mutual Security: A New Approach to Soviet–American Relations* (1991) and to *NATO and the Warsaw Pact in the 1990s* (1991). He is a 1992 Salzburg Seminar Alumnus.

Daria Fane (USA) is a US foreign service officer who has specialized in nationalities issues in the former USSR. She is currently assigned to the US Embassy in Moscow.

James E. Goodby (USA) is Distinguished Service Professor of International Peace and Security at Carnegie Mellon University. During a 35-year career as a foreign service officer, he was head of the US delegation to the Stockholm Conference on Disarmament in Europe, Vice Chairman of the US delegation to the Strategic Arms Reduction Talks (START), and Ambassador to Finland.

Fred Charles Iklé (USA) was Under Secretary of Defense for Policy in the Reagan Administration and is currently a Distinguished Scholar at the Center for Strategic and International Studies, Washington, DC.

David Kaiser (USA) is a Professor in the Strategy Department of the Naval War College, Newport, Rhode Island. He is the author of *Politics and War: Economic Diplomacy and the Origins of the Second World War* (1980), and numerous articles on the history of European international relations.

Steven Kull (USA) is a Senior Scholar at the Center for International Security Studies at the University of Maryland and a Senior Research Associate at Global Outlook in Palo Alto, California. A psychologist as well as a political analyst, he is the author of *Minds at War: Nuclear Reality and the Inner Conflicts of Defense Policymakers* (1988) and *Burying Lenin: The Revolution in Soviet Ideology and Foreign Policy* (1992).

Irving Lachow (USA) is a Ph.D. candidate in the Department of Engineering and Public Policy at Carnegie Mellon University. His research is performed under the auspices of the Program on International Peace and Security. He holds a B.S. in physics and a B.A. in political science from Stanford University. His current research focuses on the impact of global positioning technologies on missile proliferation.

Steven E. Miller (USA) is Director of Studies at the Center for Science and International Affairs in the John F. Kennedy School of Government at Harvard University. He is also Editor of the quarterly *International Security*. Previously he was Senior Research Fellow at the Stockholm International Peace Research Institute and taught defence and arms control studies at the Massachusetts Institute of Technology.

Benoit Morel (France) received a Ph.D. in physics in Geneva before continuing as a postdoctoral fellow at Harvard and the California Institute of Technology. He was a Science Fellow in the Center for International Security and Arms Control at Stanford University before he joined the faculty at Carnegie Mellon University as Associate Professor in the Department of Public Policy. His research focuses on high technology and its impact on defence policy, arms control and international security.

William W. Newmann (USA) is a Ph.D. candidate at the Graduate School of Public and International Affairs at the University of Pittsburgh, and Adjunct Professor of Political Science at Virginia Commonwealth University. He holds an M.A. and a B.A. in political science from Drew University and the University of Pennsylvania, respectively. His research focuses on US defence and foreign policy.

Sergey Rogov (Russian Federation) is Deputy Director of the Institute of USA and Canada (Moscow). He is the founding director of a new, independent institute focusing on arms control.

Judyth L. Twigg (USA) is a Ph.D. candidate in the Defense and Arms Control Studies Program at the Massachusetts Institute of Technology, and an Assistant Professor in the Department of Political Science at Virginia Commonwealth University. She holds an M.A. in political science from the University of Pittsburgh and a B.S. in physics from Carnegie Mellon. Her research focuses on US, Soviet and Japanese weapon procurement policies, and Soviet military affairs.

Index